Contents

Acknowledgments

Thanks to all of my former coworkers and bosses at Number Six Software, for their support, reviews, and insights. Special thanks are due to the cofounders, Rob Daly and Brian Lyons, for creating an amazing environment in which to work and to stretch professionally. Special thanks to Susan Cardinale, Greg Gurley, Kevin Puscas, Hugo Scavino, and Eric Tavella for their feedback and encouragement.

Thanks to John Haynes for his careful review and commentary.

Thanks to Mike Janiszewski and Jennifer Horn, for their review, encouragement, and support. Friends in need are friends in deed.

Many thanks to the fine professionals from John Wiley and Sons; Terri Hudson, Kathryn Malm, Angela Smith, Janice Borzendowski, and Brian Snapp. Kathryn deserves special recognition for her ability to edit technical material while keeping an exhausted author motivated.

Thanks to the Wrights, for their consistent friendship, encouragement, and lawn advice. We couldn't ask for better neighbors.

Thanks to my parents, for fostering a lifetime obsession with the printed word.

I will never be able to sufficiently thank my family for permitting me this most selfish endeavor. How many evenings and weekends did I take away? How many mornings did I wake bleary eyed and grumpy from too little sleep and too little progress? This book truly was a once in a lifetime opportunity for the skinny (formerly) kid who read too much, and you two made it possible. Thank you!

About the Author

CT Arrington has spent the last nine years developing client-server software systems ranging from currency options valuation to barge scheduling to complex corporate intranets. Over the last five years, he has become convinced that the combination of Object Oriented Analysis and Design and good Software Engineering practices can yield excellent systems in a sane work environment.

CT's focus over the last few years has been architecting and developing systems in Java. These tended to be 3+ tier server side applications for use in corporate intranets. His favorite technologies for such systems include Servlets, XML, EJB, and Object to Relational persistence frameworks. He also had the good fortune to be the lead developer for a slick Java data visualization tool for barge scheduling. This project used Swing and a commercial 2D graphics framework and convinced him that Java applications can meet demanding performance goals.

In these pursuits, CT has depended heavily on books on OO design, design patterns, software engineering, Java, CORBA, EJB, and XML. While he has read and enjoyed many great books over the years, he cannot imagine developing software without Grady Booch's *OOAD with Applications*, the Gang of Four's *Design Patterns*, Steve McConnell's *Rapid Development* and of course, Patrick Chan's *The Java Class Libraries*.

CT is an architect and development manager with Capital One in Northern Virginia.

CT is a former Rational Software certified instructor and a Sun certified Java Programmer, Developer, and Architect. He holds a Bachelor's in Applied Mathematics from the University of Maryland at Baltimore County.

OMG Press Advisory Board

OMG Press Books in Print

(For complete information about current and upcoming titles, go to www.wiley
.com/compbooks/omg/)

- *Building Business Objects* by Peter Eeles and Oliver Sims, ISBN: 0471-191760.
- *Business Component Factory: A Comprehensive Overview of Component-Based Development for the Enterprise* by Peter Herzum and Oliver Sims, ISBN: 0471-327603.
- *Business Modeling with UML: Business Patterns at Work* by Hans-Erik Eriksson and Magnus Penker, ISBN: 0471-295515.
- *CORBA 3 Fundamentals and Programming, 2nd Edition* by Jon Siegel, ISBN: 0471-295183.
- *CORBA Design Patterns* by Thomas J. Mowbray and Raphael C. Malveau, ISBN: 0471-158828.
- *Enterprise Application Integration with CORBA: Component and Web-Based Solutions* by Ron Zahavi, ISBN: 0471-32704.
- *Enterprise Java with UML* by CT Arrington, ISBN: 0471-386804
- *The Essential CORBA: Systems Integration Using Distributed Objects* by Thomas J. Mowbray and Ron Zahavi, ISBN: 0471-106119.
- *Instant CORBA* by Robert Orfali, Dan Harkey and Jeri Edwards, ISBN: 0471-183334.
- *Integrating CORBA and COM Applications* by Michael Rosen and David Curtis, ISBN: 0471-198277.
- *Java Programming with CORBA, Third Edition* by Gerald Brose, Andreas Vogel, and Keith Duddy, ISBN: 0471-247650.
- *The Object Technology Casebook: Lessons from Award-Winning Business Applications* by Paul Harmon and William Morrisey, ISBN: 0471-147176.

- *The Object Technology Revolution by Michael Guttman and Jason* Matthews, ISBN: 0471-606790.

- *Programming with Enterprise JavaBeans, JTS and OTS: Building Distributed Transactions with Java and C++* by Andreas Vogel and Madhavan Rangarao, ISBN: 0471-319724.

- *Programming with Java IDL* by Geoffrey Lewis, Steven Barber and Ellen Siegel, ISBN: 0471-247979.

- *UML Toolkit* by Hans-Erik Eriksson and Magnus Penker, ISBN: 0471-191612.

About the OMG

The Object Management Group (OMG) was chartered to create and foster a component-based software marketplace through the standardization and promotion of object-oriented software. To achieve this goal, the OMG specifies open standards for every aspect of distributed object computing from analysis and design, through infrastructure, to application objects and components.

The well-established CORBA (Common Object Request Broker Architecture) standardizes a platform- and programming-language-independent distributed object computing environment. It is based on OMG/ISO Interface Definition Language (OMG IDL) and the Internet Inter-ORB Protocol (IIOP). Now recognized as a mature technology, CORBA is represented on the marketplace by well over 70 ORBs (Object Request Brokers) plus hundreds of other products. Although most of these ORBs are tuned for general use, others are specialized for real-time or embedded applications, or built into transaction processing systems where they provide scalability, high throughput and reliability. Of the thousands of live, mission-critical CORBA applications in use today around the world, over 300 are documented on the OMG's success-story web pages at http://www.corba.org.

CORBA 3, the OMG's latest release, adds a Component Model, quality-of-service control, a messaging invocation model, and tightened integration with the Internet, Enterprise Java Beans and the Java programming language. Widely anticipated by the industry, CORBA 3 keeps this established architecture in the forefront of distributed computing, as will a new OMG specification integrating CORBA with XML. Well-known for its ability to integrate legacy systems into your network, along with the wide variety of heterogeneous hardware and software on the market today, CORBA enters the new millennium prepared to integrate the technologies on the horizon.

Augmenting this core infrastructure are the CORBAservices which standardize naming and directory services, event handling, transaction processing, security, and other functions. Building on this firm foundation, OMG Domain Facilities standardize common objects throughout the supply and service chains in industries such as Telecommunications, Healthcare, Manufacturing,

Transportation, Finance/Insurance, Electronic Commerce, Life Science, and Utilities.

The OMG standards extend beyond programming. OMG Specifications for analysis and design include the Unified Modeling Language (UML), the repository standard Meta-Object Facility (MOF), and XML-based Metadata Interchange (XMI). The UML is a result of fusing the concepts of the world's most prominent methodologists. Adopted as an OMG specification in 1997, it represents a collection of best engineering practices that have proven successful in the modeling of large and complex systems and is a well-defined, widely -accepted response to these business needs. The MOF is OMG's standard for metamodeling and metadata repositories. Fully integrated with UML, it uses the UML notation to describe repository metamodels. Extending this work, the XMI standard enables the exchange of objects defined using UML and the MOF. XMI can generate XML Data Type Definitions for any service specification that includes a normative, MOF-based metamodel.

In summary, the OMG provides the computing industry with an open, vendor-neutral, proven process for establishing and promoting standards. OMG makes all of its specifications available without charge from its website, http://www.omg.org. With over a decade of standard-making and consensus-building experience, OMG now counts about 800 companies as members. Delegates from these companies convene at week-long meetings held five times each year at varying sites around the world, to advance OMG technologies. The OMG welcomes guests to their meetings; for an invitation, send your email request to info@omg.org.

Membership in the OMG is open to end users, government organizations, academia and technology vendors. For more information on the OMG, contact OMG headquarters by phone at +1-508-820 4300, by fax at +1-508-820 4303, by email at info@omg.org, or on the web at www.omg.org.

Introduction to Modeling Java with the UML

As Java completes its move from a novelty language to the language of choice for Web-enabled enterprise computing, Java developers are faced with many opportunities as well as many challenges. We must produce systems that scale as the underlying business grows and evolves at Web speed. Our customers' appetite for functionality, scalability, usability, extensibility, and reliability rises each year.

Fortunately, Java provides a lot of support as we struggle to meet these demands. First and perhaps foremost, Java is a small, tightly written object-oriented language with excellent support for exception handling and concurrency built in. Of course, this language runs on a platform-independent virtual machine that allows Java systems to run on everything from a PalmPilot to a Web browser to an AS400, with about a dozen operating systems in between. From this solid foundation, Sun built and evolved one of the most impressive class libraries you could ever ask for, including support for internationalization, calendar management, database access, image manipulation, networking, user interfaces, 2D and 3D graphics, and more. Finally, Enterprise JavaBeans and Java 2 Enterprise Edition provide specifications for true cross-platform enterprise computing. Many of the problems that have plagued enterprise developers for decades, such as object-to-relational persistence, object caching, data integrity, and resource management are being addressed with newfound vigor. These specifications, and the application servers that implement them, allow us to leverage a wealth of academic research and practical experience. We are better equipped to develop enterprise systems than ever before.

However, powerful tools do not guarantee success. Before developers can harness the enormous power of enterprise Java technology, they need a clear understanding of the problem and a clear plan for the solution. In order to develop this understanding, they need a way to visualize the system and communicate their decisions and creations to a wide audience. Fortunately, the last few decades have also seen dramatic progress in our ability to understand and model object-oriented systems. The Unified Modeling Language (UML) is an open standard notation that allows developers to build visual representations of software systems. These models enable developers to devise elegant solutions, share ideas, and track decisions throughout the entire development cycle. Also, tools for creating, reverse-engineering, and distributing software models in UML have matured greatly over the past two years, to the point where modeling can be a seamless part of a development lifecycle.

This book describes software modeling with the UML, and demonstrates how developers can use UML throughout the software development process to create better enterprise Java systems and more livable enterprise Java projects. The remainder of this chapter discusses software modeling in more detail and presents some object-oriented terminology and UML notation as a foundation for the rest of the book.

NOTE This is a book for Java developers who are interested in modeling software before they build it. It is based on my own practical experience as a software developer, both painful and euphoric.

When you finish this book, you will be able to:

- Communicate an understanding of OO modeling theory and practice to others.
- Communicate an understanding of UML notation to others.
- Critically review a wide variety of UML software models.
- Use UML to create a detailed understanding of the problem from the user's perspective.
- Use UML to visualize and document a balanced solution using the full suite of Java technologies.
- Use UML to describe other technologies and class libraries.

What Is Modeling?

A model is a simplification with a purpose. It uses a precisely defined notation to describe and simplify a complex and interesting structure, phenomenon, or relationship. We create models to avoid drowning in complexity and so that we can understand and control the world around us. Consider a few examples from the real world. Mathematical models of our solar system allow mere mortals to calculate the positions of the planets. Engineers use sophisticated modeling techniques to design everything from aircraft carriers to circuit boards. Meteorologists use mathematical models to predict the weather.

Models of software systems help developers visualize, communicate, and validate a system before significant amounts of money are spent. Software models also help structure and coordinate the efforts of a software development team. The following sections describe some characteristics of models and how they contribute to software development.

Simplification

A model of a system is far less complex, and therefore far more accessible, than the actual code and components that make up the final system. It is much easier for a developer to build, extend, and evaluate a visual model than to work directly in the code. Think of all the decisions that you make while coding. Every time you code, you must decide which parameters to pass, what type of return value to use, where to put certain functionality, and a host of other questions. Once these decisions are made in code, they tend to stay made. With modeling, and especially with a visual modeling tool, these decisions can be made and revised quickly and efficiently. The software model serves the same purpose as an artist's rough sketch. It is a quick and relatively cheap way to get a feel for the actual solution.

The inherent simplicity of models also makes them the perfect mechanism for collaboration and review. It is very difficult to involve more than one other developer during the coding process. Committing to regular code reviews requires a great deal of discipline in the face of ubiquitous schedule pressure. A particular piece of a software model can be reviewed for quality, understandability, and consistency with the rest of the model. Preparation time for reviews of a model is dramatically lower than for a comparable code walkthrough. An experienced developer can assimilate a detailed model of an entire subsystem in a day. Assimilating the actual code for the same subsystem can easily take weeks. This allows more developers to collaborate and review more of the whole model. In general, collaboration and review of software models leads to lower defect rates and fewer difficulties during integration. Also, software models dramatically decrease the time required to assimilate and review code.

Varying Perspectives

A single model of a software system can describe the system from different perspectives. One view might show how major parts of the system interact and cooperate. Another view might zoom in on the details of a particular piece of the system. Yet another view might describe the system from the users' perspective. Having these different views helps developers manage complexity, as high-level views provide context and navigation. Once the developer has found an area of interest, he or she can zoom in and assimilate the details for that area. Newly acquired developers find this especially useful as they learn their way around a system.

We use this technique in the real world. Consider the common street map, which models the streets and buildings of a city. One part of the map might show the major highways and thoroughfares of the entire city, while another part might zoom in on the downtown area to show each street in detail. Both views are correct and valuable, in different ways.

Common Notation

A common notation allows developers to move past arguments over the meaning of a proposed solution and focus on the merits of the solution. Of course, this requires consistent use and understanding of the common notation. Many other disciplines use a common notation to facilitate communication. Experienced musicians do not argue over the meanings of their symbols. They can depend on the notation to provide a precise description of the sounds, which frees them to collaborate to find the right sounds.

A precise software model in a common notation allows developers to combine their efforts and to work in parallel. As long as each contribution fits the model, the parts can be combined into the final system. Modern manufacturing uses this technique to lower costs and decrease production schedules. Based on a vehicle design, an automotive manufacturer can purchase parts from hundreds of suppliers. As long as each part meets the specifications described in the design model, it will fit nicely into the final product.

UML

The Unified Modeling Language (UML) is a language for specifying, visualizing, constructing, and documenting the artifacts of software systems. UML provides the precise notation that we need when modeling software systems. It is important to note that the UML is not just a way to document existing ideas. The UML helps developers create ideas, as well as communicate them.

The UML was not the first notation for modeling object-oriented software systems. In fact, UML was created to end the confusion between competing notations. Many of the best and brightest academics and practitioners in the field of object-oriented software development joined together in the mid- to late-1990s to create a common notation. It is now the international standard for modeling object-oriented systems.

The UML is an open standard controlled by the Object Management Group (OMG), rather than any one individual or company. This book uses and discusses version 1.3 of the UML, which is the current version. The next major release of UML, 2.0, is expected sometime in 2002.

The Basics

Before we dive into modeling your system using UML, there are a few object-oriented concepts that you need to understand before you start.

Abstraction

An *abstraction* is a simplification or model of a complex concept, process, or real-world object. As humans, we need abstractions to survive. Abstractions allow us to simplify our understanding of the world so that our understanding is useful without becoming overwhelming. Do you thoroughly understand personal computers, televisions, CD players, or even a simple transistor radio? Can the same person understand these electronic devices and also conquer the mysteries of cellular biology and human physiology? How about the details of any two human endeavors, such as coal mining and professional football?

An abstraction is a simplification or mental model that helps a person understand something at an appropriate level. This implies that different people would build radically different abstractions for the same concept. For example, I see my refrigerator as a big box with a door, some food inside, and a little wheel that lets me set the temperature. A design engineer sees my refrigerator as a complex system with an evaporator fan, an evaporator, a defrost heater, a compressor, and a condenser fan, all working together to move heat from the inside of the equipment to my kitchen. The design engineer needs this rich view of the fridge to design an efficient and effective refrigerator. I, on the other hand, am needlessly burdened by such details. I just want a cold glass of soda.

A good abstraction highlights the relevant characteristics and behavior of something that is too complex to understand in its entirety. The needs and interests of the abstraction's creator determine the level of detail and emphasis of the abstraction.

Abstractions are even more useful when they help us understand how different parts of a larger model interact together. In the object-oriented world, the interacting parts of a model are called *objects*.

Encapsulation

According to my dusty old copy of Webster's, to encapsulate means "to enclose in or as if in a capsule." For object-oriented systems, the specifics of the data and behavioral logic are hidden within each type of object. Think of encapsulation as a counterpoint to abstraction. An abstraction highlights the important aspects of an object, while encapsulation hides the cumbersome internal details of the object. Encapsulation is a very powerful tool in our effort to make reusable, extensible, and comprehensible systems.

First, encapsulating the nasty details inside of a system makes the system easier to understand and to reuse. In many cases, another developer may not care how an object works, as long as it provides the desired functionality. The less he or she needs to know about the object in order to use it, the more likely that developer is to reuse it. In short, encapsulation reduces the burden of adopting a class or class library for use in a system.

Also, encapsulation makes a system more extensible. A well-encapsulated object allows other objects to use it without depending on any internal details. Consequently, new requirements may be met by changing the encapsulated details, without affecting the code that uses the object.

Object

An object is a particular and finite element in a larger model. An object may be very concrete, such as a particular automobile in a car dealer's inventory system. An object may be invisible, such as an individual's bank account in a banking system. An object may have a short life, such as a transaction in a banking system.

It is important to distinguish between the abstraction that similar objects in a system share and the objects themselves. For example, the abstraction comprising cars in a dealer's inventory system certainly includes the make, model, mileage, year, color, purchase price, and condition. The object, which is a particular car in the inventory, might be a light blue 1996 Honda Accord, in good condition, with 54,000 miles on the odometer.

All objects have *state*, which describes their characteristics and current condition. Some characteristics, such as make and model for the car, never change. Other parts of a car's state, such as mileage, change over time.

Objects also have *behavior*, which defines the actions that other objects may perform on the object. For instance, a bank account may allow a customer object to withdraw money or deposit money. A customer initiates a withdrawal, but the logic for performing the withdrawal lives inside of the account object. Behavior may depend on an object's state. For example, a car with no gas is unlikely to provide desirable behavior.

Moreover, each object in a system must be uniquely identifiable within the system. There must be some characteristic or group of characteristics that sets each object apart. To continue the car example, each car has a unique vehicle identification number.

In the UML, an object is represented as a rectangle with the name underlined, as in Figure 1.1

The work in an object-oriented system is divided up among many objects. Each object is configured for its particular role in the system. Since each object has a fairly narrow set of responsibilities, the objects must cooperate to accomplish larger goals. Consider a customer who wants to transfer money from one account to another at an ATM. This fairly trivial example requires a user interface object, a customer object, a checking account object, and a savings account object. This combination of narrow specialization and cooperation allows the objects to stay simple and easy to understand. A *method* is a service or responsibility that an object exposes to other objects. Thus, one object can call another object's methods. A method is loosely analogous to a function or subroutine in procedural programming, except that the method is called on a specific object that has its own state. This tight integration between data and behavior is one of the key distinguishing features of object-oriented software development.

Class

A class is a group of objects that have something in common. A class captures a particular abstraction and provides a template for object creation. By convention, class names start with an uppercase letter and use mixed case to mark word boundaries. Each object created from the class is identical in the following ways:

- The type of data that the object can hold. For instance, a car class might specify that each car object have string data for the color, make, and model.
- The type and number of objects that the object knows about. A car class might specify that every car object know about one or more previous owners.
- The logic for any behavior that the object provides.

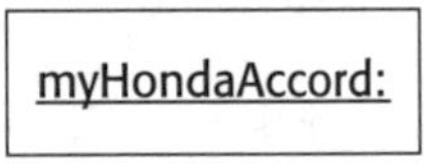

myHondaAccord:

Figure 1.1 A car object.

The actual values for the data are left to the objects. This means that one car may be a blue Honda Accord with one previous owner, while another car might be a green Subaru Outback with two previous owners. Also, since the behavior may be state-dependent, two different objects may respond differently to the same request. However, two objects with identical state must respond identically.

Consider a more detailed and completely silly analogy. Toy soldiers are created by melting either green or brown plastic and injecting the molten plastic into little molds. The shape of the mold determines the height and shape of the toy soldier, as well as its ability to grasp a tiny rifle and carry a radio on its back. The purchaser cannot change the height of the toy or outfit it with a flamethrower. The class—I mean mold—does not support these configurations.

However, there is still work for purchasers of the toy soldier. They may provide or withhold the rifle and radio, and they may organize the toys into squads for deployment against the hated Ken doll. They are configuring the objects—oops, I mean soldiers—and determining the associations between them.

Objects provide the real value in an object-oriented system. They hold the data and perform the work. Classes, like molds, are important for the creation of the objects, though no one ever plays with them.

In the UML, a class is represented as a rectangle with the name in the top compartment, the data in the next compartment, and the behavior in the third compartment. Figure 1.2 shows a UML representation of the ToySoldier class. Notice that unlike the UML representation of an object, the name is not underlined.

Relationships between Objects

Object-oriented systems are populated by many distinct objects that cooperate to accomplish various tasks. Each object has a narrowly defined set of responsibilities, so they must work together to fulfill their collective goals. In order to cooperate, objects must have relationships that allow them to communicate with one another.

Recall that the state and behavior for an object is determined and constrained by the object's class. The class controls the state that the object possesses, the behavior that it provides, and the other objects that it has relationships with. With this in mind, it is logical to describe the relationships between objects in a class diagram.

There are four types of relationships:

- Dependency
- Association

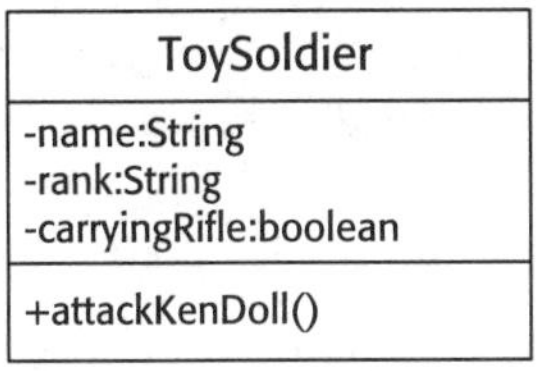

ToySoldier
-name:String -rank:String -carryingRifle:boolean
+attackKenDoll()

Figure 1.2 The ToySoldier class in the UML.

- Aggregation
- Composition

Dependency

Dependency is the weakest relationship between objects. An object depends on an object if it has a short-term relationship with the object. During this short-lived relationship, the dependent object may call methods on the other object to obtain services or configure the object. Real life is full of dependency relationships. We depend on the cashier at the grocery store to sell us food, but we do not have a long-term relationship with that person. In the UML, dependency is represented by a dashed line with an arrow pointing to the depended upon class.

Dependency relationships in object-oriented systems follow a few common patterns. An object may create an object as part of a method, ask it to perform some function, and then forget about it. An object may create an object as part of a method, configure it, and pass the object to the method caller as a return value. An object may receive an object as a parameter to a method, use it or modify it, then forget about it when the method ends.

Figure 1.3 shows a dependency relationship between the Customer class and the Cashier class. This relationship reads as: "Each Customer object depends on Cashier objects." Changes to interface of the Cashier class may affect the Customer class.

Association

An association is a long-term relationship between objects. In an association, an object keeps a reference to another object and can call the object's methods, as it needs them. Real life is replete with association relationships. Consider people with their automobiles. As long as they remember where they left their car, the car will let them in and take them to their destination. In the UML, association is represented by a solid line between the two classes.

In some cases an object may instantiate another object and keep a reference to it for future use. An object may also receive an object as a parameter to a configuration method and keep a reference to the object.

Figure 1.4 shows an association relationship between the Person class and the Car class. The relationship is read as: "Every Person object is associated with an unspecified number of Car objects," and "every Car object is associated with an unspecified number of Person objects." It may help to think of this as a "knows-about-a" relationship, as in "each Person object knows about some Car objects."

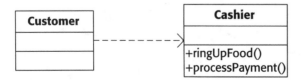

Figure 1.3 Sample dependency relationship.

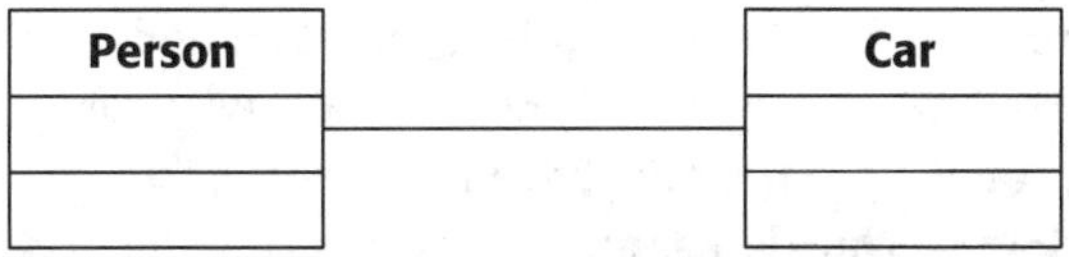

Person		Car	

Figure 1.4 Sample association relationship.

Aggregation

An aggregation relationship indicates that an object is part of a greater whole. The contained object may participate in more than one aggregation relationship, and exists independently of the whole. For example, a software developer may be part of two project teams and continues to function even if both teams dissolve. Figure 1.5 shows this aggregation relationship.

In the UML, aggregation is indicated by decorating an association line with a hollow diamond next to the "whole" class. The relationship is read as: "Each ProjectTeam object has some SoftwareDeveloper objects," and "each SoftwareDeveloper object may belong to one or more ProjectTeam objects."

Composition

A composition relationship indicates that an object is owned by a greater whole. The contained object may not participate in more than one composition relationship and cannot exist independently of the whole. The part is created as part of the creation of the whole, and is destroyed when the whole is destroyed. In the UML, composition is indicated by decorating an association with a solid diamond next to the "whole" class.

Consider a small gear deep in the oily bowels of an internal combustion engine. It is inextricably part of the engine. It is not worth the cost of removal when the engine finally expires, and it is not accessible for replacement. Figure 1.6 shows this composition relationship. The relationship is read as: "Each Engine object always contains a SmallGear object," and "Each SmallGear object always belongs to a single Engine object."

Figure 1.5 Sample aggregation relationship.

Figure 1.6 Sample composition relationship

> **TIP**   It may be difficult to remember which relationship is aggregation and which is composition. I offer a simple and somewhat silly mnemonic device for aggregation. Aggregation sounds a lot like congregation, as in members of a church. People may exist before joining a church. People may belong to more than one church, or they may change churches. Likewise, people continue to exist after leaving the church or after the church disbands or merges with another church. As for composition, well, it is the other one. Sorry.

Navigability

Relationships between objects are often one-sided. For instance, in any car that I can afford, the Car object controls the Wheel objects, but the Wheel objects are unable to control the Car. Figure 1.7 shows an association relationship between the Car class and the Wheel class. The arrow pointing to the Wheel class indicates that the Car may send messages to the Wheel but that the Wheel cannot send messages to the Car. This means that a Car object may call the getSpinSpeed method on its Wheel objects and that the Wheel object may return a value from that method; but the Wheel does not have a reference to the Car object, so it cannot call the startEngine method.

According to the UML specification, an association line with no arrows can have one of two meanings. Developers on a project may agree that the absence of arrows means that the association is not navigable. Alternatively, developers on a project may agree that the absence of arrows means that the association is bidirectional.

Since there is no reason to have an association that is not navigable, the first interpretation of an association with no arrows generally means that the navigability has not been determined. In this case, an arrow on each side of the line indicates bidirectional navigability.

Developers on a project may agree that a line with no arrows represents bidirectional navigability. In this case, the double-arrow notation is never used and there is no way to indicate an unspecified or not-navigable association.

For this book, I use double arrows to indicate bidirectional navigability. I prefer this option because it allows me to defer consideration of the navigability of an association without confusion.

Multiplicity

One object may have an association with a single object, with a certain number of objects, or with an unlimited number of objects. Figure 1.8 shows several relationships

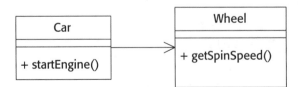

Figure 1.7 Sample association with one-way navigability.

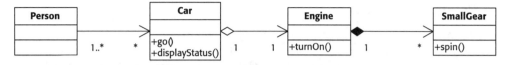

Figure 1.8 Sample associations with multiplicity.

with the multiplicity determined. In the UML, the multiplicity describes the object that it is next to. So, an Engine object may have many SmallGear objects, but each Small-Gear object belongs to exactly one Engine object. Each Car object is associated with one or more Person objects, and each Person object may be associated with several Car objects. Also, each Car object has exactly one Engine object, and different Car objects never share an Engine object.

NOTE There is no default multiplicity. The absence of a multiplicity for an association indicates that the multiplicity has not been determined.

Interface

An interface defines a set of related behavior, but does not specify the actual implementation for the behavior. To be more specific, each interface completely specifies the signature of one or more methods, complete with parameters and return type. An interface captures an abstraction, without addressing any implementation details.

A class realizes an interface by implementing each method in the interface. The interface defines a set of behavior. The class makes it real.

Interfaces provide flexibility when specifying the relationship between objects. Rather than specifying that each instance of a class has a relationship with an instance of a specific class, we can specify that each instance of a class has a relationship with an instance of some class that realizes a particular interface. As we will see throughout this book, creative use of this feature provides an amazing amount of flexibility and extensibility.

For instance, a game might contain a sound simulator object that is responsible for collecting and playing the sounds that emanate from various objects in a virtual world. Each SoundSimulator object is associated with zero or more objects whose classes realize the INoiseMaker interface. From the SoundSimulator's perspective, the specific type of noisemaker is completely irrelevant. Figure 1.9 shows this relationship.

Figure 1.9 Sample interface.

Polymorphism

Polymorphism, according to my dictionary, means having more than one form. In object-oriented circles, polymorphism refers to multiple implementations of a single abstraction. Abstractions are captured in classes and in interfaces. So, we can get polymorphism by having more than one class inherit from a base class. Each class could simply override the default implementation provided by the base class. We can also get polymorphism by having more than one class realize an interface. Each class must provide an implementation for each method in the interface.

To continue our sound simulator example for polymorphism through interfaces, consider two classes that make noise, Trumpet and Tiger. Both implement the makeNoise method and realize the INoiseMaker interface. Each SoundSimulator object is associated with some objects whose classes realize INoiseMaker. The sound simulator does not need to know the specific class for each object. Instead, the sound simulator just asks the object to make some noise. Figure 1.10 shows the two classes that realize the INoiseMaker interface and the relationship between SoundSimulator and INoiseMaker.

Multiple implementations of an abstraction can also be achieved by having more than one subclass override the default implementation provided by the base class. Figure 1.11 shows an alternative approach in which each SoundSimulator object is associated with some objects that instantiate SimulationElement or a subclass of SimulationElement. As before, the SoundSimulator knows that the object on the other end of the association implements the makeNoise method, but does not know what sound to expect.

Polymorphism has two very significant benefits. First, polymorphism allows unlimited flexibility within a running system. Different implementations of an abstraction can be mixed and matched to achieve very interesting affects. The second benefit is long-term extensibility for the system. As long as the abstraction is unchanged, new implementations can be introduced without affecting the code that depends on an interface. For example, adding a new class that realizes INoiseMaker does not affect the SoundSimulator class in any way.

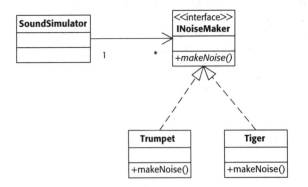

Figure 1.10 Polymorphism through realization.

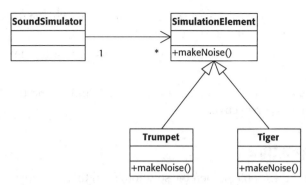

Figure 1.11 Polymorphism through inheritance.

Modeling Software Systems with the UML

UML enables developers to build a single coherent model that describes a software system from several perspectives. This combination of internal consistency and distinct views means that a variety of participants can use the same model and speak the same language throughout the development process. Granted, some participants will only use part of the model, but they can still follow the overall structure of the model.

The Customer's Perspective

Most customers are relatively disinterested in technology. They are far more interested in the value that the system provides for them, that is, how it increases their productivity and makes their lives easier. Developers should gather requirements from the customer's perspective, considering how the customer will interact with the system to obtain value. This allows the customer to review and validate the requirements from a very natural perspective, his or her own. The customers can also measure development progress from an individual perspective.

UML provides several mechanisms for documenting system requirements from the user's perspective. They are the use case diagram, a text description for each use case, and an activity diagram for each use case.

- A *use case* defines and describes a discrete way in which users get value from the system. A user might perform a series of fairly complex steps to obtain a desirable result, such as withdrawing funds from an ATM or purchasing a book online. Alternatively, a user may simply press a large red button labeled Run Quarterly Sales Report. User effort is not the determining factor. Instead, the independent usefulness of the result is the key. A *use case diagram* models all interactions between the user and a system in a single high-level diagram. This diagram allows customers and developers to capture the intent and scope of the system in a very accessible format. The use cases can then be used to track development progress and to guide development activities.

- The *text description* of each use case describes the use case, including the details of the interactions between the user and the system.
- An *activity diagram* is a visual description of the interactions between the system and the user for a use case.

Together, these diagrams help the customers and developers to fully understand the system problem from the customer's perspective.

The Developer's Perspective

Developers must first understand the problem, then the solution, from their own perspective. Object-oriented systems force developers to describe a system in terms of objects that cooperate to provide functionality to the users, so object-oriented developers focus on the objects that populate the system and the classes that define the objects.

UML provides several mechanisms for documenting a system from the developer's perspective: class diagrams, state chart diagrams, package diagrams, sequence diagrams, and collaboration diagrams.

- A *class diagram* defines and constrains a group of objects in detail. It shows the state, behavior, and relationships with other objects that are mandated for each object that instantiates the class.
- A *state chart* describes the state-dependent behavior for a class. Specifically, it describes how an object responds to different requests depending on the object's internal configuration.
- A *package diagram* describes how different parts of a system depend on one another based on the relationships between objects that reside in different parts of the system.
- A *sequence diagram* shows how objects interact with one another to provide functionality. A sequence diagram clearly indicates the order of the interaction; it is less useful for determining the relationships between objects.
- A *collaboration diagram* also shows how objects interact with one another to provide functionality. Collaboration diagrams provide a counterpoint to sequence diagrams by clearly revealing the relationships between objects. However, they are less useful for determining the sequence of interactions.

Modeling Process

UML is used to gradually evolve the understanding of a system. First, the developers and customers use the UML to understand the problem from the customer's point of view. Next the developers use UML to understand the problem from their own point of view. This clear understanding of the problem allows the developers to use UML as they invent a solution to the problem. Finally, the UML model is used as a resource by the implementers of the system. The chapters in this book mimic the stages of the modeling process.

Requirements Gathering

When gathering requirements, developers seek to understand the problem from the customer's perspective, without concern for technology or system design. This ensures that the developers are focused on the correct problem. While no system is immune to requirements change or "scope creep," adopting this perspective can prevent misunderstandings and dramatically reduce the severity of requirements changes.

In this process, developers create use case diagrams, text use case descriptions, and activity diagrams. I introduce requirements gathering in Chapter 2, "Gathering Requirements with UML." In Chapter 3, "Gathering Requirements for the Timecard Application," I begin gathering requirements for a sample application.

Analysis

In analysis, developers seek to understand the problem from their own perspective, still without concern for technology. Building on the understanding of the problem created during requirements gathering, they discover the roles and responsibilities that must be filled in the system. This builds a solid foundation for technology selection and design of the system.

In the analysis process, developers create class diagrams, sequence diagrams, and collaboration diagrams. I introduce analysis in Chapter 4, "A Brief Introduction to Object-Oriented Analysis with the UML." In Chapter 5, "Analysis Model for the Timecard Application," I demonstrate analysis in an example.

Technology Selection

During technology selection, developers categorize the system in terms of its technological requirements, then select the most appropriate technologies to fulfill these well-defined needs. This orderly and disciplined approach to selecting technology trades a fairly large upfront effort for decreased risk over the life of the project.

In the technology selection process, developers use all of the existing documents and diagrams. They produce a high-level summary of the technological requirements and a list of appropriate technologies for the system. No additional UML diagrams are produced.

Technology selection is covered in several chapters. In Chapter 6, "Describing the System for Technology Selection," I explain the process for describing the technology needs of a system, and reinforce these ideas by example. In Chapters 7 ("Evaluating Candidate Technologies for Boundary Classes") and 8 ("Evaluating Candidate Technologies for Control and Entity Classes"), I present different technologies and describe their suitability, before selecting appropriate technologies for the example system.

Architecture

In architecture, developers describe the system at a high level, and decompose the system into smaller parts, such as subsystems. Relationships between parts are highlighted, while the details of each part are deferred. Technology selections are clearly shown as part of the architecture. Providing a high-level view of the system and its component parts makes it possible for a large number of participants to evaluate the feasibility of the architecture. Also, during design and implementation, the architecture serves as an invaluable high-level guide to developers as they struggle to understand the system as a whole.

Architecture builds on the cumulative understanding of the system as described in the use case model and in the technology selection. During architecture, developers produce primarily class diagrams and package diagrams.

I cover architecture in a single chapter: Chapter 9, "Software Architecture," explains the process and demonstrates it through the sample system.

Design and Implementation

In design, developers use all of the results from the previous steps as they create an intricate model of the objects that interact to provide the system's functionality. A detailed design provides the last chance to validate the solution before the extremely expensive and labor-intensive implementation process begins. In about a day, a small group of developers who are familiar with UML and with the system can prepare for a thorough design review of a major subsystem. Compare this to the weeks that are required to read and understand the code for a major subsystem. A detailed design can be created, reviewed, and revised in a fraction of the time it takes to write the code.

Once the design is complete, it serves as a valuable foundation for implementation. Developers are free to focus their efforts on the details of the implementation technologies, without constantly worrying whether their efforts will fit within the larger system. As long as they follow the design, or reconcile any changes to the design with other developers, their work will not be wasted. I cover design and implementation in the remainder of the book: in Chapter 10, "Introduction to Design," I explain the process; I dedicate Chapters 11 ("Design for the Timecard Domain and Timecard Workflow") and 12 ("Design for HTML Production") to designs for different parts of the system.

WHAT'S ON THE CD-ROM

The book's companion CD-ROM contains all the design documents and the source code for the sample Timecard application that you'll work on through out the book. You'll also find instructions for installing and running the sample Timecard application with Sun's J2EE reference implementation. Use these files as you go along through the book exercises.

The Next Step

Now that we have established a basic understanding of the terminology and the processes involved, we can start with requirements gathering, which seeks to understand the problem from the customer's perspective.

Gathering Requirements
with UML

The first step to designing any enterprise application is to gather requirements for the system. A system's requirements consist of a document (or a collection of documents) that describes the functionality that the system provides. It is an agreement between the end user, the developer, and the system's sponsor as to what the system should and can do.

Requirements gathering is an interactive process whereby business analysts and developers gather system requirements by interacting with end users, domain experts, and other stakeholders. This highly iterative process is a combination of problem discovery and consensus building that lays the foundation for the project's success.

In this chapter, I'll show you how the Unified Modeling Language (UML) can be used in a requirements-gathering process. I'll outline several classic paths that lead to poor requirements, then suggest ways that you can detect and avoid them.

> **NOTE** The UML notation and requirements-gathering techniques introduced here will be used to capture requirements for a sample application in Chapter 3, "Gathering Requirements for the Timecard Application." I use this sample application throughout the book, so even if you are an expert in requirements gathering, it might be useful to skim this chapter and read Chapter 3.

Are You Ready?

Before you can gather requirements, you need to do two things:

1. Create a clear vision of the system.

2. Determine who has the decision-making authority for the project.

The first step is to create a clear vision for the system. This vision is described in the *vision document,* a text document that presents an extremely high-level explanation of the goals and scope of the system. The vision document can be in any format. In one company, the vision document may be two paragraphs transferred from the napkins that were handy during the dinner when the principals spawned the idea for the company. In another organization, it may be a formal document that presents an exhaustive business case, complete with revenue projections, return-on-investment calculations, and four-color graphs on fancy paper. However it is presented, a successful vision document describes the system, its goals, and how the organization benefits from it. The system goals are described at a fairly detailed level to give the developers and the customers the flexibility to clarify the system vision. The document also highlights any known scope limitations.

The second step is to identify a *sponsor* or *sponsors* for the project. Gathering requirements without sponsors is painful at best and disastrous at worst, because they are the people who make final decisions regarding budget, features, and schedule. Ideally, the sponsors form a small decisive group that has the authority and vision needed to settle disputes and to keep a clear focus for the project. In any system, compromises must be made. For example, some desired functionality might be deferred to a later release to meet the schedule. Different groups of users may have different needs and goals that pull the system in different directions. Without a clear decision-making authority, it is difficult to resolve issues and to keep them resolved. When decisions are made and remade in a frustrating cycle in an attempt to please everyone, developers often end up over-committing themselves and, subsequently, end up disappointing everyone.

What Are Good Requirements?

Good requirements clearly and unambiguously state what the system does and for whom. They answer questions such as: Who uses the system? What value do users receive from their use of the system? These questions must be answered before considering technology selection, architecture, and design, otherwise, developers will be doomed to solve the wrong problems and be unable to make informed decisions about technology and architecture.

Requirements gathering involves five key steps:

1. Find the people who can help you understand the system.

2. Listen to these stakeholders and understand the system from their perspective.

3. Capture the way customers want to use the system, along with the value provided, in an accessible model.

4. Create a detailed description of the interactions between the system and the customers and between the system and other external systems.

5. Refactor the detailed descriptions to maintain readability and accessibility.

These steps are repeated until a solid consensus on what the system should do is reached. Notice that the goal is a *solid* consensus, not a 100 percent, perfect, consensus. Gathering requirements, like any creative and collaborative endeavor, never reaches a clear conclusion, as each iteration raises new subtleties and a new layer of details. Requirements must not become an end in themselves. Requirements are useful only as a form of communication and as a consensus-building process; they are not artistic works with intrinsic value. Each additional refinement of the requirements yields less and less value. At some point, the project must move on.

Find the Right People

In order to gather requirements, you must solicit input from people at different levels within the organization or user group. One group may understand the problem domain and strategic goals, but they may not actually use the system. Another group may not see the big picture, but may be intimately familiar with the day-to-day activities. These people are the system's stakeholders, those who have a significant interest in the project's direction and success. Stakeholders include everyone from the end user to the development team to the senior managers who control the budget. It is up to you to establish a reasonable rapport with a wide variety of stakeholders, for they will provide you with the information you'll need to develop the requirements document.

Domain Experts

The domain experts are the strategic thinkers. They understand the organization and the system. They set the goals for the system as well as lend insight to their particular domain. These people are usually easy to identify, as they generally have a high profile and occupy nice offices. They may have advanced degrees, many years of experience in their field, and a senior position, such as CEO, vice-president, or senior research fellow. Unfortunately, they also tend to be incredibly busy, talk too fast, and assume that everyone else knows and loves their field. To build the system that they need, you must understand them. To achieve that, you must make sure that they appreciate this simple truth and be confident that you will treat their time with care. Whenever possible, prepare by learning the relevant terminology and concepts inherent to their field before meeting with them, then baseline their expectations by explaining your limited background.

Subsequently, it is a good idea to verify your understanding of the conversations by paraphrasing them back to the source, preferably both verbally and in writing. Persistence and humility are key ingredients to your success.

End Users

Another important source of information is the actual end user. After all, it is the end users who must accept and use the final product. Their importance seems obvious, yet, remarkably, many organizations fail to solicit their input. Therefore, in some cases, you may need to push for access to a representative group of users. Sometimes the reluctance of management to grant access to the end users is evidence of an honest effort to protect the end users' time. In other cases, institutional traditions and rigid hierarchies erect the barrier. A medical doctor, for example, may balk at the idea that a licensed practical nurse may have valuable insights into the actual use of a medical data-tracking system. A manager with 20 years of experience may not realize that it has been 15 years since he or she actually did the work, and that a new hire may have a valuable perspective.

Be firm; excluding the actual users is not a viable option. Remember, developers must understand the day-to-day pragmatics as well as the strategic value of the system.

WARNING   **Never forget the end user.**

Listen to the Stakeholders

Developers need insight and knowledge from the stakeholders. To facilitate this dialogue, you must temporarily suppress your own perspective and inclinations so you can hear these stakeholders. In most cases, domain experts and end users are not concerned with cool technologies or object-oriented design principles; they want to know how they will benefit from the system. They are not interested in scarce technical resources or the risks of adopting new technology; they need a solid schedule that they can plan around. They are not interested in user interface design techniques; they just want a system that makes them more efficient.

Until you can clearly restate the customer's needs in your own words, do not plan the solution or consider the impact on the schedule. Above all, be positive, and try to think of the system in terms of the value that it provides to people. This is not an intuitive perspective for most developers, myself included. Our training and natural inclinations often make the solution more interesting than the problem. Also, there is a natural tendency to consider the impact on our personal and professional lives. We must overcome this mind-set—at least long enough to understand the needs of the people on the other side of the table.

It is important to remember that considering the other stakeholders' perspective does not mean committing to an impossible system or schedule. It means that developers are obligated to completely understand the requests and needs before contemplating feasibility and negotiating schedule.

TIP   **Gathering requirements sets the stage for development, and makes—or breaks—every development team's relationship with the customer and domain experts.**

Considering the customer's point of view in this initial stage often yields amazing dividends. In addition to high-quality requirements, you can gain the trust and goodwill of the stakeholders. Then, later in the process, stakeholders may consider the developer's perspective when considering requests to defer features or adjust the schedule.

The dialogue between you and the clients should be captured via meeting notes or transcribed recordings. Transcribed recordings are more accurate, but may make many people uncomfortable. In any case, a written dialogue that can be verified and built upon is an essential tool.

Develop Accessible Requirements

Requirements are useful if and only if people use them. If the user finds them turgid and/or incomprehensible, then they cannot tell you if you are specifying the right system. If developers find them obtuse and irrelevant, then the actual system will radically deviate from the requirements. While even the best requirements document is unlikely to find itself on the *New York Times* best-seller list, a requirements document must be readable and accessible to a wide audience. Describing how the system is used at a high level is an important step toward this goal.

TIP　Requirements are useful if and only if people use them.

The high-level diagrams within the use case model in UML provide an excellent mechanism for this purpose. *Use case diagrams* show discrete groups of system users as they interact with the system. There are three steps to creating a use case model.

1. Identify the groups of people who will use the system.
2. Determine how these groups of people will get value from the system.
3. Provide a simple and accessible view of the users and their use of the system.

The next sections take a closer look at each of these steps.

Find Actors

The first step to requirements gathering is to identify the distinct groups of people who will use the system. In UML, a distinct group is referred to as an *actor*. Other systems that use the system or are used by the system are also actors. So, an actor is a group of people or a system that is outside of the system and interacts with the system. To qualify as an actor, the group must use the system in a different way.

It is important to note that differences in the real world may not be relevant within the system requirements. For example, managers often are considered a distinct group of people in the real world, whereas in many systems, they are not separate actors because they do not use the system in a manner that is different from the way an employee uses the system. Consider a simple timecard system, in which every employee enters his or her hours. A select few add valid charge codes. It is possible that some employees who add charge codes are managers, but that some are not. So managers, in this case, do not need separate representation. Examples of reasonable actors from various domains will help clarify this distinction. The following groups are separate actors in the given problem domain.

- Bank customers and bank tellers are separate actors because they have very different needs and privileges in a banking system. For instance, customers cannot see other customers' records.

- Traveling salespeople and back-office personnel are separate actors because they have different needs and different access methods for a sales-tracking system.

- Students and the registrar are separate actors because they have very different needs and privileges in a course registration system.

The following groups do not need to be treated as separate actors.

- Republicans and Democrats do not need to be treated as separate actors in a system that gathers votes for an election. Party affiliation might be noted for each voter, but it does not change the way voters use the system.

- Doctors and nurses do not need to be treated as separate actors in a system that records quantitative medical data, such as heart rate, blood pressure, and temperature. Both groups are well qualified to obtain and record the information, and there are no differences in the way that they perform the activities.

- Men and women do not need to be treated as separate actors in most computer games.

Once you have identified the actors, you are ready to move on to the next step.

Find Use Cases

The next step is to identify the ways the actors get value from the system. In the UML, the manner in which the system provides a discrete value to an actor is called a *use case*. A user might perform a series of fairly complex steps to obtain a desirable result, such as withdrawing funds from an ATM or purchasing a book online. Alternatively, a user may simply press a large red button labeled Run Quarterly Sales Report. User effort is not the determining factor. Rather, the independent *usefulness* of the result is the key.

It is important to keep each use case well focused, with a single, clear purpose. Use cases divide the requirements into sections, so focused use cases make the documents easier to navigate and to understand. Use cases are also used for scheduling and estimation, so tightly focused use cases facilitate accurate estimation and precise tracking. Each use case is also used as a basis for a test case, so well-focused use cases convert nicely to a useful test plan and provide the basis for objective progress tracking. Monolithic use cases mean fewer divisions in the requirements documents and fewer milestones.

If you can answer yes to the following questions, a use case is well focused. Otherwise, the use case may need to be split into several use cases.

- Does the use case provide a single discrete benefit?
- Can you describe that benefit in 20 to 30 words, without adding several occurrences of "and" or "or"?
- Does the actor tend to complete the use case in a single session or sitting?
- Can you imagine the use case as a single test case in a coherent test plan?

Each use case must be significant and provide value in isolation. A use case may depend on other use cases or be part of a larger workflow, but the user must obtain a significant value from the use case alone. Individual steps, such as accepting user input, validating user input, retrieving data from a database, and formatting a result are not good candidates for use cases. They simply do not make sense separately.

If you can answer yes to the following questions, then the use case is probably significant and well isolated. Otherwise, the use case may really be part of some other use case.

- Does the actor either gain significant information or change the system in some measurable way?
- Could an actor perform the use case and then stop using the system for a significant time? This may not be the normal case, but it must be plausible.

Let's take a look at the use cases for a banking system as an example. A banking system with the functions enter amount, select account, withdraw funds, deposit funds, select source account, select destination account, and transfer funds as separate use cases is too granular. The use cases do not make sense in isolation. For example, no user would select an account and then walk away satisfied. Each of these activities is actually part of one or more use cases.

The same system with a single use case—manage money—is too ambiguous. A good use case provides specific value to one or more specific actors. Manage money sounds like a vision for any number of systems, not a particular use case in a banking system.

Instead, a bank system might reasonably have these use cases: deposit funds, withdraw funds, and transfer funds. Each of these use cases provides concrete benefit to the bank customer, as each moves the customer's money around in a useful and distinct way. Each of these use cases makes sense in isolation. For instance, the user might comfortably walk away from the system after depositing money, and return some other day to withdraw funds.

Describe Actors and Use Cases

Once you have identified the actors and use cases for the system, the next step is to indicate which actors depend on which use cases. In the UML, a stick figure represents an actor, and a labeled oval represents a use case. A solid arrow pointing from an actor to a use case indicates that the actor initiates the use case. Figure 2.1 shows that the Customer actor uses the Purchase Book use case.

This type of diagram serves as a very accessible view of the overall use of the system. It allows developers and stakeholders to keep their bearings as they navigate through a large requirements document. It also helps end users to identify areas that affect them, so they can efficiently contribute to those areas. As we will see in the next section, the full requirements document contains a wealth of information for each use case.

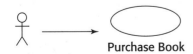

Figure 2.1 An example use case diagram.

Describe Detailed and Complete Requirements

There are two ways to describe the requirements: use a text document to describe the use case in detail, along with the interactions between the actor and the system for each use case; or describe the requirements using a UML *activity diagram*. The UML activity diagram shows the same interactions as described in the text document, but in a visual form. The two documents have a similar purpose and contain similar information, and reinforce one another quite well. Certainly, different people learn in very different ways, so having a readable text description and a highly precise visual description is an advantage.

Each use case includes three elements:

- Use case description
- One or more flow of events
- Activity diagram

Let's take a look at each of these elements.

Use Case Description

A use case description provides an overview of the use case, and specifies any special features, such as preconditions, postconditions, performance requirements, security requirements, and deployment constraints. Preconditions include any use cases that must be completed before the actor may start the use case. Postconditions include any changes to the system that must be accomplished during the use case. Finally, deployment constraints describe limitations on how the use case is accessed. For instance, the actor may need to interact with the system through a firewall or from a highly portable device. These constraints specify needs while leaving the solution as open as possible.

Flow of Events

A flow of events describes a sequence of interactions that occurs as the actor attempts to complete the use case. A flow of events does not describe different variations; instead, it follows a single path all of the way through the use case. Other paths through the use case are described by other flows of events.

Each interaction in the flow is a text description of the actor's input and the response from the system. Consider the interactions involved in the Withdraw Funds use case from a banking system when the actor does everything right and the system performs as expected.

1. Customer inserts card and enters his or her personal identification number. The system greets the customer by name, and presents a list of options, consisting of withdraw funds, deposit funds, and transfer funds.

2. User selects withdraw funds. The system presents a list of accounts for the customer to choose from.

3. The customer chooses an account. The system asks the user to enter the amount of money for withdrawal.

4. The customer enters a positive multiple of $20. The system asks the customer if the amount is correct.

5. The customer responds that the amount is correct. The system thanks the user, distributes the money, prints a receipt, and returns the customer's card.

To restate: This first flow of events describes the interactions when everything goes well. Certainly, there are other less favorable possibilities, but it is often best to describe the normal flow before tackling the details of other possible flows, including disaster scenarios. For example, think about when you give driving directions to a new arrival to your town or city. Most people describe the most direct route first, then provide alternative routes on request. This logic holds for use cases. Someone who is new to the system needs to understand the normal flow before he or she considers more complex flows.

There are three types of flows through every use case:

Normal, or baseline flow. Captures the purpose of the use case by describing the interactions when everything proceeds according to plan. The flow above for the Withdraw Funds use case is an example of a normal flow.

Alternative flows. Describes variation by the actor. For example, the actor may abort the session or become confused and wander through the system for a while. Or the actor may enter invalid data and be forced to correct it before he or she can continue. One use case may require several alternative flows. Alternative flows for the Withdraw Funds use case include the entry of an invalid PIN and a request to overdraw the account.

Exception flows. Describes variation by the system. Since systems are generally prized for their consistency, these variations are errors. For example, the system may be prevented from completing its normal response due to network failure, disk errors, or resource limitations. Most use cases have at least a few exception flows.

Activity Diagrams

An activity diagram is a UML diagram that shows all of the flows of events for a use case in one place. To accomplish this, activities diagrams show different activities that the system performs and how different results cause the system to take different paths. Activity diagrams depict a start state, activities that the system performs, decisions that determine which activity is performed next, and one or more end points. Activity diagrams also have notation to describe activities that are performed in parallel.

Figure 2.2 shows the activity diagram for the Withdraw Funds use case. The solid circle represents the start of the use case; the round-corner rectangles represent activities that the system performs. Each arrow represents a transition from one activity to another. So, the first activity is the system asking the actor to enter his or her pin, as shown in the Ask for PIN activity. The labeled arrow from the Ask for PIN activity to

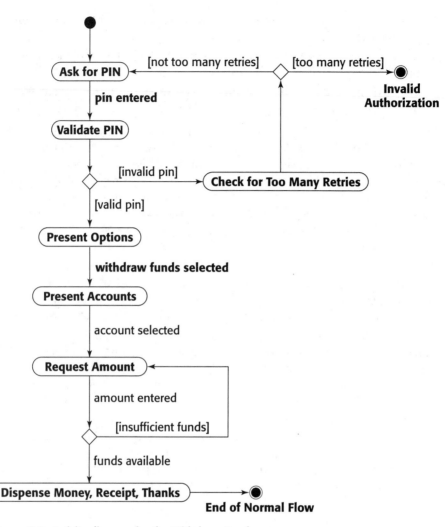

Figure 2.2 Activity diagram for the Withdraw Funds use case.

the Validate PIN activity represents the transition between the two activities that occurs when the actor enters his or her PIN. Since there are two outcomes from the Validate PIN activity, the next transition includes a diamond-shaped decision symbol. Each of the outcomes is labeled with the associated decision criteria. If the PIN is valid, the transition goes to the Present Accounts activity; otherwise, the transition goes to the Check for Too Many Retries activity. Following the path straight down, the actor selects an account to transition from the Present Accounts activity to the Request Amount activity. From there, the actor enters an amount to cause the transition from the Request Amount activity. This transition contains a decision, with one outcome leading back to the Request Amount activity and the other outcome leading down to the Dispense Money activity.

The straight path from the Ask for PIN activity to the Dispense Money activity is the normal flow. The side paths for invalid logins and for overdrawn accounts are alternative flows. No exception flows are shown.

> **NOTE** An activity diagram is not a flowchart. While they look very similar and share much of the same notation, they have very different purposes. Flowcharts help implementers develop code by precisely describing the control logic for the code. An activity diagram helps stakeholders understand the requirements at a very precise level, and helps developers design the system, by precisely describing how the actor uses the system and how the system responds. Flowcharts describe the solution; activity diagrams describe the problem.

Some project teams limit the creation of activity diagrams to very complex use cases. This is generally not a good idea. If the use case really is simple, developing an activity diagram is straightforward and does not consume much time. Also, creating the activity diagram often unearths interesting issues that might not surface in a text description of the interaction. Finally, creating activity diagrams for the simple use cases also familiarizes developers and stakeholders with the mechanism on easy use cases.

Refactor the Use Case Model

After each use case is fleshed out, the requirements gatherers must revisit and often revise the use case model as a whole. Using the guidelines for isolation and focus, use cases may need to be split up, merged, or clarified. Excessively complex use cases must be identified and fixed.

In some cases, a use case may seem well focused and isolated, but still be too complex. This is often found in use cases that consist of complex workflows. The system may not provide any value unless the entire workflow is completed, yet it may be difficult to comprehend the entire process at once. For example, consider the process of ordering a book online. The use case that provides the value is Purchase Book. That does not, however, specify the steps involved: The customer must find a book, consider any reviews, enter his or her payment information and shipping information, and, finally, purchase the book. No mere mortal could understand the activity diagram for this monolithic use case. Few organizations own a sufficiently large plotter to print it. Writing or even reading this huge flow of events from the beginning to the end would be exhausting. Finding a specific issue in a flow of events would be difficult. Despite the theoretical correctness of the use case, it fails the ultimate test; it is not useful to the stakeholders.

There are several mechanisms that manage this sort of complexity. The first splits up the use case and uses preconditions to describe the workflow. Another mechanism uses the *include* and *extend* relationships as specified by the UML. Also, variability can be expressed by actor and use case generalization. Let's consider these mechanisms as applied to a simple book-ordering example.

Split Up the Use Case

First, an unwieldy use case may be deleted and its functionality split into several use cases. These use cases are connected by preconditions and postconditions. Preconditions include any use cases that must be completed before the actor may start the use case. Postconditions include any changes to the system that must be accomplished during the use case. Figure 2.3 shows the Purchase Book use case split into many use cases. Find a Book allows the customer to search for a book by different criteria; it has no preconditions. View Reviews displays the reviews for a selected book; it has successful completion of Find a Book as a precondition. Since each customer must enter payment information at least once and each customer may buy many books, the Enter Payment Information use case is an optional part of the workflow. The same is true of Enter Shipping Information. The Complete Purchase use case has completion of the Enter Payment Information use case and the Enter Shipping Information use case as preconditions. All preconditions for a use case are described in the description of that use case.

This approach has several advantages. First and foremost, it breaks the use case model into manageable pieces. Each new use case has significantly smaller flows of events. The activity diagrams for the use cases no longer require an expensive plotter and a magnifying glass. The overall use case model is far easier to navigate and to understand.

Unfortunately, some information is hidden in this process. A reviewer must check the preconditions to determine the order and dependencies of the use cases in the workflow. There is no way to determine which use cases are optional and which use cases are essential to the workflow. While the layout of the diagram provides some visual clues, it is not a precise or clear description.

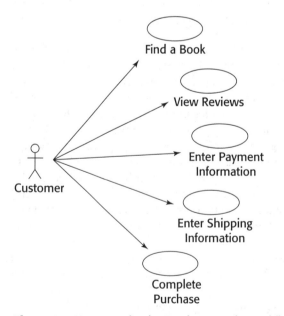

Figure 2.3 Use cases for the Purchase Books workflow.

Use of Include and Extend Relationships

The UML provides two powerful and, at times, confusing relationships between use cases. The *extend* relationship allows a use case to be included as an option in another, or base, use case. The other relationship, *include*, allows a use case to always include another base use case.

Include

In an include relationship, the base use case depends on the included use case because it absorbs its behavior. An include relationship is represented by a dashed arrow pointing from the base use case to the included use case. The relationship is stereotyped by enclosing the word "include" within double angle brackets. The flow of events proceeds along in the base use case until the inclusion point is reached. At this point, the flow of events for the included use case is followed until it completes. After completion of the included use case, the rest of the base flow of events is followed to completion. The inclusion is not optional; when the base use case reaches the inclusion point, the included use case takes over the flow. Also, the included use case may be abstract, such that different forms of the use case can be included without changing the base use case.

Include has two major advantages. First, the base use case is simplified, since the included use case is pulled out. Second, a use case may be included in more than one base use case, so that common flows can be abstracted out. However, in order to qualify, the included use case must fit the definition of a use case. Specifically, it must provide some isolated value to the actor.

Extend

In an extend relationship, the base use case does not include the subordinate use case. Instead, the extension use case depends on the base use case and optionally adds its flow of events to the base use case's flow of events. An extend relationship is represented by a dashed arrow pointing from the extension case to the base use case. The relationship is stereotyped by enclosing the word "extend" within double angle brackets. The base use case defines one or more extension points in its flow of events. Each extension use case specifies the extension point at which it may be inserted, along with the conditions that must hold for the insertion to take place. As the base use case's flow of events progresses to an insertion point, the conditions are checked for the extension use case. If the conditions are met, the extension use case's flow of events is followed to completion. Next, the base use case's flow of events picks up just after the extension point.

In an extend relationship, the dependency is from the extension use case to the base use case, as opposed to an include relationship, in which the dependency is from the base use case to the included use case. Extend use cases are optional, while included use cases must take over the flow if the base use case reaches the inclusion point.

Example

Let's take a look at an example. Figure 2.4 shows the Customer actor initiating the Purchase Book use case. The include relationship between the Purchase Book use case and the Find a Book use case indicates that the flow of events for the Purchase Book use

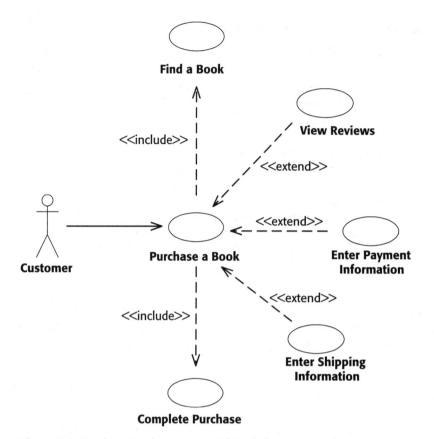

Figure 2.4 Purchase Books use case with include and extend.

case always includes the flow of the Find a Book use case. Similarly, the include relationship between the Purchase Book use case and the Complete Purchase use case indicates that the flow of events for the Complete Purchase use case is always followed, if the flow of events for the Purchase Book use case reaches the inclusion point.

The extend relationships between the Purchase Book use case and the remaining use cases indicate that they are optional. For instance, the customer may have already entered shipping and payment information and be quite content with it.

There are advantages to using the include and extend relationships. The original use case is simplified because the flows of events in the base use case implement the included or extended use cases. Also, the relationships between the original use case and the subordinate use cases are far more precise and visually apparent than is the case for independent use cases and preconditions.

However, the precision of include and extend comes with a price. It is not always easy to explain the concepts; and, as noted earlier, a use case must be written for a wide audience. Imagine a requirements review with 30 people in attendance. Now picture trying to explain the include and extend relationships on the spot. If your use case model benefits from this more advanced notation, then it may be necessary to educate the stakeholders in small groups. Alternatively, it may be possible to show a simplified use case model that omits the inclusion and extension use cases to the wide audience, and reserve the more complex model for carefully targeted groups.

Use Case Generalization

In some situations, a use case may have several distinct paths. For example, there may be two ways in which to find a book. Customers who have a clear idea of their needs can search by title, subject, or even ISBN. Otherwise, customers browse in broad categories, such as mystery novels or home and garden. They may jump from book to book, by following links to similar books.

This combination of searching and browsing in one use case makes the Find a Book use case very difficult to develop and to understand. Fortunately, UML provides a mechanism for exactly this situation. The Find a Book use case is converted into an abstract use case, which means that it defines the value that is obtained by the actor, but does not specify the interactions that are used to reach the goal. Next, multiple concrete use cases are written, with each one specifying a set of interactions that reach the goal defined by the abstract use case. For the Find a Book use case, one concrete use case might be Search for a Book and the other might be Browse for a Book. Figure 2.5 shows the abstract Find a Book use case as a generalization of the two concrete use cases.

Use case generalization can help divide a complex use case into more manageable pieces. In many cases, just the act of creating the activity diagram identifies good candidates for use case generalization. Look for parallel paths that have the same basic purpose.

WARNING Do not implement use case generalization based on use case size and complexity alone.

It is often tempting to split up a use case as the activity diagram and flow of events becomes unwieldy. Discipline and an understanding of the different mechanisms must temper this natural instinct. Arbitrary use of sophisticated mechanisms leads to confusion and eliminates many of the benefits of use cases.

When appropriate, use case generalization makes a use case model more precise without making it much more complex. It is an excellent mechanism when there are high-level alternatives in a use case, but both alternatives serve the same basic purpose.

That said, as with include and extend, use case generalization requires more sophistication from the consumers of the use case model. In my experience, the concept is significantly easier to explain than include and extend. Also, it is very easy to produce a high-level use case model that simply excludes the concrete use cases.

Actor Generalization

In many use case models, one actor is very similar to another actor, yet still has additional obligations or responsibilities. In the UML, an actor is shown as a special type of

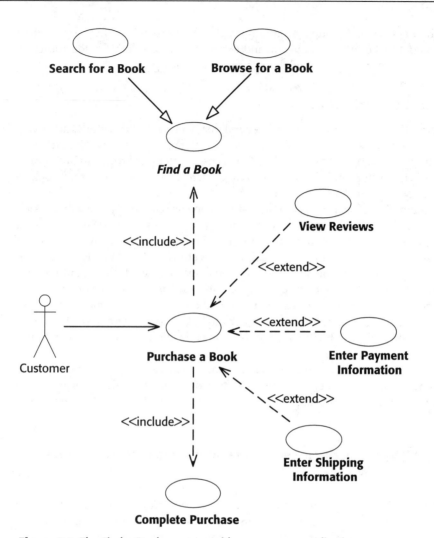

Figure 2.5 The Find a Book use case with use case generalization.

another actor by drawing a generalization arrow to the more general actor. The generalization relationship is intended to document real-world differences and similarities between user groups. The more specific actor must initiate all of the use cases that the more generic actor initiates; thus the more specific actor is actually a type of the generalized actor.

Consider a simple hiring process, in which managers and employees both participate in the interview and selection processes, but in which only the manager discusses salary and makes the final hiring decision. Both perform the Interview Candidate and Evaluate Candidate use case, but only the manager performs the Tender Offer and Reject Candidate use cases. Figure 2.6 shows the first two use cases initiated by the Employee actor and the second two use cases initiated by the Manager actor. But note, since the

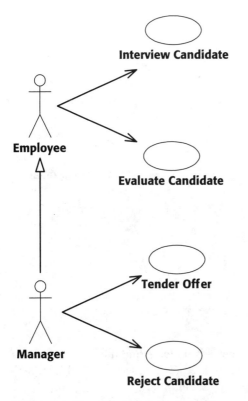

Figure 2.6 Use of actor generalization.

Employee actor is a generalization of the Manager actor, the Manager actor also initiates the Interview Candidate and Evaluate Candidate use cases.

Actor generalization is appropriate only if the actor uses all of the use cases that the generalized actor uses, thus really is a special type of the generalized actor. Consider an example with technical experts and managers. In most companies, there is no generalization relationship between the actors. Not all managers are technical experts and not all technical experts are managers. There is no reason to force this into a generalization relationship. Instead, simply show the actors separately, as in Figure 2.7.

WARNING Actor generalization can become needlessly complex. Don't impose a relationship where none exists. Remember, you can always eliminate the actor generalization and simply show the relationships between each actor and use case.

Actor generalization can simplify a use case model, especially if a new version of an actor adds a few use cases while initiating many existing use cases. However, actor generalization does add complexity and demand some incremental sophistication from the consumers of the use case model. If the actors' names are well chosen, and the

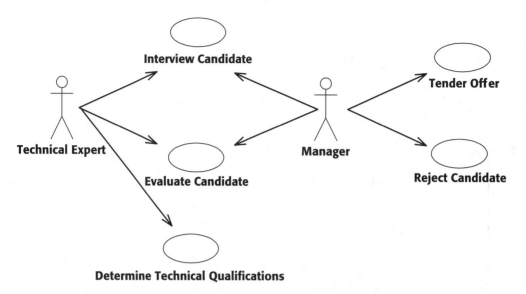

Figure 2.7 Separate actors, no generalization.

relationships are not excessively complex, most stakeholders find the underlying idea quite reasonable. After all, the relationships between actors reflect and highlight real-world differences and similarities between user communities.

Guidelines for Gathering Requirements

It is important to keep the requirements at a consistent level of detail and to be thorough. That said, it is also important to make sure the requirements-gathering process does not become an end unto itself. Striking this balance between too little and too much will result in a solid foundation for the entire development process. The following guidelines give general advice on the requirements-gathering process as a whole.

Focus on the Problem

Remember to concentrate on what the system does, and ignore questions about how it works. For example, it is inappropriate to choose between two competing technologies in a requirements document, but it is necessary to include any known deployment constraints. The customer may require access to certain functionality from a Web browser, which is a requirement and so must be noted for each use case. However, the decision to use Java servlets as opposed to JavaServer Pages (JSP) is inappropriate in a requirements document. Later, when the project focuses on technology selection and architecture, the requirements provide valuable information that shapes these difficult and crucial decisions. Attempting to make the decisions while still gathering requirements leads to hasty decisions that are based on incomplete information.

Don't Give Up

Perseverance is often the hardest part of use case modeling. A large system may have dozens of use cases with several flows of events for each use case. There is an activity diagram for each use case. Be complete, and strive to maintain a consistent level of quality and detail. The collective understanding of every system evolves over time, and requires countless hours of review of the meeting notes and updates to the use case model.

It often helps to develop the requirements in stages. First, develop the high-level use case model, which identifies the actors and use cases. Validating this model with the user builds consensus and clarifies the boundaries of the system. Next, develop descriptions and flows of events for some strategically important use cases. It may be appropriate to review this material with some of the stakeholders as you proceed. Continue this process until you have at least a description and the normal flow for each use case in the model. After validating this model with the stakeholders, identify a few use cases for further exploration and dig in. At this stage, it is appropriate to spend several days on each use case, developing alternate and exception flows of events and consolidating the flows in an activity diagram. After a few use cases have elaborated, it may be necessary to refactor the high-level use case model, using techniques such as the include and extend relationships between use cases or use case generalization. After reviewing this block of work with the stakeholders, you must decide to design and develop the well-defined use cases or elaborate additional use cases.

A commitment to complete requirements does not preclude other concurrent efforts. For instance, once each use case has been described and reviewed, parallel efforts for screen design, technology selection, and architecture may coexist with refinement of the use case model. Obviously, these processes must not start too early; but judicious overlapping of these activities is relatively safe and often provides valuable insight. On the other hand, it is very dangerous to consolidate the various documents or consolidate the efforts. Each effort has separate goals and deserves a separate schedule and separate reviews.

Don't Go Too Far

Authors and speakers, myself included, use statistics to frighten developers into gathering comprehensive requirements. Having seen the effects of inadequate requirements, I believe that this tactic is justifiable. Nevertheless, requirements gathering can be over-emphasized and drawn out past its usefulness. Remember, requirements are not an end unto themselves. They are a foundation for the rest of the development process. Foundations must be strong and durable; they do not need to be artistic masterpieces.

In some cases the requirements-gathering process drags on and on due to a reluctance to move forward or a desire to achieve perfect requirements. This tendency may be exacerbated by a demanding or indecisive customer or by uncertainty about the next step. Developers are especially vulnerable on their first project with a new methodology or with new technology. I have seen some projects become mired in requirements long after the benefits stopped, because it was easier to continue to impress the stakeholders with another round of requirements than to face an uncertain future. Of course, this never works out well, as the next step must eventually be taken, and time spent endlessly refining requirements cannot be used on prototyping or technology training that might remove some of the uncertainty.

Believe in the Process

Solid requirements are essential to your project's success. Without them, you are doomed to solve the wrong problems, repeat your efforts, and anger your customer. Attempting to save time by neglecting requirements invariably leads to extending the duration of the project and higher costs. As Benjamin Franklin put it, "Haste makes waste." Discovering a missing or misunderstood requirement during system test is often catastrophic. Fixing an omission or mistake may require weeks or months of development. In the meantime, marketing schedules are destroyed, expensive production hardware sits unused, business opportunities are missed, and credibility is lost forever. In some cases, projects, jobs, even entire companies are lost. At best, developers pour their hearts into a year's effort and produce a system that the customers think they can live with, although they don't really see what that one screen is for and they really wish that it worked differently.

Poor requirements lead to project failure in several ways:

Customer confidence in the development process and the developers erodes with each misunderstanding. Each failure raises the pressure for the next attempt; hence, communication between developers and stakeholders deteriorates rapidly. Once communication breaks down, the misunderstandings grow, and an adversarial cloud settles over the project. It is very difficult to reverse this trend once it starts.

The software base bloats as it expands to accommodate an ever-changing view of the system. New requirements and new understandings of existing requirements add layer after layer to the implementation. Continued over months and years, this process can mean a tedious death of a project by a thousand cuts.

Developer morale collapses as they realize that they are spending more and more time but accomplishing less and less. Each time a developer spends time solving the wrong problem, his or her faith in the process and hope for success diminishes.

On the other hand, a good use case model is a solid foundation for the rest of the project:

Developers begin analysis, architecture, and design with confidence. They know that the requirements will not shift radically beneath their feet, and they have a clear source of information as they proceed. Certainly they expect to ask questions and refine the requirements as they go, but the core value is complete. This allows them to focus their attention on the solution. Technology selection and architecture decisions are based on complete information. Also, since the overall problem is well understood, developers may comfortably focus on a few use cases at a time.

Project managers treat each use case as a unit of work for scheduling, risk tracking, and estimation. Developers produce effort estimates and identify risks for each use case in turn. This allows the project manager and the senior technical staff to develop a very sophisticated project plan that identifies and attacks risks early in the project, by targeting particular use cases. For example, one use case may be identified as a high priority due to its complex processing or to a challenging user interface. Also, many project teams are new to the solution technologies. Selecting simple use cases for the initial development effort may help alleviate this common and serious risk. It is better to build on success than to overreach and live with failure. So, project managers should leverage the use case model as they estimate and schedule development, manage risks, and grow their team.

Testers treat each use case as a basis for a section in the test plan. A well-written flow of events form easily evolves into a test case. Remember, the flow of events describes the interactions between the actor and the system. In the test case, the actor's requests and inputs become test directions, and the system's responses become the expected result. Of course, the use case is written without consideration for particular screens or technology, so additional instructions must be added. However, the basic structure and narrative flow often remains unchanged in the evolution from flow of events to test case. This creates an interesting side effect: People with experience developing test plans may be very proficient at reviewing and writing use cases.

Stakeholders track progress objectively; either the latest release supports a use case or it doesn't. Objective measurement tends to reduce tensions between developers and stakeholders. Clearly understood bad news is still better than being completely in the dark. Completing three out of the five use cases is a clear, if partial, success. Everyone knows what is complete and what is not complete. Compare this to the equivalent measurement of a milestone being 60 percent complete. Stakeholders tend to feel frustrated and mislead, as the system progress is a mystery to them, and the percent-complete numbers never quite move as expected.

How to Detect Poor Requirements

If gathering requirements is key to project success, then everyone must be doing it. Tragically, this is not the case. Many organizations, both large and small, skim past requirements or develop them so poorly that all benefit is lost. There are several common rationalizations for this negligence:

- Excessive schedule pressure
- No clear vision
- Premature architecture and design

The following sections describe these common paths to poor requirements, including symptoms and remedies.

Path 1: Excessive Schedule Pressure

Excessive schedule pressure is the most common rationale for skipping or skimming through the requirements-gathering process. It is also the worst possible combination: The development team does not know what it is trying to accomplish, but they are working too fast to notice. The pressure to get something, anything, out the door is overwhelming. In the end, very bright people spend nights and weekends paying the price.

There are two distinct variants on this path. In one, management is almost completely uninvolved. Their only concern is the final milestone, so the constant refrain is "When will you be done?" The alternative version is micromanaged pressure. In this version, management obsessively tracks the schedule and misuses schedule-oriented practices, such as commitment-based scheduling and time-boxing.

Symptoms

- Hard deadlines are determined before the objectives are defined.
- Developers make feature decisions as they code.
- Everyone is coding, but there is no coherent or readable requirements document.

Solution

Education, redirection of energy, and verification are the keys to avoiding this path. Managers, developers, and the stakeholders must understand the process and importance of gathering requirements; and requirements reviews must be used to ensure that requirements are complete before moving forward. If the schedule is truly important, managers and the entire development staff must redirect their energies toward practices that do work.

First, both developers and managers need to understand that trying to save time by skimping on requirements is a dangerous and counterproductive practice. Reinforce the following points:

- Incomplete requirements lead to expensive and time-consuming rework.
- Work that is invalidated by a new requirement or a new interpretation is completely wasted.
- The longer it takes to catch missing or incorrect requirements, the longer it will take to undo the damage.
- Committing to gathering solid requirements prevents rework, thereby shortening the actual schedule.
- Fostering positive relations with the other stakeholders during requirements gathering sets the stage for win-win compromises on schedule and features.

Once everyone understands the need for good requirements, they must commit to producing them. Specifically, managers must schedule time for requirements gathering, and ensure that the requirement gatherers have access to the right stakeholders. The requirement gatherers must be thorough and persistent. Requirements must be reviewed for quality and completeness at scheduled intervals. At least some of these reviews must include a wide range of stakeholders. Gathering requirements takes skill and a great deal of persistence.With a little practice and a lot of willpower, every project team can excel at this process.

Path 2: No Clear Vision

In this situation, the development team gathers requirements for a poorly defined system. Without a solid system scope and vision, requirements tend to change and grow at each requirements meeting. If there is no clear system sponsor, requirements change as developers attempt to please various potential sponsors. A lack of vision often leads to requirement artifacts of unusually large size. These intricate creations grow, but rarely improve. I have seen over $1 million (U.S.) spent gathering requirements and prototyping, all without a clear vision of the system. At best, the time is simply wasted. At worst, the final set of requirements actually impedes progress because it is burdened by obsolete or contradictory requirements. Ironically, the requirements-gathering process and the developers often receive the blame.

Symptoms

- Requirements documents are very large and very convoluted.
- Requirements are contradictory.
- Frequent changes are made to requirements.
- Requirements are unstable: They are included, excluded, and reinstated in a bizarre birth, death, and reincarnation cycle.
- Corporate politics are an integral part of requirement meetings.

Solution

Developers can raise awareness of the risks associated with gathering requirements without a clear vision. Unfortunately, the underlying political barriers to commitment may be very real. Perhaps the budget is fragmented among different departments. Perhaps the most likely sponsor swore off commitment to risky software development projects as part of a New Year's resolution.

The first goal is to find or create a sponsor. In some cases, there are stakeholders who face severe consequences if the project does not succeed. These stakeholders may listen to reason and become the sponsor. As always, finding receptive people and educating them about risks and dangers is a delicate task. But the alternative is worse.

If no sponsor can be found, the developers may still be able to bring some order to the chaos. Rather than having one set of requirements that has pieces of each vision, try to maintain a distinct document for each major vision. This may help the stakeholders see the dilemma. At the very least, the developers' lives will improve, as each document stays relatively simple.

Path 3: Premature Architecture and Design

In times of adversity, we revert to what we know and believe. Is it surprising when developers forsake tedious and often contentious requirements meetings in favor of technology selection, design, and code? It is difficult to spend endless hours establishing the details of the system requirements when design and code beckon with the promise of quick progress, objective results, and intellectual stimulation. As a result, requirements documents either atrophy from neglect or evolve to resemble architecture and design documents. Either way, the quick progress is often illusory, because it is progress in a poorly defined direction.

Symptoms

- The requirements-gathering process ends, with no closure or consensus.
- Requirements documents contain implementation details.

Solution

There are two solutions to this situation. First, educate and encourage developers to make requirements a priority. Second, make gathering requirements as easy as possible for developers.

Developers must understand the benefits of requirements and the dangers of developing software without them.

Reinforce the following points at every opportunity:

- Incomplete requirements lead to poor technology selection and architecture decisions. The time spent making these decisions and implementing them cannot be recovered.
- Solid requirements make estimation, scheduling, and testing possible. All of these activities help the developer coexist with the other stakeholders, by baselining expectations and providing project visibility.

These messages are especially powerful when combined with commitment-based scheduling. In this scenario, a developer develops requirements for part of a system, then produces an effort estimate based on the requirements. This allows developers to benefit from their own diligence.

In many organizations, gathering requirements is unnecessarily burdensome for developers. For instance, tedious formatting standards can be relaxed or the work may be shifted to other personnel. Dedicated business analysts can interact with the customer and start the process.

The Next Step

This chapter established a number of steps and guidelines for gathering requirements, including gathering raw requirements, creating a high-level view of the requirements, and describing the details of the requirements. Chapter 3 introduces a simple sample application to demonstrate how you can use these techniques.

Gathering Requirements for the Timecard Application

In this chapter, we'll simulate the requirements-gathering process for a simple time-tracking application, using the process introduced in Chapter 2, "Gathering Requirements with UML." We'll use this example throughout this book.

NOTE For the purposes of this book, I had to keep the example simple, so please keep in mind that while this book describes techniques that are appropriate for much larger systems, demonstrating these real-world techniques against a fairly small problem often forced me to over-engineer the sample solutions. Another caveat: To keep the example small, the simulated customer is unbelievably compliant and helpful.

In this example, the developer discovers that the primary stakeholder is the operations manager who manages the time-tracking process for the client organization. Next, the developer works with the operations manager and an end user to understand the system, then describes the system in a high-level use case model. Based on feedback from the customer, the developer refines the use case model and increases the level of detail. Finally, the developer refactors the use case model to improve readability and accessibility.

The final product of this chapter is a use case model, complete with a high-level use case diagram for navigation, as well as a detailed description of each use case. Together, these elements combine to form a model that is both accessible and complete. Both factors are critical, as stakeholders review the use case model to validate the proposed system, and the development team treats the use case model as a basis for the entire development process, from effort estimation to design and test.

Listen to the Stakeholders

Remember, a system is defined by the value that it provides to people. So, our goal during this phase is to understand the system from the customer's perspective. This section describes a somewhat idealized dialogue between a developer, the operations manager who is responsible for time tracking, and an employee who uses the system. Their goal is to describe the system's functionality and purpose. Certainly, in the real world, such a meeting would involve 5, 10, or even 20 people, all with different needs and perspectives. It might take many meetings over several weeks to reach the first solid understanding of the system.

TIP Raw requirements are the foundation for the whole development process. There is only one way to get them: Go forth and ask—nicely. Then ask if you got it right.

SAMPLE NOTES FROM INITIAL MEETING

DEVELOPER: Who will use the application?

CUSTOMER: Employees will use it to record their billable and nonbillable hours.

DEVELOPER: From where? Here and home and client sites? Behind firewalls?

CUSTOMER: Here at the office. Sometimes from home. Definitely from client sites that are behind firewalls.

DEVELOPER: Okay, that helps. Well, what does the timecard application look like now?

CUSTOMER: It is an Excel spreadsheet for each half-month. Each employee fills in his or her copy and then emails it to me. It is pretty standard: charge codes down the side and days across the top. The employee is able to comment any entry.

DEVELOPER: Where do the charge numbers come from?

CUSTOMER: A separate spreadsheet has a list of valid charge codes, organized by client and activity.

DEVELOPER: So, each charge code has a name, a client, and a project?

CUSTOMER: Yes, and also a type, like billable or nonbillable.

DEVELOPER: Do you think you would ever need a deeper hierarchy?

CUSTOMER: What?

DEVELOPER: Sorry, right now you have client, project, and activity. Would you ever need subprojects or subactivities?

CUSTOMER: No, I wouldn't think so.

DEVELOPER: Who manages charge codes?

CUSTOMER: Well, I add them as needed, and individual managers tell their people what to bill to. They never really go away.

DEVELOPER: Are there any special cases you can think of? For instance, do employees fill in ahead of time or anything like that?

CUSTOMER: Oh, I see. The employee doesn't. If someone is going to be on vacation for a long time, or in the hospital, I take care of his or her timesheets.

DEVELOPER: How will the data be used once it is collected?

CUSTOMER: I'm going to export each month's hours to our new billing system.

DEVELOPER: Should the system automatically select the data range and all of the employees?

CUSTOMER: If possible, I would like to select the date range, clients, and employees that are included in the export.

DEVELOPER: Okay. The billing system has an existing data format?

CUSTOMER: Yes, it expects XML.

DEVELOPER: Okay; we should be able to handle that. I'll see if I can track down the details for that.

DEVELOPER: Thank you very much for your time; I think we have something to work with…. Can we meet again on Tuesday?

CUSTOMER: Sounds good.

In this dialogue, the customer and the developer discovered and refined the customer's needs for the system. Notice that the developer asks a question, listens to the answer, then either summarizes the response or asks a clarifying question. In most cases, the customer does not know exactly what he or she wants, and certainly is not expected to anticipate the level of detail required for software development. So, it is up to the developer or requirements analyst to shape the discussion and ensure that the necessary information is gathered.

Based on this dialogue, the developers can begin creating the actual system requirements documents, starting with a high-level use case diagram.

Build a Use Case Diagram

Building a high-level use case diagram has three steps: identify the actors, identify the use cases, and finally determine the relationships between the actors and use cases.

Remember from Chapter 2:

- An actor usually represents a group of people who gain value by interacting with the system. An actor may also represent a system that is outside of the system and that gains value or provides value by interacting with the system. In the UML, actors are shown as stick figures. There is no distinction between human actors and external systems.

- A use case describes a set of interactions between an actor and the system that provides a discrete benefit or value to the actor. The value must be independently significant, yet well focused. In the UML, a use case is shown as a labeled oval.

- There are only two reasons for an actor to be associated with a use case. First, all use cases are initiated by at least one actor. In order to initiate a use case, the actor must be associated with it. In the UML, this is shown by a solid arrow from the actor to the use case. Once a use case is initiated, it may send notifications to other actors or request information from other actors. This dependence on the other actor(s) is represented in the UML by a solid arrow drawn from the use case to the actor.

Find the Actors

Actors are discovered by reading the raw requirements notes, culling out participants, and determining the distinct groups of users. This first attempt invariably contains redundant names for the same actor, and may miss some actors entirely.

Find Candidate Actors

From the raw notes, the developer highlights the following dialogue:

> **DEVELOPER: Who will use the application?**
>
> **CUSTOMER:** Employees **will use it to record their billable and nonbillable hours. Each employee fills in his or her copy and then emails it to me.**
>
> **DEVELOPER: Who manages charge codes?**
>
> **CUSTOMER: Well, I** (operations manager) **add them as needed, and individual** managers **tell their people what to bill to. They never really go away.**

From these excerpts, it appears that the candidate actors are employee, operations manager, and manager.

Refine the Actors

Refining the list of actors is an interactive process. In many cases, the customers have a clear view of the roles within their organization. Subsequent meetings will be greatly simplified if developers adopt the users' terminology. Also, developers may need to probe a bit to determine whether there are differences in the way different types of people use the system. Remember, actors are determined by their use of the system, not by differences in job title or organizational hierarchy.

The first actor seems clear. Employees use the system to record their time. The next, operations manager, seems essential, but the name indicates a single person in the organization. What if that person goes on vacation or needs to delegate his or her responsibilities as the organization grows? A brief flurry of emails with the operations manager determines that the actor's real name is "administrative user," with the understanding that currently only one person is filling this role.

A face-to-face meeting is needed to decide whether managers are separate actors. They certainly have a role in the process, as employees must know which projects they can bill to. However, under the current requirements, the managers do not use the system to enforce these decisions. After some discussion, the customers agree that determining who has permission to bill to a charge code is not a requirement for the system. So, managers are eliminated as an actor.

This leaves the following actors: employee and administrative user.

Find the Use Cases

Use cases are found by identifying candidate use cases from the raw notes and asking what additional use cases are needed to support the obvious use cases. Then the guidelines established in Chapter 1, "Introduction to Modeling Java with the UML," are applied to the candidates. These guidelines lead developers to split, merge, and eliminate use cases until a solid set of use cases is identified.

Find Primary Use Cases

These are the use cases that characterize the system. From the raw notes, the developer highlights the following dialogue:

> **DEVELOPER: Who will use the application?**
>
> **CUSTOMER: Employees will use it to** record their billable and nonbillable hours.
>
> **CUSTOMER: It is an Excel spreadsheet for each half-month. Each employee fills in his or her copy and then emails it to me. It is pretty standard: charge codes down the side and days across the top. The employee is able to** comment any entry.
>
> **DEVELOPER: Who manages charge codes?**

> **CUSTOMER:** Well, I (operations manager) add them **as needed, and individual managers tell their people what to bill to. They never really go away.**
>
> **DEVELOPER: How will the data be used once it is collected?**
>
> **CUSTOMER: I'm going to** export each month's hours **to our new billing system.**
>
> **DEVELOPER: Should the system automatically select the data range and all of the employees?**
>
> **CUSTOMER: If possible, I would like to select the date range, clients, and employees that are included in the export.**
>
> **DEVELOPER: Okay. The billing system has an existing data format?**
>
> **CUSTOMER: Yes, it expects XML.**
>
> **DEVELOPER: Okay; we should be able to handle that. I'll see if I can track down the details for that.**

The first excerpt leads to the Record Time use case. The second leads to the Comment Time Entry use case. The third excerpt leads to the Create Charge Code use case. Finally, the last excerpt leads to the Export Time Entries use case.

TIP   Use short active phrases when naming a use case. When reading the use case diagram, a reviewer should be able to say the name of the actor followed by the use case and have it sound almost like a sentence. For example, a diagram that shows the Employee actor initiating the Record Time use case reads as "the employee records time."

Find Supporting Use Cases

Supporting use cases are not mentioned in the dialogue. They are found by asking what the system needs before it can accomplish each use case. Consider the Record Time use case. Before an employee can record his or her hours, the system needs a list of charge codes and a list of employees. The first part, the charge codes, is already provided by the Create Charge Code use case, but the existence of the employee is unexplained. So, a new use case, Create Employee, is needed. The other use cases, Comment Time Entry and Export Time Entries are supported by the Record Time use case.

The new list of candidate use cases includes Create Employee, Create Charge Code, Record Time, Comment Time Entry, and Export Time Entries.

Evaluate Use Cases

Each use case must meet the isolation and focus guidelines as described in Chapter 2. To summarize, each use case must be significant, so that it has value in isolation. However, it must also be well focused, so that it does not provide more than one distinct benefit to the actor. Each use case is considered independently before checking the whole use case model for consistency.

The Create Employee use case has a single benefit, as it only allows an administrator to add an employee to the system. So, the Create Employee use case meets our guidelines for focus. It is easy to imagine an administrative user receiving a request from a new hire's manager and adding the new hire to the system as a single task. Also, the system is significantly changed, as it has gained a new end user, so the Create Employee use case meets our guidelines for independent value.

The Create Charge Code use case also has a single benefit, as it only allows the administrative user to add a charge code to the system. It is easy to imagine the administrative user receiving a request from a project manager and adding the new charge code as a single task. Also, the system is significantly changed, as it has gained a new charge code that may be used by the end users. So, the Create Charge Code use case meets our guidelines.

The Record Time use case seems slightly less focused, as it allows an employee to view, update, and add time entries. However, none of these activities seems independently valuable. Record Time has a single distinct value, despite its distinct subactivities. When a use case seems too large, but the subactivities are clearly too small, it is wise to keep the high-level use case. As we will see later in this chapter, there are several techniques that simplify complex use cases without losing their coherence. Certainly the Record Time use case has value in isolation, as it is the motivation for the entire system.

The Comment Time Entry use case certainly meets the guidelines for focus, as it has a very concrete benefit. However, it fails the test for value in isolation. Commenting an entry is part of a larger activity, recording time. So, the Comment Time Entry use case is deleted as a use case and becomes part of the details for the Record Time use case.

The Export Time Entries use case clearly has a well-defined and valuable purpose, as it allows the administrative user to export the system's data

This process trims our list of use cases to Create Employee, Create Charge Code, Record Time, and Export Time Entries.

Determine the Actor-to-Use-Case Relationships

Each actor initiates one or more use cases, and each use case is initiated by one or more actors. Our final step in creating the high-level use case diagram is to describe these relationships for the actors and use cases. A solid arrow from the actor to the use case indicates that the actor initiates the use case.

Consider each actor in turn. Based on the dialogue with the customers, the Employee actor cannot initiate the Create Employee, Create Charge Code, or Export Time Entries use cases. Certainly, the Employee actor must initiate the Record Time use case on a regular basis.

The Administrative User actor clearly initiates the Create Employee, Create Charge Code, and Export Time Entries. The person who fills the role of the Administrative User actor is almost certainly an employee of the organization and therefore must record his or her time. However, he or she does so in the role of an employee. The only

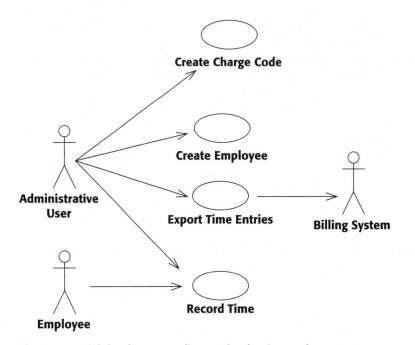

Figure 3.1 High-level use case diagram for the timecard system.

reason a person would need to record time as an Administrative User would be to record another employee's time. Revisiting the meeting notes, it is clear that this is a requirement, as the administrative user records time for sick or vacationing employees.

Figure 3.1 shows these relationships; it is the first draft of the high-level use case diagram. At this point, you should confirm the accuracy of the model with the customer. The customer must recognize all of the actors and use cases. At this meeting, your customer should provide a valuable sanity check, and point out any missing features. Remember, a good use case model serves as a friendly and readable entry point into your requirements. Your customer must be able to easily understand it.

Describe the Details

A use case diagram provides a high-level view of the entire system, but this is not a sufficient foundation for design. For each use case, you need to determine exactly how the customer uses the system. Again, the emphasis is on the value and the workflow, not on specific solutions.

Guidelines for Describing the Details

Any known deployment constraints are included at this point. For instance, if the end user accesses the system from behind a firewall or from a portable device, you must capture that requirement for any affected use cases. However, technology selection decisions are not included, so it would be inappropriate to propose solutions to the deployment constraints. Another common mistake is to think of a use case in terms of screen design. This is dangerous, because some screens may support many use cases and one use case may use several screens in the final design.

Developing a flow of events requires a developer or requirements analyst to play the role of the end user and ask a series of questions. How does the flow start? What information does the system demand from the actor? How does the system respond? How does the flow end? The answers are captured in a list of inputs to the system and responses from the system. A flow of events resembles a test plan without any details about the screens or the format of the responses. In some cases, the developer can interact with the end users during this process, understanding their needs for each use case. Otherwise, the developer must develop reasonable flows of events and have the end users validate them.

It is a common belief that you come away with a very clear understanding of the system after the initial meeting with the customer. In fact, often, filling in the details for each use case is a humbling and enlightening experience. As you develop each flow of events and attempt to describe the preconditions and deployment constraints, you will discover relevant questions and open issues. These can be listed as part of the use case documentation and resolved at the first review of the entire use case model.

Each use case should follow a template. Though no two projects follow the same template, it should look something like this:

Name of use case. A brief active phrase that captures the purpose of the use case.

Description. A brief paragraph that explains the purpose of the use case, with an emphasis on the value to the actors. If this information cannot be conveyed in a brief paragraph, the use case may not be clearly focused.

Preconditions. A brief paragraph that lists any use cases that must be succeed before the use case is initiated and that describes the dependency.

Deployment constraints. A brief paragraph that describes how the system will be used to fulfill the use case. For instance, a particular use case may be initiated by an Employee actor who is behind the firewall that protects the employee's client. As neglecting this sort of constraint can have serious consequences, the information must be captured as early as possible.

Normal flow of events. An ordered list of interactions that describes all inputs to the system and responses from the system that make up the normal path through the use case. The normal flow of events captures the intent of the use case by showing the interactions when everything proceeds according to plan. This flow of events is also referred to as the *happy flow*.

Alternate flow of events. An ordered list of interactions that describes all inputs to the system and responses from the system that make up a single alternative path through the use case. An alternative flow of events captures the system's response to variations by the user, such as entering invalid data or attempting to perform steps in a workflow in an unusual order. This section is repeated for each alternate flow of events.

Exception or error flow of events. An ordered list of interaction that describes all inputs to the system and responses from the system that make up a single exception path through the use case. An exception flow of events captures the system's response to errors, such as unavailable system or external resources. This section is repeated for each exception flow of events.

Activity diagram. Shows all of the flows of events for the use case in one diagram. It complements the flows of events and provides a valuable way to measure the complexity of a use case.

Nonfunctional requirements. A brief paragraph or two that describes any success criteria for the use case that are not easily embedded in the flows of events. For instance, the system might need to provide a response for the use case in less than three seconds; or there might be an upper limit of seven mouse clicks to navigate through any flow of events for the use case.

Notes (optional). A list of resolved issues that don't fit well in any other category. These may include restrictions on the system's functionality.

Open issues (optional). A list of questions for the stakeholders.

Let's take a look at the use case documentation for our timecard application.

Sample Use Case Documentation for Create Charge Code

Name of use case. Create Charge Code

Description. The administrative user actor uses the Create Charge Code use case to populate the time-tracking system with charge codes. Once added, a charge code is available to all employees as they enter their hours.

Preconditions. None

Deployment constraints. None

Normal flow of events. Add a charge code to an existing project.

1. The administrative user sees a view of existing charge codes. Charge codes are activities organized by client and project.

2. The administrative user adds a charge code to an existing project. The new charge code appears in the view, and may be used by employees.

Alternate flow of events. New charge code for a new project for a new client.

1. The administrative user sees a view of existing charge codes. Charge codes are activities organized by client and project.

2. The administrative user adds a client. The new client appears in the view.

3. The administrative user adds a project to the new client. The new project appears in the view.

4. The administrative user adds a charge code to the new project. The new charge code appears in the view and may be used by employees.

Alternate flow of events. Duplicate charge code.

1. The administrative user sees a view of existing charge codes. Charge codes are activities organized by client and project.

2. The administrative user adds a charge code to an existing project. The charge code already exists for the project.

3. The system informs the administrative user that the charge code already exists. No change to the view.

Exception flow of events. System is unable to add the charge code due to a system or communication error.

1. The administrative user sees a view of existing charge codes. Charge codes are activities organized by client and project.

2. The administrative user adds a charge code to an existing project. The system is unable to complete the addition, due to a system or communication error.

3. The system informs the administrative user of the error, complete with available details. The view reverts to the previous state.

4. If possible, an error is added to a log.

Activity diagram. See Figure 3.2.

Nonfunctional requirements. None

Open Issues.

- Is there a default set of activities?
- Can an employee bill to a project without specifying the activity?
- Is there information other than the name of the client, project, or activity?

Sample Use Case Documentation for Create Employee

Name of use case. Create Employee

Description. The Create Employee use case allows the administrative user to add an employee to the time-tracking system. Once employees have been created, they are able to use the system to record their time.

Preconditions. None

Deployment constraints. None.

Normal flow of events. The administrative employee adds an employee.

1. The administrator sees a view of all existing employees by name.

2. The administrator adds an employee, with a name, email address, and password.

3. The new employee appears in the view. The employee can record his or her hours.

Alternate flow of events. Employee exists.

1. The administrative user sees a view of all existing employees by name.

2. The administrative user adds an employee, with a name, email address, and

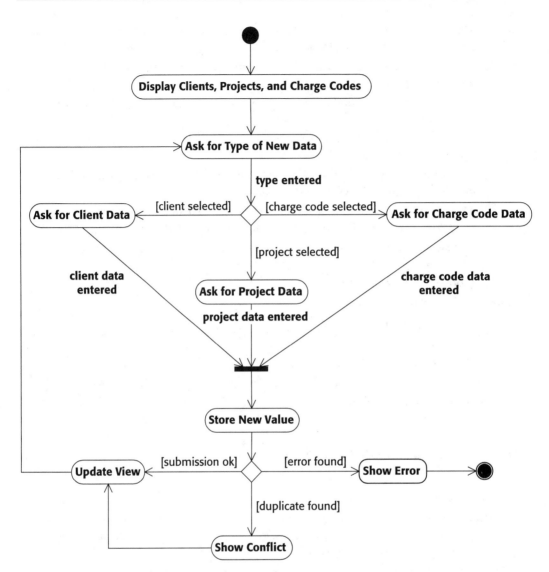

Figure 3.2 Activity diagram for Create Charge Code use case.

password.

3. The administrative user is notified of the conflict. No change to existing data.

Exception flow of events. System is unable to add the employee due to a system or communication error.

1. The administrative user sees a view of all existing employees by name.

2. The administrative user adds an employee, with a name, email address, and password. The system is unable to complete the addition, due to a system or communication error.

3. The system informs the administrative user of the error, complete with available details. The view reverts to the previous state.

4. If possible, an error is added to a log.

Activity diagram. See Figure 3.3.

Nonfunctional requirements. None

Open issues.

- Is there information other than the employee's name and password?
- Will the employee need to change his or her password?
- Are employees organized by department or category?

Sample Use Case Documentation for Record Time

Name of use case. Record Time

Description. The Record Time use case allows employees to track the hours that they work. The Record Time use case allows an administrative user to record hours for any employee.

Preconditions. None

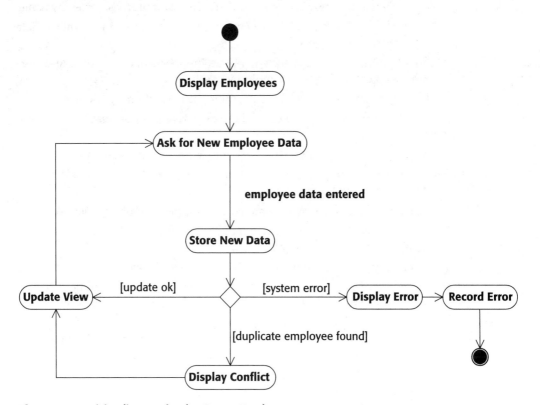

Figure 3.3 Activity diagram for the Create Employee use case.

Deployment constraints. The Record Time use case must be accessible from client sites and the employees' homes. In the case of client sites, they will often be behind the client's firewall.

Normal flow of events. An employee records his or her time.

1. The employee sees previously entered data for the current time period.

2. The employee selects a charge number from all available charge numbers, organized by client and project.

3. The employee selects a day from the current time period.

4. The employee enters the hours worked as a positive decimal number.

5. The new hours are added to the view and are seen in any subsequent views.

Alternate flow of events. An employee updates his or her time.

1. The employee sees previously entered data for the current time period.

2. The employee selects an existing entry.

3. The employee changes the hours worked.

4. The new information is updated in the view and is seen in any subsequent views.

Alternate flow of events. An administrative user records time for an employee.

1. The administrative user is presented with a list of employees, sorted by name.

2. The administrative user selects an employee and sees previously entered data for the current time period.

3. The administrative user selects a charge number from all available charge numbers, organized by client and project.

4. The administrative user selects a day from the current time period.

5. The administrative user enters the hours worked as a positive decimal number.

6. The new hours are added to the view and are seen in any subsequent views.

Exception flow of events. System is unable to add the update to the timecard due to a system or communication error.

1. The employee sees previously entered data for the current time period.

2. The employee selects a charge number from all available charge numbers, organized by client and project.

3. The employee selects a day from the current time period.

4. The employee enters the hours worked as a positive decimal number. The system is unable to complete the addition, due to a system or communication error.

5. The system informs the administrative user of the error, complete with available details. All additions and edits are undone together. The view reverts to the previous state.

6. If possible, an error is added to a log.

Activity Diagram. See Figure 3.4.

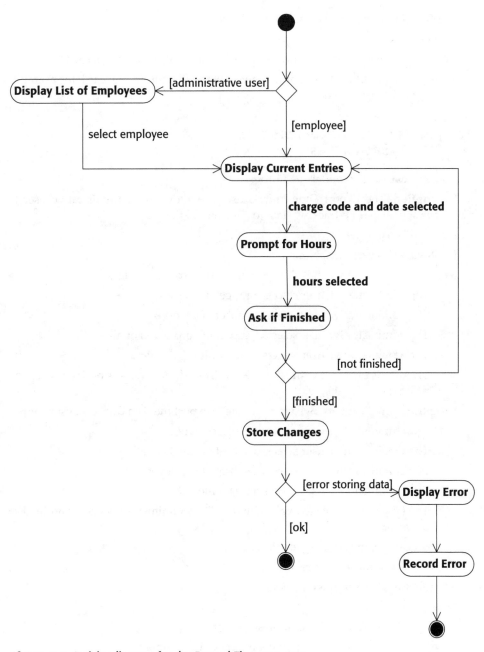

Figure 3.4 Activity diagram for the Record Time use case.

Nonfunctional requirements. None

Open issues.

- Can an employee enter hours or edit hours in a previous timecard?
- Can an employee enter hours or edit hours in a future timecard, for example, just before a vacation?

Sample Use Case Documentation for Export Time Entries

Name of use case. Export Time Entries

Description. The Export Time Entries use case allows the administrative user to save specified time-tracking data to a formatted file.

Preconditions. None

Deployment constraints. None

Normal flow of events. The administrative user exports the data.

1. The administrative user selects a range of dates.
2. The administrative user selects a subset of clients or all.
3. The administrative user selects a subset of employees or all.
4. The administrative user selects a target file.
5. The data is exported to the file as XML. The administrator is notified when the process is complete.

Exception flow of events. System is unable to export the data due to a system error.

1. The administrative user selects a range of dates.
2. The administrative user selects a subset of clients or all.
3. The administrative user selects a subset of employees or all.
4. The administrative user selects a target file.
5. The system is unable to export the data. The administrative user is notified of the error.
6. If possible, the error is recorded to a log.

Activity Diagram. See Figure 3.5.

Nonfunctional requirements. None

Open issues.

- Are the data selection criteria sufficient?
- Are the data selection criteria unnecessarily complex?
- Do other export formats exist?

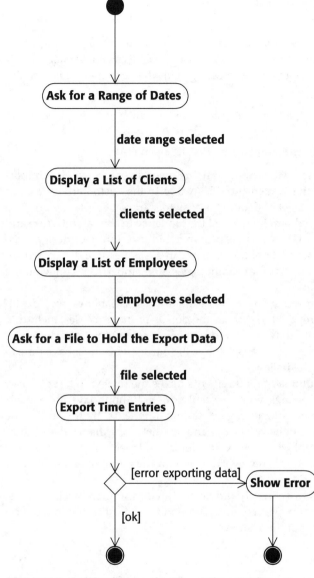

Figure 3.5 Activity diagram for Export Time Entries.

Gathering More Requirements

Creating the detailed flow of events for use cases clarifies your understanding of the problem domain and raises many issues. At some point, you accumulate enough new questions to justify a requirements review meeting with the customer. This meeting has two goals:

- To validate and improve the current use case model, which includes the flows of events.
- To resolve most of the outstanding questions and open issues.

The key is to understand the system from your customer's perspective. It is important to stay focused on how the system provides value to the customer. But as you describe the system at a lower level of detail, it is easy to start contemplating possible solutions, so it is essential to be disciplined; resist the tendency to start architecture and design at this point. To this end, it is very helpful to avoid user interface design. Discussions concerning the look and feel of the system can easily become discussions of what is and is not possible with particular technologies. Remember, focus on what the customer needs from the system.

This requirements review meeting covers all of the use cases that have been developed. Participants must be prepared to discuss the details of the use cases, including the flows of events, the activity diagram, the deployment constraints, and any open issues. In order to ensure this level of preparedness, the participants must have time to review the documents before the review meeting.

In many cases, the sheer volume of requirements forces the review to be split over several meetings. Marathon meetings, with consecutive 8- to 10-hour days, are impressive-sounding, but result in uneven coverage of the requirements. By the end of the second day, the participants are either worn out and apathetic or exhausted and combative. Either way, the time is not well spent. Consider instead meeting every other day or performing smaller more frequent reviews throughout the requirements-gathering process.

As before, the results of the meeting should be captured in written meeting notes, which should be validated by the participants. These notes will form the foundation for the common understanding of the system.

SAMPLE NOTES FROM FOLLOW-UP MEETING

DEVELOPER: Let's start with the Create Charge Code use case. Does the primary flow make sense?

CUSTOMER: Yes. I don't think we would ever need to add a charge code directly to the client. If we do, we can just add a "general" project.

DEVELOPER: Are there other data associated with clients or projects—purchase orders, contact information?

CUSTOMER: Yes, of course, but they are not part of this system.

DEVELOPER: Is there a default set of activities that are common to all projects?

CUSTOMER: No two projects have exactly the same activities, but there are some commonly occurring activities. Could the administrator select some from a list of common activities and type others? That would save a lot of time and avoid using alternate spellings or synonyms for the same activity.

DEVELOPER: I'll add that. Can an employee bill to a project without specifying the activity? Or directly to a client?

CUSTOMER: If an employee needs to bill without a project and activity…well then we probably have a problem.

DEVELOPER: Are billing rates set for different activities for each client?

CUSTOMER: Bill rates vary by client, project, activity, and employee. But we really don't want that in the timecard system.

DEVELOPER: Excellent; it helps to know where the system stops. Great. Let's move to the Add Employee use case. What do you think of the main flow?

CUSTOMER: I agree that the employees would be organized by name. There is no need to organize people by department for this application. We haven't thought much about passwords or security. I know I personally hate assigned passwords; people always write them down and post them on their monitors.

DEVELOPER: So, should employees be able to change their passwords? Should they be required to do so on their first login?

CUSTOMER: That would be great. And most of them will be used to that flow from other systems.

DEVELOPER: Okay, I'll add that. Is there other information that we should be tracking—billing rates, contact information?

CUSTOMER: No; we may want to integrate that sort of thing in later, but for now we want to keep it very simple.

DEVELOPER: Okay. Is there any other functionality we need here?

CUSTOMER: Well…I don't know how hard this would be, but could the system email the new users? Maybe to tell them they can start using the system and to give them their password?

DEVELOPER: We can add that. It's much better to add it to the requirements now.

CUSTOMER: Thanks.

DEVELOPER: Any other issues with this use case?

CUSTOMER: No, I think we have it.

DEVELOPER: Great. Let's move to the Record Time use case. What do you think of the main flow?

CUSTOMER: It makes good sense to me.

DEVELOPER: Can an employee edit previous timecards?

CUSTOMER: That is a tough question. I worry that if we don't let them do it, we will be getting calls from employees saying, "Please, just this one time, I need to add three hours…" And if they don't record them, we can't bill for them. I think that they should be able to look at their previous timecard. They'll need to submit when they are done.

DEVELOPER: Okay; how about editing future timecards?

CUSTOMER: Yeah, I know that sounds useful, especially for vacations and stuff. On the other hand, we want to avoid prebilling. We definitely should not allow them to fill in next week's timecard. Also, it should not be possible for people to fill in tomorrow's timecard. It may be a pain, but some customers audit our billing practices, and this would really help.

DEVELOPER: Okay, I'll add that. Will a manager or administrator need to add entries for sick or vacationing employees?

CUSTOMER: Oh; I guess so. If the employee is out more than a week, then an administrator needs to fill in the timecard.

DEVELOPER: Can any administrator do any employee's timecard?

CUSTOMER: Sure; let's keep it simple.

DEVELOPER: Any other functionality or issues?

CUSTOMER: No. Interestingly, I thought that was the easy use case, but it brought up a lot of issues.

DEVELOPER: Isn't that just the way? What do you think of the Export Time Entries use case?

CUSTOMER: I like it. It will make it easy to generate the raw data for different reports. It would be nice to filter by project within client.

DEVELOPER: Oh, of course. Any other output formats?

CUSTOMER: No, I can't think of any.

DEVELOPER: Finally, a use case that was as simple as it looked.

CUSTOMER: A nice way to finish out the meeting. Thanks.

DEVELOPER: Thank you; you have really improved my understanding of the system.

In this dialogue, the customers and the developer refined their collective under-standing of the system. Specifically, they discovered some missing functionality, excluded other functionality, and validated a significant portion of the use case model. Following the meeting, the use case model must be updated to reflect the new under-standing of the system.

Revising the Use Case Model

In many cases, a healthy dialogue with the customer will completely change your understanding of the system. Remember, both you and the customer are discovering and inventing the system as you go. You should notice a shift from discussing basic terms to delving into relatively subtle points. The first meeting and use case model builds a common vocabulary and reaches a consensus on what the system should and should not do. The second meeting uncovers missing pieces and resolves the special cases. This section shows how the use case diagram and the details for each use case are updated from the dialogue.

Revise the Use Case Diagram

Adding new information to the use case diagram follows the same pattern as during its original. First, mine the dialogue for new actors and new use cases. Then validate the candidate use cases against the guidelines for narrow focus and independent value. Finally, look for new relationships between actors and use cases.

For this example, the dialogue does not reveal any new actors, so we'll move on to the new use cases.

Find New Use Cases

The following excerpts indicate a need for some new use cases.

> **CUSTOMER: We haven't thought much about passwords or security. I know I personally hate assigned passwords; people always write them down and post them on their monitors.**

> **DEVELOPER: So, should employees be able to** change their passwords? **Should they be required to do so on their first** login?

> **CUSTOMER: That would be great. And most of them will be used to that flow from other systems.**

The new candidate use cases are Login and Change Password

Evaluate Candidate Use Cases

Change Password is well focused and certainly has value in isolation, as it protects the employee's privacy and security. So we add the Change Password use case to the model.

Login is less clear. It is well focused, but it does not provide much value on its own. In general, employees log in as a precursor to some more interesting task, such as recording their time. On the other hand, most people describe it as a separate step, as in "I log in, then record my time." Many development teams and UML gurus have spent many hours disputing the status of Login as a use case. That said, no project has ever failed because the wrong choice was made. For now, we'll consider it as a separate use case that is used as part of many more valuable use cases.

Find New Relationships

The following excerpts provide insight into the interactions between the system and the actors.

> **CUSTOMER: Well . . . I don't know how hard this would be, but could the** system **email the new users? Maybe to tell them they can start using the system and to give them their password?**
>
> **DEVELOPER: We can add that. It's much better to add it to the requirements now.**
>
> **CUSTOMER: We haven't thought much about passwords or security. I know I personally hate assigned passwords; people always write them down and post them on their monitors.**
>
> **DEVELOPER: So,** should employees be able to change their passwords? **Should** they (the employees) be required to do so on their first login?
>
> **CUSTOMER: That would be great. And most of them will be used to that flow from other systems.**

The first excerpt indicates that the Create Employee use case interacts with the Employee actor by sending him or her an email. This is represented in Figure 3.6 by the solid line from the Create Employee use case to the Employee actor. You can verbalize this as, "The Administrative User actor initiates the Create Employee use case. As part of the use case, the system sends information to the Employee actor."

The second excerpt shows that the Employee actor initiates the Change Password use case. Also, the Change Password use case is always included in the Login use case if it is the employee's first login. This is shown by the include relationship (dashed line) from the Login use case to the Change Password use case. Remember, the extend relationship indicates that the subordinate use case is optional. An included use case is always performed if the flow of events reaches the inclusion point.

The second excerpt also reveals that the Employee actor initiates the Login use case. While it is not explicitly stated, it is reasonable to expect administrative users to log in and change their passwords.

At this point, you update the use case diagram to match your new understanding of the system. The updated high-level use case diagram is shown in Figure 3.6.

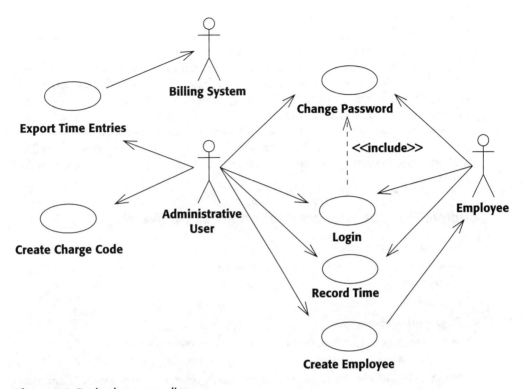

Figure 3.6 Revised use case diagram.

Revising the Use Case Documentation

In many cases, the flow of events for a use case evolves radically from the initial draft. Oddly enough, they never get shorter. Updating a flow of events is a fairly mechanical process of reviewing meeting notes and incorporating the changes. Perseverance is the key. If the list of open issues does not shrink over time, it may be a sign that you lack a clear and stable system vision.

The discussion of the Create Charge Code use case clarified the system scope. The customer clearly sees the timecard system as a simple and isolated system. It may seem odd to explicitly exclude functionality in requirements. After all, requirements describe what the system does, right? In my experience, it is well worth the effort to document any known limitations of the system as they are discovered. This simple discipline avoids countless arguments in which the customer contends that certain functionality is clearly within the current schedule while the developers stare blankly as they consider weekends about to be lost. The flow of events for the Create Charge Code use case limits each client to a name and a list of projects. Each project consists of a name and a charge code. Nothing else is included—no purchase orders, no contact information. This sort of restriction encourages precise thinking by developers and customers. The message should be "speak now or be willing to talk schedule later."

Review of a flow of events may introduce completely new requirements. For example, the Administrative User Actor now is able to pick charge codes from a list of previously defined activities. This must be added to the flow of events.

You can see how discussions with the user can lead us to revise existing use cases, add new use cases, place limits on system functionality, and add completely new functionality. In general, this is a positive sign. Hopefully, by this point, everyone's understanding of the system is maturing and converging to a common view. Conversations are increasingly productive, as different parties agree on general principles and common meanings for domain terms. The following samples demonstrate how requirements evolve; they also serve as a foundation for the ongoing sample timecard application.

Sample Use Case Documentation for Login (New)

Name of use case. Login

Description. The Login use case allows employees and the administrative user to access the system.

Preconditions. None

Deployment constraints.

1. Employees must be able to log in from any computer, including home, client sites, and on the road. This access may be from behind a client's firewall.

Normal flow of events. The administrative user or employee's username and password are valid.

1. The administrator or employee supplies a username and password.
2. The user is authenticated as either an administrator or an employee. This is not a choice during the login; it is determined by the username.

Alternate flow of events. First Login

1. The administrator or employee supplies a username and password.
2. The user is authenticated as either an administrator or an employee. This is not a choice during the login; it is determined by the username.
3. The user is instructed to change his or her password.
4. Include the Change Password use case at this point.

Alternate flow of events. Invalid authentication information.

1. The administrator or employee supplies a username and password.
2. The user is notified that he or she has entered incorrect login information.
3. The failure is logged by the system.
4. The user is allowed to try again indefinitely.

Activity diagram. See Figure 3.7.

Nonfunctional requirements.

1. The user's password must not be passed as plaintext.

Open Issues. None

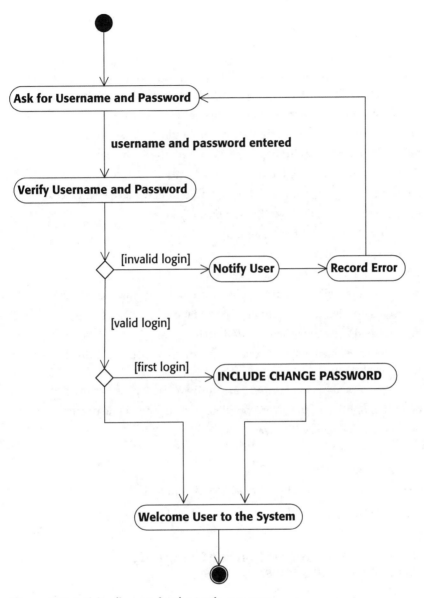

Figure 3.7 Activity diagram for the Login use case.

Sample Use Case Documentation: Change Password (New)

Name of use case. Change Password

Description. The Change Password use case allows employees and administrative users to change their password.

Preconditions.

1. The user must have logged in to the system.

Deployment constraints.

1. Employees must be able to log in from any computer, including home, client sites, and on the road. This access may be from behind a client's firewall.

Normal flow of events. Employee changes his or her password.

1. The user enters his or her current password and new password twice.
2. The user is notified that his or her password has been changed.

Alternate flow of events. Invalid current password.

1. The user enters his or her current password and new password twice.
2. The user is notified that his or her attempt failed.
3. The failure is logged by the system.
4. The user is allowed to try again indefinitely.

Alternate flow of events. New passwords do not match.

1. The user enters his or her current password and new password twice.
2. The user is notified that his or her attempt failed.
3. The user is allowed to try again indefinitely.

Exception flow of events. System is unable to store new password due to a system or communications error.

1. The user enters his or her current password and new password twice.
2. The user is notified of the error, complete with any available details.
3. The failure is logged by the system.

Activity Diagram. See Figure 3.8.

Nonfunctional requirements.

1. The user's password must not be passed as plaintext.

Open Issues. None

Sample Use Case Documentation for the Create Charge Code Use Case (Revised)

Name of use case. Create Charge Code

Description. The Create Charge Code use case allows the administrative user to add a new charge code to the system so that employees can bill to the charge code. Since each charge code is specific to a client and a project, the administrative user may need to add a client or project first.

Preconditions.

1. The user must be logged in as an administrative user.

Deployment constraints. None

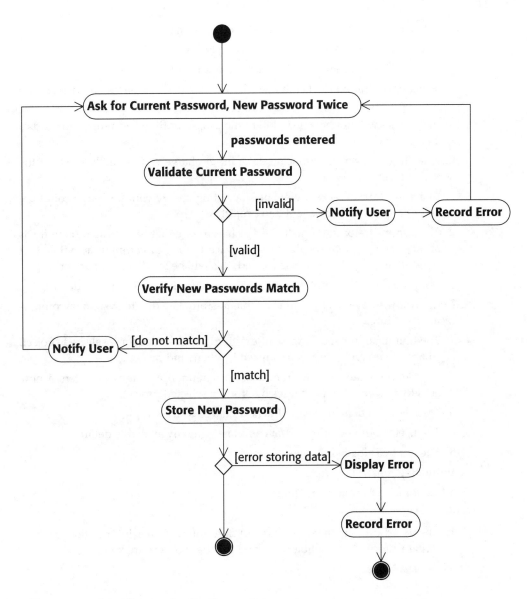

Figure 3.8 Activity diagram for the Change Password use case.

Normal flow of events. Add a charge code to an existing project.

1. The administrator sees a view of existing charge codes for a selected project. Charge codes are activities organized by client and project.

2. The administrator selects from a list of common activities or enters a new activity to create a new charge code for the selected project.

3. The new charge code appears in the view and may be used by employees.

Alternate flow of events. Administrator adds a new client and project.

1. The administrator sees a view of existing clients.

2. The administrator enters the name of a new client.

3. The administrator selects the new client and enters the name and description for a new project.

4. Employees will not be able to bill to the project until the administrator adds a charge code.

Alternate flow of events. Duplicate data; input charge code already exists at the specified level.

1. The administrator sees a view of all existing charge codes. Charge codes are activities organized by client and project.

2. The administrator attempts to add a charge code that has the same activity as another charge code for the project. Once the list of common activities that does not include duplicates is created, this will be less likely to happen.

3. The administrator is notified of the conflict. No change to existing data.

Exception flow of events. System is unable to store data due to system or communications failure.

1. The administrator sees a view of existing charge codes for a selected project. Charge codes are activities organized by client and project.

2. The administrator selects from a list of common activities or enters a new activity to create a new charge code for the selected project.

3. The system is unable to store the new charge code.

4. The user is notified of the error, complete with any available details.

5. The failure is logged by the system.

Activity diagram. See Figure 3.9.

Nonfunctional requirements. None

Notes.

1. Client and projects have a name and description. Other information, such as contact information, billing rates, and purchase orders are kept elsewhere.

Open issues. None

Sample Use Case Documentation for Create Employee (Revised)

Name of use case. Create Employee

Description. The Create Employee use case allows the administrative user to add an employee to the system, so that the employee may enter his or her hours into the time-tracking system.

Preconditions.

1. The user must be logged in as an administrative user.

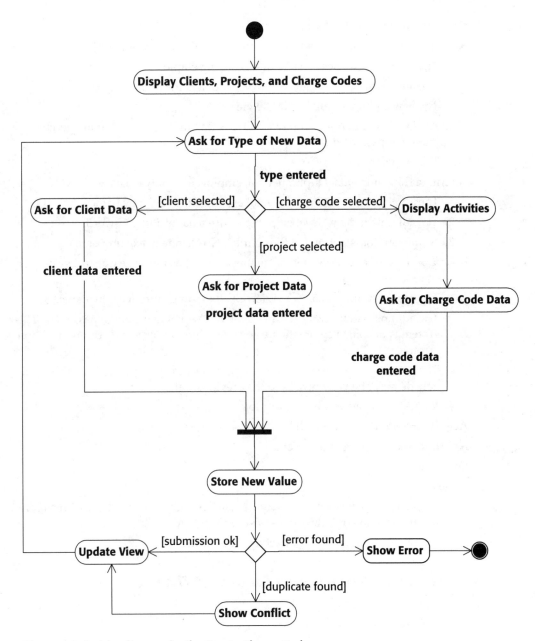

Figure 3.9 Activity diagram for the Create Charge Code use case.

Deployment constraints. None

Normal flow of events. The administrative user adds a new employee.

1. The administrator sees a view of all existing employees by name.
2. The administrator adds an employee, with a name and password.
3. The new employee appears in the view.
4. An email is sent to the employee, instructing him or her to log in and change his or her password.
5. The employee can log in.

Alternate flow of events. Duplicate data; employee already exists.

1. The administrator sees a view of all existing employees by name.
2. The administrator adds an employee, with a name and password.
3. Administrator is notified of the conflict. No change to existing data.

Exception flow of events. System is unable to add the employee due to a system or communication error.

1. The administrative user sees a view of all existing employees by name.
2. The administrative user adds an employee, with a name and a password. The system is unable to complete the addition, due to a system or communication error.
3. The system informs the administrative user of the error, complete with available details. The view reverts to the previous state.
4. If possible, an error is added to a log.

Activity diagram. See Figure 3.10.

Nonfunctional requirements. None

Open issues. None

Notes.

1. Each employee has a name and password. All other information, such as contact information or billing rates is kept elsewhere.
2. Employees will not be organized by department.

Sample Use Case Description for Record Time (Revised)

Name of use case. Record Time

Description. The Record Time use case allows any employee to track his or her own hours. Administrative users can record hours for any employee.

Preconditions.

1. The user must be logged in.

Deployment constraints.
The Record Time use case must be accessible from client sites and the employees' homes. In the case of client sites, they will often be behind the client's firewall.

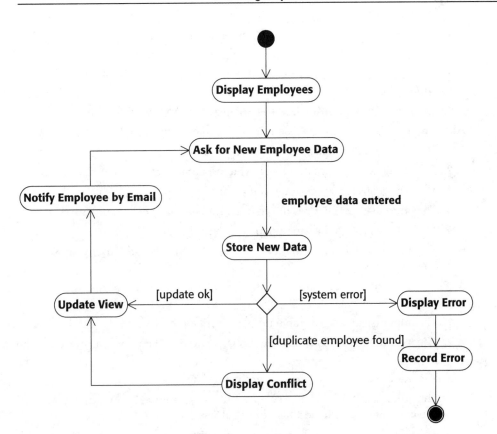

Figure 3.10 Activity diagram for the Create Employee use case.

Normal flow of events. An employee records his or her own time.

1. The employee sees any previously entered data for the current time period.
2. The employee selects a charge number from all available charge numbers, organized by client and project.
3. The employee selects a day from the time period.
4. The employee enters the hours worked as a positive decimal number.
5. The new hours are added to the view and are seen in any subsequent views.

Alternate flow of events. Employee edits existing data.

1. The employee sees previously entered data for the current time period.
2. The employee selects an existing entry.
3. The employee changes the charge number and/or the hours worked.
4. The new information is updated in the view and is seen in any subsequent views.

Alternate flow of events. Employee submits timecard as complete.

1. The employee sees any previously entered data for the current time period.
2. The employee elects to submit the timecard.
3. The employee is asked to confirm his or her choice and warned that he or she will not be able to edit his or her entries.
4. The timecard is submitted; it is no longer available for editing.

Alternate flow of events. Administrator edits an employee's timecard.

1. The administrator selects an employee from a list.
2. The administrator sees previously entered data for the current time period.
3. The administrator selects an existing entry.
4. The administrator changes the charge number and/or the hours worked.
5. The update is logged as an unusual activity
6. The new information is updated in the view and is seen in any subsequent views.

Alternate flow of events. Administrator submits an employee's timecard as complete.

1. The administrator selects an employee from a list.
2. The administrator sees any previously entered data for the current time period.
3. The administrator elects to submit the timecard.
4. The administrator is asked to confirm his or her choice and warned that he or she will not be able to edit his or her entries.
5. The submission is logged as an unusual activity
6. The timecard is submitted; it is no longer available for editing.

Activity diagram. See Figure 3.11.

Nonfunctional requirements. None

Notes.

1. The employee can only enter data for one timecard at a time. If he or she has not submitted a previous timecard, he or she will not be able to enter hours for the current timecard.
2. Once a timecard has been submitted, it cannot be edited again.
3. Employees cannot enter time for days that have not started.

Open issues. None

Sample Use Case Documentation for Export Time Entries (Revised)

The only change for this use case is the addition of Login as a precondition.

Name of use case. Export Time Entries

Description. The Export Time Entries use case allows the administrative user to save specified time-tracking data to a formatted file.

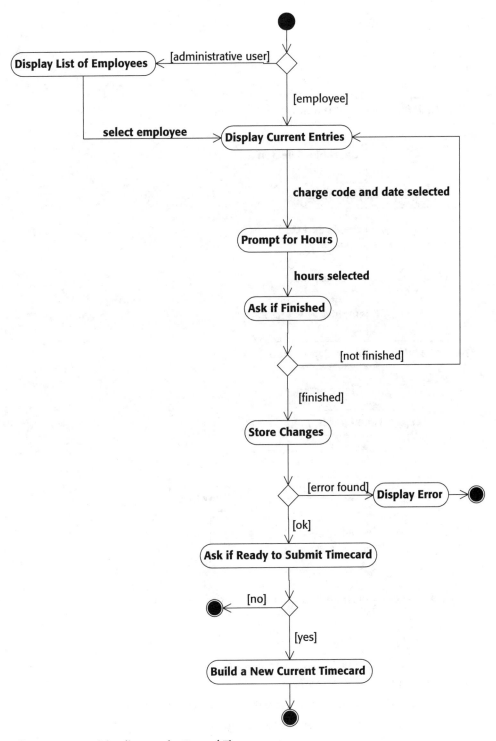

Figure 3.11 Activity diagram for Record Time use case.

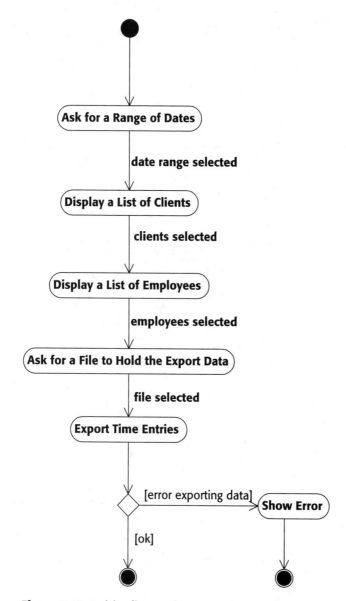

Figure 3.12 Activity diagram for Export Time Entries use case.

Preconditions.

1. The user must be logged in as an administrative user.

Deployment constraints. None

Normal flow of events. The administrative user exports the time entries.

1. The administrative user selects a range of dates.

2. The administrative user selects a subset of clients or all.

3. The administrative user selects a subset of employees or all.

4. The administrative user selects a target file.

5. The data is exported to the file as XML. The administrator is notified when the process is complete.

Exception flow of events. System is unable to export the entries due to a system error.

1. The administrative user selects a range of dates.

2. The administrative user selects a subset of clients or all.

3. The administrative user selects a subset of employees or all.

4. The administrative user selects a target file.

5. The system is unable to export the entries. The administrative user is notified of the error.

6. If possible, the error is recorded to a log.

Activity diagram. See Figure 3.12.

Nonfunctional requirements. None

Open issues. None

The Next Step

This chapter demonstrated the power of the UML for gathering requirements. A high-level use case diagram makes it fairly easy to understand the system's purpose and its benefit to the people who use it. At a far lower level of detail, the flows of events and activity diagrams for each use case allow developers and stakeholders to reach a consensus on the behavior of the system. The UML provides a precise and expressive notation for building and sharing a collective understanding of the problem that the system must solve.

Now that the problem is well understood from the customer's point of view, the developers can continue development from a solid foundation. There will always be misunderstandings and requirements changes due to new business needs, but the number of surprises can be contained to a reasonably low level. This enables developers to work in a more stable and successful environment. In the next step, analysis, the developers build an understanding of the problem from a developer's perspective.

A Brief Introduction to Object-Oriented Analysis with the UML

The preceding chapters demonstrated how the UML is used to view a problem from the customer's and end-user's perspective. During analysis, though the focus is still on the problem, it is from the developer's perspective. Analysis describes what the system needs to do; it does not determine how it will do it. Thus the emphasis is still on understanding the problem, rather than selecting technology to solve the problem. These details are determined later, in architecture, technology selection, and detailed design.

> **NOTE** My view of object-oriented analysis and design is influenced by the Rational Unified Process, my experiences teaching Rational's object-oriented analysis and design course, and many fine texts by Grady Booch, Martin Fowler, and Peter Coad. Any misinterpretations or oversimplifications are, of course, my own.

Performing analysis for a system is somewhat analogous to staffing a brand new company. Before collecting resumes and performing interviews, you have to figure out what roles need to be filled. In analysis, you determine the roles and responsibilities of different parts of the system before you evaluate candidate technologies and actually build or purchase the parts.

In this chapter, we will walk through the analysis phase of the project. In Chapter 5, "Analysis Model for the Timecard Application," we'll use the concepts introduced here when we create the analysis model for the Timecard application.

Are You Ready?

Object-oriented analysis is the art and science of finding and documenting the objects that cooperate to meet the system's goal. In analysis, this effort is limited to determining the responsibilities of each object and the interactions among the objects. Analysis is a technology- and implementation-independent description of the objects' roles and interactions, which is then used as a basis for technology selection, architecture, and design.

There are two key steps to prepare to begin analysis. First, you must ensure that the requirements are solidly and consistently defined. Next, if the project is large enough to merit multiple iterations, you must prioritize the use cases based on risk, significance, and the abilities of your project team.

Solid Requirements

To begin analysis, the requirements must be solid, with a high-level use case diagram and documentation for each use case. At a minimum, the documentation for each use case must contain the normal flow of events. Many use cases should be fully specified, with alternate and exception flows of events. However, it is important to recognize that though the requirements are solid, they are not complete.

Working with poorly formed requirements or attempting to achieve perfect requirements ensures failure. Balance is the key. If you discover radically new use cases during analysis, it means you quit the requirements-gathering phase too soon and that your requirements were not solid. That said, you might find a new use case that supports an existing use case, or realize that an existing use case must be refactored into several use cases. Certainly, you must expect to refine your understanding of each use case during analysis.

Prioritizing Use Cases

Analysis may be performed for all of the use cases at once or for a targeted subset of use cases, as in iterative development. In iterative development, all of the use cases are described during a comprehensive requirements-gathering phase. Next a set of use cases is identified and a mini-system is developed to meet these requirements. This mini-system is created by performing analysis, architecture, technology selection, design, code, and test for the selected use cases. The process of building the mini-system is an iteration. The entire system is built incrementally, with a new set of use cases added in each iteration.

Prioritizing the use cases makes it possible to attack the most important ones together in the first iteration. Once this first iteration is completed, the remaining use cases are reprioritized, and the process continues. By dividing the use cases in this manner, the overall project risk is minimized, and the project can build a large success from a series of smaller successes, or overcome small failures rather than succumb to one large failure.

TIP   It is always better to plan a series of small successes and accept the occasional minor setback. Planning for one giant success often results in one catastrophic failure.

Risk

Risk provides an important criterion when ordering use cases. It often makes sense to attack risks early in the project. In this approach, a risky use case may cause the first iteration to fail. On the bright side, there is plenty of money left in the budget and plenty of time in the schedule so you can try other approaches. If the total schedule is going to lengthen, it is better to find out early. Either way, this approach ultimately reduces risk and increases the predictability of the schedule.

There are many types of risk. A use case may push the state of the art for computer science, depend on an intricate set of interactions with the end user, or have very restrictive nonfunctional requirements. Consider a brief example: A credit card company is developing a Web-enabled system that allows customers to check their outstanding balance, view the last month's transactions, pay the current bill, and apply for more credit. Experience and focus groups determine that there is no speed requirement for the first two use cases, View Balance and View Transactions. People are used to waiting several seconds for this sort of information.

In contrast, most people become anxious when money is changing hands. They want the transaction completed and a printable receipt produced. So, the Pay Current Bill use case is risky because it must meet demanding performance requirements. The last use case seems to have a lot of risk, because it requires a computer to apply a complex set of rules to a large amount of data, and produce an important answer. However, this is hardly a new problem in the credit card industry, so in practice there may not be much risk involved.

Significance

Some use cases capture the intent of a system, while other use cases play a supporting role. In many systems, it is important to develop the more significant use cases in the first iteration. The supporting use cases can often be deferred by populating the system with fake data. By developing the more significant use cases first, developers give the other stakeholders a chance to see the system while there is still time and budget to change it.

Team Competency and Team Building

While it is important to pick use cases based on risk and significance, you must not forget the developers. Ignoring team competencies can jeopardize both the project's success and the long-term stability of the development team. Teams that are new to one another, new to object-oriented development, and new to some of the candidate technologies must start with a small simple set of use cases.

What Is Object-Oriented Analysis?

Since objects do the work in an object-oriented system, object-oriented analysis must discover the objects that make up the system, describe their responsibilities, and determine their interactions. Again, this is done without considering the development language or technology that will be used for the objects.

There are two key advantages to deferring technology selection. First, it allows you to solve a simpler and more generic problem. It is easy to become absorbed in the intricacies of a particular technology; and focusing on these details prevents a designer from seeing larger patterns. Also, an implementation-independent analysis model allows for more flexibility as the solution evolves. Strange combinations of technology shortcomings and new requirements can lead to changes in the implementation strategy. An implementation-independent analysis model helps developers to create clear designs and provides insurance against radical changes in the system architecture.

If analysis is not concerned with the specific technologies of the system, then what questions does it answer? Analysis discovers the objects that interact to form the system. When the analysis is completed, you have an understanding of what the objects in the system need to do and, at a logical level, how they will do it. As you discover and evolve this detailed understanding of the system, you invariably notice weak areas in the requirements. It is very common for developers to revisit some use cases with the other stakeholders during analysis.

The Analysis Model

An *analysis model* contains two types of diagrams, which describe the objects and their interactions. These diagrams are organized according to the use case model, with each use case leading to several diagrams.

The first diagram used for analysis is the *class diagram.* This diagram captures each type of object in detail. Remember that the template for creating all objects of a particular type is called a class. So, a class diagram shows the state and describes the behavior that typifies the objects. The second type of diagram is an *interaction diagram.* This diagram describes the interaction between objects. It shows how one object configures another object and how other objects use an object to reach an objective.

These diagrams form two very different views of the objects that make up a system. The first, the class diagram, shows the templates for the objects in great detail. The second diagram, the interaction diagram, shows the object in motion.

Relationship to Use Case Model

Analysis builds on requirements gathering, so the analysis model builds on and is structured by the use case model. Specifically, each use case in an iteration leads to a class diagram that shows all of the different types of objects that participate in the use case. Also, each flow of events for a use case leads to an object interaction diagram that shows how individual objects cooperate to perform the flow of events. Finally, all of the classes from all of the use cases are organized into groups, for consistency.

Considering each use case separately also helps decrease the total effort for analysis. Obviously, developers must consolidate and refactor their model of the system as additional use cases are considered, which adds to the effort. But the benefits of a divide-and-conquer approach far outweigh the effort spent on refactoring. After all, finding all of the objects for a moderately large system in one pass is impossible for most people. Perhaps there is one genius in a million who, like a chess grand master or brilliant composer, can keep the whole model in his or her head. The rest of us must be content solving the puzzle a piece at a time.

Steps for Object-Oriented Analysis

Object-oriented analysis can be broken into several discrete steps. For each use case in the current iteration, you need to:

1. Discover candidate objects.

2. Describe object interactions.

3. Describe the classes.

Let's look at each of these steps in more detail.

Discover Candidate Objects

The first step in creating an analysis model is object discovery. In this step, developers find a group of objects that contribute to the solution for a use case. These objects are used as a starting point for the next step, describing behavior.

This section has two parts. The first part enumerates some guidelines for discovering objects. The second part discusses an actual process for discovering objects. Probably, no two developers will perform this creative task in the exact same way; nevertheless, this process can serve as a reasonable starting point for most developers.

In discussing objects, it is difficult to avoid discussing classes. After all, every object is an instance of a particular class. Every class defines a type of object. In the UML, the attributes and behavior common to a group of objects are documented in a class diagram. There is no UML diagram that shows the data and behavior for an individual object. The UML diagrams that show objects are dedicated to showing interaction and cooperation between objects.

TIP   By discovering objects, you are implicitly discovering the classes that the objects instantiate.

Guidelines for Discovering Objects

Before discovering objects, you should have some guidelines for the objects and classes that you will discover. Establishing these guidelines early in the process prevents confusion between developers, and facilitates development of a coherent and consistent analysis model. The following delineations provide some criteria and checkpoints.

- Limit the responsibilities of each analysis class.
- Use clear and consistent names for classes and methods.
- Keep analysis classes simple.

Limit Responsibilities

A good class has a single clear and coherent purpose or responsibility. This makes the class easier to understand, maintain, and extend. Simplicity and clarity of purpose also make it easier for other parts of the system to use the class, which keeps the system lean and elegant. Conversely, allowing large classes with many responsibilities can cripple a project. These classes are difficult to maintain, and over time may grow beyond the comprehension of their creators. This seems to be true for all programming paradigms: If you allow too much functionality to reside in a single function, procedure, subroutine, class, module, or stored procedure, the eventual result is an incomprehensible "hot potato" that is shuffled from developer to developer until everyone retires or leaves the project.

Analysis classes may seem excessively well focused and even contrived. It may seem odd to have a class in analysis with three methods and no data. This discomfort leads many developers to combine analysis classes or to add unrelated responsibilities to an existing analysis class that appears too small. Doing so is dangerous. During detailed design and implementation, a simple analysis class may evolve into a reasonably complicated class or even a group of tightly coupled classes. User interface and system interface classes invariably explode, as their full complexity is understood. In general, creating small well-defined analysis classes is a sound philosophy. To that end, strive to answer yes to the following questions:

1. Does each class have a single clear purpose?
2. Is this purpose clear from a one-paragraph textual description?
3. Does each method fit within the responsibility of its class?

Use Clear and Consistent Names

For a class to be useful to developers, it must be easy to understand from the outside. This means that class names and responsibilities must be clear and unambiguous from the perspective of other developers and, whenever possible, other stakeholders. For instance, a class that describes part of the business problem must make sense to an industry expert. Clear class and method names allow other developers and stakeholder to understand and validate the analysis model. This allows developers and stakeholders to catch mistakes and misunderstandings before they threaten the success of the project.

By definition, an object is an independent system element, with its own data and the capability to provide services as defined by its class. With this in mind, class names should always be nouns that describe the nature or responsibility of the system element. This distinguishes classes and objects from methods. By tradition, class names start with an uppercase letter and use mixed-case letters to highlight word boundaries. Some types of objects are natural nouns. Consider a few examples from different problems, such as Employee, Timecard, LinkedList, BinaryTree, BankAccount, and Mortgage. In other cases, a class name is a distorted verb. This is often the case when a class is typified by its responsibility for some action. Again, consider a few examples from different problems, such as TaxCalculator, EventListener, PayrollProcessor, and Input-Validator. The English language is full of verbs that have mutated into nouns: People who teach are teachers; people who tend gardens are gardeners; people who program computers are programmers; people who instruct are instructors.

CHECKLIST FOR NAMING OBJECTS

✔ **Is the name of each class a noun?**

✔ **Will the name of each class and method be unambiguous to other developers who are less familiar with the system?**

✔ **Have you avoided meaningless "filler" names, such as manager, in favor of descriptive names with well-defined meanings?**

✔ **Is the name of each method a verb or a combination of a verb and a noun?**

Keep It Simple

Don't get too fancy when discovering analysis objects; that is, don't try to determine the relationships between the objects. Don't name roles or create elaborate inheritance hierarchies. Remember, this is your first attempt at a high-level solution. In short, don't spend large amounts of time perfecting the first draft. Discover some objects, review the results, and defer the details until you have found behavior.

Process for Discovering Objects

Identifying the objects that make up the system is one of the most difficult parts of analysis. The use case model is large and elaborate while the *analysis model* is just a blank sheet of paper, waiting to be filled. As with many complex and creative endeavors, the hardest part is getting started. Fortunately, the object-oriented community has identified four commonly occurring types of objects that can be used in almost every analysis model. They are:

- Entity
- Boundary
- Control
- Lifecycle

The following sections describe them in detail.

Entity Objects

Entity objects encapsulate the business data and business logic of the system [Jacobson, et al. 1999]. They are generally fairly easy to find, as they are the nouns used to describe significant parts of the problem. There are two ways to find entity objects. One approach is to consider all of the data and behavior required to solve the problem, then organize the data into related groups. The other approach is to identify the important nouns as entity objects, then determine the data and behavior that each entity object contains. While the latter is closer to object-oriented theory, reality lies somewhere in the middle for most developers. It makes sense to make a list of all data, a list of behavior, and a list of all the important-sounding nouns, then allocate the data and behavior to different types of entity objects. During this process, you may find additional entity objects, rename entity objects, or remove entity objects.

CHECKLIST FOR IDENTIFYING ENTITY OBJECTS

✔ **Is the entity object a significant noun in the problem?**

✔ **Does the entity object contain information that is used to solve the system problem?**

✔ **Does the entity object contain calculation or validation logic that is used to solve the system problem?**

✔ **Does the entity object make sense to experts who understand the system's goals?**

For example, let's find the entity objects for our reoccurring example of withdrawing funds from bank accounts, as introduced in Chapter 2, "Gathering Requirements with UML." Working through the normal flow of events and the activity diagram, there are several important-sounding nouns, some data, and some behavior.

Nouns (candidate entity objects). Customer, user, account, money, receipt

Data. Personal identification number (PIN), customer name, amount for withdrawal

Behavior. Validate PIN, withdraw funds, check for sufficient funds, dispense money, print receipt, thank customer

First, we need to clarify the nouns, data, and behavior that we extracted from the flow of events and the activity diagram. This leads us to perform the following exclusions:

- Customer and user seem interchangeable, so we discard user and keep the more descriptive customer.
- Money seems like part of a more significant entity, not an entity in its own right, so we discard it.
- Receipt does not seem very significant; it seems more oriented toward the interface with the user, so we discard it.

- Dispense money, print receipt, and thank customer all seem to be very specific parts of the interface with the user, not core parts of the terminology of the problem, so we discard them.

After these exclusions, we are left with the following nouns, data, and behavior:

Nouns (candidate entity objects). Customer, account

Data. Personal identification number, customer name, amount for withdrawal

Behavior Validate PIN, withdraw funds, check for sufficient funds

Based on these lists, we can allocate data and behavior to the candidate entity objects, as follows.

- Each customer object knows the name and PIN of the customer that it represents, and can validate the entered PIN.

- Each account object knows how much money is in the account that it represents; it provides withdrawal funds and checks for sufficient funds as services.

- No object seems appropriate to hold the withdrawal amount, so, we introduce a new entity object that represents the transaction.

We have discovered three distinct types of entity objects. Since each type of object is a class in an object-oriented system, we can use the UML notation for classes to capture the work. Figure 4.1 shows all three classes with their data and behavior. Notice the <<entity>> at the top of each class box.

WARNING In many cases, the industry's terminology may be obscure or even antiquated. You might be tempted to improve the terminology during analysis; you may want to update or generalize a term for the convenience of the developers. Don't. Maintain domain-specific terminology, and educate developers to use it. Changing the terminology makes conversations with the stakeholders difficult, and is generally impolite. After all, a term may have been around for a few hundred years and be part of the culture of the industry.

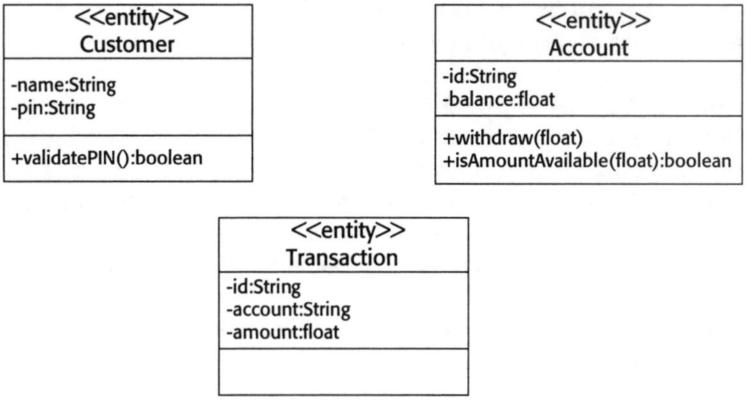

```
┌─────────────────────────┐        ┌──────────────────────────────────┐
│        <<entity>>       │        │            <<entity>>            │
│         Customer        │        │             Account             │
├─────────────────────────┤        ├──────────────────────────────────┤
│ -name:String            │        │ -id:String                       │
│ -pin:String             │        │ -balance:float                   │
├─────────────────────────┤        ├──────────────────────────────────┤
│ +validatePIN():boolean  │        │ +withdraw(float)                 │
└─────────────────────────┘        │ +isAmountAvailable(float):boolean│
                                    └──────────────────────────────────┘

                ┌─────────────────────────┐
                │        <<entity>>       │
                │        Transaction      │
                ├─────────────────────────┤
                │ -id:String              │
                │ -account:String         │
                │ -amount:float           │
                ├─────────────────────────┤
                │                         │
                └─────────────────────────┘
```

Figure 4.1 Entity classes for banking example.

Boundary Objects

In Chapter 2, the actors in the use case model were defined as those people or systems located outside of the solution system that will interact with the solution system. *Boundary objects* represent how the system will interface with the actors.

Boundary objects are identified by examining the relationships between the actors and the use cases in the use case diagram. As a rule, each actor/use case pair forms a boundary object in the analysis model. There are two types of boundary objects:

User interfaces. Allow the system to interact with humans.

System interfaces. Allow the system to interact with other systems.

For both types, boundary objects have a very narrow focus. User interface objects are responsible only for presenting data to the user and accepting input from the user. System interface objects are responsible for communicating with another system. Business data and business rules belong in entity objects, not in boundary objects [Jacobson, et al. 1999].

CHECKLIST FOR IDENTIFYING BOUNDARY OBJECTS

✔ **Does the user interface class describe the information that must be displayed and the services that are offered?**

✔ **Does the user interface class defer all user interface design details?**

✔ **Does the system interface describe the interaction with the external system?**

✔ **Does the system interface defer all protocol details?**

TIP The analysis model should not contain any user interface design details. However, user interface prototyping may be performed concurrently with analysis, as long as it is treated as a separate effort with a separate deliverable.

Consider the banking example with a Customer actor and two use cases, Withdraw Funds and Transfer Funds. According to the rule of thumb, there is a boundary object for each actor/use case pair, so there are two boundary objects. This leads to two objects withdrawFundsUI and transferFundsUI. From the normal flow of events and the interaction diagram in Chapter 2, we see that the withdrawFundsUI has the following user interface-related behavior: soliciting a PIN, displaying accounts, allowing the user to select an account, and soliciting the withdraw amount. As with entity objects, this behavior is captured in a class diagram, since it is available to all instances of the WithdrawFundsUI class. Figure 4.2 shows this behavior in a class diagram. Each method is named from the perspective of the actor or object that uses the object.

TIP Use a consistent naming scheme for user interfaces and external systems. Many projects append the suffix View or UI to the end of the use case name. If more than one actor initiates the use case, the actor's name should be incorporated.

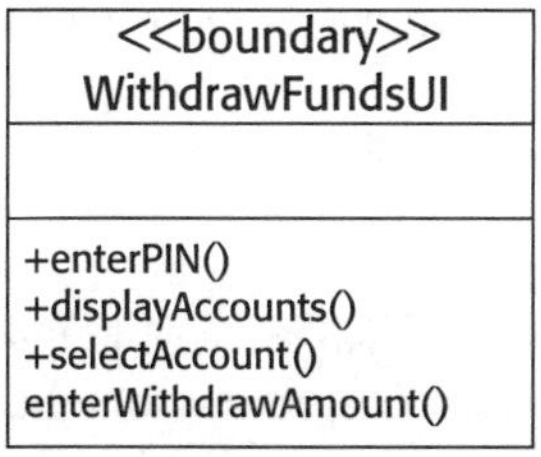

```
┌─────────────────────────────┐
│       <<boundary>>          │
│       WithdrawFundsUI       │
├─────────────────────────────┤
│                             │
├─────────────────────────────┤
│ +enterPIN()                 │
│ +displayAccounts()          │
│ +selectAccount()            │
│ enterWithdrawAmount()       │
└─────────────────────────────┘
```

Figure 4.2 WithdrawFundsUI class.

Boundary objects appear very insubstantial during analysis. They may not have any data and may have easy-sounding responsibilities, such as "display accounts." Resist the urge to discount or ignore boundary objects. In many cases, their functionality is a key criterion during technology selection, and greatly influences the design and architecture of the system. Boundary objects are only "thin" during analysis, because their responsibilities are described at a very high level.

Control Objects

Control objects provide workflow and session services to other objects. The control object bundles the complex series of requests to the entity objects into a common workflow that is easily accessed by the boundary objects. A high-level message from a boundary object to the control object is converted into a series of messages from the control object to the entity objects. This allows the boundary object to concentrate on its responsibilities while the domain object stays simple. As a rule, each use case has one type of control object in the analysis model [Jacobson, et al. 1999].

TIP The easiest way to identify control objects is to consider the system without them.

Entity objects are simple, with a small number of well-focused responsibilities. This means that a boundary object with a complex objective must send a complex series of requests to the simple well-focused entity objects. The trade-off is unpleasant: either to have heavy and less flexible entity objects or to have complex boundary objects that are tightly coupled with the entity objects. Neither option is acceptable. Entity objects must be simple and flexible, so that they can provide business logic and business data for many use cases. Even well-defined user interface and system interface objects tend to be difficult to extend and to maintain, so adding even more complexity is quite dangerous.

Fortunately, a control object serves as an intermediary between the boundary objects and the entity objects that cooperate in a particular use case. This allows the entity objects to provide a simple set of services while the boundary objects defer the complexity of interacting with the entity objects to the control object. Several boundary objects may use a single type of control object for a particular use case. For example, a Web interface and a client server interface might share a common type of control object.

Perhaps a real-life example will make this rather abstract idea more concrete. Consider a customer ordering lunch in a sub shop on North Broad Street in Philadelphia, specifically, a nice cheese steak on a freshly baked sub roll with mayo, mushrooms, fried onions, and sweet peppers, but no tomatoes, no lettuce. But I digress. The customer does not shout his or her order to the short order cook; most shops would frown on such a breach of etiquette. Instead, a designated order taker or cashier accepts the request, queries the customer for additional drink and side preferences, settles the bill, writes down the order on a little piece of paper, and clips it to the greasy range hood.

This interaction is very simple and convenient for the customers. They do not need to get the cook's attention or direct their efforts in any way. They do not need to separately request fries or the drink from busy employees. Once the order is completed, they wait in quiet anticipation.

The little piece of paper also simplifies the staff's tasks. The fry guy can fill drinks and dish up some fries without worrying whose order it is. The cook is similarly free to concentrate on the details of sub making; getting the ingredients together and in proper balance, ignoring the customer's preferences, and wrapping the finished product. In the end, the customer gets a delicious cheese steak with mayo, hot peppers and tomato and lettuce.

So, a simple single point of contact, the order taker, simplifies life for the customer and allows the other employees in the shop to stay focused on their individual tasks. This is exactly the role of a control object. A control object encapsulates the interactions with entity objects so that the boundary object can focus on the actor without making additional demands on the entity objects.

CHECKLIST FOR IDENTIFYING CONTROL OBJECTS

✔ **Does the control class model the application or workflow logic for the use case?**

✔ **Does the control class delegate the actual business logic to the entity classes?**

Consider the Withdraw Funds use case. Our simple rule of thumb indicates that there is a single type of control object for each use case. Since the use case describes a simple workflow for withdrawing money, it seems appropriate to introduce a WithdrawFundsWorkflow class, as in Figure 4.3.

The behavior for this type of control object is determined by isolating the behavior that is exposed by the entity objects and used by the boundary objects for the use case. The behavior consists of validating the entered PIN, checking for sufficient funds, and withdrawing funds. Remember, a control object does not actually verify the PIN or withdraw funds. Instead, the control object finds and uses one or more entity objects to process each request.

Object Lifecycle Classes

Object lifecycle classes keep track of entity objects. Object-oriented systems contain hundreds or even thousands of entity objects. These objects must be created, located, and

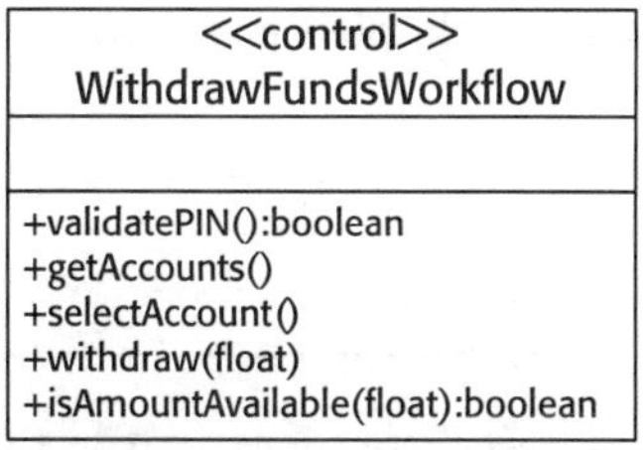

```
            <<control>>
      WithdrawFundsWorkflow

+validatePIN():boolean
+getAccounts()
+selectAccount()
+withdraw(float)
+isAmountAvailable(float):boolean
```

Figure 4.3 The WithdrawFundsWorkflow class.

sometimes destroyed. Control or entity objects may need to locate an entity object by different criteria. For example, a WithdrawFundsWorkflow object needs to locate a specific Customer object, given the name or ID of the actual customer. There may be several ways to create an entity object. Since the logic for creating, finding, and destroying a particular type of entity object may be used in many use cases, it is handy to have a single type of lifecycle object for each type of entity object. As the developer considers each use case in turn, the lifecycle class accumulates additional behavior. As a general rule, there is a lifecycle class for each entity class.

> **NOTE**   Entity, boundary, and control classes have a long history as analysis classes. Lifecycle classes, at least by this name, lack this pedigree. In fact, as far as I know, I just made up the term. In my experience, almost all designers introduce something similar either late in analysis or very early in design. Most designers use names from the intended implementation technology or from their design experience. Some common examples include *home*, *factory*, and *container*. None of these names seems appropriate for an analysis model, as they all include design assumptions. While in general I frown upon the practice of authors creating their own terms to describe existing ideas, it seems that there is a vacuum to be filled here. So, I refer to such classes as *lifecycle classes*.

CHECKLIST FOR IDENTIFYING LIFECYCLE OBJECTS

✔ **Does the lifecycle class locate, create, or destroy entity objects?**

✔ **Is each lifecycle class dedicated to a single type of entity object?**

For the Withdraw Funds use case, both customer and account objects are located by particular criteria. Figure 4.4 shows that CustomerLocator lifecycle objects can locate

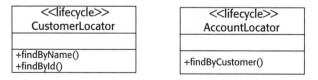

Figure 4.4 The CustomerLocator class.

Customer objects by ID or name. Similarly, the AccountLifecycle objects can locate accounts for a specified customer.

Describe Behavior

Once you've identified entity, boundary, and controller classes, the next step is to determine how the associated objects interact, to realize the use cases.

This section has two parts. The first part enumerates some guidelines for describing behavior. The second part discusses an actual process for describing the interaction between objects. As noted before, probably no two developers will perform this creative task in the exact same way, but this process can serve as a reasonable starting point for most developers.

UML uses two diagrams to describe the interactions between objects: sequence diagrams and collaboration diagrams. *Sequence diagrams* show how objects interact over time. A sequence diagram allows you to track complex message sequences easily, but does not show how objects are connected. *Collaboration diagrams* show connections between objects, but are not very readable for complex sequences.

Objects interact by calling methods in other objects. Objects use this mechanism to send information, request a service, or request information. In object-oriented terminology, these interactions are described as *messages*, which are sent from one object and received by another. While messages are named from the perspective of the calling object, it is important to remember that the implementation is in the receiving object. Think of the receiver as providing some standardized service that can be called by other objects.

> **TIP**   To preserve your sanity, I recommend considering use cases one at a time, developing sequence diagrams and a view of participating classes for each use case in turn. As you add more use cases, you inevitably revise your earlier work. For instance, your understanding of the responsibilities of a particular class often changes as you consider its role in various use cases.

Guidelines for Finding Behavior

There are four rules to follow as you identify the behavior of objects as they cooperate to fulfill a use case:

- Make sure the messages for each type of object fit together.
- Clearly name each message.
- Completely satisfy the functionality for the use case.
- Keep it simple.

The following subsections explain these guidelines in detail.

Ensure Cohesion between Methods

The methods for a class must form a coherent group, and they must fit the stated responsibilities of the class. For instance, makeToast, makeEggs, and makeJuice are closely related behaviors that combine to fulfill the "make breakfast" responsibility. They make perfect sense as methods in a Cook class. If we add the changeOil method, the methods no longer form a single coherent responsibility.

You will be tempted to add a responsibility to an object that does not fit with the existing responsibilities. The short-term convenience is not worth the long-term confusion.

Use Clear and Unambiguous Method Names

Each method must be named clearly and unambiguously from the perspective of the calling object. A developer who wishes to use your object should not need to read your source code to determine what the methods do. For instance, a class that has getQuantity and getValue as its methods is not likely to earn popularity awards for its developer. You must remember that the audience for your method names includes other current developers, future developers, and *you* after a long vacation.

Most method names can indicate the return type of the method. For instance, getName should return a string that is the name of the object. A method called setHeight is not expected to return anything, and almost certainly accepts a numeric parameter that changes the height of the object.

Completely Satisfy the Use Case

You must ensure that the use case is completely realized by your objects. This requires perseverance and good bookkeeping. Each step in each flow of events, and each activity and conditional in the activity diagram for the use case, must be traceable to one or more methods in the objects. Since this is analysis, the method may not be well understood, but it must exist.

Keep It Simple

Don't get too fancy during analysis; that means defer any nonobvious parameters and return types until design. Also, there is no need to determine the source of each object, so don't bother creating elaborate inheritance hierarchies or arguing over the exact relationship between two objects. There is no need to get bogged down in the details when the whole landscape will change and evolve during design. For now, just use classes to hold related behaviors.

CHECKPOINTS FOR DESCRIBING BEHAVIOR

✔ **Does each method have a clear purpose?**

✔ **Is each method name a strong combination of verbs and nouns?**

✔ Have you avoided wishy-washy names?

✔ Are all methods named clearly from the perspective of the calling object?

✔ Will all method names be unambiguous to other developers?

✔ Does the method name indicate what will be returned? For instance, a getDate request might reasonably be expected to return some sort of Date object, while a repaint request would not be expected to return anything.

✔ Are the methods in each class closely related to one another?

✔ Do the methods in each class match the stated responsibility of the class?

✔ Does each class still have a single concrete purpose?

A Process for Describing Behavior

This subsection shows how to find and describe the interactions between objects as they cooperate to fulfill a use case. This process can be separated into three steps.

1. Add the previously identified participating objects to a sequence diagram.
2. Work forward from the actor, finding behavior as you go.
3. Validate the sequence from the end.

The following subsections build on the Withdraw Funds use case as introduced in Chapter 2 and on the candidate objects found in the "Discover Candidate Objects" section of this chapter.

Add Participating Objects to a Sequence Diagram

Finally it is time for the players to take the field. First, we add the actor that initiates the use case to the sequence diagram. Next, we add the boundary object, then the control object, then the entity objects. This pattern almost always holds true. Each use case is initiated by an actor, so it makes sense to put the actor on first. Likewise, there is always a single boundary object between the actor and the use case, so it makes sense to show that object next. There is always a single control object that serves as a single point of contact as the boundary object uses the entity objects. Finally, there may be many entity objects, depending on the complexity of the use case. We ignore the life-cycle objects until they are needed.

> **TIP** When arranging the actor and objects for a use case, you can derive the order based on the way objects depend on one another; or you can follow the slightly flawed mnemonic device of "simple as ABCE" for actor, boundary, control, and entity.

Figure 4.5 shows the objects arranged in this simple pattern. Each object may show its name, its type, and its stereotype. The name of an object is the underlined text to the

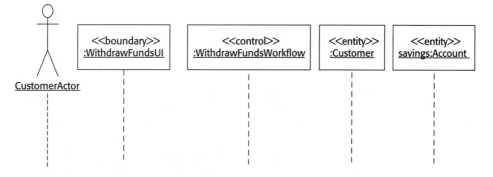

Figure 4.5 Empty sequence diagram for the Withdraw Funds use case.

left of the colon. The class that the object instantiates is the underlined text to the right of the colon. The stereotype is at the top of the object box; it is always enclosed inside angle brackets. In many cases, there is no need to name an object. For instance, in this case, there is only one object of type WithdrawFundsUI, so there is no need to name it. But because most customers have a checking and savings account, it may be useful to name the Account object.

Work Forward from the Actor

Once the objects are arranged on the sequence diagram, we can show how they inter-act with one another. Remember, in object-oriented terminology, one object sends a message to another object; the actual method implementation resides inside the receiving object. Each message is named for the method that it calls.

Since the actor always initiates the use case, it must send the first message. A message in UML is depicted as a solid arrow from one object's dashed line to another. The order of messages from top to bottom along the lines indicates the order in which they are sent.

Figure 4.6 shows a first attempt at the sequence diagram for the normal flow of events for the Withdraw Funds use case. The sequence begins when the customer enters his or her PIN. This message is received by a nameless WithdrawFundsUI boundary object that asks a nameless WithdrawFundsWorkflow object to validate the PIN. The WithdrawFundsWorkflow object, like all control objects, does not know how to perform this task directly. Instead, it knows which object to ask. It asks the Customer object that is associated with the user to validate the PIN. The return value of VALID bubbles up to the WithdrawFundsUI object. The return value is explicitly shown because the value affects the sequence.

Next, the WithdrawFundsUI object needs to present a list of accounts to the user. So the WithdrawFundsUI object asks the WithdrawFundsWorkflow object for a list of accounts. The WithdrawFundsWorkflow object asks each account for its name, and returns a list. Notice that the return arrow is not shown for the getName messages, as it is obvious from the method name, and the return result does not impact the flow. The displayAccounts arrow from the WithdrawFundsUI object back to the object indicates that the object calls a method on itself to display accounts.

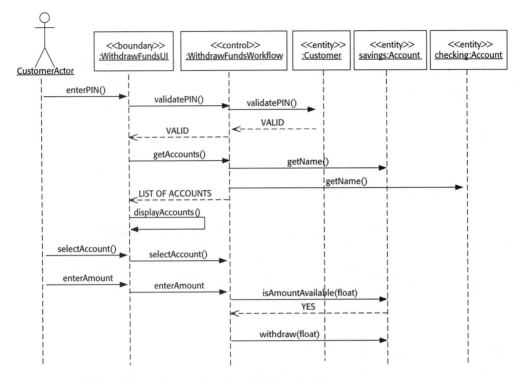

Figure 4.6 Initial sequence diagram for the Withdraw Funds use case.

Next, the customer selects an account in the WithdrawFundsUI object, which in turn selects an account in the WithdrawFundsWorkflow object. Notice that the Withdraw-FundsWorkflow simply absorbs the account selection for future use. Finally, the customer enters an amount, after which the WithdrawFundsUI passes the amount to the WithdrawFundsWorkflow object. The WithdrawFundsWorkflow object asks the savings account if the funds are available, then performs a withdrawal against the savings account.

Validate the Sequence

Finally, when you believe you have discovered the required methods, you must validate the sequence. To do this, work backward from the end of the last sequence, asking whether each object has the information that it needs to provide the desired services.

An account object certainly knows how much money it has, and can remove money from itself, so the last two methods are okay. The beginning of the sequence, where the WithdrawFundsUI object passes the amount along to the WithdrawFundsWorkflow, seems reasonable—if you assume that the WithdrawFundsUI and the Withdraw-FundsWorkflow objects are created as a pair of cooperating objects. The sequence also assumes that the WithdrawFundsWorkflow object remembers the selected account.

The previous sequence, in which the WithdrawFundsUI object passes the account selection to the WithdrawFundsWorkflow seems similarly reasonable.

Working backward from the display accounts method, it is reasonable to expect each account to know its name. It is not, however, clear how the WithdrawFundsWorkflow object found the savings and checking accounts. There are three alternatives: First, the Customer object can hold a list of its accounts; second, the WithdrawFundsWorkflow object can use a locator object to find the accounts for a given customer; third, you can defer the question until design. As long as you are consistent within your project, any of these approaches is defensible, although I prefer the locator approach, as it provides a convenient list of the ways that each type of object is located.

The first sequence raises a similar question. A Customer object can certainly validate a PIN, but how did the WithdrawFundsWorkflow object find the Customer? Figure 4.7 shows the same sequence diagram with these issues resolved.

Describe the Classes

The previous step used sequence diagrams to describe the interactions between objects for a use case. The interactions between objects require methods in classes and relationships between classes. In UML, this information is captured in a *static class diagram*.

Consider an object that sends a message to another object. In order to send the message, the sender needs a reference to the receiver. This can be a permanent link, where the sender keeps a reference to the receiver; or the sender can create a helper object, send it a few requests, and then lose track of it. Also, the method must exist in the receiving object. Since each class completely determines the data and behavior that its instances have, the method must be defined in the class that was used to instantiate the object.

This section has two parts. The first offers general guidance for describing classes and their relationships. The second part defines and demonstrates a simple process for describing classes based on object interactions.

Guidelines for Describing Classes

There are three rules to follow as you describe the classes that support a use case:

1. Be complete.
2. Keep it simple.
3. Maintain coherent classes.

Be Complete

Each message in a sequence diagram must have a corresponding method in the associated class. Remember, when an object sends a message to another object it is actually calling a method that is implemented in the receiving object's class. So, every message must match a corresponding method in a class.

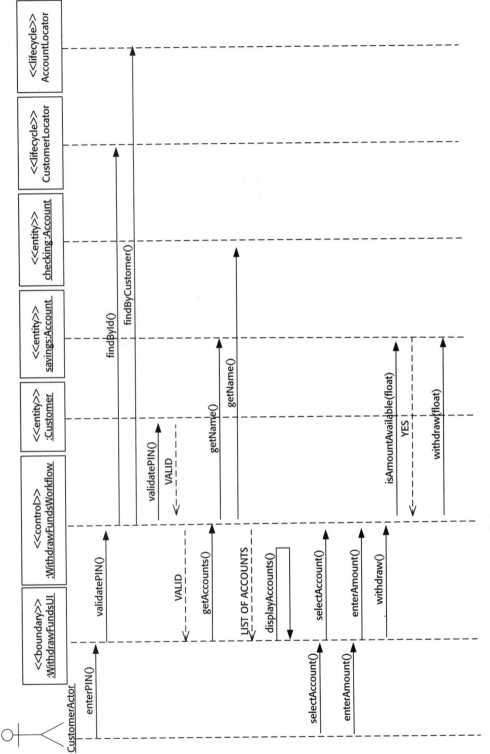

Figure 4.7 Sequence diagram for the Withdraw Funds use case.

In order to send a message, the sending object must have a relationship that is navigable toward the receiving object. The receiving object may reply with a return value without requiring navigability toward the sender.

It is important to establish the direction of relationships between classes. As the system evolves, you need to know how different parts of the system depend on one another.

Keep It Simple

You don't want to miss anything completely, and you do not want to over-analyze the problem during analysis. Remember, analysis provides a useful foundation for design, but the actual diagrams do not need to survive past design. It is simply too difficult to keep the analysis model synchronized as the design and architecture evolves.

However, you should not spend much time seeking out inheritance hierarchies or determining the multiplicity of relationships. Do not spend hours arguing over aggregation or composition for a relationship that may not even exist in the design model.

If information seems obvious, then include it; otherwise, be very conservative as you spend time in analysis. Remember, the purpose of analysis is to discover and allocate responsibilities.

TIP Think of the analysis model as a rough sketch. You must complete it before you start painting with expensive oils on an expensive canvas, but you don't frame the sketch.

Maintain Coherent Classes

Each new flow of events for each use case introduces methods for existing classes. As this effect is multiplied over many flows of events for many use cases, it is difficult to keep the methods in each class consistent. So, after the sequence diagrams are completed and the classes are updated to reflect the behavior discovered through the sequence diagrams, the classes must be reexamined. Some of the methods that accumulated in a class may not fit well together or may vary from the stated responsibility of the class. In this case, the methods must be reallocated, so that each class forms a coherent whole.

Process for Describing Classes

There are three steps in describing classes:

1. Consolidate behavior from objects to classes.
2. Refactor classes to meet guidelines.
3. Find relationships between classes.

The following subsections explain these steps and demonstrate them against the WithdrawFunds use case.

Consolidate Behavior

In the WithdrawFunds use case, there is only one sequence diagram, as shown in Figure 4.7. In real systems, there are many sequence diagrams per use case and one class diagram per use case. A class that supports more than one use case will appear in each class diagram.

The implementation for each message is located in the receiving object. Each object's behavior is completely determined by the class it instantiates. So, for each message, we identify the receiving object's class and make sure that the method is in the class. Also, if a class or a method in a class is not used in any sequence diagrams, it should be removed. Figure 4.8 shows the changes to the class diagram. The findByName method in the CustomerLocator class, the isAmountAvailable method in the WithdrawFunds Workflow class, and the entire Transaction class have all been removed. Two new methods, enterAmount in the WithdrawFundsWorkflow class and getName in the Account class are added.

Refactor Classes

You must examine each class to determine if it still has a well-focused responsibility and if the methods are cohesive. WithdrawFundsUI, AccountLocator, and Customer-Locator are all unchanged or reduced, so they pass our criteria.

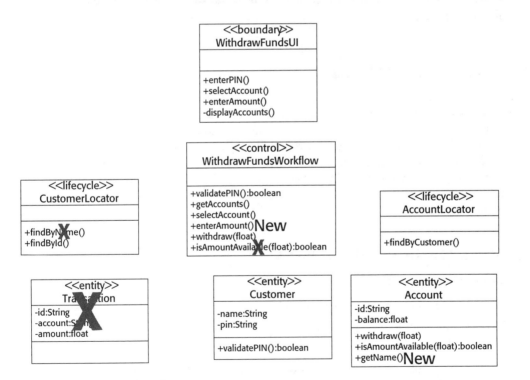

Figure 4.8 Updated class diagram.

WithdrawFundsWorkflow gained the enterAmount method and lost isAmount-Available. The responsibility and nature of the WithdrawFundsWorkflow object has not changed. It is still a simple control class that uses entity objects on the Withdraw-FundsUI object's behalf.

Account added the getName method. It seems perfectly reasonable for an account object to know and expose its own name, so Account is still okay.

Find Relationships between Classes

For each message, there is a dependency or association from the class of the sender to the class of the receiver. If the sender remembers the receiver across different messages, it is a form of association. Multiplicity can be used to describe the relationship. An object may share use of an object or may require its undivided attention.

We use the sequence diagram shown in Figure 4.7 to determine interactions between objects. There is a relationship between the WithdrawFundsUI class and the Withdraw FundsWorkflow, as the WithdrawFundsUI object calls the validatePIN, getAccounts, selectAccounts, enterAmount, and withdraw methods on the WithdrawFundsWorkflow object. This relationship is shown in the class diagram in Figure 4.9. As there are no messages from the WithdrawFundsWorkflow object to the WithdrawFundsUI object, it is a unidirectional relationship. The WithdrawFundsUI object remembers the WithdrawFundsWorkflow object over time, so it does not need to find it each time the actor enters data. It is not clear how the WithdrawFundsUI object gets an initial reference to the WithdrawFundsWorkflow object, but for now, we accept that they are a closely cooperating pair of objects.

Notice that the WithdrawFundsWorkflow object remembers information, such as the selected account and the amount to withdraw, for the WithdrawFundsUI. This implies that each WithdrawFundsWorkflow object is dedicated to a single Withdraw FundsUI. This dedication is captured by the multiplicity number, which is closest to the WithdrawFundsUI class. Reading the relationship from the WithdrawFunds Workflow to the WithdrawFundsUI results in: "Each WithdrawFundsWorkflow object is known about by exactly one WithdrawFundsUI object." Each WithdrawFundsUI needs to use the same WithdrawFundsWorkflow object every time it receives input from the actor, so it keeps a reference to exactly one WithdrawFundsWorkflow object. This is indicated by the number 1 next to the WithdrawFundsWorkflow class.

There is only one CustomerLocator object that is shared by all WithdrawFunds Workflow objects. There can, however, be more than one WithdrawFundsWorkflow object at a time, as each actor using the system gets his or her own WithdrawFundsUI object, which in turn gets its own WithdrawFundsWorkflow object. This is indicated by the asterisk (*) next to the WithdrawFundsWorkflow class and the number 1 next to the CustomerLocator class. The same logic determines the relationship between the WithdrawFundsWorkflow class and the AccountLocator class.

Clearly, there is some sort of relationship between the WithdrawFundsWorkflow class and the Customer class, as the WithdrawFundsWorkflow object sends a validatePIN method to a Customer object. However, once the validation returns, the WithdrawFundsWorkflow object never uses the Customer object again. It is possible in an alternate flow that the WithdrawFundsWorkflow object might remember the Cus-

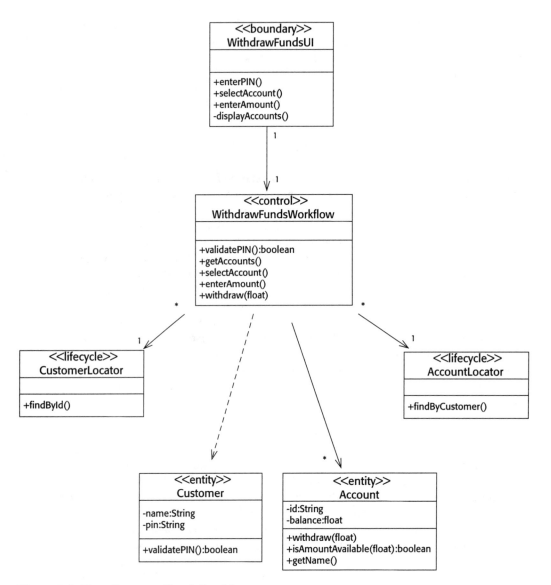

Figure 4.9 Class diagram with relationships.

tomer object, perhaps so it can retry different PINs as the actor enters them. However, we have only one sequence diagram, and it doesn't show any such memory or subsequent use. So, the relationship is a dependency.

There is clearly an association relationship between the WithdrawFundsWorkflow class and the Account class, as the WithdrawFundsWorkflow object locates some Account objects, retrieves their names, then remembers them. Notice that the multiplicity of the WithdrawFundsWorkflow objects is left unspecified. This process has just raised an interesting question: If a user can log in twice, can there be two Withdraw

FundsUI objects, each with a WithdrawFundsWorkflow object? Each Withdraw FundsWorkflow object would use the same Account objects. So, if multiple logins are allowed, the multiplicity is *; otherwise, it is 1.

The Next Step

This chapter described and demonstrated techniques for understanding the problem from a developer's perspective. Analysis describes the solution in terms of cooperating objects and the classes that define them. It focuses on the responsibilities and behavior of these objects, while ignoring the implementation technology.

This provides a solid foundation for subsequent technology selection, architecture, and design efforts. Without analysis, developers are forced to simultaneously understand the solution and the problem. This often leads to hasty or flawed decisions.

The next chapter reinforces the techniques and principles covered in this chapter, and continues the sample timecard system introduced in Chapter 2, "Gathering Requirements with UML."

Analysis Model for the Timecard Application

Now that we've walked through the steps for the analysis phase, let's walk through an example. So far, we've gathered the requirements for our timecard application. The next step is to analyze the requirements and translate them into a language that the developers can understand. Remember that we're not interested in the specific technologies yet; we're focusing on the model of how the system internals will work.

This chapter expands on the material from Chapter 4, "A Brief Introduction to Object-Oriented Analysis with the UML." It provides a small but fairly representative example of the art and science of object-oriented analysis.

NOTE The example in this chapter is continued throughout the book, so it is recommended that even experienced object-oriented practitioners at least skim the information.

Let's begin by walking through each step, from prioritizing the use cases to discovering candidate objects and interactions to, finally, describing the classes in detail.

Prioritizing the Use Cases

Each use case must be ranked according to its risk, its significance to the user and to the architecture, and its suitability given the skills of the team. Once the use cases are ranked in these categories, we must determine which subset of the use cases is most important and makes sense in the first iteration of the system. This process often involves trade-offs and compromise. For example, a use case might be very risky, which would lead us to include it in the first iteration. However, if the team is completely unprepared to succeed with that same use case, then a less risky and more achievable use case must be selected as a compromise.

The Ranking System

To make life easier, risk, significance, and suitability are forced into a simple qualitative ranking system from 1 to 5. The higher the number, the more suitable the use case is for inclusion in the first or next iteration.

In Chapter 3, "Gathering Requirements for the Timecard Application," we identified six use cases for the sample timecard application. Figure 5.1 shows the high-level use case diagram. We must describe each use case in terms of its risk, significance, and its suitability given the current state of the team.

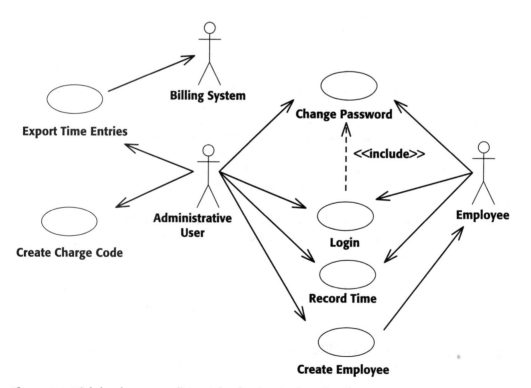

Figure 5.1 High-level use case diagram for the timecard application.

Risk

When possible, you should attack risky parts of the system early in the development cycle. Then, if the first approach fails, there is still time and opportunity to try alternatives.

Before considering the risks involved with each use case, you must develop a list of risks for the project. The following risks are common to many projects, and so can serve as a starting point as you list the risks for your project.

- Unacceptable system performance
- Unacceptable user interface
- Schedule uncertainty and schedule length
- Inability to adapt to new requirements

After some consideration, we determine that the user interface is fairly straightforward. We also realize that performance may be critical, as the end users are very busy and will not appreciate any delays due to the timecard system. Due to our experience on previous projects, we know that the stakeholders invariably increase the system's scope over time and that the stakeholders expect the new features to fit seamlessly into the existing system. Therefore, we order the risks as follows, and resolve to consider each use case with respect to the risks.

1. Unacceptable system performance
2. Inability to adapt to new requirements
3. Schedule uncertainty and schedule length
4. Unacceptable user interface

Before we rank each use case according to risk, we need a simple descriptive way of expressing different levels of risk. To that end, we ask developers if they are sure they can solve the problem on their first try, and make them pick from the following to answer:

1. Of course; our project team has solved that problem before.
2. Certainly; our organization has solved that problem before.
3. There are third-party products, training, books, or other technical resources available, but we do not have any in-house experience.
4. Maybe; we have heard of similar problems being solved.
5. I hope so, but we will be breaking new ground.

As we will see in the use case evaluations, this simple risk "spectrum" helps identify high-risk use cases that must be considered for inclusion in the next iteration.

Significance

A use case is significant to the user and to the architecture if it is close to the core vision of the system. A significant use case captures the flavor and intent of a system. Other use cases may be very important, but in a supporting role. For example, the timecard system cannot function without the Add Employee use case. On the other hand, the Record Time and Export Time Entries use cases completely capture the intent of the system.

Significance can be measured by asking developers how users would react if the use case were omitted from the iteration or replaced with simulated results. Make them pick from the following to answer this question:

1. They would barely notice, and they could easily use the system without it.
2. They would notice; but with a little imagination, the system would still make perfect sense.
3. Most of the system could exist independently.
4. Some parts of the system could exist independently.
5. The system would be impossible to use without it.

As we will see in the use case evaluations, this simple spectrum helps identify very significant use cases that must be considered for inclusion in the next iteration.

Suitability

A use case is suitable for the current project team if they can start working on it with a minimum of training and a relatively short learning curve. These two criteria are especially important when new technologies, languages, and development techniques are introduced to an organization.

Many organizations adapt to new technologies and techniques by putting their best people on a superhigh-profile project. After all, the hype says that object-oriented development and Java is the wave of the future, so why not invest in a week or two of training for the brightest people in the company and then watch them revolutionize the company under intense schedule pressure? Of course, this is backward thinking, because the company simultaneously alienates their best and brightest while making them substantially more marketable.

It takes at least six months to become proficient in a completely new way of thinking, and at least two or three months to become truly proficient in a new language and development environment. Development teams need time and practice under relatively low pressure so that they can develop proficiency and confidence in the new techniques.

Since we are picking use cases for the first iteration and have not selected any technologies yet, it may be difficult to determine exactly how much the developers will need to learn. In contrast, in the real world, project teams generally know whether they will be adopting a new technique, such as object-oriented development. Also, they generally know the language or family of languages that will be used. With this in mind, we ask the developers to describe their comfort level with the technology and techniques, and tell them to choose from the following answers:

1. The team definitely needs more seasoning before attempting this use case.
2. The team's capabilities are probably sufficient for this use case, but may improve substantially over the course of a single iteration.

3. The team's capabilities are probably sufficient and are unlikely to improve over the course of a single iteration.

4. There is no need for more seasoning. Either the team is already quite experienced or the use case is sufficiently straightforward.

5. There is no need for more seasoning. The team is experienced and the use case is straightforward. Money in the bank.

As we will see in the use case evaluations, this simple spectrum helps protect the development team by excluding inappropriate use cases from the next iteration.

For our examples, let's assume that we have a reasonably seasoned team. Most of the developers have at least a year of experience with object-oriented development, and almost everyone has at least a year of experience with Java and at least a year of experience developing software that uses relational databases.

Let's walk through each use case and evaluate them according to risk, significance, and suitability. This will tell us which use cases should be included in the first iteration.

Evaluation of the Export Time Entries Use Case

The Export Time Entries use case allows administrative users to export a specified range of time entries to a formatted XML file.

Risk

Certainly, there is some performance risk involved, since the system must extract significant blocks of data from a set of data that grows larger with every new employee and with the passage of time. This activity could be performed during off-peak hours.

- This use case must be extensible, because the criteria for extracting timecard entries may evolve and become more sophisticated over time.

- This use case is fairly easy to estimate, since it is simply a matter of finding timecard entries and writing the data to a flat file.

- The use interface is very straightforward, so there is no real risk of delivering an overly complex user interface.

Overall, the risk of the use case seems to be quite low. Level 2, "Certainly; our organization has solved that problem before," seems applicable.

Significance

This is a very significant use case. The whole point of a timecard system is to collect and retrieve timecard entries for a variety of purposes. Level 5, "The system would be impossible to use without it," is well justified.

Suitability

This use case is relatively straightforward, and the team is certainly ready. Level 4, "There is no need for more seasoning. Either the team is already quite experienced or the use case is sufficiently straightforward," seems appropriate.

Conclusion

Due to the high significance, this use case is very desirable as part of the first iteration. Including it would build credibility with the customer and provide architecturally significant functionality.

Evaluation of the Create Charge Code Use Case

The Create Charge Code use case allows administrative users to add charge codes for use by the employees as they enter their hours.

Risk

There is virtually no performance risk, since charge codes are added infrequently and contain very small amounts of data.

- The use case seems very well understood, so the extensibility risk is low.
- This use case is fairly easy to estimate, since it is simply a matter of adding data to the system.
- The use interface is very straightforward, so there is no real risk of delivering an overly complex user interface.

Overall, the risk of the use case seems to be quite low. Level 1, "Of course; our project team has solved that problem before," seems applicable.

Significance

While it is certainly very important in the final system, the Create Charge Code use case is more of a support use case. During preliminary iterations, the customer is unlikely to notice the difference between simulated charge codes and charge codes that are entered through the system. Level 1, "They would barely notice, and they could easily use the system without it," describes the likely response.

Suitability

Level 5, "There is no need for more seasoning. The team is experienced and the use case is straightforward. Money in the bank," describes the development team's readiness for this use case.

Conclusion

In the absence of any significant risk or significance, there is no compelling reason to consider this use case for the first iteration.

Evaluation of the Change Password Use Case

The Change Password use case allows any current user to change his or her password.

Risk

There is virtually no performance risk, since passwords are changed infrequently and contain very small amounts of data.

- The use case seems very well understood, so the extensibility risk is low.
- This use case is fairly easy to estimate, since it is simply a matter of changing data in the system.
- The use interface is very straightforward, so there is no real risk of delivering an overly complex user interface.

Overall, the risk of the use case seems to be quite low. Level 1, "Of course; our project team has solved that problem before," seems applicable.

Significance

Like the Create Charge Code use case, the Change Password use case provides supporting functionality. Level 1, "They would barely notice, and they could easily use the system without it," describes the likely response.

Suitability

Level 5, "There is no need for more seasoning. The team is experienced and the use case is straightforward. Money in the bank," describes the development team's readiness for this use case.

Conclusion

The relatively low risk and lack of significance indicates that this use case can be omitted from the first iteration. Certainly it is important to the project, but it can be deferred without affecting the stakeholders as they evaluate the system or the developers as they design the system.

Evaluation of the Login Use Case

The Login use case allows any current user to validate his or her identity to the system as a prerequisite to performing the other more interesting use cases.

Risk

There is some performance risk, since large numbers of users may log in at the same time. However, logging in is a fairly straightforward process and does not involve a lot of data or calculation. The performance risk is low.

- Login is a very well-understood use case, so there is little extensibility risk.
- Login does not present much schedule risk, since it is very small and well focused.
- There is no risk of an unacceptable user interface.

Level 1, "Of course; our project team has solved that problem before," describes the Login use case perfectly.

Significance

The final system would be completely unacceptable without the Login use case, but the end users could certainly evaluate the system without it. Still, the developers need to make sure that their architecture supports this use case even if it is not included in the first iteration.

Level 2, "They would notice, but with a little imagination, the system would still make perfect sense," seems appropriate.

Suitability

Level 4, "There is no need for more seasoning. Either the team is already quite experienced, or the use case is sufficiently straightforward," seems very appropriate.

Conclusion

With some reservations due to the use case's architectural significance, Login is not essential for the first iteration.

Evaluation of the Record Time Use Case

The Record Time use case allows any user to enter his or her hours for the current time period.

Risk

The performance risk is very significant, as many users will record their time in the last few working hours of each time period. Also, users are rarely willing to accept poor performance while performing "nuisance" tasks. For instance, people may be willing to wait 15 minutes for a funny video clip to download and queue up, but they become aggravated if they have to wait three minutes in a grocery store line. Filling in a time-card generally falls into the category of undesirable tasks, so performance problems must be avoided.

- The use case seems very well understood, so the extensibility risk is low.
- Any estimate for this use case will be complicated by the complexity and performance requirements.
- The user interface is fairly complex, with charge code selection, comments for entries, and an editable matrix of time entries.

The Record Time use case is fairly risky, due to the performance requirements and user interface complexity. Level 3, "There are third-party products, training, books, or other technical resources available, but we do not have any in-house experience," is appropriate.

Significance

The Record Time use case is very significant, as it captures the intent of the timecard system. It is difficult to imagine an iteration without this use case. Level 5, "The system would be impossible to use without it," seems completely justified.

Suitability

The same complexity and risk that drives us to include this use case in the first iteration also forces us to carefully evaluate its suitability for the team. Level 2, "The team's capabilities are probably sufficient for this use case, but may improve substantially over the course of a single iteration," seems appropriate.

Conclusion

Clearly, many factors encourage us to include the Record Time use case in the first iteration. However, due to its complexity, we might want to manage the stakeholders' expectations by spreading complete development of the use case over the first two iterations. For example, the first iteration might include the complete user interface but defer performance goals to the next iteration.

Evaluation of the Create Employee Use Case

The Create Employee use case allows an administrative user to add an employee to the system.

Risk

There is virtually no performance risk, since employees are added infrequently, and the process requires very small amounts of data.

- The use case seems very well understood, so the extensibility risk is low.
- This use case is fairly easy to estimate, since it is simply a matter of adding data to the system.

■ The user interface is very straightforward, so there is no real risk of delivering an overly complex user interface.

Overall, the risk of the use case seems to be quite low. Level 1, "Of course; our project team has solved that problem before," seems applicable.

Significance

Though very important in the final system, the Create Employee use case is more of a support use case. During preliminary iterations, the customer is unlikely to notice the difference between simulated employees and actual employees entered through the system. Level 1, "They would barely notice, and they could easily use the system without it," describes the likely response.

Suitability

Level 5, "There is no need for more seasoning. The team is experienced and the use case is straightforward. Money in the bank," describes the development team's readiness for this use case.

Conclusion

In the absence of any significant risk or significance, there is no compelling reason to consider this use case for the first iteration.

Select Use Cases for the First Iteration

Given a fairly seasoned development team, we can determine the use cases for the first iteration based on risk and significance. Record Time and Export Time Entries definitely belong in the first iteration. Create Employee, Create Charge Code, and Change Password should all be deferred. Login could easily be deferred, but we will include it to make the first iteration more realistic.

By putting all of the architecturally significant use cases in a single iteration, we give the stakeholders a clear impression of the system after the first iteration, while the developers can ensure the integration of the solutions to these key use cases.

Now that we have selected the use cases for the first iteration, let's perform the remaining analysis steps for those use cases.

Discover Candidate Objects

In this step, developers find candidate objects that interact to provide the functionality as described in the use cases. Remember, this process is greatly simplified by dividing objects into four categories: entity, boundary, control, and lifecycle.

While discovering objects, it is important to limit the responsibilities for each object and to use clear and consistent names for each object and for each method in each object.

Since we are just starting analysis, we will not spend time determining the relationships between objects. These relationships are clarified in the remaining steps of the process. Also, there is no point in specifying the type of every attribute or in creating elaborate inheritance hierarchies. We will keep it simple, and not try to perfect the rough draft.

Discover Entity Objects

For each use case, we search each flow of events to find nouns, data, and behavior. Nouns may become entity objects, the data may become attributes of the objects, and the behavior is allocated to one or more objects. The nouns for each use case are considered separately before considering them together.

Record Time Use Case

Working through the normal flow of events, we highlight the following candidate objects and data:

1. The **employee** sees any **previously entered data** for the current **time period**.
2. The **employee** selects a **charge number** from all available charge numbers, organized by **client** and **project**.
3. The **employee** selects a **day** from the **time period**.
4. The **employee** enters the **hours worked** as a positive decimal number.
5. The new **hours** are added to the **view** and are seen in any subsequent views.

The following pieces are highlighted in the first alternate flow of events—employee edits existing data:

1. The **employee** sees **previously entered data** for the current **time period**.
2. The **employee** selects an **existing entry**.
3. The **employee** changes the **charge number** and/or the **hours worked**.
4. The new information is updated in the **view** and is seen in any subsequent views.

The following pieces are highlighted in the next alternate flow of events—employee submits timecard as complete:

1. The **employee** sees any **previously entered data** for the current **time period**.
2. The **employee** elects to submit the **timecard**.
3. The **employee** is asked to confirm his or her choice and warned that he or she will not be able to edit his or her **entries**.
4. The **timecard** is submitted; it is no longer available for editing.

The remaining flows of events do not introduce any new information, so we move on. Next, we produce a simple alphabetic list of nouns, then judge each one. This process weeds out unneeded and duplicate entity objects. It also identifies nouns that are more appropriate as attributes inside an object as opposed to an independent object.

1. charge code
2. charge number

Clearly, charge code and charge number are synonyms. Since charge code is more common in the other documentation, we discard charge number and keep charge code as a type of entity object.

3. client

Client also seems like a reasonable type of entity object.

4. day

Day does not seem like an independent type of object. Instead, it seems like data within an object.

5. employee

An employee seems like an independent entity object.

6. existing entry

An entry in a timecard may be the object that holds the day. We tentatively make this a type of entity object.

7. hours
8. hours worked

Hours and hours worked are synonyms, but hours worked is far more descriptive, so we discard hours. Hours worked becomes data in the newly discovered entry objects. This convinces us that the entry object is justified.

9. previously entered data

Previously entered data duplicates entry, so we discard it.

10. project

Project becomes a type of entity object.

11. timecard

Timecard becomes a type of entity object.

12. time period

Time period describes a timecard, so it becomes data inside each timecard object.

13. view

View objects are boundary objects, so we reject view.

We're done with the Record Time use case. Our entity objects are: charge code, client, employee, existing entry, hours worked, project, and timecard.

Export Time Entries Use Case

Working through the normal flow of events, we highlight the following candidate objects and data for the Export Time Entries use case:

1. The **administrative user** selects a **range of dates**.
2. The **administrative user** selects a subset of **clients** or all.
3. The **administrative user** selects a subset of **employees** or all.
4. The **administrative user** selects a **target file**.
5. The **data** is exported to the file as **formatted XML**. The **administrative user** is notified when the process is complete.

Next, we produce a simple alphabetic list of nouns, then judge each one.

1. administrative user

Administrative user seems plausible as an entity object.

2. clients

Client has already been identified as a type of entity object.

3. formatted XML

This sounds more like a description of the output file than a type of entity object.

4. data

This data refers to a group of entries from a group of timecards. Since these are already entity objects, no new objects are needed.

5. employees

Employee is already a type of entity object.

6. range of dates

Range of dates sounds like data within another object. We add a new entity object; export request, even though it did not show up in the flow of events.

7. target file

This could easily be held as data inside the export request.

So, this use case gives us two new entity objects: administrative user and export request. Now, let's look at the next use case.

Login Use Case

Working through the normal flow of events, we highlight the following candidate objects and data for the Login use case:

1. The **administrative user** or **employee** supplies a **username** and **password**.
2. The **user** is authenticated as either an **administrative user** or an **employee**. This is not a choice during the login; it is determined by the **username**.

Now we produce a simple alphabetic list of nouns, then judge each one.

1. administrative user

Administrative user has already been identified as a type of entity object.

2. employee

Employee has already been identified as a type of entity object.

3. password

Password seems more appropriate as data within the employee and administrative user objects.

4. user

User is just a generic reference to an employee or administrative user.

5. username

Username seems more appropriate as data within the employee and administrative user objects.

After evaluating this use case, there are no new entity objects to add to our list.

Consolidate the Entity Objects

Our list of entity objects looks like this:

administrative user

charge code

client

employee

existing entry

hours worked

project

timecard

The only two types of entity objects that seem similar are administrative user and employee. They are both types of users, one with administrative privileges and one without. So, we decide to eliminate both types of objects and add user.

The class diagram in Figure 5.2 shows the different types of the entity objects.

Discover Boundary Objects

Our next step is to identify the boundary objects for our use cases. Remember the rule for boundary objects in analysis: one boundary object per actor/use case pair.

For the Export Time Entries use case, this leads to a boundary object that serves as an interface between the administrative user and the system. It also leads to a boundary object that serves as an interface between the system and the external billing system.

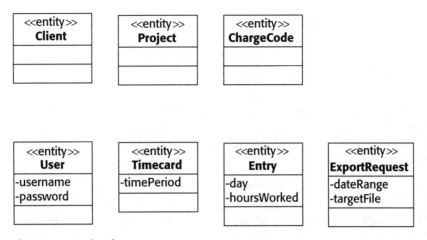

Figure 5.2 Entity classes.

For the Record Time use case, the rule leads to two boundary objects, one that serves as an interface between the administrative user and the system and one that serves as an interface between regular employees and the system. This is true despite our earlier decision to merge the administrative user and the employee into a single entity object. Boundary objects are discovered based on the way people or external systems use the system, not on how they are represented inside the system.

For the Login use case, the rule leads to two boundary objects, one that serves as an interface between the administrative user and the system and one that serves as an interface between employees and the system.

Following a standard naming convention simplifies this process. We use UI as a suffix for any user interface objects and SystemInterface for any system interfaces. If more than one actor initiates the use case, the boundary classes must be named distinctly. Applying these guidelines to the preceding decisions leads to the boundary classes in Figure 5.3.

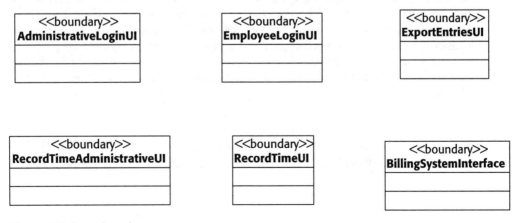

Figure 5.3 Boundary classes.

Discover Control Classes

The rule for control classes in analysis is one type of control object per use case. A control object encapsulates the workflow for the use case. This allows the entity objects to stay well focused while the control object provides a simple interface to the boundary objects.

When devising a name for a type of control object, remember to keep it simple. It makes sense to pick a reasonable suffix, such as Workflow and stick with it. In many cases, simply adding Workflow to the use case name is sufficient. No points are given for style. Simplicity and consistency are far more important.

- For the Export Time Entries use case, this leads to a control class called Export-TimeEntriesWorkflow.
- For the Record Time use case, this leads to a control class called RecordTime-Workflow.
- For the Login use case, this leads to a control class called LoginWorkflow.

Figure 5.4 shows these control classes.

Discover Lifecycle Classes

There is no easy rule for discovering lifecycle classes. A lifecycle object is used to create, locate, and destroy entity objects. In analysis, a lifecycle class allows developers to consolidate the different ways a certain type of entity object is located and created.

In many cases, it makes sense to see how entity objects are used before creating lifecycle classes. Therefore, we will not attempt to discover any lifcycle classes at this point. Instead, we will defer their discovery to the next step, describe object interactions.

Describe Object Interactions

In this step, we use sequence diagrams to model the interaction and cooperation between objects as they fulfill a use case. This requires a sequence diagram for each flow of events and a class diagram for each use case. The class diagram shows all of the classes that define the objects that participate in the sequence diagrams.

During this step, we use the flows of events and the activity diagram for the use case, as well as the entity, boundary, and control classes that we discovered in the previous step.

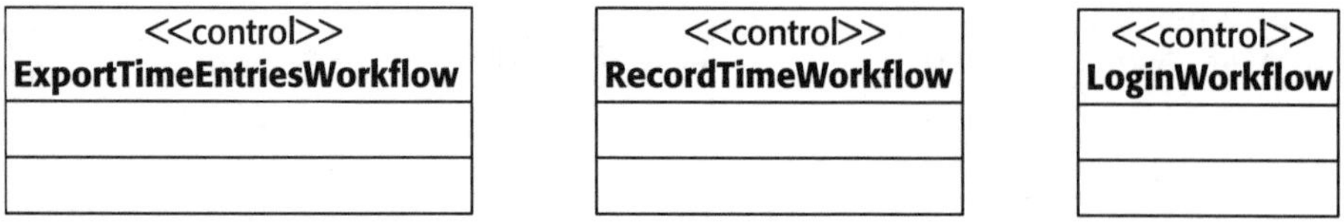

<<control>> **ExportTimeEntriesWorkflow**	<<control>> **RecordTimeWorkflow**	<<control>> **LoginWorkflow**

Figure 5.4 Control classes.

It is often helpful to discover some behavior for each class before starting the sequence diagrams. These methods often help shape the sequences, and they can always be moved or removed if they do not fit. This is especially true for developers who are migrating to object-oriented development from procedural development. Novice object-oriented developers tend to mutate the objects into verbs and the methods into data, as in a data flow diagram. Finding the objects and some methods in a separate step helps prevent this natural tendency.

WARNING   Objects should be nouns, and methods should be verbs. If your sequence diagram has verbs for the objects and nouns for the methods, you are reverting to procedural habits by creating data flow diagrams.

Add Tentative Behavior for Login

Walking through the normal flow in the activity diagram, we see that the system asks for the username and password. Clearly, this must be performed by the LoginUI objects, as they handle all interactions with the external actors. So we add a display-LoginForm method to both user interface classes.

Next, the actor enters values for the username and password. The actor must somehow indicate that he or she is done, so we add a submitNameAndPassword method to the user interface classes.

In the next activity, the system verifies the username and password. Clearly, this business logic does not belong in the boundary objects. We give the responsibility to the LoginWorkflow objects by adding the validateLogin method to the LoginWorkflow class. However, the LoginWorkflow object will not actually know whether a particular name and password pair is valid. Since the user objects already have this information, we make the LoginWorkflow object find the right user and ask him or her to validate the login, so we add a validateLogin method to the User class. For the LoginWorkflow object to find the right user, we need a lifecycle object that searches for users by username, so, we create a UserLocator class with a findByName method.

In the final activity of the normal flow, the system welcomes the user, so we add a displayWelcome method to the user interface classes.

Walking through the activity diagram lets us find behavior and allocate methods to the classes identified earlier. All of these decisions are captured in Figure 5.5. Next, we must use a sequence diagram to visualize and verify this behavior.

Build Sequence Diagrams for Login

Now that we have identified several types of objects, and allocated responsibilities to them, we must show how the objects work together. First, we arrange the initiating actor and the objects on a sequence diagram. Since the actor initiates the sequence, we place the actor in the top left. Since the actor interacts with the system through the boundary object, we place the boundary object to the immediate right of the actor. Since the control object serves as a single point of contact between the boundary object and the entity objects, we place the control object between them.

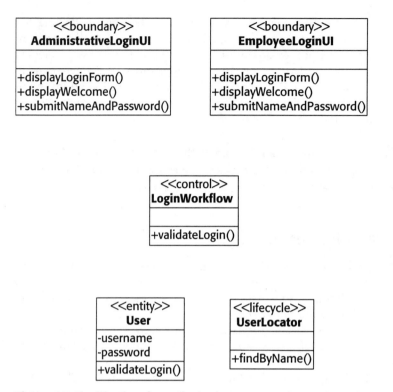

Figure 5.5 Participating classes for Login.

We repeat this process for the normal flow and some of the alternate flows. At some point, the sequence diagrams become repetitive, so we stop making them. Deciding when to stop is a delicate balancing act; including too few sequence diagrams leads to missed behavior, while too many sequence diagrams leads to extra work, as each sequence diagram must be kept up to date and improved throughout the analysis and design process.

Normal Flow for Login

The actor asks the boundary EmployeeLoginUI object to display the login form. The actor then fills in username and password and submits them to the system. The EmployeeLoginUI object asks the control LoginWorkflow object to validate the login workflow. To satisfy this request, the LoginWorkflow object asks the UserLocator object to find the User object that corresponds to the name. Once the LoginWorkflow object gets the right User object, it asks it to validate the password. Once the Login-Workflow object receives a response, it passes it back to the EmployeeLoginUI object. When the EmployeeLoginUI object receives the valid response, it displays a welcome message, and the flow is complete. Figure 5.6 shows this sequence.

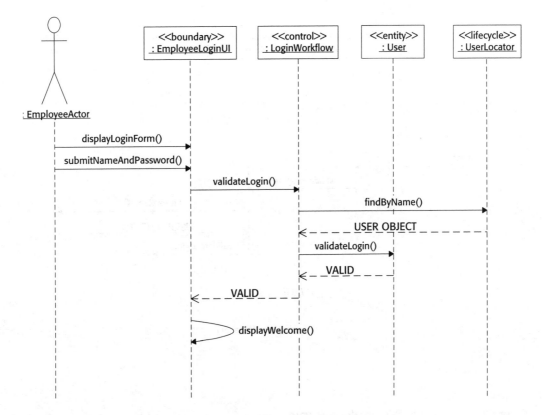

Figure 5.6 Sequence diagram for the normal flow of Login.

Alternate Flow for Invalid Password

This sequence proceeds exactly as in the normal flow, until the User object responds with INVALID to the validateLogin method. This response is propagated up to the EmployeeLoginUI, which must display an invalid password message to the actor. Since there is no method in the EmployeeLoginUI, we add one, displayError message. Figure 5.7 shows the complete sequence.

Alternate Flow for Unknown User

This sequence proceeds exactly as in the normal flow, until the UserLocator responds with a NULL when asked to locate the user by his or her name. Obviously, the Login-Workflow cannot ask an unknown User object to validate the password, so it returns INVALID to the EmployeeLoginUI object. As in the sequence for the invalid password, the EmployeeLoginUI calls its own displayErrorMessage method.

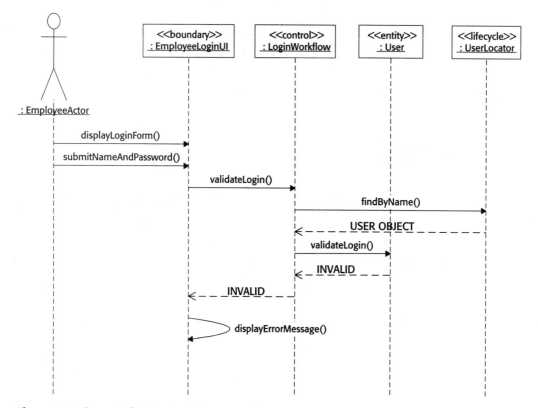

Figure 5.7 Alternate flow for invalid password.

Validate Sequences for Login

In the previous sequences, we found behavior by following the flow of events forward. Now we must verify the sequences by going backward through each sequence. At each step, we determine whether the object has the information it needs to respond to the request.

Normal Flow

The last method call is displayWelcome from the EmployeeLoginUI to itself. Certainly, the EmployeeLoginUI can greet the user by his or her username.

The previous method is from the LoginWorkflow object, which asks the User object to validate the login. The LoginWorkflow object knows about the User object because it just asked the UserLocator object to find it. Since each User object has a username and a password, it can easily determine whether the password matches.

The previous method is the LoginWorkflow, which asks the UserLocator to find the User object that corresponds to the username. Though it is not clear how the LoginWorkflow object knows the UserLocator object, it is safe to assume that any object can use the dedicated User-

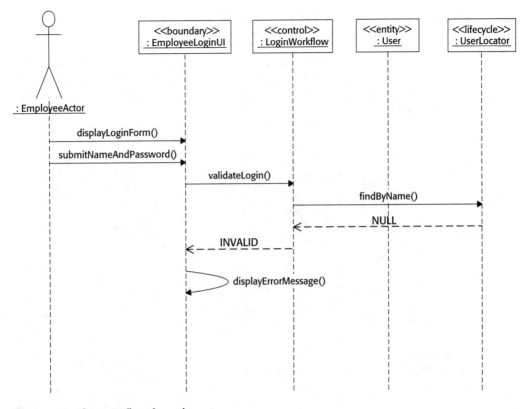

Figure 5.8 Alternate flow for unknown user.

Locator object. The details are deferred until design. Certainly, the UserLocator must be able to locate any User object; that is its job.

The previous method is the EmployeeLoginUI object, which asks the LoginWorkflow object to validate the login. Though it is unclear how the EmployeeLoginUI object knows about the LoginWorkflow object, it is reasonable to assume that these two objects are a cooperating pair, and that either the EmployeeLoginUI created the Login-Workflow or they were both created by the same application-level object. Again, this detail is deferred until design. While the LoginWorkflow cannot perform this task on its own, it knows where to go for this information. This is the nature of control objects.

Certainly, the EmployeeLoginUI object knows how to display the login form and accept user input. It is unclear how the actor and EmployeeLoginUI are hooked together. This depends on the implementation strategy, and may be profitably deferred until design.

Sequence Diagrams and Class Diagrams for the Remaining Use Cases

The sequence diagrams and class diagrams for the Export Time Entries and Record Time use cases are shown in Figures 5.9 through 5.13 with little explanation. These diagrams complete the analysis model that is used as a basis for the remainder of the book, but they do not introduce any new techniques or issues.

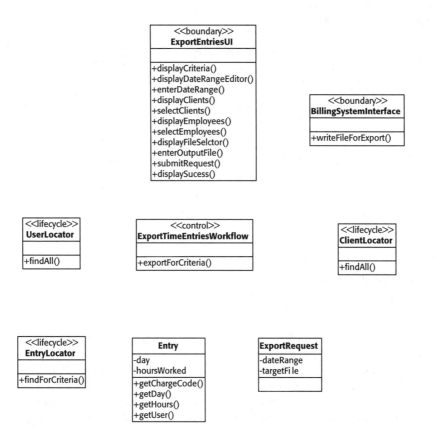

Figure 5.9 Participating classes for Export Time Entries.

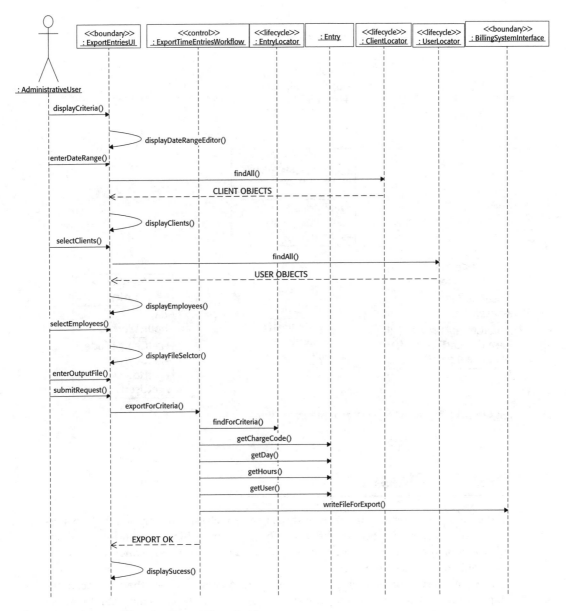

Figure 5.10 Normal flow for Export Time Entries.

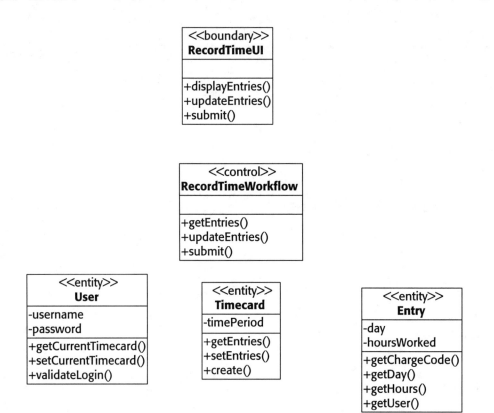

Figure 5.11 Participating classes for Record Time.

Describe Classes

In this step, we determine the relationships between classes that are required to support the interaction between objects in the flow of events. This is accomplished by creating a class diagram for each use case. This means that several sequence diagrams contribute to each class diagram.

Remember, each time an object calls a method in another object there is a relationship between the objects. This relationship is captured in the class diagram. In analysis, we want to fully specify the relationships between entity classes while loosely specifying the relationships between boundary and control classes and between control and entity classes. Of course, we should determine that a relationship exists and determine its direction. However, any decisions as to multiplicity or type of association are pure speculation. Different technologies and different techniques lead to different patterns of association.

Determining the need for a relationship is simple bookkeeping. Every message from one object to another requires a relationship from the sending object's class to the receiving object's class. Determining the type of the relationship is a bit more complex.

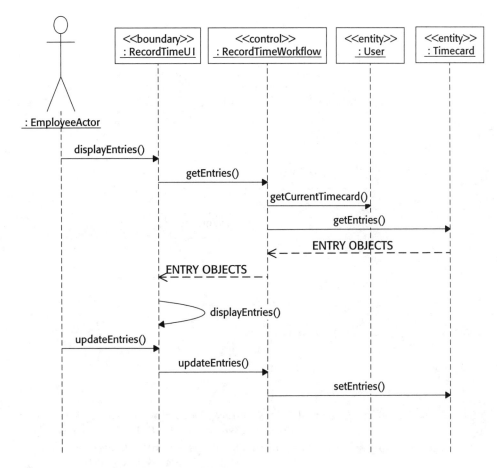

Figure 5.12 Normal flow for Record Time.

It is a dependency if the sending object creates the receiving object, uses it, then loses it, or if the sending object receives the receiving object as a method parameter, uses it, and fails to keep it. During analysis, this may be difficult to determine, as there are no method parameters. Fortunately, these decisions are not important during analysis.

Find Relationships for Login

We find relationships by working forward in the sequence diagram for the normal flow of the Login use case. The EmployeeLoginUI object calls the validateLogin method in the LoginWorkflow object. This implies a relationship from the EmployeeLoginUI class to the LoginWorkflow class. There is also a relationship from the LoginWorkflow class to the User class and the UserLocator class. The return values do not indicate relationships, since an object does not need a reference to provide a response.

Now that we have determined the direction of the relationship, we consider the type of each relationship. At first, it seems as if there is no reason for the EmployeeLoginUI

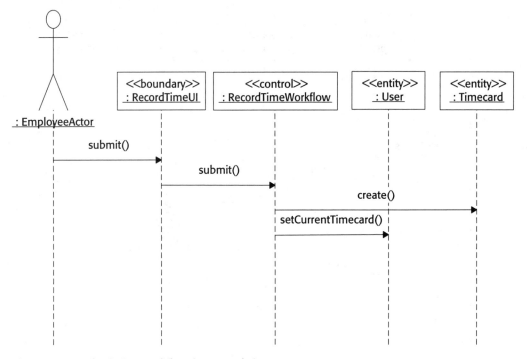

Figure 5.13 Submit timecard flow for Record Time.

object to keep a reference to the LoginWorkflow object. However, a quick glance at the activity diagram for the Login use case shows that the EmployeeLoginUI allows the user to reenter his or her username and password. It makes sense for the EmployeeLoginUI object to keep a reference to the LoginWorkflow object, so the relationship is an association.

The relationship between the LoginWorkflow object and the UserLocator object follows the same logic. The LoginWorkflow object should keep a reference in case it needs it for subsequent login attempts, so the relationship is an association.

The LoginWorkflow object does not need to keep a reference to the User object, as the LoginWorkflow object looks up the User object each time, so the relationship is a dependency.

Figure 5.14 shows these relationships.

Find Relationships for Export Time Entries

The ExportEntriesUI object uses the ClientLocator object and the UserLocator object. It also uses the ExportEntriesWorkflow object. The ExportEntriesWorkflow object uses the EntryLocator object, the BillingSystemInterface object, and many Entry objects. No object is reused, so all of the relationships may be treated as dependencies.

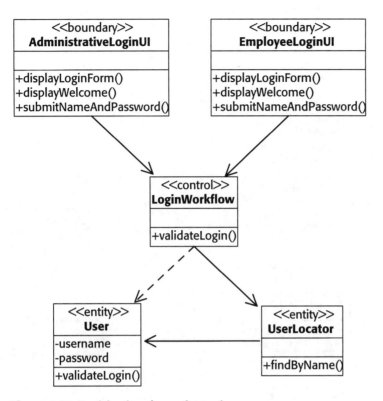

Figure 5.14 Participating classes for Login.

Notice that the ExportEntriesUI object interacts directly with the ClientLocator and the UserLocator, rather than going through the control object. The class diagram highlights this deviation from our normal pattern.

Figure 5.15 shows these relationships.

Find Relationships for Record Time

The RecordTimeUI object uses the RecordTimeWorkflow object, which in turn uses the User object and the Timecard object.

The RecordTimeUI object keeps a reference to the RecordTimeWorkflow object, and uses it to update the entries, so the relationship is an association.

The RecordTimeWorkflow object keeps a reference to the User object. This object is used when the RecordTimeWorkflow object submits the old timecard and replaces it with a new timecard, so the relationship is an association.

The RecordTimeWorkflow object keeps a reference to the Timecard object. This object is used when the RecordTimeWorkflow object sets the entries for the Timecard object, so the relationship is an association.

Figure 5.16 shows these relationships.

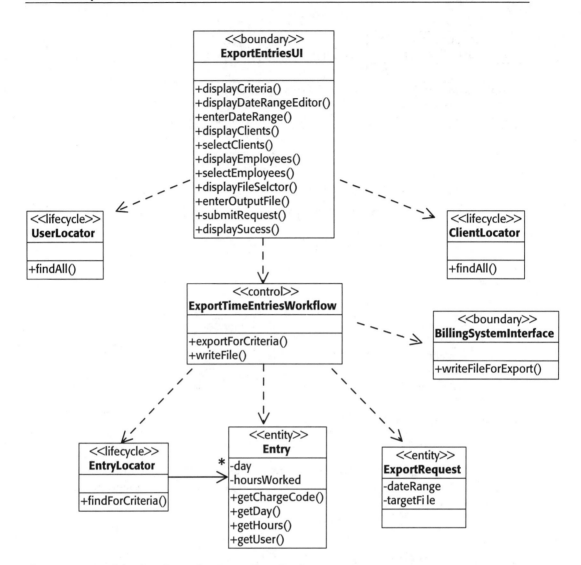

Figure 5.15 Participating classes for Export Time Entries.

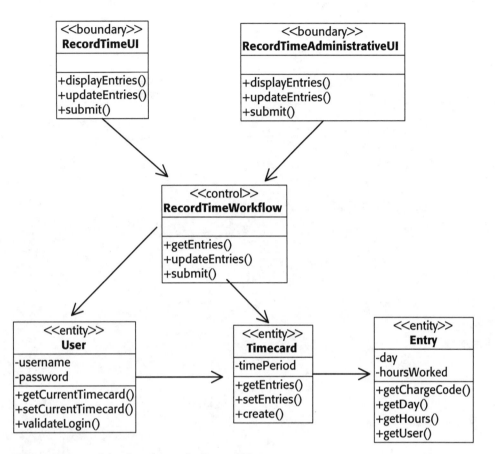

Figure 5.16 Participating classes for Record Time.

The Next Step

This chapter focused on some of the use cases, based on their risk, significance, and suitability. For each of these use cases, we used the flows of events to find some entity, control, and boundary objects. In the next step, we use sequence diagrams to describe the interactions between the objects. Finally, we use class diagrams to show the relationships between objects.

At this point, we have a good understanding of the system from the stakeholders' and the developers' point of view. This understanding provides a solid foundation as we invent the solution in the remaining processes.

Describing the System for Technology Selection

The previous chapters detailed how to use a consistent process and the UML to understand a system from the stakeholders' and developers' perspective. That effort leads to a very complete and detailed view of the problem. In this chapter, you'll learn how to describe and categorize the system so that technology experts can determine the most suitable technologies, without being overwhelmed by the intricacies of the problem.

In some cases, the developers who gather the requirements and develop the analysis model may also determine the best technologies. In other cases, the developers may use a variety of resources within and even outside of the organization. Having a higher-level description of the proposed system allows more and a wider variety of people to contribute to the technology selection process.

Perhaps a real-world example is in order. Architects can select materials and building technology for a proposed structure without understanding exactly how the building will be used. They do, however, need to know if the building is planned for residential, commercial, or industrial use, and they need a rough estimate of its size or capacity. They don't need to know what each room will be used for or who will occupy each space. Based on this limited and high-level view of the building, an architect can choose between wood, concrete, or steel for the building's skeleton. The same holds true for a computer system; the technology experts need to know only the basics about the system in order to choose the right technology to make the system work.

Are You Ready?

In order to describe the system for technology selection, you must have a clear understanding of the system. Without this understanding, developers are doomed to solve the wrong problem or to deliver unusable solutions. For example, a technology may meet all of the functional requirements but fail to function in the user's actual environment, due to hardware limitations, nonstandard operating systems, or network topology.

These misunderstandings can be avoided by gathering requirements, complete with deployment constraints and nonfunctional requirements for each use case. The analysis model helps developers identify common parts of the system that can be considered together during technology selection. In some cases, the developers must gather additional information, such as the expected the number of concurrent users, the expected volume of data, and the deployment environment.

There are two significant steps to create a description of the problem for technology selection:

1. Group analysis classes.
2. Describe each group.

Let's look at each of these.

Group Analysis Classes

In the previous chapters, we developed an analysis model that identified entity, control, boundary, and lifecycle classes for each use case. Before performing technology selection, we will group similar analysis classes together. This allows developers to consolidate the decision making process and helps ensure a coherent solution.

Different types of analysis classes connect in different ways, so you need to consider each of the following separately:

- Boundary classes between humans and the system
- Boundary classes between an external system and the system
- Control, entity, and lifecycle classes

Boundary (User Interface)

The boundary classes between humans and the system are more commonly known as the user interface. There are three main criteria for grouping user interface classes for technology selection:

- User group
- Deployment constraints
- Complexity of the user interface

Whenever possible, you should use a single technology for all user interface classes in the system. If this is impossible, all of the user interface classes for each group of users should use the same technology. Limiting and consolidating the user interface technologies greatly decreases deployment costs such as distribution, training, and support. Systems that depend on a patchwork quilt of different technologies tend to be difficult for new users to learn and for developers to maintain, extend, and support.

Unfortunately, varying deployment constraints and user interface complexity often complicates this goal. If the user interface classes in a group have radically different deployment constraints, then it may be necessary to split up the group. The same process must be followed for user interface complexity.

User Group

In the UML, actors in the use case model represent distinct user groups. This makes it very easy to identify a group of user interface classes: just group the boundary classes that are used by an actor.

For example, a banking system may use one presentation technology to allow customers to pay bills online, and another technology to allow bank tellers to manage new and existing accounts. This enables the developers to select one technology for the customers based on their needs for low deployment cost and universal access, while selecting the other technology based on the bank tellers' needs for ease of use and full functionality.

Deployment Constraints

When dividing the user interface classes into groups, it is important to consider deployment constraints. In order to be suitable for all of the user interface classes in a group, the technology must meet the most restrictive deployment constraint. If one class has more restrictive deployment constraints, it should be split out to a separate group.

The deployment constraints are found in the description of the use case that led to the creation of the user interface boundary class during analysis. For instance, a use case may specify that it must be accessible from behind a firewall or from any computer that is connected to the Internet.

User Interface Complexity

The complexity of the user interface must be considered when dividing the user interface classes into groups. If most of the user interface classes involve simple data entry, a sophisticated data visualization class may need to be considered separately when selecting technologies. Attempting to push a technology past its strengths often will cause headaches as the system evolves and expands. A technology that is just barely capable of supporting the current user interface may not support future desires for more user interface sophistication. Therefore, it is important to consider user interface complexity in grouping user interface classes.

User interface complexity can be derived from the flows of events for each use case and by examining the responsibilities of each user interface boundary class.

Boundary (System Interface)

Each boundary class that controls the system's interaction with another system must be considered separately. While it is desirable to use the same technology for all system interface classes, it may not be possible. In many cases, existing external systems dictate the interface. For example, a system may expose its functionality through CORBA or RMI, or support a standard protocol such as HTTP or FTP. External systems may require special formatting for the data, such as XML or a proprietary data structure.

It is easy to group the system interface classes, as each is its own group. Later, after technologies have been selected, it may be possible to combine system interface classes or share common functionality.

Remember, system interface classes encapsulate the interactions between your system and an external system. So, when describing a boundary class, use the flow of events and the responsibilities in the system interface class to derive the technology needs for the boundary class.

Control, Entity, and Lifecycle

Recall the different responsibilities held by control, entity, and lifecycle classes. Control objects convert high-level messages from the boundary objects into many simple messages to entity objects. This allows the entity objects to stay very focused and as simple as possible while providing a convenient interface to the boundary objects.

Entity objects hold the persistent business data and business rules for the system. Lifecycle objects create, locate, and destroy entity objects. All control, entity, and lifecycle classes in a system should use the same technology or related technologies. After all, they are closely related, as control objects use lifecycle objects to obtain references to entity objects, then interact with those entity objects to fulfill the functionality for a use case. A lot of data and object references are passed about. In many cases, transactions must be started and completed. The alternative, a patchwork quilt of technologies, is often unpleasant to develop and extend. With these factors in mind, it is highly desirable to select a single technology or a closely related family of technologies for all of the control, lifecycle, and entity classes. There may be some esoteric exception to this rule, but I have never encountered it.

Describe Each Group

Once you have identified some groups of classes, you can describe each group's characteristics with respect to technology requirements. For example, you might categorize a group of user interface classes according to the complexity of the interface and according to its deployment constraints. Every user interface can be loosely located in a spectrum of complexity that ranges from simple data entry to slick interactive graphics. It can also be located in a spectrum for deployment constraints.

The real payoff comes when you use the same descriptive spectrums to describe the strengths and weaknesses of each technology. For instance, a user interface technology may be perfectly adequate for one level of complexity, but be inappropriate for a more complex level. Using the same descriptive spectrum to describe both the problem and the prospective solutions greatly simplifies the technology selection process and removes much of the uncertainty and guesswork.

I suggest a spectrum of descriptions for the following areas:

- User interface complexity
- Deployment constraints for user interfaces
- Number and type of users
- Available bandwidth
- Types of system interfaces
- Performance and scalability

Let's examine each spectrum in detail.

User Interface Complexity

GUI complexity is the most important criterion to consider when selecting a technology for user interface classes. It is incredibly important to be clear on what your user wants and needs before making this decision. It would be horrible to be 80 percent done with a year's worth of tedious HTML and JavaScript generation only to find that you cannot satisfy your customer with an HTML-only solution. It would be equally painful to discover that you have completely overdesigned the interface and that what they really need is tabular data that will load into their PalmPilot's Web browser. It is often difficult to extract such decisions from a user community that may not even know, collectively, what it wants. I offer my empathy, along with the caveat that the following section is completely useless if you cannot establish solid requirements.

In describing the complexity of a user interface, it is helpful to have some descriptive categories to which to compare. With this goal in mind, consider a range of complexity from simple data entry to interactive graphics:

Simple data input. A simple data input user interface allows a user to enter data into the system. It may help the user by presenting a list of choices or by performing simple field-level validation for dates or numbers. At the very least, the technology must allow text entry, as with a command prompt or text entry field. However, most users expect a little more; consequently, simple data input in our modern era often includes some not-so-simple widgets, such as drop-down selectors, selectable lists, radio buttons, checkboxes, and scrollable text entry fields. Field-level validation, such as a check for valid dates or numeric data, may also be included.

Static view of data. A static view of the data can be a table, tree, or graph that is unaffected by changes in the underlying system data. It is equally unresponsive to the user's desire to see more or less data or to change a sort order. The view is essentially a snapshot of some underlying data in the system. If users want to vary the presentation or see the latest data, they must have the system regenerate the entire view. For example, consider a list of books and prices from an online bookseller. The data is constant; customers must resubmit their request whenever they need the latest information. Also, if customers want to exclude some books, they must enter new search criteria.

Customizable views. A customizable view allows a user to customize the presentation of static data without making a new request to the server. For example, given tabular data, the system user may filter the data, select the sort order, and hide particular columns. Given a graph, the system user may zoom in on one part of the graph or filter the data to create a new graph. The data is constant; only the presentation changes. For example, if you have a table of 50 used cars, a user can sort and re-sort by price, manufacturer, or cargo capacity, all without submitting a new request to the server.

Dynamic view of data. A dynamic view of data is automatically refreshed to stay current with the underlying system data changes. There is no need for the user to request an updated view. Either the view is updated whenever the underlying data changes or the view is periodically updated. A news ticker is a good example. The user does not request the updated information. It simply appears unbidden and, often, unwanted.

Interactive graphics. Interactive graphics are similar to dynamic views; the graphical view is automatically updated as the underlying system data changes. However, interactive graphics take this one step further. The user can update the underlying data by manipulating the graphics. This level of interaction can be very useful for visualizing resource allocation, interactive simulations, and developing collaborative designs.

A networked version of the game Doom is a good, if extreme, example. Each player uses interactive graphics to view and change the underlying data in the system. By keeping all of the remote views synchronized, the system allows the player to interact with one another and with the computer-generated players.

Other systems use interactive graphics to allow a user to change data visually, then see the effects as calculated by the system. Microsoft Project is an excellent example of this type of application. A user can change the scheduled end date for an activity by dragging it to the right on a timeline. The application determines if the change has a ripple affect on other activities. If so, it updates both the underlying data and the visual display. This gives the user access to an intuitive visual interface to evaluate complex project scheduling options.

These categories describe a spectrum of user complexity from very simple to very complex. A similar spectrum can be used to describe deployment constraints.

Deployment Constraints for User Interfaces

It is impossible to characterize a group of user interface classes without considering how the classes will be deployed. For most systems, the deployment constraints are as important as the complexity of the user interface. After all, great functionality does not help anyone if the intended audience cannot use the system.

When you describe the deployment constraints for a user interface, it is helpful to have some descriptive categories to which to compare. With this goal in mind, consider a range in deployment scenarios from a handheld device accessing the system over the Internet to a few dedicated workstations accessing the system on a high-speed LAN:

Handheld device. This deployment constraint requires the user interface to work on a handheld device, such as a PalmPilot or perhaps even a cellular phone. While this requirement is quite rare today, it may become more and more common, as wireless technology improves and tiny user interfaces mature.

Any Web browser on the Internet. This deployment constraint requires the user interface to perform acceptably on any browser, on any computer, over the slowest possible dial-up connection. Some browsers may not support images, much less dynamic HTML, so the user interface must be presented or at least presentable in a text-only form. While rare, this constraint is a reality, especially for government sites that provide access to people with disabilities. In other cases, the computer may be old, slow, and behind a corporate firewall, or old, slow, and connected to a painfully slow modem. In both cases, the system must perform adequately, despite the restrictions. There also is no limit to the number of concurrent users in this scenario.

Late-model Web browser on the Internet. This deployment category relaxes the constraints a bit, by ensuring that each Web browser is no more than a few generations old. If this assumption is true, we know that the computer is also no more than one or two generations old, since significantly older computers cannot support resource-hungry late-model browsers. There is also no limit to the number of concurrent users in this scenario. This is the target deployment scenario for most commercial Web sites.

Late-model browser on a network. This deployment category assumes a late-model Web browser and a reasonably late-model computer on the same network that contains the system. The number of concurrent users is certainly fewer than the total number of users on the network. This is a common deployment scenario for systems that are deployed on corporate intranets.

Specific browser on a network. This deployment category restricts the users of a system to a single version of a specific browser. The number of concurrent users is certainly fewer than the total number of users on the network. This is a slightly less common deployment scenario for systems that are deployed on corporate intranets.

Dedicated workstations on a network. In this scenario, users implement software installed on workstations to access the system. This allows the developers to completely control the software on both the server and the client. The number of clients that are installed limits the number of concurrent users. This is a traditional client/server approach.

These categories describe a spectrum of deployment constraints from very restrictive to completely under the control of the developers. A similar spectrum can be used to describe the number and type of users.

Number and Type of Users

The number of users influences technology selection in two ways. First and foremost, a high number of users forces the technology for the entity, control, and lifecycle classes to scale well. A high number of users also influences the selection of user interface technology. A larger audience makes ease of deployment and support costs major factors.

A system with many users must keep the incremental distribution, deployment, and support costs low. Distribution and deployment costs can be reduced, by allowing users to download the client software or by offering the entire service as a Web site. Support costs encourage simplicity over flash and extra functionality.

The type of users also influences the technology selection. An enthusiastic group of users who gain a lot by using the system will accept a slightly more difficult deployment process. Their vested interest in the system makes them more accommodating and flexible. On the other hand, users who have little to gain or who are forced to use a system to perform a nuisance task, such as filling in their timecard or paying personal property taxes, are less accommodating, in which case, the technology must be easy to use.

In describing the expected number and type of users for a system, it is helpful to have some descriptive categories to which to compare. With this goal in mind, consider a range from a few users within an organization to a mass market:

Small number of dedicated users. This is a small group of users who help define the system and who directly benefit from the system. Distribution, installation, training, and support may be cost-effectively customized to fit their needs. Functionality is usually the priority, as these groups are often willing to invest their own time and energy as they learn the system. In many cases, the users spend much of each working day intertwined with the system.

While this seems like an esoteric category, examples can be found in many industries. Air traffic controllers use immensely complex systems to visualize the location and path of commercial air traffic. Stock traders use highly customized and proprietary systems to analyze risk and determine values for securities. Resource planners in the oil industry use complex systems to keep expensive refineries operating at high efficiencies while keeping inventory costs low and fulfilling contracts. Call center systems allow people to handle huge volumes of calls for customer or technical support.

General use within an organization. This is a much larger group of users, who are generally less motivated with respect to the system. In some cases, almost everyone in a company with tens of thousands of employees on three continents depends on a system. These systems tend to support the organization, rather than contributing directly to the core business. Examples include time tracking, benefits management, safety compliance, and information sharing.

Large audience with high interest. In this scenario, a system must serve a large audience of very involved participants. The users may be geographically scattered and otherwise unconnected from one another. The users may log on to the system to exchange information or to collaborate. The Internet was actually started by one form of this audience, researchers who needed to share data and information in a loose collaborative environment.

This audience is generally willing to accept some inconvenience, as the system holds great value for them. For example, researchers may be willing to download and install fairly complex software if it will help them visualize mathematical models for weather or burning buildings, for example. An audiophile may be willing to do almost anything to hear his or her favorite recording artist's new track a week early.

In many cases, this audience is virtually self-supporting, as the community members help one another through the inevitable pitfalls of installing and using the software.

Huge audience with low interest. In this scenario, a system must attract and serve a relatively fickle audience. This, of course, is the audience for most consumer Web sites. Visitors are alienated easily by systems that start slowly or that waste their time in any way. Both potential and existing customers want a very pleasant and efficient experience, and they are certainly not going to accommodate the system in any way.

These categories describe a spectrum of users from a small number of dedicated users to a large number of relatively disinterested users. A similar spectrum can be used to describe the available bandwidth.

Available Bandwidth

Available bandwidth is another key factor when selecting technologies. Some combinations of technologies allow the developers to meet low bandwidth restrictions, while other technologies exacerbate bandwidth constraints. The descriptive categories for bandwidth ranges from a dial-up connection to an Internet service provider at one end and a dedicated network at the other:

Dial-up Internet connection. This is still the most common type of connection to the Internet. Supporting speeds from roughly 26 KBaud (thousand bits per second) to 56 KBaud, a dial-up connection is suitable for systems that let users view text and images, listen to streaming audio, and enter text data. It is painfully slow for any sort of real-time video or other media.

Fast Internet connection. Fast Internet connections include a variety of technologies, including digital data transmission over phone lines, cable and satellite transmission, and shared direct transmission lines to the Internet backbone. These connections allow users to view text, images, and even streaming video without significant discomfort.

Dedicated network between client and server. A dedicated network allows the client and the server to exchange data at very high speeds. Even an inexpensive home network can easily support 100 million bits per second over relatively short distances.

These categories describe a spectrum of bandwidth from dial-up connections to a dedicated network. A similar spectrum can be used to describe different types of system interfaces.

Types of System Interfaces

In some cases, the technology for a system interface is determined by an existing external system. Otherwise, you must describe the system interface, then select an appropriate technology. Obviously, this process must be coordinated with the development team for the external system. System interfaces divide into three categories:

Data transfer. Many system interfaces exist solely to transfer large blocks of information from system to system. Such interfaces are traditionally referred to as Electronic Data Interchange (EDI) interfaces. The exchange of data may be performed at preset intervals or it may be performed on demand. In any case, one system takes a snapshot of its internal data, formats it for the other system, and sends it to the other system. The receiving system must read the information and update its own internal information. Each interaction has its own agreed-upon data structure, so that both sides can read and write the records.

Data transfer interfaces are very common in business and financial systems. Semi-independent branch office systems retrieve the latest data from the home office. The home office collects the day's transactions from its satellite offices. Money flows from bank to bank. Business partners exchange data and make commitments.

Services through a protocol. The next form of system interface allows a system to make requests through an agreed-upon protocol. A server allows a client system to authenticate itself and request data or services by sending predefined codes and values. This arrangement allows very structured access to the server, with substantially more flexibility than a simple data interchange.

Some protocols have been standardized for widespread use. For example, the File Transfer Protocol (FTP) allows clients to move files to and from the server. The HyperText Transfer Protocol (HTTP) allows a client to retrieve data from a Web server and to post requests to a Web server. Many organizations develop their own protocols to provide services and exchange more arbitrary information. Protocol-based interfaces use many of the same techniques as data interchange interfaces. It may even be difficult to distinguish between a simple protocol and a complex data interchange. However, protocol-based interfaces generally allow more flexibility and add behavior to the data. For instance, a data interchange interface sends a large block of data and lets the receiver determine the next step. A protocol-based interface might send a small block of data as part of a command, then wait for the response before deciding what to do next.

Direct access to system services. This type of interface allows a client system to directly call designated methods in the server. The server exposes certain methods for remote access. The client passes the name of the method and any input arguments as a request to the server. The server calls the actual method and passes the result back to the client.

Procedural versions of this type of interface are called Remote Procedure Calls (RPCs), while object-oriented versions of this system use the open standard Common Object Request Broker Architecture (CORBA), Microsoft's Distributed

Common Object Model (DCOM), or Sun's semi-open standard Remote Method Invocation (RMI).

This type of interface can provide a very flexible and intuitive interface between two systems. In many cases, it is infinitely easier to expose parts of an existing system in this manner than to implement an entire protocol between two systems.

These categories describe a spectrum of system interfaces from simple data transfer to remote access to the system's functionality. A similar spectrum can be used to describe the performance and scalability issues for a system.

Performance and Scalability

Performance and scalability requirements are increasingly important factors in the selection of technology for control, entity, and lifecycle classes. Performance must be balanced against data integrity in any multiuser system, and there aren't many single-user systems left. Also, as concurrent users and data are added to the system, the system must scale well so that the user experience stays tolerable.

Several factors complicate the development of high-performance and scalable systems. Certainly, the amount of data and the number of concurrent users impact the performance. However, high-performance databases can handle large amounts of data with ease, and high-speed networks minimize the impact of additional users. One factor that dramatically affects performance is concurrent access and updates of data. Some systems must contend with multiple users modifying the same data. In order to keep the data intact while meeting performance requirements, these systems must use sophisticated locking strategies.

There are several descriptive categories that affect scalability and performance:

Read-only. Some systems allow users to view the system data, but do not allow them to update it. While this sounds quite restrictive, many very important systems fit this description. For instance, a system may allow a stockbroker to analyze and visualize the risk in his or her portfolio, without allowing him or her to buy or sell securities. A safety compliance system may allow a user to search for safety regulations, without allowing that person to change the regulations. In fact, many systems allow a mass audience to view data, while narrowly restricting changes to the data.

Isolated updates. In many systems, many users change the system's data, but the changes do not conflict with one another. An online store may have many customers, but they cannot change one another's billing or shipping preferences. Of course, this example falls apart if two people are allowed to log in as the same user, at the same time.

Concurrent updates. In other systems, many users change the system's data, with some of the changes affecting the same data. An online airline reservation system allows many users to reserve a seat on a particular flight. Since a flight holds a limited number of passengers, each reservation affects a very important piece of data, the number of remaining seats on the flight.

These categories describe a spectrum of factors that affect the performance and scalability of a system. Now we have several descriptive spectrums that allow us to describe a system's technology needs.

Technology Requirements for the Timecard Application

Now that we have the descriptive spectrums, let's apply them to our Timecard system. This section divides the analysis classes into groups and uses the descriptive categories to describe the technology requirements for each group. These descriptions will be used in subsequent chapters, when we select technologies for each group.

Find Groups of Analysis Classes

There are at least three distinct groups for the Timecard application: the user interface classes, the system interface for the external time entry repository, and the control, entity, and lifecycle classes.

While the deployment constraints for the employee's user interface classes are more restrictive than the administrative users' user interface classes, the user interface complexity is exactly the same. Therefore, any technology that satisfies the employees, with their additional requirements for remote access, will also satisfy the administrative users. Treating all of the user interface classes as a single group will greatly simplify the Timecard application.

There is only one external interface class, the BillingSystemInterface. It must be treated as a separate group.

Unless there is some compelling reason, the control, entity, and lifecycle classes should be treated as a single group. This group contains all of the application logic and business logic for the system.

These decisions leave us with the following groups of analysis classes:

- All user interface classes
- The system interface for the external billing system
- All application and business logic classes

Let's focus on the user interface classes first.

User Interface Complexity

To determine the complexity of the user interface, we need to consider each user interface class in turn. Since all of the user interface classes are grouped together, the selected technology must support the most complex user interface class.

The descriptive categories for user complexity are:

- Simple data input
- Static view of data

- Customizable views
- Dynamic view of data
- Interactive graphics

The group includes the following analysis classes we documented in Chapter 5, "Analysis Model for the Timecard Application":

AdministrativeLoginUI. The AdministrativeLoginUI allows the users to enter their username and password as proof that they are authorized to use the system. Examining the class and its methods, as shown in Figure 6.1, it is clear that the purpose of the AdministrativeLoginUI class is best described as simple data input.

EmployeeLoginUI. Since the EmployeeLoginUI class provides the identical functionality as the AdministrativeLoginUI class, it must have the same user interface complexity: simple data input. Figure 6.2 shows the methods for the class.

ExportEntriesUI. The ExportEntriesUI class allows administrative users to export time entries to the Time entry repository. Examining the class and its methods, as shown in Figure 6.3, it is clear that the ExportEntriesUI class both displays existing data, such as a list of clients, and allows export criteria to be entered. There is no indication that the data is dynamically updated, so we conclude that the purpose of the ExportEntriesUI class is best described as simple data input and static view of data.

RecordTimeAdministrativeUI. The RecordTimeAdministrativeUI allows administrative users to enter hours for any employee. Examining the class and its methods, as shown in Figure 6.4, it is clear that the RecordTimeAdministrativeUI class displays existing time entries, and allows the user to enter new time entries and update existing time entries. We conclude that the purpose of the RecordTimeAdministrativeUI class is best described as simple data input and static view of data.

RecordTimeUI. The RecordTimeUI allows employees to enter their hours. Since the RecordTimeUI class provides less functionality than the RecordTimeAdministrativeUI class, we conclude that it has the same description, simple data input and static view of data. Figure 6.5 shows the methods for the class.

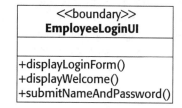

<<boundary>> **AdministrativeLoginUI**
+displayLoginForm() +displayWelcome() +submitNameAndPassword()

Figure 6.1 AdministrativeLoginUI class.

<<boundary>> **EmployeeLoginUI**
+displayLoginForm() +displayWelcome() +submitNameAndPassword()

Figure 6.2 EmployeeLoginUI class.

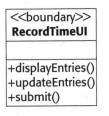

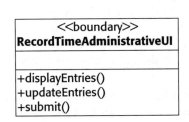

Figure 6.3 ExportEntriesUI class.   **Figure 6.4** RecordTimeAdministrativeUI class.

Figure 6.5 RecordTimeUI class.

Deployment Constraints for User Interfaces

Examining the use case descriptions covered in Chapter 3, "Gathering Requirements for the Timecard Application," there seem to be two distinct sets of deployment constraints. The Login and Record Time use cases for the employee must be accessible from almost anywhere, while the use cases for the administrative user have no such restrictions.

Recall that all of the user interface classes have been grouped for technology selection. So, one user interface technology will be selected, and it must meet the most restrictive deployment constraints.

First we survey the use case descriptions to determine the individual deployment constraints. Based on this information, we select a descriptive category that fits all of the use cases. Revisiting the use case descriptions in Chapter 3, we find the following deployment constraints:

Login use case. Employees must be able to log in from any computer, including home, client sites, and on the road. This access may be from behind a client's firewall.

Record Time use case. The Record Time use case must be accessible from client sites and employees' homes. In the case of client sites, they will often be behind the client's firewall.

Next, we need to pick the descriptive category. The descriptive categories for deployment constraints are:

1. Handheld device
2. Any Web browser on the Internet
3. Late-model Web browser on the Internet
4. Late-model browser on a network
5. Specific browser on a network
6. Dedicated workstations on a network

Since the employee must be able to access the system from home and client sites, we can exclude categories 4, 5, and 6. There is no indication that handheld devices are used, so we can exclude category 1. This leaves us with option 2, "any Web browser on the Internet," and option 3, "late-model Web browser on the Internet." The deployment constraints in the use case descriptions do not determine which of these two options is most appropriate.

In this case, we might ask the stakeholders, or use a simple email survey to clarify the issue. For our example, let's assume that all of the employees already use late-model browsers, so we choose option 3, "late-model Web browser on the Internet."

Number and Type of Users

The number and type of users can usually be deduced from the use case model. Remember, each distinct group of users is represented by an actor in the use case documentation. In the Timecard application, there are only two actors, employee and administrative user. The employee actor represents all employees who use the system to record their time. The administrative actor represents people who administer the system.

The descriptive categories that describe users are:

1. Small number of dedicated users
2. General use within an organization
3. Large audience with high interest
4. Huge audience with low interest

Since all employees use the system to record their hours, category 2, "general use within an organization," seems very appropriate for the user interfaces that support the Login and Record Time use cases. Option 1, "small number of dedicated users," seems more appropriate for the user interface that supports the Export Time Entries use case. However, we have decided to pick a single user interface technology that supports the most restrictive case, so we select the more challenging option, number 2, "general use within an organization."

Available Bandwidth

Available bandwidth can usually be deduced from the deployment constraints on specific use cases and from the descriptions of the actors. For example, if all the actors use the system at a single facility, bandwidth may not be an issue. If some actors use the system from remote facilities, from home, or while traveling, bandwidth may be an important factor.

The descriptive categories for bandwidth are:

1. Dial-up Internet connection
2. Fast Internet connection
3. Dedicated network between client and server

From the deployment constraints in the use case descriptions, we see that the employee must be able to use the system from "any computer, including home, client sites, and on the road." This clearly excludes the last two categories and leaves us with "dial-up Internet connection."

Types of System Interfaces

System interfaces are best described by examining the complexity of the interaction as documented in the flow of events for the use case(s) that use the external system. We must ask questions such as: What data is exchanged? Which services are obtained? How flexible is the interface?

The descriptive categories for system interfaces are:

1. Data transfer
2. Services through a protocol
3. Direct access to system services

The only system interface, the BillingSystemInterface, does not demand any services of the billing system. Instead, it simply sends a block of time entries to the external system. Category 1, "data transfer," is clearly the right choice.

Performance and Scalability

The performance and scalability factors are generally found by examining the class diagrams and sequence diagrams from the analysis model. These diagrams describe the data access and update patterns that influence performance and scalability. Unfortunately, these diagrams cover a single use case at a time. It is up to the developers to consider the effects of several use cases occurring concurrently.

The descriptive categories for performance and scalability are:

1. Read-only
2. Isolated updates
3. Concurrent updates

To determine the most appropriate category, we must consider how multiple users performing the use cases simultaneously affects each entity object. In many cases, a cursory glance at the activity diagram and sequence diagrams for a use case is suffi-cient. In other cases, developers must examine the sequence diagrams to see exactly how the entity objects are used. It seems profitable to consider each use case in turn before considering the impact of users performing different use cases simultaneously on the categorization. The following sections each describe the performance and scala-bility factors for an individual use case.

Login use case. In the Login use case, the system locates the user entity object that corresponds to the actual employee. Once the object is located, it must determine if the password is valid. This requires the system to read the password from some sort of persistent store. No data is updated, so "read-only" is the appropriate description. The sequence diagram in Figure 6.6 shows this interaction between the objects.

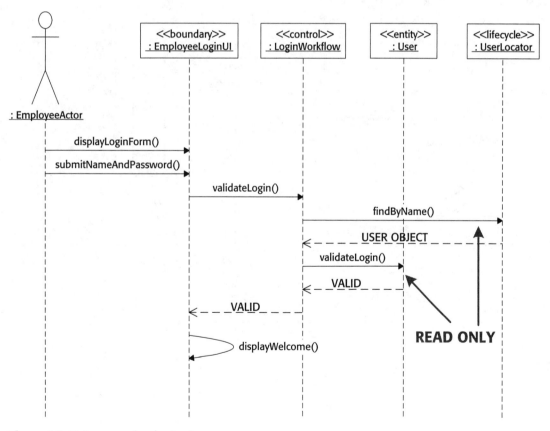

Figure 6.6 Data access for the Login use case.

Export Time Entries use case. In the Export Time Entries use case, the system locates client, user, and time entry objects. It also retrieves the details for each time entry object. It does not update any system data, so "read-only" is the appropriate description. Figure 6.7 shows these interactions.

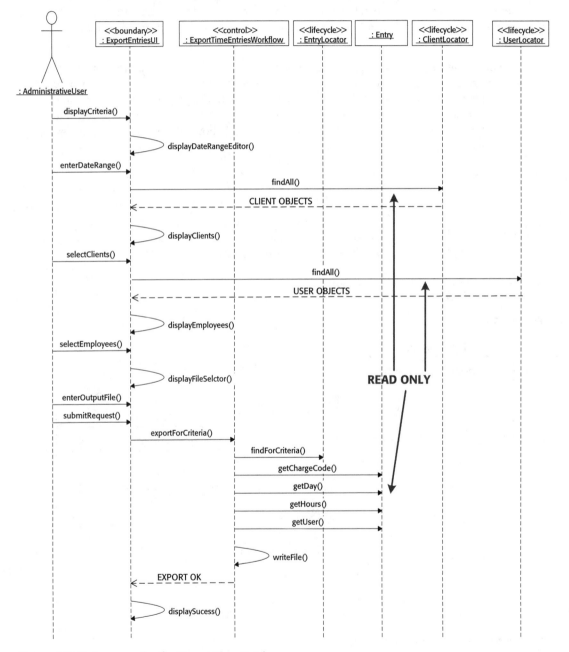

Figure 6.7 Data access for the Export Time Entries use case.

Record Time use case. In the Record Time use case, the system retrieves and displays the time entry objects. After the user updates the entries, the system must update its data with the new data. Therefore, the use case must be described with either "isolated updates" or "concurrent updates."

Each employee can only record his or her own hours, so there is no danger of concurrent updates due to different employees using the system at the same time. We can easily preclude the same employee from logging in twice, so there is no danger of the same employee recording hours in multiple sessions. However, the administrative user can initiate the Record Time use case on behalf of any employee. So, two administrative users or one administrative user and the actual employee could record time for the same employee at the same time. The Record Time use case does introduce a risk of "concurrent updates." Figure 6.8 shows these interactions.

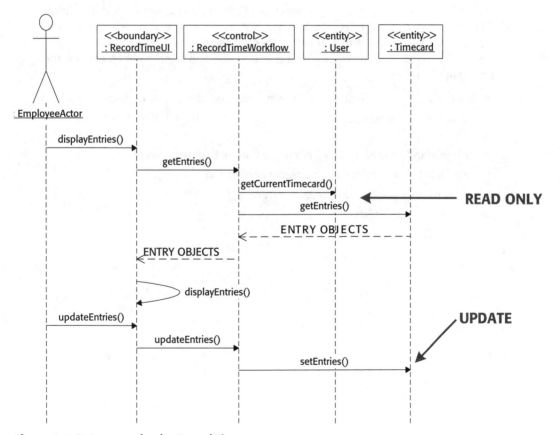

Figure 6.8 Data access for the Record Time use case.

The Next Step

Describing the technology requirements of a system forces you to carefully examine the requirements and analysis model for the system. For real-world systems, this is a very daunting prospect. Hundreds of pages of documentation must be read and understood as the system is gradually categorized. However, the result is well worth the effort, as the technology requirements for a complex system, with many interesting nuances and subtleties, can be summarized in a few paragraphs.

This summary is used to facilitate technology selection and to enable the participation of more people in the selection process. For instance, developers with experience in a given technology can easily use the summary to evaluate the suitability of that technology. They can share their expertise without spending countless hours learning the system. Summarizing the technology requirements for a system is also useful if you are *not* using outside expertise. By producing the summary before considering technology, developers avoid any urge to pick a technology and then justify its suitability for the system. It is very common for developers to semi-consciously select a technology before evaluating its suitability. This leads them to see the areas where the technology fits, while and sometimes glossing over the areas where it does not.

The next two chapters use the following to describe and select technologies for the Timecard application:

- User interface complexity: Simple data input and static view of data.
- Deployment constraints for user interfaces: Late-model Web browser on the Internet
- Number and type of users: General use within an organization
- Available bandwidth: Dial-up Internet connection
- Types of system interfaces: Data transfer
- Performance and scalability: Concurrent updates

Evaluating Candidate Technologies for Boundary Classes

Now that we've grouped our classes and described each group, we're ready to examine the classes and select the technologies that will achieve our system requirements.

This chapter describes how to describe and evaluate candidate technologies for boundary classes. It begins with an introduction of a standard format for describing a technology that we can use. Then, we'll apply the template to several technologies. Once this is done, we'll use the technology requirements from Chapter 6, "Describing the System for Technology Selection," and the technology descriptions to find the right technologies for the boundary classes in the Timecard system.

Technology Template

When learning a new technology, it is easy to become absorbed in the details and miss important information. Most developers, myself included, lose objectivity as they learn about the latest and slickest technology. Given a shiny new hammer, all I see are nails. The following template helps me focus my efforts and stay grounded as I assimilate a new technology. I suspect that, with some modifications, it may serve you in a similar way.

Each technology description contains the following elements:

Name and description. This section provides the name, acronym, and origin of the technology, before briefly summarizing it. The emphasis is on the nature and purpose of the technology, rather than any of the details.

Gory details. This section uses class diagrams, sequence diagrams, and code samples to describe how the technology works and how it is used. While full coverage of each technology is not possible, this section does capture the flavor and general use of each technology. For more information about specific technologies discussed here, refer to Appendix B, "Additional Resources."

Strengths. This section describes areas and uses in which the technology excels.

Weaknesses. This section describes any pitfalls or limitations of the technology.

Compatible technologies. This section discusses common combinations of technologies that leverage the strengths of the candidate technology.

Cost of adoption. This section quantifies the costs of adopting the technology. Special emphasis is given to the difficulty of acquiring expertise in the technology. It also mentions any product costs or licensing issues.

Suitability. This section uses the descriptions established in Chapter 6 to describe the situations for which the technology is suitable.

With a reasonable template for describing technologies in hand, we can explore several technologies that can be used to implement boundary classes.

Swing

Swing is Sun's framework for GUI development. It continues to receive well-deserved accolades for fulfilling Sun's "write once, run anywhere" philosophy for user interface development and for its object-oriented design. A Swing application, or applet, looks and behaves the same on any compliant Java Virtual Machine (JVM). Since JVMs exist for Microsoft Windows, most flavors of UNIX, and Linux, developers have a lot of freedom in developing and deploying Swing-based products. I continue to be impressed when the code I write at night on my PC runs fine under Solaris the next morning. While far from perfect, Swing is a solid implementation of a great vision.

Another, less-hyped, characteristic of Swing is its clear separation of model and view classes. Swing provides many valuable model classes that can be used with Swing view components, with other presentation implementations, or as independent data structures in a model. Once a model object is constructed, it can be wired to one or more view objects. The view objects are kept in sync with the model by an event model. For example, consider a list component that is wired to an underlying list model object. Updates to the model are automatically reflected in the list component. Similar model and view pairs are available for pull-down lists, trees, and tables, to name a few.

In an effort to make the view and model separation even more flexible and powerful, Swing's architects made each model an interface, and provide a default implementation. Custom implementations of the model interface work seamlessly with the corresponding view objects. For example, a developer could provide a fancy implementation of ComboBoxModel that keeps the elements in alphabetical order.

Many of Swing's early weaknesses, such as poor IDE support, poor performance, and unsettling instability in the API, have been resolved. Undoubtedly, it will continue to improve incrementally, it is now a stable and legitimate alternative for GUI development. I predict that Swing will complete its move from a leading-edge technology to a mainstream technology over the next few years.

Gory Details

Swing is an incredibly large and rich class library. It is impossible to do it justice here. However, I can cover some important facets of Swing that, hopefully, will capture its elegance and its versatility.

Separation of Model and View

In our analysis model, user interface classes are carefully separated from entity classes, because they have very different responsibilities. Encapsulation is the key goal. Business data and business logic are encapsulated in the entity classes so that they are easy to find, easy to extend, and easy to reuse. Presentation logic and user interaction logic are encapsulated in the boundary class, so that they are easy to find, and can be extended without affecting other classes. Also, this separation allows developers to specialize; one set of developers acquires knowledge of the business while another focuses on user interface design and the details of the presentation technology.

Swing has built-in support for this separation. Like all user interface class libraries, Swing comes with a rich array of widgets, including everything from text entry to progress bars to tree controls. However, Swing also includes classes that represent the data in a view-independent way. These classes are called *model classes*, based on the common synonym for entity classes. Swing model classes organize data into lists, trees, and tables, just to name a few. These models are completely independent of the view, and may be useful even if no view is involved. This is especially true of the DefaultTreeModel, which provides methods for adding nodes to a tree, removing nodes from a tree, traversing a tree, and generating a list of nodes from a leaf node to the root node.

By design, Swing model classes are highly extensible. In each case, Swing provides an interface that defines the behavior for the model, as well as a default implementation. This approach allows developers to solve straightforward problems with little effort, while allowing developers to handle more complex modeling problems with proportionally more effort.

Consider a list of objects and the corresponding graphical widget for displaying the objects in a pull-down combo box. In Swing, all concrete combo box model classes must implement the ComboBoxModel interface if they intend to be used by graphical combo box components. The class JComboBox contains all of the presentation and user interaction logic for producing combo box widgets. Each JComboBox object has a unidirectional association with exactly one object, whose class implements the ComboBoxModel interface. The JComboBox object is completely protected from the implementation details of the model; as long as the object supports all of the methods in the ComboBoxModel interface, the JComboBox object's needs are satisfied. Notice that one ComboBoxModel can support many JComboBox objects. Figure 7.1 shows these relationships. Sun provides the DefaultComboBoxModel as a quite reasonable

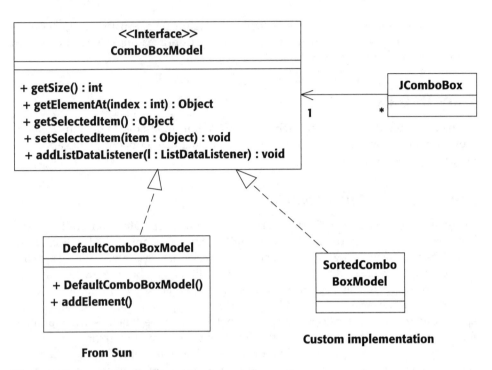

Figure 7.1 ComboBoxModel and implementations.

implementation of the ComboBoxModel interface. More complex implementations, such as a list model that sorts its contents, must implement the ComboBoxModel interface.

Event Model

In many applications each graphical view object must stay up to date with its underlying model object. The most obvious approach is to have the model object notify each view object when a change occurs. However, this introduces a dangerous mutual association between the model object and the view objects, as shown in Figure 7.2 for the JComboBox and its associated model class. The JComboBox object calls the getSize and getElementAt methods on the ComboBoxModel object, and the model object calls the intervalAdded notification method on the view object whenever an object is added to the model. This mutual association makes it impossible to reuse the model class without also reusing the view class, which is often inappropriate. Also, allowing a model class to access one method in the view class may lead developers to use other methods, until the two classes are tightly coupled.

The architects of the Swing class libraries needed a way to update view objects to reflect changes to the model objects' state, without introducing direct dependencies from the model classes to the view classes. Fortunately, there is a well-defined and well-respected design pattern that solves this exact problem, called Observer [Gamma 1995]. In this pattern, the observer class implements an interface that contains all of the

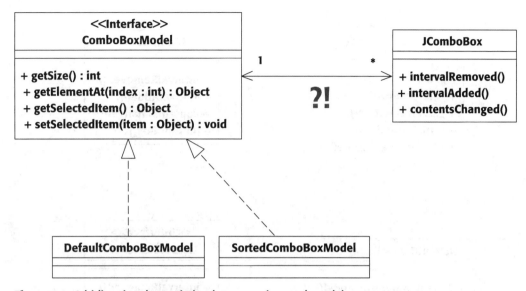

Figure 7.2 A bidirectional association between view and model.

notification methods. An observer object is registered with the observed object. When a change occurs, the observed object must notify each registered observer. However, the observed object does not depend directly on the observers; it just knows that they implement the observer interface.

In Swing, this pattern is implemented by requiring the view objects to register themselves as listeners on the model objects. Swing adds an additional twist, as the JComboBox does not know the specific implementation of ComboBoxModel. It only knows that the model object implements the ComboBoxModel interface. Since JComboBox implements ListDataListener, it is able to add itself as a listener to the model object. Once the model object has a reference to the listener, it can use the intervalAdded or contentsChanged methods to notify the listener of changes. The bidirectional association is avoided, because the model object does not know about JComboBox objects, just ListDataListeners. Figure 7.3 shows the way in which Swing's event model works for JComboBox objects and the underlying model.

The Observer pattern allows the objects to communicate with one another while keeping the model independent of the view and providing an amazing amount of flexibility. An application can create a particular type of ComboBoxModel, such as a DefaultComboBoxModel. The application can then create a JComboBox object that receives a reference to the model object in its constructor. However, the JComboBox object does not know or care which concrete implementation of ComboBoxModel it receives. JComboBox's constructor calls the addListDataListener method on the ComboBoxModel object. This registers the JComboBox as a listener on the model. Finally, the JComboBox object extracts the current state of the ComboBoxModel and uses the information to populate itself.

When the DefaultComboBoxModel object receives new elements, it notifies each registered ListDataListener object by calling its intervalAdded method. In the case of

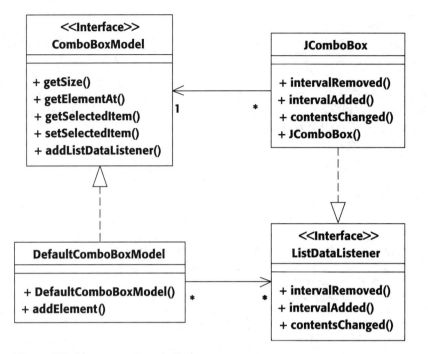

Figure 7.3 Observer pattern in Swing.

the JComboBox object, it knows to repopulate itself to reflect the model. Figure 7.4 shows the interaction between objects, while ignoring the interfaces.

Combining User Interface Components

Swing includes almost 50 user interface classes, from entire tables to tiny tooltips and everything in between. While many of these classes are independently impressive, any real user interface requires developers to connect user interface objects in sophisticated combinations. A user interface might include a tree control and a detail editor that allows the user to view and update the data for the item that is selected in the tree control. This navigation and editing tool might live inside of a larger user interface that includes a menu bar and a toolbar with icons.

The key to Swing's power and flexibility lies in the breadth and sophistication of the user interface classes themselves and in the ease with which developers can assemble a complicated whole from relatively simple parts. In providing this functionality, the Swing classes make excellent use of the Composite design pattern [Gamma 1995]. A JPanel is a Swing class that extends JComponent. Figure 7.5 shows how a JPanel object can hold any number of other JComponent objects, including other JPanels. This gives Swing developers full freedom to compose several components into a group, then use several groups to build a still larger user interface.

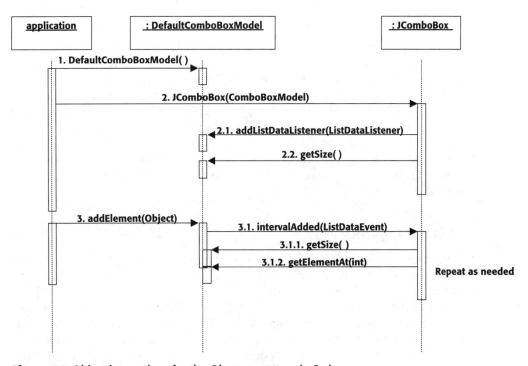

Figure 7.4 Object interactions for the Observer pattern in Swing.

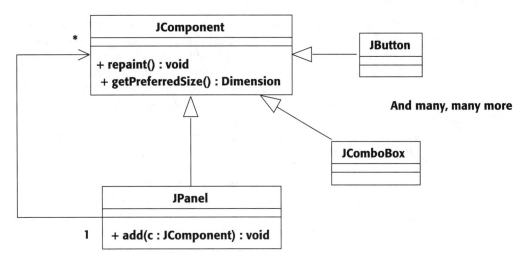

Figure 7.5 Use of Composite design pattern.

Layout Managers

Combining many components to form a coherent user interface requires the developer to determine how the components will be organized relative to one another, and how each component handles changes to the size of the enclosing window. Swing provides several classes, known as *layout managers*, that allow developers to control the layout of components within a container. Each JPanel object has exactly one layout manager object, which is an instance of a class that implements the LayoutManager interface. As shown in the one-to-one relationship between JPanel and LayoutManager in Figure 7.6, each LayoutManager object is dedicated to a single JPanel. Since the JPanel has a reference to the LayoutManager interface, it can use any concrete implementation of LayoutManager without modification.

Putting It Together

Swing makes excellent use of the Observer pattern to keep the model and presentation classes separate while keeping the views in sync with the model. It also uses the Composite pattern to allow the incremental construction of arbitrarily complex user interfaces. Flexibility is constantly increased through the creative use of interfaces. In fact, as you can see in Figure 7.7, every single association relationship is to an interface or to a base class, rather than directly to a concrete implementation class. This means that any JPanel can contain any number of different components, and use any layout manager. A JComboBox can use any model that implements the ComboBoxModel interface, and a DefaultComboBoxModel object can keep any object up to date, as long as the object's class implements the ListDataListener interface. Swing's developers clearly designed with flexibility and extensibility in mind.

A Small Sample

The following sample application shows how several JComboBox objects can present the elements of the same ComboBoxModel object. A separate text entry frame is used to add items to the model. Each time an object is added as an item in the ComboBoxModel object, it is immediately available in all of the JComboBox objects.

Let's take a look at the files that produce the combo boxes and the entry widget. The UpdatedChooser's constructor receives a reference to an object that realizes the ComboBoxModel interface. This UpdatedChooser's only job is to pass the model object along to the JComboBox and display the JComboBox inside of a frame. It is not at all involved in the Observer pattern.

The main method of UpdatedChooser, which as you know serves as a static entry point into this little application, constructs a new DefaultComboBoxModel and passes it to the constructor of a few UpdatedChooser objects. Notice that the constructor for the UpdatedChooser objects only knows that the parameter is an object whose class implements the ComboBoxModel interface. The main method could use any other implementation of ComboBoxModel, without affecting the code for the UpdatedChooser.

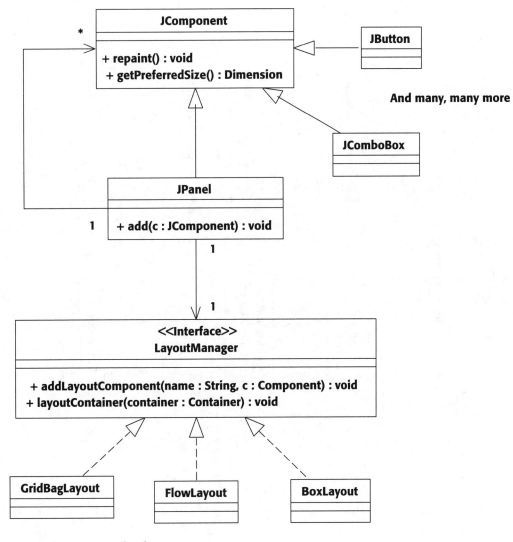

Figure 7.6 Layout managers.

UpdatedChooser.java

```
package com.wiley.compBooks.EJwithUML.SwingExamples;

import javax.swing.*;

/**
 *
 * Each instance of UpdatedChooser consists of a JFrame with a
```

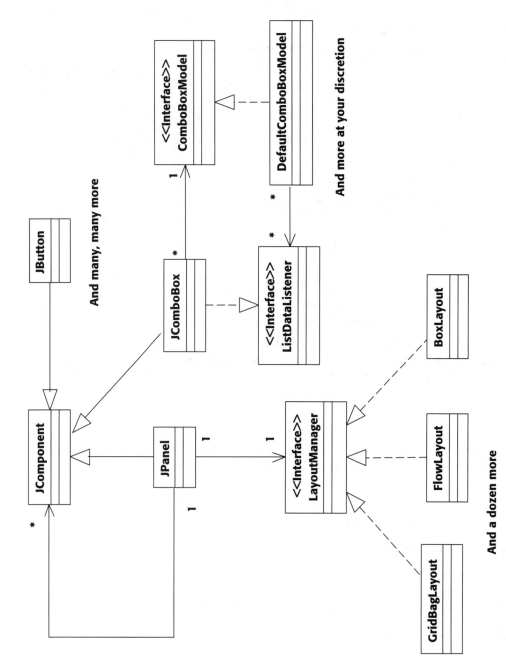

And many, many more

And more at your discretion

And a dozen more

Figure 7.7 All together now.

```
 * JComboBox inside of it. The JComboBox allows the user to
 * select from the items in a ComboBoxModel.
 *
 * The ComboBoxModel is passed in as a parameter to the
 * constructor and is used to construct the JComboBox. This
 * allows the JComboBox to register itself as a listener on
 * the model.
 *
 *
 */
public class UpdatedChooser extends JFrame
{
  public UpdatedChooser(ComboBoxModel model)
  {
    super("Updated Chooser Exampple");

    // construct a JComboBox that displays the model
    JComboBox chooser = new JComboBox(model);

    // add the JComboBox to the main container for this JFrame
    this.getContentPane().add(chooser);
    this.pack();

    this.addWindowListener(new ExitListener());
    this.setVisible(true);

  }

  public static void main(String[] args)
  {
    /* create a combo box model and pass it along to a few
       presentation and update objects */
    DefaultComboBoxModel model = new DefaultComboBoxModel();
    new UpdatedChooser(model);
    new UpdatedChooser(model);
    new TextEntryFrame(model);
    new TextEntryFrame(model);
  }

}
```

The TextEntryFrame keeps a reference to the DefaultComboBoxModel object, which it receives in its constructor. The constructor also adds a text field and an OK button to the frame, and registers the TextEntryFrame object as an action listener on the button. When the OK button is pushed, Swing's framework calls the TextEntryFrame object's actionPerformed method, which reads the text field and adds the resulting string to the model.

TextEntryFrame.java
```
package com.wiley.compBooks.EJwithUML.SwingExamples;
```

```java
import javax.swing.*;
import java.awt.event.*;
import java.awt.*;

/**
 * Each instance of the TextEntryFrame class contains a text
 * field and an "OK" button. Each instance also receives a
 * DefaultComboBoxModel object as a parameter to its
 * constructor.
 *
 * Whenever the user presses OK, the TextEntryFrame reads
 * the text field and adds the contents to the
 * DefaultComboBoxModel.
 *
 */
public class TextEntryFrame extends JFrame implements
                                        ActionListener
{
  private JTextField field;
  private JButton button;
  private DefaultComboBoxModel model;

  public TextEntryFrame(DefaultComboBoxModel model)
  {
    super("Entry Frame");

    // initialize instance variables
    this.model = model;
    field = new JTextField(15);
    button = new JButton("OK");
    button.addActionListener(this);

    // Get a new box container
    Box box = Box.createVerticalBox();
    box.add(field);
    box.add(button);

    // Add the box container to the main container of this JFrame
    this.getContentPane().add(box);
    this.pack();
    this.addWindowListener(new ExitListener());
    this.setVisible(true);
  }

  /** Implement behavior for ActionListener interface */
  public void actionPerformed(ActionEvent ae)
  {
    // read the text field and add it to the model
    String text = this.field.getText().trim();
```

```
      model.addElement(text);

      this.field.setText("");
   }
}
```

This fairly small sample shows how the Observer design pattern works behind the scenes in Swing. All the developer has to do is wire the right objects together using the addXXXListener methods.

Now that we have explored some of the inner workings of the Swing classes, let's continue to discuss the strengths and weaknesses more specifically.

Strengths

Swing's strengths lie in its limitless flexibility and richness, its cross-platform nature, and in the clear separation of model classes from view classes. The first two strengths allow developers to create incredibly slick user interfaces that look and behave the same on dozens of platforms, from Microsoft Windows to Linux to high-end UNIX workstations. Used effectively, the clear separation of model classes from view classes allows developers to write extremely extensible and readable code.

Swing has very reasonable performance and usability characteristics. Certainly, no one is writing the next commercial 3D point-and-shoot game in Swing and Java 3D, but Swing is quite suitable for business applications or even interactive data visualization. In fact, several popular arcade games from the 1980s have found new life as Swing applets.

Weaknesses

Swing is not a low-end GUI solution. Some organizations buy an IDE, send their PowerBuilder and Cobol programmers to a week of Java training and a week of Swing training, and expect to be up and running the next week. It is not possible. Learning to develop Swing applications takes time, and is easier with a strong background in object-oriented user interface development. Consequently, Swing may be precluded due to a lack of expertise.

Compatible Technologies

Swing applications, or applets, integrate well with all server-side Java technologies, such as RMI, JDBC, and EJB. For example, a boundary object that is implemented in Swing can interact with remotely deployed control or entity objects that are implemented with RMI or Enterprise JavaBeans. It is also possible to locate the boundary, control, and entity objects in the same virtual machine. For example, a Swing boundary object may talk directly to control and entity objects that use JDBC to retrieve information from a relational database.

Cost of Adoption

Swing is provided free as part of the standard JDK, but there are costs of adoption. First and foremost, to be successful with Swing, your project must fill the roles of *UI designer, architect,* and *Swing developer.*

UI Designer

It is always good to have a user interface designer who can address usability and human factors. A UI designer devises alternative interface strategies that meet the requirements, and works with the stakeholders and the developers to determine which approach is most suitable for the project. Deliverables range from screen shots in a drawing program to thin prototypes.

Architect

Swing user interfaces can degenerate into a series of unconnected works, with no two screens following the same format or using the same components. An architect can reduce this effect by establishing reusable components, such as button panels, layouts for input forms, and default windows. This allows developers to easily change the look of the entire application by altering the reusable components. The alternative requires each screen to be laboriously edited, perhaps for something as trivial as the background color or the space between buttons.

The architect can also keep the code base sane, and avoid costly rework by establishing standards for exception handling, error logging, and the use of layout managers.

The architect for a Swing-based user interface must have a strong knowledge of object-oriented principles, extensive design experience, and a clear grasp of the Swing architecture and event model.

Developer

At minimum, a Swing developer needs a solid understanding of the event model, layout managers, and some basic components. However, every Swing project needs at least one developer who knows the full breadth of classes that make up Swing. Almost any GUI component you can dream up can be built from Swing's classes. The trick is knowing where to start.

Developers who have solid object-oriented skills and a strong background in user interface development can migrate to Java and Swing without too much difficulty. However, it does take time and practice. A C++ developer with Motif experience would need a few months before he or she was truly comfortable with Java and the Swing class libraries. An experienced Java developer with GUI development experience in some other language might take considerably less time.

Developers who are migrating from a procedural background to Java and Swing may be overwhelmed by the challenge of learning object-oriented development, Java, and the intricacies of Swing. Most developers in this situation should gain experience with Java before tackling Swing.

Suitability

In Chapter 6, we discovered the following descriptive categories:

- User interface complexity
- Deployment constraints for user interfaces
- Number and type of users
- Available bandwidth

Let's evaluate Swing to see if it is a suitable choice for our system.

User Interface Complexity

Swing is certainly capable of handling simple data input and static data presentation tasks. It comes with a full array of input widgets, including text entry fields, pull-down selectors, radio buttons, scrollable lists, and nifty sliders. Presentation classes include tables, tree controls, and image maps. In addition:

- Swing also easily supports customizable views, such as sorted tables and filtered tables.
- Dynamic views of data are incredibly easy to implement in Swing, as its architecture has built-in support for change propagation, and stresses a clear separation between the data and the presentation of the data. Once a view object is connected to an underlying data or model object, any changes to the model object automatically cause changes to the view object.
- Swing can be combined with the Java 2D or Java 3D graphics frameworks to produce some very impressive interactive graphics. By manipulating the view, a user can update the underlying data.

In summary, Swing supports the entire spectrum of user interface complexity, from simple data input to interactive graphics.

Deployment Constraints for User Interfaces

The first two deployment constraints, handheld devices and any Web browser, clearly are not supported by Swing. However, most late-model Web browsers do include support for Swing applets, either directly or through the Java plug-in. Almost every workstation, from UNIX to Linux to Microsoft Windows, has a Java virtual machine, and therefore supports Swing applications.

Number and Type of Users

Swing is easily appropriate for a small number of dedicated users. Deployment and support of a Swing applet or dedicated application may easily be justified for low numbers of users.

Swing may also be appropriate for general use within an organization, if the complexity of the user interface makes Swing a desirable choice. However, Swing does have some incremental support costs. Swing applications must be installed on each user's workstation, complete with the appropriate Java virtual machine. Swing applets do not need to be individually installed, but an appropriate browser or Java plug-in must be present.

Similar considerations apply to using Swing for a large audience with high interest. If the complexity of the user interface and the system is sufficiently compelling, users will install the Java virtual machine, Java plug-in, and appropriate browser.

Swing is completely inappropriate for huge audiences with low interest. Any users who do not have a suitable configuration will not take time out of their day to install new software.

Available Bandwidth

Swing can be a very attractive option even for low-bandwidth scenarios. Swing applets do require the client browser to download the class files before running the application. However, the class files for a reasonably complex application are still smaller than three large images.

Once it starts running, a Swing applet can actually use less bandwidth than other user interface technologies. The server does not need to control the presentation; instead, the server can send the smallest possible amount of data or even compressed data.

With a little creativity, Swing is appropriate for all bandwidth categories, from dial-up connections to dedicated networks.

Java Servlets

The Servlet API is Sun's flexible and extensible framework for server-side development. Within the Servlet API, the HTTP package protects developers from tiresome HTTP protocol details and allows them to focus on their own unique data presentation problems. Servlets are used in conjunction with a Web server to create dynamic content based on the user's input.

There are a several key terms that are critical to an understanding of servlets. These are:

HyperText Transfer Protocol (HTTP). Specifies a communication protocol between Web clients and Web servers. It specifies valid request and response formats, error codes, and datatypes. By complying with HTTP, a Web browser is able to communicate with millions of Web servers, regardless of their hardware, operating system, or Web server vendor.

HTTP is a *connectionless protocol*, in that the browser does not keep a connection open nor send multiple requests across it. Instead, each request requires a new socket connection to the Web server. The connection is closed as soon as the request is complete.

HTTP request. A group of data sent from the browser to the Web server. An HTTP request includes the name of the requested page, descriptive information about the browser, acceptable datatypes for the response, any cookies that were dropped by the target server, and any data as entered by the user. In a nutshell, each HTTP request packages a request from the user into a format that any Web server can understand.

HTTP response. A group of data sent from the Web server to the Web browser in response to a request. An HTTP response includes descriptive information about the server, an expiration date for the response, and formatted data. The formatted data might be plaintext, formatted HTML, an image or even binary data. The browser is responsible for displaying the formatted data.

Form data. HTTP allows Web browsers to collect data from the user and pass it along to the Web server as a list of strings. The user fills in an HTML form in his or her browser and submits the data. The browser packages the form data as part of the HTTP request and passes it to the Web server as part of a HTTP request.

Cookie. When a browser loads a page, the page may ask the browser to save a relatively small chunk of data on the client machine. This chunk of data is called a cookie. If the browser accepts the cookie, then the browser stores the data and the name of the site that "dropped" the cookie.

When a browser sends a request to a Web server, it appends all of the cookies previously dropped by that site. This allows the Web server to keep track of each user so it can simulate a continuous interactive session.

HTTP servlet. A Java class that accepts an HTTP request and fills in an HTTP response. Servlets extend javax.servlet.http.HttpServlet, which protects them from the messy details of parsing HTTP headers, retrieving form data, and formatting HTTP data for the response.

The actual processing occurs inside of the servlet's doGet or doPost method, which accepts the HTTP request and HTTP response objects as method parameters. The doGet or doPost method uses the HTTP request object to retrieve any form data, then builds the formatted response data.

Servlet engine. Allows a Web server to redirect incoming requests to a deployed servlet. The Web server must be configured to associate certain relative URLs with servlets. When the Web server receives an HTTP request for one of these URLs, it captures the request and passes it along to the servlet engine. If the servlet is not already active, the servlet engine loads the servlet class and instantiates it. Next the servlet engine creates a response object and wraps the request data in a request object. These well-encapsulated and easy-to-use objects are gift-wrapped and presented to the servlet's doGet or doPost method. The servlet uses the request and any other resources at its disposal, including database connections, Enterprise JavaBeans, and HTML formatting code to fill in the response. The response from the servlet can be an HTML page, an image, or a file.

For more detailed information about any of these technologies, refer to the additional resources in Appendix B.

Gory Details

Servlets make life easier for developers by retrieving form data in a convenient form and by managing sessions and session data. However, a lot of work remains for the developer, who must build huge quantities of HTML and keep the system safe despite concurrent access from the Web server.

Retrieving Form Data

When a request is received from the Web server, the servlet engine creates the HttpServletRequest object, parses the form data out of the raw request, and adds the form data to the HttpServletRequest object. This encapsulates the logic for reading HTTP in the servlet engine. The doPost or doGet methods of the processing servlet can use the getParameterNames and getParameter methods of HttpServletRequest to extract each piece of form data.

Sessions

Servlet engines use cookies or hidden form data to keep track of different users by unique identifiers and to simulate a continuous session. Remember, each request is a distinct connection, and contains any cookies that have been dropped by the Web server onto the client. If there is no identifying data accompanying the request, then the servlet engine creates a new session. If identifying data exists, the servlet engine verifies that the session is still active. If so, it treats the request as part of a continuing session.

Consider a real-world analogy. When you make a flight reservation with an airline by phone, the booking agent gives you a confirmation number at the end of the call. It is up to you to write this number down and make sure that you do not confuse it with the confirmation number for your rental car. If you need to make changes to your flight, you simply call the airline and provide the confirmation number. This enables the booking agent to easily find the relevant transaction out of tens of thousands of similar transactions. To complete the analogy: You are the Web browser; the booking agent is the servlet engine; and the confirmation number is the cookie.

When the servlet engine receives a request from the Web server, it constructs a HttpServletRequest object that encapsulates the request information. The servlet engine also attaches the HttpSession object to the HttpServletRequest. This session object is especially valuable to servlet developers, as it allows them to store references to any object in a map of name and value pairs. This makes it really easy to associate different useful objects with a user and to retrieve them by name when processing subsequent requests. Figure 7.8 shows how the session and request information is packaged and delivered to the doGet and doPost methods of the servlet.

HTML Production

Servlets usually obtain a PrintWriter from the HttpServletResponse. This allows the servlet to send a stream of formatted text data back to the Web browser. Most servlets fill the response stream with HTML, lots and lots of gruesomely complex HTML. For many projects, this leads to a series of one-of–a-kind works of art, with each developer

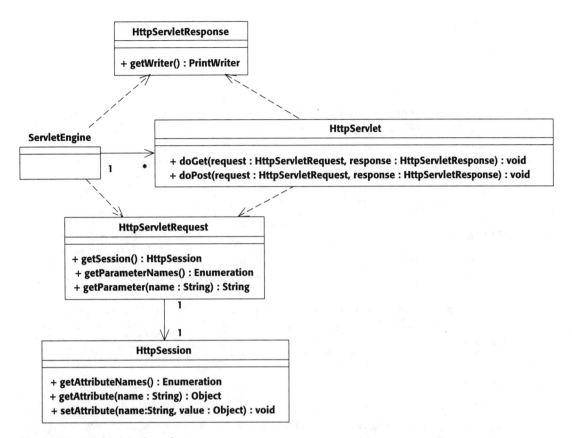

Figure 7.8 Sessions and servlets.

embedding hundreds or even thousands of lines of hard-coded HTML tags and JavaScript in each servlet. This brute-force approach is survivable until the developers receive a requirement for a new look or behavior that affects many dynamically generated Web pages. It could be something as simple as applying a new look to every table. Developers must comb through each servlet, searching for tables and making the desired change. Each new work exacerbates this problem, until it becomes prohibitively expensive to make any wholesale changes.

Producing complex pages of HTML in a clean and reusable manner is a challenge that all servlet projects must accept. The project team must create a reusable set of HTML production classes that are used throughout the project. For instance, there might be a single class for creating HTML tables and another for creating a group of radio buttons. These classes must be configurable so that they can be used in a variety of situations, yet be simple to use. In some cases, a separate class or subclass must be created to accommodate a specific browser. This approach has three major advantages: First, the code base stays small and is easier to understand and to extend. Second, applicationwide changes affect only a few classes. Finally, since each HTML production class is reused throughout the application, sufficient time can be spent on efficiency, quality, and appearance.

NOTE   For one approach to this challenge, see Chapter 12, "Design for HTML Production."

Concurrent Access

In developing servlets, it is easy to forget that the code in their doGet or doPost methods may be called by more than one thread at a time. However, since all production servlet engines process requests concurrently, this is an unavoidable reality. It is up to the servlet developer to make sure that any resources that are shared between servlet instances are thread-safe, by synchronizing the appropriate methods or code blocks.

Strengths

Servlets are incredibly simple to learn. A simple "hello world" servlet takes only a few lines, and once developers understand the session management logic, a shopping cart servlet is quite trivial.

Servlets protect developers from the HTTP's complexity, as all of the nasty details of parsing and building HTTP headers and payloads are hidden within the HTTP servlet classes.

Weaknesses

Though servlets are technically very sound and very easy to learn, by having a separate servlet for each dynamically generated page, and by lumping data access and HTML production into the doGet or doPost method, it is also very easy to create a maintenance and extensibility nightmare. Despite the simplicity of the servlet classes, servlet-based systems must still be designed with extensibility and flexibility in mind.

Compatible Technologies

Servlets are very compatible with Web technologies, such as HTML, DHTML, JavaScript, and XML. Servlets are often used to create elaborate, dynamically generated Web pages that produce content in these forms.

Servlets are also quite compatible with server-side technologies, such as JDBC, RMI, and EJB. A servlet boundary object can easily access a remote control or entity object using RMI or EJB. As with Swing, the variations are limited only by your architectural imagination.

Cost of Adoption

The servlet classes are provided free as part of the enterprise edition of Java, and most commercial quality Web servers include a servlet engine. However, there are other costs of adoption. First and foremost, to be successful with servlets, your project must fill the roles of UI designer, architect, and servlet developer.

UI Designer

It is always good to have a user interface designer who can address usability and human factors. A UI designer devises alternative interface strategies that meet the requirements, and works with the stakeholders and the developers to determine which approach is most suitable for the project. Deliverables range from screen shots in a drawing program to thin prototypes.

This is especially important in servlet development, where user interfaces are limited by the capabilities and idiosyncrasies of the users' browsers. Creativity and persistence are definitely required. Also, the user interface designer for a servlet-based interface must constantly refresh his or her skills, as browsers and Web technologies evolve and mutate at a disturbingly quick pace. At the very least, designers must know or be on a sharp learning curve for HTML, DHTML, JavaScript, XML, and XSL.

Architect

Servlet-based user interfaces can degenerate into a series of unconnected works, with no two following the same format or producing HTML in the same way. An architect can reduce this effect by establishing reusable HTML production classes to produce everything from tables and trees to frames and the enclosing page. This allows developers to easily change the look of the entire application by altering the reusable HTML production classes. The alternative requires each servlet to be laboriously edited, perhaps for something as trivial as the background color or the space between buttons.

The architect can also keep the code base sane and avoid costly rework by establishing standards for exception handling, concurrency, error logging, and the use of session data.

The architect for a servlet-based user interface must have a strong knowledge of object-oriented principles, extensive design experience, an understanding of Web technologies, and a clear grasp of the servlet architecture.

Servlet Developer

Compared to Swing, servlets require substantially less object-oriented sophistication, and frequently have a significantly shorter learning curve. This is especially true when the architect or other senior developer defines the intent of each servlet, and the UI designer prototypes the HTML and associated Web scripting. Given these assumptions, servlet development may serve as an excellent first project for a budding Java developer.

If the architect and user interface designer roles are not filled, then the servlet developer is forced to know everything from object-oriented design to DHTML to JavaScript. This requires a strong object-oriented Java developer who understands Web technologies and who can visualize usable interfaces.

Suitability

In Chapter 6, we identified the following descriptive categories:

- User interface complexity
- Deployment constraints for user interfaces
- Number and type of users
- Available bandwidth

Let's see how suitable servlets are for each of these requirements.

User Interface Complexity

Servlets, in combination with HTML, can easily support simple data input and static views of data. First, a servlet formats the HTML for a customized form. When the user submits the form, the form data is sent to a servlet for processing. The servlet can use any other data sources, such as database connections, Enterprise JavaBeans, or external systems, to create a response. The response is usually formatted HTML, although it could be a file or an image.

Customizable views, in which the user can manipulate the view without making a separate request to the server, are more difficult. Remember, the servlet responds to each request with a single block of data that is interpreted by the browser. So, the formatted response must include some combination of more complicated Web technologies, such as JavaScript and DHTML. These solutions depend on the browser to correctly render them, and they must be customized for each browser vendor and browser version. Therefore, creating customizable views using servlets is a complex undertaking that requires patience and a sophisticated understanding of Web technologies.

Dynamic views of the data are equally problematic. Remember, a dynamic view keeps current with the underlying model, either by receiving notification when a change occurs or by periodically retrieving the new data. With servlets and Web browsers, the first option is impossible; the server does not maintain a connection to the Web browser and therefore cannot notify it when the data changes. The second option can be achieved by using JavaScript to reload the entire page or a frame at suitable intervals. Of course, this is not very efficient, as all of the data, not just the updates, must be retrieved. As with customizable views, creating dynamic views using servlets is a complex undertaking that requires patience and a sophisticated understanding of Web technologies.

Interactive graphics, in which the user sees changes as they occur, and updates the underlying data by interacting with the graphics, are not possible with servlets and an unmodified Web browser. Just rendering the graphics requires some form of plug-in, such as a VRML or ActiveX viewer. Propagating changes back to the server is even more problematic.

Servlets are most appropriate for simple data input and static views of data. Customizable views and dynamic views of data are quite possible, but depend on browser-specific Web technologies, such as JavaScript and DHTML. Interactive graphics are not possible with servlets and standard Web browsers.

Deployment Constraints for User Interfaces

Servlets can support the entire range of deployment scenarios; the hard part is to generate HTML that presents well for the different users. For instance a micro-Web browser on a handheld device will not present large images very well, so the HTML produced by the servlet must include an alternative textual description in place of the image.

Number and Type of Users

Servlets are very appropriate for all user communities. The users should not even notice that servlets are being used. They will know that they requested information from a Web server and that they received information in response. They do not need to alter the configuration of their Web browser or accommodate the system in any way.

Available Bandwidth

Servlets are generally appropriate for all bandwidth levels. However, there are some limitations when attempting to stretch the capabilities of the browsers while constrained by low bandwidths. Remember, the browser simply renders the formatted HTML as sent by the Web server and servlet engine. This HTML contains data, presentation instructions, and any special processing logic, all in a form that the browser can interpret. In some cases, this may lead to an amazingly large quantity of HTML. For instance, implementing a customizable view by making each option a separate layer may replicate most or all of the data for each layer. Similarly, implementing a dynamically updated view by reloading the page periodically forces the servlet to send all of the data and presentation instructions each time.

XML

The eXtensible markup language (XML) is a rare example of an extremely hyped technology that really is worth the hoopla. Since its specification by the World Wide Web Consortium (W3C) in 1998, XML has become the standard mechanism for storing and exchanging descriptive data via electronic data interchange (EDI). Industry groups and government agencies are establishing XML document formats to describe everything from astronomical data to job descriptions to workflow management. Other common uses include configuration files, flexible data storage, and language-independent object serialization.

XML documents are valuable for people as well as computers. XML documents are precise enough for computers to create, read, and update them. Most people find them fairly easy to work with, especially with the aid of an XML authoring tool. For example, authors might use XML to divide a document into sections and to describe the suitability of the document for various audiences, based on their language and organizational role. An XML-based document management system can tailor each user's view of the documents based on the user's profile and this suitability description.

Before continuing this discussion in more depth, there are a few key terms that must be defined:

Element. XML divides a document into elements. Each element may contain data, attributes, and other elements. Conceptually, elements are rather like nodes in a tree.

Document type definition (DTD). Defines the structure of a set of documents. Specifically, a DTD defines which elements can be part of each element, and how many and in what order. The notation is reasonably simple and consistent with other pattern definitions, such as regular expressions.

Parser. Breaks a document into a tree of elements, and validates the document's structure against the DTD. Note that the validation tests for presence of the correct elements, attributes, and data within defined elements. It does not test data against an allowable range, or even differentiate between letters and numbers.

Authoring tool. Helps a human read and write XML documents that are valid for a particular DTD. Authoring tools save typing and your sanity, so you want one of these.

Now we can plunge into the details of XML.

Gory Details

XML allows people and computers to create and read documents that present data and describe themselves. This section discusses the structure of XML documents and the technology for creating and parsing XML documents.

Self-Describing Documents

Every piece of data in an XML document is inside of an element or is a named attribute of an element. As long as the author of the DTD picks explanatory names for elements and attributes, the XML document is self-describing. This eliminates an entire class of errors that have plagued EDI developers for decades. Traditionally, a protocol or data interchange format described the meaning and allowable values for each position in each record. Imagine the resulting chaos if a program reads field 11, which is Social Security number, as field 12, which is age in seconds since 1970. Also, changing the interchange format may ruin existing documents; you certainly cannot safely delete a field or insert one in the middle.

Now consider a self-describing document format, such as XML. There is never any argument over the identity of a piece of data. The name literally surrounds the data. Of course, there may be arguments over the associated units or how to interpret the data, but this is hardly the technology's fault. Also, a new element can be added anywhere in the document. As long as it is optional, no existing documents break. This really helps when different organizations create documents that are similar but not identical in structure.

For example, XML can be used to describe a transaction in a form that is easy to read and unambiguous for both humans and computers. Consider the following brief snippet of XML that describes a single transaction in which someone gets very lucky on February 1, 1999.

```
<transaction>
 <date>
  <day>1</day>
```

```
    <month>Febuary</month>
    <year>1999</month>
  </date>
  <amount>
    <value>1000000</value>
    <units>USD</units>
  </amount>
</transaction>
```

Consider the alternative approach of simply allocating a particular number of bytes for each field. Tiny disagreements in the size or starting index of a field can lead to strange and sometimes difficult-to-diagnose problems. The following densely packed line shows the same data as in the preceding XML sample; however, the meaning of each byte is left to the human or computer that reads the line.

```
01Febuary    19991000000USD
```

Parsers

Parsers come in two flavors and use two parsing methods. First, parsers either validate the document against the DTD or they don't.Thus, parsers are often described as validating or nonvalidating. The first parsing method, the Simple API for XML (SAX), is an event-based parser that deserves recognition for its elegance and the fact that its acronym encapsulates two other acronyms. The second parsing method, the Document Object Model (DOM), builds a tree of elements in memory.

SAX

As a SAX parser works its way through a XML document, it notifies the registered document handler whenever an element begins and ends. This allows the handler to react to the content a piece at a time, so it can build objects or perform any required actions. Any extraneous information is discarded, with no wasted memory. Also, it is easy to stop parsing at any point. For instance, an application might parse through a document looking for the first valid record. With a SAX parser, it is easy to stop because it is processing one record at a time.

Writing applications that use a SAX parser can be somewhat tedious, however, as each event must be caught, identified, and processed. This is especially painful when the processing depends on where the element occurs in the tree.

DOM

DOM parsers are generally built on top of a SAX parser; they provide an extra level of convenience. A DOM parser builds a tree structure from the document. Once the entire document has been parsed, this tree structure can be navigated and explored at length. Also, an application can modify the DOM tree and save it as a new XML document. So, for many applications, a DOM parser is the clear choice.

Unfortunately, this convenience may come at a price. The entire document is parsed and held in memory before the tree of elements is returned to the application. DOM parsers are notoriously wasteful if the document is large and the application needs only a fraction of the data. Or are they? Some DOM parsers accept event handler objects and notify them when certain events occur. For instance, IBM's venerable, and horribly named, xml4j parser allows an application to register element event handler objects with the parser. These handlers are notified when matching elements are completely parsed. In this scheme, the element handler can do nothing, replace the element with another element, or consume the element completely. If the parser supports this sort of scheme, then developers get the convenience of a nice DOM tree without the wasted space.

NOTE IBM's xml4j has been integrated into Apache's open source toolkit for XML. It is now called Xerces. While the name is undeniably cool, it is even less explanatory.

Strengths

XML greatly improves data interchange between peer systems and between people and systems. It dramatically decreases development time and minimizes the risk of translation errors. In short, it actually deserves its hype.

Weaknesses

If network bandwidth is a very high priority, then an XML document with more bytes spent on element names than on the actual data values may be a foolish luxury. Otherwise, it is a great way to exchange data.

Another less obvious weakness of XML is its natural hierarchical structure. While XML is perfect for treelike data, it is not such a natural fit for webs of interconnected nodes. Relationships must be stored as data. This may seem awkward, and prove to be error-prone, as deleting a data element requires the deletion of the associated relationships.

Compatible Technologies

XML can be used by any Java application, applet, or servlet. It is used to store information on both clients and servers, and to communicate between different parts of the same system and between different systems. It truly is well on its way to ubiquity.

Cost of Adoption

Use of XML requires several, some, or all of the following roles.

DTD Author

DTD authors determine the structure of XML documents. At a minimum, they need a mastery of the data that is described in the document, and a facility with the syntax and idioms of DTDs. Fortunately, DTDs are fairly straightforward, and there are many excellent texts on the pragmatics and theory of DTD construction. Also, an effective DTD author needs a strong vision for the future of the document.

In some cases, the DTD author may not have sole control over the document's structure. In many cases, XML documents help diverse organizations exchange information. Each organization promotes certain perspectives and interests as the document structure evolves by consensus. A DTD author in such a situation needs patience and persistence in unusually large quantities, as well as skills in negotiation and compromise.

Document Author

Once the DTD solidifies, actually authoring XML documents is fairly straightforward. Tools automate much of the drudgery, and prevent invalid XML based on a particular DTD. This frees the document author to concentrate on the actual data.

In some cases, humans do not create XML documents. Instead, XML documents are generated by a system. For instance, a system may extract data from a database and convert it into XML. In this case, there is no need for a human document author.

Developer

XML development requires developers to learn at least one parser technology. Fortunately, documentation and sample code for XML parsers is readily available. XML development does not generally require extensive knowledge of the Java class libraries.

Suitability

Recall from Chapter 6 that system interfaces can be divided into three categories: data transfer, services through a protocol, and direct access to system services. This section explores XML applicability for these three categories.

Data Transfer

XML is very useful for data transfer between systems. XML was created in part as a more flexible and easy-to-use alternative for electronic data interchange. One system may extract data from a database or two, use a XML parser to build an XML document, and send the document across to the other system. The receiving system can use a parser to recover the document. Once a system has recovered a document, it can process each element individually or build a set of interrelated objects.

XML is an excellent choice for system interfaces that emphasize data transfer.

Services through a Protocol

XML is also very useful for system interfaces that allow one system to receive services through series of requests and responses. One system builds an XML document and sends it over a socket connection to the server system. The server parses the request, performs any required actions, builds a response XML document, and sends it back to the client system. The same flexibility and extensibility characteristics that make XML an ideal EDI technology are assets in this situation. Also, the readability of XML is very helpful when debugging the interactions between the client and server.

Direct Access to System Services

This type of system interface exposes some of its methods for remote access. XML is gaining acceptance as an object serialization mechanism for use with language-independent remote method invocation. Hopefully, this will allow greater interoperability between EJB and CORBA systems in the near future.

Technology Selections for the Timecard System

Now that you have an understanding of the different technologies available for boundary classes, let's use the technology requirements from Chapter 6 and the technology descriptions from this chapter to select technologies for the Timecard system's boundary classes. We'll also need to consider the cost of adopting the technology.

The boundary classes break into two groups: user interface classes and the system interface with the billing system.

User Interface Classes

Recall from Chapter 6 that we lumped all of the user interface classes for the system into a single group for technology selection. Also, we characterized those user interface classes in several areas.

- User interface complexity: Simple data input and static view of data
- Deployment constraints for user interfaces: Late-model Web browser on the Internet.
- Number and type of users: General use within an organization.
- Available bandwidth: Dial-up Internet connection.

Based on these descriptions, we must choose between servlets and Swing. Let's examine them individually.

User Interface Complexity

Both technologies are perfectly capable of supporting simple data input and static views of data. Neither technology has an advantage. We will have to base our decision on other criteria.

Deployment Constraints for User Interfaces

Servlets can be used to produce dynamic Web pages for display in any late model browser. Swing is also appropriate for deployment as an applet under these same circumstances, since all late model browsers either have a built in Java virtual machine or supported the Java plug-in. This may require the user to install the Java plug-in or change the configuration of their browser.

While these accommodations seem trivial to developers and other power users, some users may resist, due to security concerns, lack of time, or for sheer perverse pleasure. Making any additional demands on the user results in extra demands on the development or deployment staff for the system, so servlets have a slight advantage over Swing.

Number and Type of Users

Servlets are appropriate for any number of users. Swing applets are appropriate for general use within an organization. However, there must be some advantage to using Swing, to offset the incremental support costs that result from deploying an applet to a large and often unmotivated audience. In this case, there does not seem to be any advantage to using Swing, as the user interface seems straightforward. Therefore, the advantage is to servlets.

Available Bandwidth

The Timecard system must support low-bandwidth scenarios, such as traveling employees using a slow dial-up connection. On the other hand, updating a timecard does not require much data. Either Swing or servlets are perfectly appropriate. There's no advantage to either technology. We will have to base our decision on other criteria.

Cost of Adoption

The cost of adopting servlets for this application is quite low, as the user interface is fairly straightforward. The UI designer and servlet developers should have a reasonably easy time. As far as user interface classes go, this project is appropriate for developers with low to moderate experience in Web technologies and Java development.

The cost of adopting Swing for this application could be a bit higher, due to the complexity of Swing development. Unless the developers already know Swing, and do not know any Web technologies, the cost of adoption is clearly higher for Swing. Servlets, therefore, have the advantage.

Conclusion

The Timecard application could reasonably be implemented with either Swing or servlets. However, there are no indications for choosing Swing over servlets. In the absence of any strong preference on the part of the development staff or the users, we will use servlets.

System Interface with the Billing System

Recall from Chapter 6, that the interface with the billing system is simple data transfer. Finally, we get an easy decision. XML lets us create a flexible data interchange format;

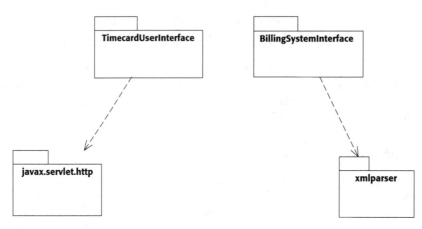

Figure 7.9 Package dependencies and technology selection.

and it comes with free tools and parsers. We happily follow the rest of the industry and select XML.

The Next Step

UML provides package dependency diagrams that show the relationships between large parts of the system. In this case, we can show that the user interface classes depend on the servlet classes, while the billing system interface depends on an XML parser of undetermined origins. Figure 7.9 shows our technology selections for the two groups of classes.

Now that we have selected technologies for the boundary classes, we can turn our attention to the control and entity classes.

Evaluating Candidate Technologies for Control and Entity Classes

The control and entity classes comprised the second group of analysis classes we identified in Chapter 6, "Describing the System for Technology Selection." In this chapter, we'll use the template I introduced in Chapter 7, "Evaluating Candidate Technologies for Boundary Classes," to describe and evaluate the candidate technologies for implementing this group of classes. The first step is to apply the simple descriptive template to several technologies, before using the technology requirements descriptions from Chapter 6 to find the right combination of technologies for the control and entity classes in the Timecard application.

The technologies we'll evaluate are Remote Method Invocation (RMI), Java Data-Base Connectivity (JDBC), and Enterprise JavaBeans (EJB). However, we evaluate the suitability of RMI and JDBC together, since they are often used together.

RMI

Remote Method Invocation (RMI) was added to version 1.1 of the Java Development Kit (JDK) to allow remote access to objects. It is important to understand RMI both as an alternative to EJB for simple applications and as a technology that directly supports EJB.

RMI has a simple and wonderful purpose. It allows a client object on one host to call methods on an object that resides on another host. The client objects use a *stub object* to communicate with a *skeleton object* on the server. Fortunately, RMI and its tools provide the stub and skeleton objects, which do all of the hard work. Figure 8.1 shows communication between a client and an RMI server. While the client thinks it is calling a method on a remote object, it is actually calling a method on a stub object in the same virtual machine (VM). The client stub converts the method parameters into data and sends them across to the waiting server skeleton. (Note: The client stub and the server skeleton live in different virtual machines and may even be located on different continents, so the communication between the stub and the skeleton is over a network connection.) The client stub then waits for a response. Once the skeleton receives the data, it converts the data back into parameter objects and calls the same method on the implementation object. The return value, if any, is converted into data and sent back across the socket connection to the waiting client stub that converts it back into an object and passes it along to the client.

Gory Details

RMI consists of a handful of classes and interfaces and a few simple tools. Thanks to this simplicity, a reasonably experienced Java developer can learn enough to have a remote HelloWorld server up in a few hours. However, designing an efficient and effective RMI server is a bit more challenging. RMI developers must consider what data is passed for each remote method, and protect against concurrent access to their RMI server's objects. As explained in the next section, RMI is both very simple and very complex.

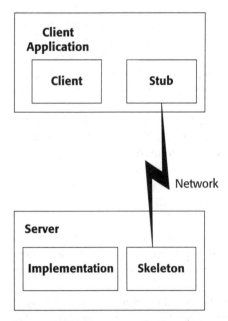

Figure 8.1 RMI communications between clients and servers.

Classes and Interfaces

Consider a user interface that uses RMI to access some functionality on a remote server. Each ClientView object has a reference to an object that implements the Some-RemoteInterface interface. For the client, the object that implements the SomeRemote-Interface interface is an instance of ClientStub. When one of the interface methods is called, the ClientStub object converts each parameter and sends it over the socket to the server. It then waits for a response. The response is either a return type or an error. If it is an error, then the ClientStub converts the raw data into a RemoteException and throws the RemoteException to the calling client. Otherwise, it converts the returned data and returns it to the calling client. Figure 8.2 shows the classes and interfaces for this simple scenario.

On the server, the SomeImplementation class extends UnicastRemoteObject and implements the SomeRemoteInterface. A ServerSkeleton that has a socket connection to the ClientStub has a reference to the actual implementation. When the ServerSkeleton receives data from the socket, it converts the data to parameters and calls the correct method on the SomeImplementation object. If any RemoteExceptions are thrown, they are converted to data, and the data is sent back across the socket. Otherwise, the return value is converted to data and sent back across the socket.

Fortunately, developers do not need to write the complex code that dwells inside of the stubs and skeletons. Sun Microsystems provides a tool, called rmic, as part of the JDK, which produces the stub class files based on your class files. It is up to you to bundle the class files so that the client and server applications can find them.

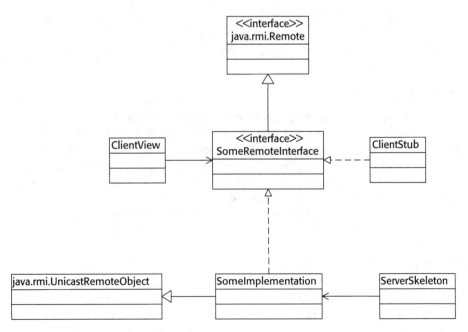

Figure 8.2 Classes and interfaces for RMI.

NOTE   In JDK 1.1, rmic also produced custom skeleton class files. As of JDK 1.2, the skeleton is part of the RMI server.

Remote Object Registration

Before a client can reference a remote object, the RMI registry must be running on the server, and the remote object must be registered with the RMI registry. The RMI registry is simply a Java application that listens on a port for incoming requests. When it receives a request for a particular object, it tries to match the request against all of the implementation objects that have registered. A remote object is instantiated by a Java application, which then uses the static bind or rebind method in the Naming class to register the object with the RMI registry.

The following code snippet shows how a remote object for the example in Figure 8.2 is instantiated and registered.

```
public static void main(String[] args)
{
    try
    {
      System.setSecurityManager(new RMISecurityManager());

      SomeImplementation remoteObject = new SomeImplementation();
      Naming.rebind("SomeServer", remoteObject);
    }
    catch(Exception e)
    {
      e.printStackTrace();
    }
}
```

Parameter Passing

So far, I have glossed over a great deal of complexity by ignoring how parameters and return types are converted to and from data. Consider what happens when a client object calls a method on a remote object reference. Before the client stub can pass the request to the server, it must convert the parameters into data. This is known as *serialization*. When the response is received, the client stub must convert the data back into a return value. This is known as *deserialization*.

There are three types of serializable data that can be used as parameters or return types in RMI: *primitive data, serializable objects,* and *remote references*.

Primitives

Primitive data types are very convenient for use with RMI, as there is no need to convert primitive data types to data; they are already simple data. They allow remote clients to configure the remotely accessible object and to request data from the remotely accessible object.

Serializable Objects

The client stub must convert each parameter object into data. If the object contains primitive data, then this process is fairly straightforward. The stub simply serializes the object by sending the name of the object's class and all of the object's data. However, if the object contains other objects, then they must be serialized also. So, serializing a single object can lead to the serialization of an entire network of connected objects.

Java provides two mechanisms that help developers manage the serialization process. First, an attribute can be marked as *transient* in the class. Transient data is ignored during serialization. Also, in order for an object to be serialized, the class must implement the Serializable interface, which has no methods. By allowing a class to implement Serializable, a developer is stating that objects of that type are reasonable for serialization.

Each object that is serialized on the client was instantiated from a particular class. When the skeleton on the server receives the serialized data, it instantiates an object of the same class and loads the data into it. This requires that the same version of the class exist on both the client and the server.

In remote method calls, a serialized copy of the object is passed to the server, so any changes to the passed object's state on the server do not affect the original object on the client.

Remote References as Parameters

When the stub is converting the parameters, it checks for objects that implement java.rmi.RemoteObject. These parameters are not serialized. Instead, their stubs are serialized and sent in their place. Thus, the server receives as a parameter a stub object that connects back to the remote object on the client machine.

Thread Safety

When an object is registered with the RMI registry, it is open for access by concurrent threads. RMI, like most distributed architectures, allows more than one client to access the server at the same time. So, the remote object and every object that the remote object has a reference to must be designed with thread safety in mind. It is up to the developer to make sure that any resources that are shared among client requests are thread-safe, by synchronizing the appropriate methods or code blocks.

Development and Deployment

Applications based on RMI have a reasonable, if somewhat tedious, development and deployment cycle. In order to develop and deploy a RMI-based system, you need to follow these steps:

1. Write remote interfaces and implementations for the server.
2. Use the rmic command to generate stub classes.
3. Write client applications.
4. Distribute stub classes and any common domain classes to the client.
5. Start the RMI registry.

6. Run the main application to register the remote objects with the registry.

7. Start the clients.

Most of these steps can be automated in a build or make file.

Common Uses of RMI

RMI is a fairly simple and very flexible technology. There are three ways in which RMI can expose business logic to clients:

- Remote object that hides entity objects
- Direct access to entity objects
- Direct access to entity objects with event notification

The following sections describe these common uses in more detail.

Remote Object That Hides Entity Objects (Strict Layering)

In many cases, it is possible to completely isolate the user interface objects from the entity objects. As discussed in Chapter 3, "Gathering Requirements for the Timecard Application," this separation helps simplify the user interface while keeping the entities well focused. When the user interface objects are distributed, the control object may expose its methods through RMI. Figure 8.3 shows the UpdateTimecardControl as a remote interface that is implemented by the UpdateTimecardControlImpl class. The UpdateTimecardControl object keeps track of the employees and receives the employee ID as the first argument of each method. This allows the UpdateTimecardControl object to get the current timecard from the correct employee and call the appropriate method on that timecard.

There is only one remote object, the UpdateTimecardControl. None of the entity objects are exposed as remote objects. All of the parameters and return types are simple objects, primitives, or enumerations of simple objects.

Hiding the entity objects keeps the remote client isolated from the remote objects. All interactions funnel through a very straightforward interface. This reduces the deployment burden, because as long as the UpdateTimecardControl interface remains the same, the domain objects can be altered without impacting the clients.

Direct Access to Entity Objects (Relaxed Layering)

An alternative design allows the user interface to directly access the entity objects. Since the user interface and entity objects are on different hosts, RMI is used to expose the entity objects as remote objects. A locator object is registered as a remote object. The locator object's methods allow the user interface to find Timecard objects. Rather than receiving a serialized copy of the timecard object, the user interface receives a remote object reference to the specified timecard object. Thereafter, the user interface communicates with the timecard object via RMI. Figure 8.4 shows the classes and interfaces for this alternative.

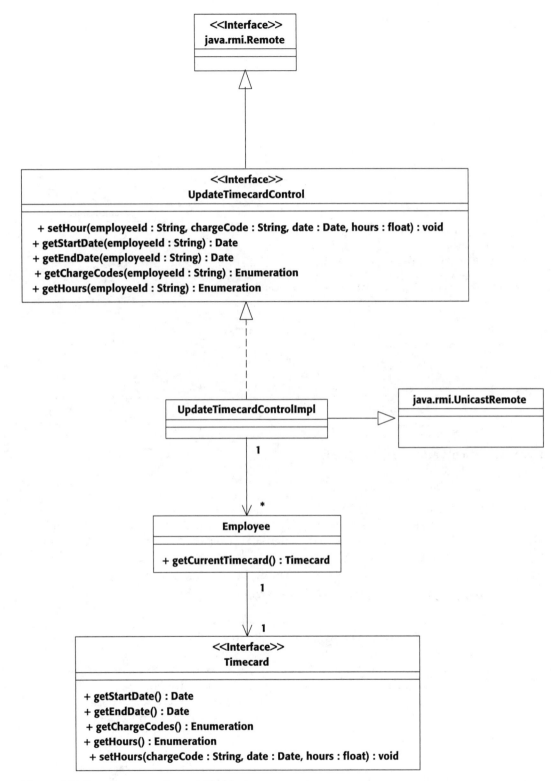

Figure 8.3 Remote access to control object.

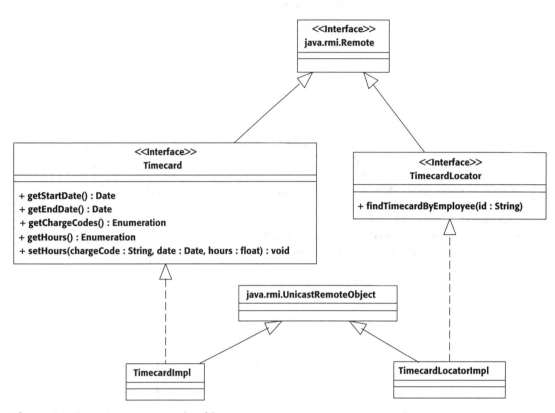

Figure 8.4 Remote access to entity objects.

Notice that each change to the Timecard interface requires a new deployment. It is important to note that changes to the internal implementation of the Timecard class may not require redeployment.

Direct Access with Event Notification

It is common for objects to track the state of another object. This allows a view to stay in sync with an underlying entity, or one entity to monitor a group of entities. Fortunately, the Observer design pattern [Gamma 1995] allows an object to receive an event notification whenever the state of another object changes. The object of interest does not know the specific type of each registered observer. Instead, the object of interest keeps references to any object that implements a simple notification interface.

Java uses the Observer pattern both in JavaBeans with PropertyChangeListeners and in AWT and Swing with different types of listeners for different events.

NOTE For a more thorough description of the use of the Observer design pattern in Swing, see the *Gory Details* section for Swing in Chapter 7.

In some cases, the observer object and the observed object may reside in different virtual machines, perhaps on different continents. One solution to this scenario extends the JavaBeans event model to notify remote clients of changes in an entity object's state. For example, an object might provide a remote method to register remote property change listeners. The property change listener must also be remotely accessible, so that the object of interest can notify it of changes. Figure 8.5 shows some classes and interfaces that illustrate this scenario. An InterestingThing object is registered with the RMI registry. Once a client gets a reference to the InterestingThing, it can register a listener object. Whenever a client changes the state of the InterestingThing by calling its changeSomething method, the InterestingThing must call the propertyChanged method on each registered listener.

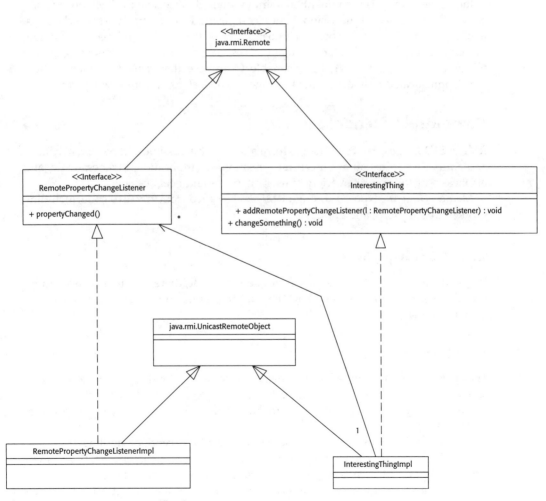

Figure 8.5 Remote event notification.

Strengths

RMI is a great starting point for distributed applications. It makes distributed computing palatable to developers by hiding the nasty details of serializing and deserializing parameters and return values. There are not many classes or interfaces to learn, and the rmic and rmiregistry tools are very easy to use. Also, the error handling is fairly straightforward, assuming a basic knowledge of exception handling in Java. It is a very elegant and easy-to-assimilate technology. Moreover, it works between any hosts that have a compliant virtual machine. For example, a client on a PC can easily access a remote object on a UNIX server.

Weaknesses

RMI leaves scalability, fault tolerance, load balancing, and data integrity concerns up to the developers. This is an intentional limitation in Sun's vision for RMI, not a weakness in the execution of the vision. In any case, using RMI for an enterprise class system requires developers to consider a host of issues, from object and resource pooling to redundancy to thread safety. In many cases, designing and implementing simple solutions for these issues may be reasonable. Otherwise, the architecture must include more sophisticated technology that leverages RMI, such as Enterprise JavaBeans.

Compatible Technologies

RMI and JDBC are often combined to form a remotely accessible and persistent control and entity layer. This allows a central repository of application, business logic, and business data to support a variety of user interfaces and peer systems.

Methods that are exposed through RMI can be called from any Java code, including servlets, applications, and applets.

Cost of Adoption

While RMI is provided free as part of the standard JDK, there are other costs of adoption. In order to be successful with RMI, your project must fill the roles of architect and RMI developer.

Architect

The architect for a RMI-based system needs a clear understanding of the performance and scalability issues involved with different design choices. Choices between strict and relaxed layering and for event notification need to be made early in the development cycle.

Also, the architect must establish clear guidelines for exception handling, error logging, and naming for different types of common RMI classes and interfaces. This upfront effort yields huge dividends in the form of a smaller and more readable code base.

The architect must have a strong background in distributed object-oriented development and in Java.

RMI Developer

RMI developers need to understand distributed development, threads, and concurrency. A clear understanding of these issues is more important than the actual Java classes and programming techniques, which are actually fairly straightforward. A developer with the right experience can easily pick up the RMI specifics from a few examples. So, a system or subsystem that is dominated by domain data and RMI may serve as an excellent entry point for a developer who is transitioning to Java from, say, C++ and CORBA.

RMI developers do need a strong understanding of synchronization, exceptions, serialization from the java.io package and, of course, the java.rmi package.

JDBC

Java DataBase Connectivity (JDBC) was introduced in JDK 1.1. JDBC is a thin, object-oriented wrapper around the full functionality of SQL. You can create, read, update, and delete the schema and the data; execute stored procedures, commit or roll back transactions, and even fiddle with isolation levels. If you can do it in SQL, you can do it with JDBC.

Using JDBC to save a few objects to a database is very easy. You just figure out the mapping from the object's data to the table's fields, and the rest is straightforward drudgery.

Real systems tend to be a bit more complex. Problems begin to crop up when you have different flows through the system that all update an object but that all have different transaction boundaries. Where do transactions originate? Where is each transaction committed? Who creates database connections, and can they be reused? Also, no useful object is an island. How do you store the relationships between objects? When you load an object, do you load all of the objects that the object knows about, or do you wait until they are needed? How many objects can you store in memory?

Fortunately, a lot of very smart people have dedicated their careers to solving the puzzles inherent in object-to-relational persistence. This body of work can be consumed and leveraged by absorbing the theory and by using commercial object-to-relational mapping products. Also, EJB servers are becoming increasingly sophisticated in this area.

Gory Details

JDBC allows developers to write database-independent code while still getting the performance of drivers, which are written and tuned by the vendor.

As you explore the technology in this section, be alert for creative uses of object-oriented principles, such as encapsulation, interfaces, and polymorphism. In addition to its technical merits, JDBC is valuable and accessible example of object-oriented theory as applied to a very real problem.

Drivers, Connections, and Statements

JDBC derives much of its appeal from the freedom it gives developers to almost completely ignore the differences between databases. JDBC requires the code to load one or more drivers and to request a specific connection from the DriverManager. After that, the rest of the code is entirely generic. Many projects use a configuration file to hold the connection information and the driver class names that must be registered. This means all of the code can be blissfully unaware of the database specifics. Let's examine some of the classes and interfaces that perform this rather impressive feat.

The Driver interface defines the methods that are required to determine if a driver is suitable and to open a connection. If it is, database vendors must provide a specific implementation class for the Driver interface, which encapsulates the details of opening a connection to their specific type of database, and provides information about the supported features for their database and their driver.

The thoughtful developers at Sun also protect developers from worrying about the individual drivers by supplying a class, DriverManager, that collects drivers and determines which one fits a particular situation. When a concrete implementation of the Driver interface is loaded, it must register with the DriverManager class by calling the static registerDriver method. Later, when an object needs a connection to a database, it calls the static getConnection method on the DriverManager class. This method searches the DriverManager's list of drivers until it finds one that matches the requested database type. It then asks the driver to open a connection to the database by calling the connect method on the driver. Assuming that all goes well, this connection is returned to the requesting object. Figure 8.6 shows the sequence diagram as an application first registers two drivers and then obtains a connection that fits the second driver.

Notice that this connection is really a vendor-specific implementation of the Connection interface. Connection objects allow full control over the current transaction, through the commit and rollback methods. If the database allows it, they also allow configuration of the isolation level for subsequent transactions on the connection.

Consequently, the code that you or I write deals solely with the DriverManager and the Connection and Statement interfaces. We are protected from all of the database-dependent variations that are hidden inside of the vendor-supplied implementation classes. Figure 8.7 shows the classes and interfaces required to obtain a Connection object and a Statement object. The vendor must supply a chain of database-dependent implementation classes, as shown on the right, that implement the chain of interfaces shown on the left. This elegant scheme simplifies development for application developers, as well as driver writers.

New and Improved Result Sets

In JDBC 2.0, the createStatement method in the Connection interface accepts two new integer parameters. The first determines how the result set can be traversed. In previous versions of JDBC, the result set is traversed from beginning to end, with each row seen exactly once. This is one option for the first parameter. Another option allows the result set to be traversed in any order, and for multiple visits for each row. The next parameter determines if the result set can be updated.

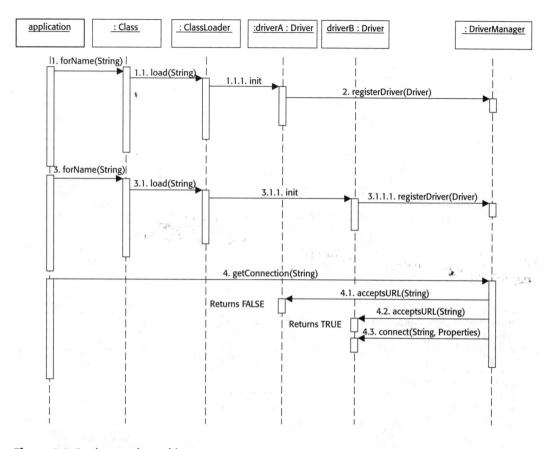

Figure 8.6 Register and use drivers.

The result set contains several distinct types of methods. These methods traverse the result set, retrieve data from the result set, update data in the result set, and refresh the result set from the database.

The traversal methods move the current row within the result set. In older versions, the only traversal method is next. Each record is seen once, from top to bottom. The new version adds methods to move about the result set in both directions, jump to arbitrary rows, and revisit rows.

The data retrieval methods are very similar to previous versions. Support has been added for additional datatypes, but the pattern is the same.

An entirely new set of methods has been added to update the data. The current row can be deleted or have its data changed. A new row can be added by moving to the insert row, which serves as a buffer, and by updating each column for the new row. After changes have been made, the updateRow method submits the changes to the database.

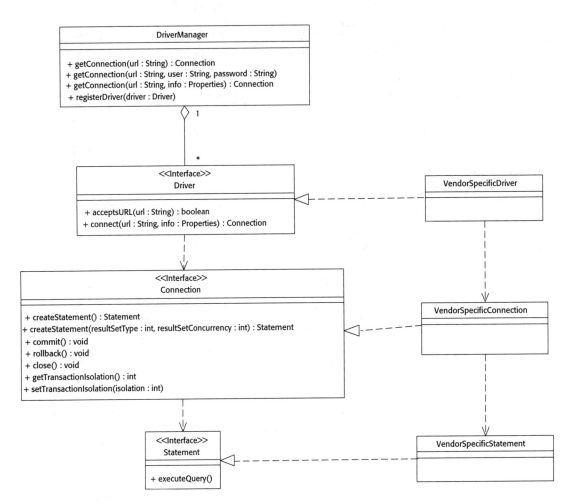

Figure 8.7 JDBC classes.

Another completely new method, refreshRow, has been added to reread the current row from the database.

Figure 8.8 shows the classes for retrieving and using a result set. As before, the vendor must supply a chain of database-dependent implementation classes, as shown on the right. These classes implement the chain of interfaces on the left.

Strengths

Like RMI, JDBC is a great starting point; database-independent code is easier than ever. As long as there is a JDBC driver for your favorite databases, and as long as you stick to SQL-compliant datatypes and syntax, you can change databases with ease. The class libraries are easy to understand, and behave as expected.

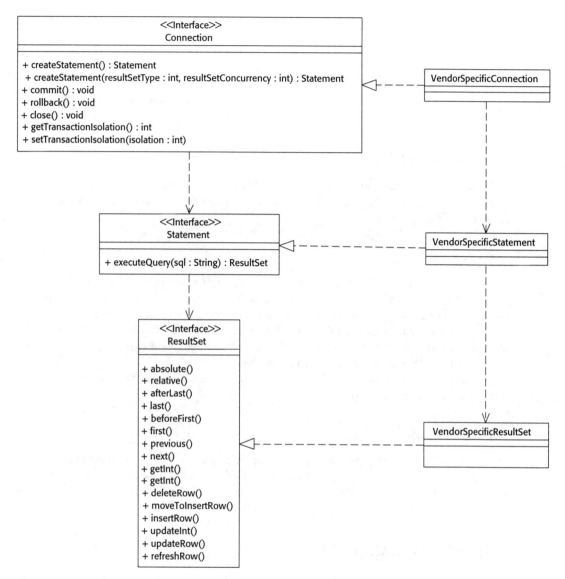

Figure 8.8 Result sets.

Weaknesses

Like RMI, JDBC leaves many issues to the developer. Larger datasets and more complex transactions require caching, transaction management, and connection pooling. In many cases, designing and implementing simple solutions for these issues may be reasonable. Otherwise, the architecture must include more sophisticated technology that leverages JDBC, such as a commercial object-to-relational framework or Enterprise JavaBeans.

Compatible Technologies

RMI and JDBC are often combined to form a remotely accessible and persistent control and entity layer. This allows a central repository of application, business logic, and business data to support a variety of user interfaces and peer systems.

JDBC can be used to access a database from any Java code, including servlets, applications, and applets.

Cost of Adoption

JDBC is provided free as part of the standard JDK, but there are other costs of adopting it. In order to be successful with JDBC, your project must fill the roles of architect and JDBC developer.

Architect

Architects for JDBC-based systems must be familiar with many performance, scalability, and data integrity issues. Database connections, which are fairly expensive to establish, must be used efficiently. Transactions must be started and completed. Mappings from objects to database tables must be established in a flexible and extensible manner. The simple class library makes JDBC development look easy, but there are many subtleties that, if ignored, can cripple a project.

The architect must have a solid object-oriented background and some experience with object-to-relational persistence.

JDBC Developer

Developing JDBC-based applications is generally straightforward. The class library is extremely clear and easy to use. A basic understanding of transactions and SQL is needed. Developers who are migrating to Java may find JDBC to be a comfortable starting point.

Suitability of RMI and JDBC

In Chapter 6, we identified two descriptive categories:

- Number and type of users
- Performance and scalability

Let's evaluate how RMI and JDBC perform in these categories.

Number and Type of Users

RMI and JDBC are certainly a valid choice for the first three audiences: a small number of dedicated users, general use within an organization, and a large audience with high interest. As the number of users and the data accessed grows, developers will need to cache objects and pool resources, but these are common problems in large-scale development.

This combination is less applicable for huge audiences. At some point, the performance characteristics of RMI, like any distributed technology, will be overwhelmed by the demands of a mass audience. Unfortunately, RMI does not support any form of load balancing across servers. In some cases, it may be possible to create a simple architecture that spreads the load across several hosts. However, this is not an easy task. Really large audiences usually require a more formal and scalable solution, such as EJB, which leverages both RMI and JDBC.

Performance and Scalability

A combination of RMI and JDBC is certainly a reasonable choice for read-only systems and for systems that allow isolated updates. These systems do not require any special design for transaction management or data integrity. The combination is also appropriate for systems that allow concurrent updates of data. However, in this case, the developers must supply their own architecture for coordinated transaction management on top of the simple control provided by JDBC.

EJB 1.1

The Enterprise JavaBeans specification, which is part of the Java 2 Enterprise Edition, completely specifies a framework that exposes business objects to remote clients. It builds heavily on the lessons and innovations of CORBA, while defining a more comprehensive suite of services, including object caching, transaction management, object-to-relational persistence, and security. Any developer who has struggled to implement these services for his or her own distributed application knows that doing so is both painful and risky.

EJB implementations tend to depend heavily on the technologies described so far. They use RMI to provide distributed access, JDBC as a basis for persistence, and XML to describe the deployment decisions.

Several terms are essential to understanding of EJB. These are:

- Entity bean
- Home interface
- Session bean
- Remote interface
- Implementation
- Deployment descriptor
- Bean-managed persistence
- Container-managed persistence

- Transaction boundaries
- Container
- Persistence

The following sections give a general overview of these terms. Resources for more information on these topics can be found in Appendix B.

Entity Bean

Entity beans are remotely accessible components that expose business data and business logic for an EJB system. Each entity bean represents a single independent and persistent entity in the domain. An individual employee and an employee's timecard are both appropriate entity beans.

Individual pieces of data, such as a name or contact information, may be contained within entity beans, but they are not good candidates for separate entity beans. Lists or collections of entities do not need to be wrapped inside of another entity bean. This role is played by the home interface, as explained next.

Entity beans generally evolve very cleanly from entity objects in the analysis model.

Home Interface

Entity beans are only useful if clients can create, locate, and destroy them. This is the role of the home interface. Each home interface specifies remotely accessible methods for the creation, location, and destruction of one type of entity bean. For example, if a system has entity beans for employees and for timecards, then the system has separate home interfaces for employees and for timecards. Home interfaces generally evolve nicely from the object lifecycle analysis objects.

Session Bean

Session beans are remotely accessible components that expose high-level business logic and workflow logic that spans multiple entity beans. Session beans simplify and support access to entity beans in several ways. A session bean translates an individual high-level request into many requests to many entity beans. In translating the request, the session bean may protect the caller from knowledge of the entity beans by returning simple data or collections of simple data.

Session beans do not generally update domain data directly. They frequently call methods on entity beans that change the persistent state of the entity bean.

Despite the superficial similarity in names, EJB session beans are completely distinct from HTTP sessions. A single HTTP session may use many session beans to accomplish many subtasks during a single login.

Session beans typically evolve fairly cleanly from control objects in the analysis model.

Remote Interface

Each entity and session bean has an interface that defines its remotely accessible methods. When a call to a bean's home interface returns an entity object, it is actually returning a reference whose type is the corresponding remote interface. All access to the entity bean is accomplished through this remote interface reference.

Implementation

Each entity and session bean has an implementation that realizes the EntityBean or SessionBean interface. The implementation contains the Java code for the business logic for entity beans, and the workflow logic for session beans. It does not implement the home and remote interfaces. The implementation also defines persistent instance data.

Deployment Descriptor

The deployment descriptor is an XML document that describes how the entity and session beans are deployed. It describes everything from the location of class files to decisions about persistence, transactions, and security.

Container

An EJB container holds entity and session beans. It is responsible for a variety of housekeeping activities, from object caching to transaction management to managing resource pools. The interactions between beans and their enclosing container are tightly defined in the EJB specification. The following are some interesting aspects to the relationship between beans and their enclosing container.

Object caching. A large-scale enterprise system may hold data for thousands or even millions of entity beans. However, at any point in time, most entity beans are not being accessed. It is up to the container to determine which entity beans need to be active due to current or recent usage. When the container takes beans in or out of service, it notifies the bean via callback methods, such as ejbPassivate and ejbActivate.

Concurrent access. In order to preserve data integrity, the container controls access to each entity bean. Many clients or session beans may have access to the same bean, but each method call must complete before another method call can start on that bean. Notice that a series of calls from different clients may be interleaved. Also, calls to different beans of the same type may be executed simultaneously.

WARNING The EJB specification precludes developers from using the synchronized keyword in beans or code that is called from beans.

Transaction management. The container also enforces any transaction requirements specified in the deployment descriptor. By moving the decisions out of the developer's code and requiring the container to enforce it, the EJB specification gives the developer a lot of flexibility and opportunity to procrastinate or experiment. For example, developers can defer any serious thoughts on transaction boundaries until late in a project without disturbing existing code.

Persistence. The container also determines when each entity bean needs to be saved, and in the case of container-managed persistence, uses the mapping in the deployment descriptor to save the data.

Bean-Managed Persistence

In bean-managed persistence, the entity bean loads and saves its own data. The entity bean does not need to determine when it is time to load or save. Bean-managed persistence requires developers to embed JDBC code within the bean's implementation.

Container-Managed Persistence

In container-managed persistence, the developer specifies a mapping between each piece of persistent data and a field in a table in the database. This mapping is stored in the deployment descriptor.

Transaction Boundaries

The container determines transaction boundaries based on decisions that are recorded in the deployment descriptor. For each remotely available method, developers specify if the method should join an existing transaction, start its own transaction, or execute outside of any transaction.

Gory Details

Enterprise JavaBeans is a fairly complex technology, with lots of terms, concepts, rules, classes, and interfaces to learn. However, one thing is certain: using EJB is infinitely better than trying to produce your own scalable remote object framework.

Classes and Interfaces

In order to gain all of the benefits of an EJB system, the developer must create classes and interfaces that fit within the specification. Specifically, for each Enterprise Java-Bean, the developer must provide a remote interface, a home interface, and an implementation class. Each remote interface, which defines the public face of the bean, must extend the EJBObject interface as provided by Sun. Each home interface must extend the EJBHome interface, also provided by Sun. Each implementation class must realize the EntityBean interface.

Notice that the implementation class does not implement the home and remote interfaces. This is a good thing, as you really do not want to write code for some of the methods in EJBObject and EJBHome. These tasks are left to the vendor, who supplies a proxy class that implements your remote and home interfaces. Since these interfaces extend Sun's interfaces, the proxy must provide behavior for your business behavior, as described in your remote interface, the bean lifecycle behavior, as described in your home interface, and the behavior defined by Sun in the EJBObject and EJBHome interfaces.

Obviously, the container vendors cannot be expected to anticipate your business logic, yet their proxy class is expected to implement your remote interface. This forces the proxy to delegate each request for a business method to an instance of the implementation class.

Figure 8.9 shows the classes and interfaces that are provided by Sun, the application server vendor, and the developers.

Stateful Session Beans

Session beans are divided into two distinct categories, *stateless* and *stateful*. A stateful session bean maintains a dialogue with the client application, in which the session bean remembers past requests, and uses them to simplify subsequent requests. For example, a stateful session bean for an online store might allow the customers to select a product, enter their billing information, then enter their shipping information, and finally confirm the purchase. This allows each interaction to stay simple, while useful information builds up in the session bean.

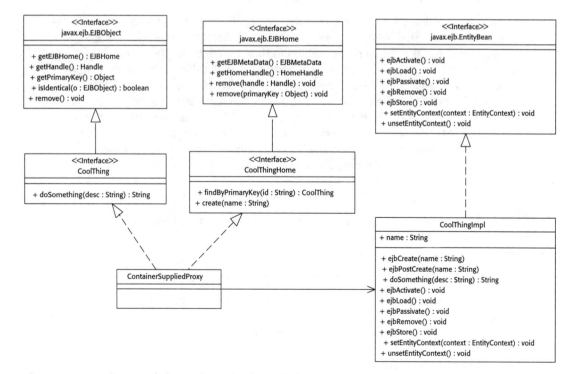

Figure 8.9 Interfaces and classes for a simple entity bean.

This convenience comes with a price. The stateful session object takes up memory, and must be managed by the container until the session is completed by the client application. If the container runs low on memory, it must serialize the bean and recover it when the client makes another request. Also, there is no guarantee that the client will gracefully end the session. This forces the container to worry about timeouts and cleanup for orphaned stateful session beans.

Control objects that provide a conversational workflow for the client are generally very appropriate as stateful session beans.

Stateless Session Beans

A stateless session bean is not required to remember any conversational state from request to request. In fact, the same client making multiple requests to the same stateless session bean may actually receive a different instantiation each time.

This is very efficient, as the container can keep a small pool of stateless session beans for use by many clients. There is no need for the container to manage relationships between the session beans and the client application.

Stateless session beans often evolve from control objects, which convert a single method into a series of smaller requests, and consolidate the results.

Development Workflow, Assuming Container-Managed Persistence

As a system is designed and implemented with EJB, development breaks into fairly distinct pieces. First, developers determine the business data that resides in each entity bean, along with the remotely accessible interface that exposes the data. At the same time, session beans are identified from control objects in the analysis model. They encapsulate the high-level business logic and workflows that span multiple entity beans. After these two efforts solidify, a separate effort maps the data in the entity beans to fields in a relational database. The mapping is held in a deployment file, not in the code itself. As these efforts mature and are exercised against actual data and usage scenarios, developers can determine the most appropriate transaction boundaries and permissions for remotely accessible methods. Again, these decisions are kept in a deployment file, not in the code.

So, development of an EJB system breaks into the following primary steps:

1. Allocation of business data, business logic, and control logic to entity and session beans.

2. Mapping entity data to persistent data store.

3. Determining transaction boundaries and security.

The key is that each step does not affect the previous steps. For instance, the code for the entity beans and session beans is completely unaffected by the mapping from the data to the database. Even the data mappings are independent of the decisions regarding transaction boundaries and security.

This clear division between software development activities may be EJB's greatest contribution to enterprise development. By allowing developers to defer and revisit different steps without destroying the existing work, use of EJB technology can dramatically decrease project risk.

Strengths

By providing a coherent framework of services and standards, EJB greatly simplifies the development of enterprise systems. EJB allows developers to leverage several decades of research and innovation in transaction management, object-to-relational persistence, object caching, and resource management. Standing on the backs of giants allows us to approach formidable projects with confidence. The following section discusses some specific advantages of EJB.

Object Lifecycle Management

Object lifecycle management includes creating, locating, caching, and deleting objects. In EJB, the methods for performing these tasks are defined in the home interface. In most cases, no code is written by the developer to realize these methods. Instead, the container uses SQL statements and database mappings as defined in the deployment descriptor to realize them at runtime.

This approach has two tremendous advantages. First, developers save a great deal of effort that would otherwise be spent writing tedious JDBC code to load and save objects, as well as complex and error-prone code for caching objects. Also, entity beans can easily be reused in other systems, since developers follow standard conventions.

Transaction Management

In EJB development, transaction boundaries may be handled within the code or described in the deployment descriptor. The first approach gives developers limitless flexibility, while the later approach is incredibly easy to use and allows developers to revisit their decisions without disturbing the existing code base.

Security

EJBs provide security by allowing developers to specify which users can access each method. This approach allows developers to control system access with a great deal of precision and at a fine granularity. Of course, the user interface must handle invalid requests gracefully or prevent users from attempting to access forbidden functionality.

Persistence

As with transaction management, EJB development offers limitless flexibility for beans that require custom persistence code or easy point-and-click descriptions of the mapping from entity bean data to database fields. While this is certainly not unique to EJB, it is still a huge advantage.

Vendor Neutrality

Since the relationship between the container and the enclosed beans is very well determined by the EJB specification, a set of beans can be redeployed within a different compliant container with proportionally little effort. This allows developers to scale their system by changing the container, not the code. For instance, a system might be developed within a free or cheap container, initially deployed inside of a midrange container, and then redeployed to a fancy cluster of high-performance EJB servers. Also, containers may be selected based on particular strengths, such as superior transaction management or scalability.

Portability and Reuse

By definition, every EJB developer follows the same specification. This greatly increases reuse potential. There is no worry that a bean will not fit the persistence or security scheme of the new system. So, a bean that fits nicely with the new system's domain can never be excluded due to implementation decisions.

Weaknesses

While EJB development has many advantages, it is not without a price. Application servers that provide substantial value come with substantial price tags. Also, Enterprise JavaBeans require developers to comply with the EJB specification, master the application server's deployment tool, and endure painful code-deploy-test cycles.

Compatible Technologies

Enterprise JavaBeans can be accessed from any kind of application, applet, or servlet. It can be used to create entity and control objects that are accessed from almost any sort of boundary objects.

Cost of Adoption

Commercial-quality application servers with EJB support are quite expensive. You pay the vendor so that you will not have to solve the rather nasty problems associated with enterprise development. If your project really needs the strengths of EJB, the costs of not using it may be incredibly high. Your development team must provide solutions for the object caching, persistence mapping, and transaction control needs of a scalable enterprise system. On the other hand, using EJB should decrease risk and speed up the development cycle.

> **TIP** If you worry that finding or cultivating EJB developers is difficult and expensive, consider the option: finding the developers who are qualified to develop an alternative solution to each of the problems that EJB solves.

In order to be successful with EJB, your project must fill the roles of architect, bean developer, and deployer.

Architect

Architects for EJB systems need knowledge of the EJB specification, the J2EE platform, distributed computing, object-to-relational persistence issues, transaction management, concurrency, exception handling, and architectural patterns. Experience with CORBA or another distributed computing technology may be helpful. This role requires a wide breadth of knowledge, as well as practical low-level experience.

Bean Developer

In many cases, bean development is fairly straightforward. Knowledge of transaction basics, exceptions, and the Java language is essential. No particular breadth of knowledge of the Java class libraries is required.

Deployer

A bean deployer needs a basic understanding of transactions, concurrency, resource pools, and security. A deployer does not need to implement any of these areas in code; instead, he or she must make deployment decisions that maximize performance while protecting data integrity.

In-depth knowledge of the application server and its associated deployment tool is also essential. Expertise in the Java programming language is not necessary.

Bean deployment is not like other design and code activities. It is closer to system administration or database administration.

Suitability

In Chapter 6, we identified two descriptive categories:

- Number and type of users
- Performance and scalability

Let's take a look at how EJB meets these criteria.

Number and Type of Users

EJB is certainly a valid choice for all four types of audience: a small number of dedicated users, general use within an organization, a large audience with high interest, and a huge audience with low interest. As the number of users and the amount of data accessed grows, the capability of an EJB server to cache objects and pool resources becomes increasingly important.

While load balancing and clustering will never be easy, vendors of commercial application servers are already focusing on this challenge. It is important to note that several of the application server vendors, including BEA, IBM, and Sun, have extensive experience with enterprise system development and clustering technology.

Performance and Scalability

EJB is not always a reasonable choice for read-only systems and systems that allow isolated updates. These systems make use of a small set of EJB's strengths, such as object caching. And if the system has demanding performance requirements, using EJB may actually increase overall project risk.

EJB really starts to show its value when faced with concurrent updates of the system data. The combination of object caching and transaction management is more efficient than 99 percent of all in-house efforts. Also, EJB developers and deployers can manipulate the transaction boundaries without altering a single line of code. This is invaluable when attempting to achieve just the right balance between data integrity and performance.

Sample Technology Selection

This section uses the technology requirements from Chapter 6 and the technology descriptions from this chapter to select technologies for the Timecard system's control and entity classes. It also considers the cost of adopting the technology.

One choice is a custom implementation based on RMI and JDBC. The other choice is an EJB implementation.

Let's review the Timecard application's technology requirements as developed in Chapter 6 and proceed from there.

Technology Requirements

The relevant areas for control and entity classes are number and type of users and performance and scalability. The results were:

- Number and type of users: General use within an organization
- Performance and scalability: Concurrent updates

Based on these descriptions, we must choose between the custom combination or EJB.

Number and Type of Users

RMI and JDBC certainly make a valid combination for general use within an organization. As the number of users and the data accessed grows, developers will need to cache objects and pool resources, but these are common problems in large-scale development.

Recall that RMI and JDBC do not provide any clustering or load-balancing framework. However, it seems unlikely that any one company's Timecard application will require a cluster of servers to meet demand, so this is not a factor.

EJB is certainly appropriate for general use within an organization. It has the object-caching and resource-pooling capabilities that greatly simplify system development. Conclusion: EJB has a slight advantage.

Performance and Scalability

A combination of RMI and JDBC is appropriate for systems that allow concurrent updates of data. However, in this case, the developers must supply their own architecture for coordinated transaction management on top of the simple control provided by JDBC.

EJB is designed with concurrent updates in mind. Supporting them in this case should not require any great effort or creativity. EJB has the advantage.

Cost of Adoption

This category is more difficult and subjective to assess. First, for most systems, the licensing cost is not financially significant when compared to payroll. Certainly, application servers are expensive. However, reducing the project staff by one person over a year or reducing the schedule by a month or two is worth a lot of money. Such modest reductions in effort are very reasonable when comparing EJB with RMI/JDBC for a challenging project.

Now let us consider the remaining cost of adoption: assembling a team. EJB has one huge advantage over RMI/JDBC in this area. With EJB, you must acquire one or two experts who understand the technology and the application servers. With RMI/JDBC, you must acquire one or two experts who must develop a framework and usage guidelines for persistence, resource pooling, and object caching. Either way, to avoid chaos, you must allow most developers to work within a fairly narrow and well-documented framework. However, with EJB, the framework and guidelines already exist, along with books, seminars, and online tutorials. Even the best in-house solutions cannot reach this level of sophistication. Therefore, EJB reduces the workload on the architect while making all of the developers more productive.

If EJB is technically suitable for an application, it seems wise to use it. While it is difficult to balance salaries against licenses, the advantages of EJB seem fairly clear.

Conclusion

The Timecard system could clearly be implemented with RMI/JDBC or EJB. However, given the slight advantage for EJB in each category, it seems prudent to select EJB.

WARNING Some companies are selecting EJB as an implementation technology even before they establish their requirements. Unfortunately, not all systems are appropriate for EJB, and choosing EJB when the technical requirements do not indicate it may be very risky. For instance, some systems place a high premium on speed, but do not have data integrity issues. Using EJB for such a system may decrease development time but fail to meet the performance requirements.

The Next Step

We selected technologies for the boundary classes in Chapter 7, and for the control and entity classes in this chapter, we are ready to move forward with our understanding of the solution. Next, in architecture, we elaborate and structure our growing understanding of the solution.

Software Architecture

In previous chapters, we discussed techniques for understanding a problem from the users' and developer's perspective. In Chapters 6 ("Describing the System for Technology Selection"), 7 ("Evaluating Candidate Technologies for Boundary Classes"), and 8 ("Evaluating Candidate Technologies for Control and Entity Classes"), we discussed a disciplined approach to technology selection and selected technologies for each group of analysis. Finally, we have the information we need to describe a viable solution to the system problem. The software architecture is exactly that: It is a high-level structural description of the solution for the system.

A software architecture composes groups of classes into a coherent solution, and shows how the pieces are structured with respect to one another. The emphasis is on the structure and relationships, not on the details of each piece. This is similar to a blueprint for a building, which shows the dimensions of the building and indicates the building materials, while omitting details about the interior of the building and the actual construction techniques.

As they work on their specific parts, a software architecture allows developers to understand the entire system as a coherent whole. More people can understand and review the solution before it is implemented, and this helps to minimize confusion and facilitates a more orderly development process. A solid architecture diffuses confusion and creates a clearly defined goal. This has a significant effect on developer morale and productivity. Just as a blueprint helps separate teams of carpenters, electricians, and masons to contribute efficiently to a greater goal, a software architecture helps developers coordinate their efforts around a common and consensual understanding of the solution.

I am continually shocked at how little emphasis is placed on architecture in our industry, especially compared to other industries. No builder would commit to a project without reviewing detailed plans, yet even sophisticated software companies often spend more money on catering than on the software architecture. The result is all too common and all too predictable: Developers flounder about, unsure how their efforts contribute to the whole system. Periodically, the code from different developers and from different teams is merged and tested. At this point, a host of incompatible interfaces and inconsistencies brings the entire process to a halt. After the finger-pointing subsides, the developers resolve their integration issues as quickly as possible and describe the changes as "bug fixes." Not a pretty sight.

Are You Ready?

Before you can create a software architecture for your system, you must have a clear understanding of the problem and a clear understanding of the technologies that will be used.

Clear Understanding of the Problem

You need solid requirements, analysis classes, and sequence diagrams for a representative subset of the use case model. This model of the system forms and documents your understanding of the problem that will be solved. Failing to understand the problem from the users' perspective leads to the dreaded, "That's nice, but..." reaction at the first large-scale demonstration. Failing to understand the problem from the developers' perspective often leads to a brittle architecture that cannot easily meet the functional requirements of the system.

Clear Understanding of the Technology

You need a clear understanding of the technologies, including their strengths, weaknesses, and compatibilities. This information is invaluable as you organize the solution. In some cases, technologies may not be directly compatible. For example, you may create an additional piece of the system solely to adapt a commercially available class library for use in your system. In other cases, the technology may not support a desired relationship. Time spent upfront understanding the technologies prevents a wide array of difficulties, and greatly lowers your risk of spectacular failure.

You should also consider the difficulties in adopting a technology when dividing a system into parts. After all, actual humans, who may not know all of the technologies involved, must implement each part. You must ensure that each part is sufficiently limited in the technology it uses, so that a reasonably small group of your organization's developers can master the required technologies.

TIP Never forget the developers. At first, it seems that architecture is all about technology and object-oriented theory. Certainly these factors are important, but an elegant and technologically impressive solution may still fail if your organization is not prepared to implement it. As a professional, with obligations to customers and to your peers, it is better to succeed quietly than to fail spectacularly.

Goals for Software Architecture

A good software architecture is also the result of an endless series of compromises and trade-offs. Moving closer to one goal may inadvertently move the architecture away from another goal. For example, increasing the scalability of a system usually makes the system more complex and more difficult to maintain. Using a new technology may reduce technical risk, but increase schedule risk as developers scramble to adopt the technology. In short, perfect architectures are sought, but are never found.

TIP Architecture, like politics, is the art of the possible.

Most software architectures have some or all of the following goals, either implicitly or explicitly, but it is better to spell out the goals explicitly, so that they can be prioritized and monitored. This does not need to be an elaborate process; it can even be a simple list for internal use.

We will refer back to these goals as we discuss various techniques for creating a high-quality software architecture.

Extensibility

Enterprise systems are expected to provide value over many years. Over time, a successful system evolves to meet the changing needs of the customer. Completely new functionality may be added, or existing functionality may change radically. A good system architecture must easily assimilate small changes, gracefully adapt to large changes, and survive radical changes. In order to produce an architecture that handles change well, the architect must have a solid vision about what can change and what is truly fixed.

Maintainability

Over a decade, a large enterprise system may be developed and maintained by 50 or even 100 different people. The original developers often leave the project to create the next big thing, perhaps with an entirely different organization. In those 10 years, even stalwart maintenance developers are promoted or retire. Therefore, bug fixes and requirements may have to be made with little or no help from the original system architect and developers. This means that the system architecture must be accessible to an entirely new group of developers. Simplicity and clarity may need to be balanced against extensibility or performance goals.

Reliability

Many systems have nonfunctional requirements that specify the reliability of the system. These requirements may limit system downtime or prohibit any downtime. Reliability certainly constrains shape as well as the technology selection and architecture for the system.

Scalability

Many systems have goals for the number of concurrent users and the amount of data that the system will contain. These scalability goals must be considered when developing the system architecture. Otherwise, the system may meet the functional requirements but fail to scale as the business it serves grows. This often leads to a series of desperate attempts to improve performance, followed by unchecked finger-pointing, and finally to a complete redesign of the system.

With these goals in mind, we can consider some theory and pragmatic techniques that will help you develop strong software architectures.

UML and Architecture

Architecture is all about managing complexity by dividing the solution into small pieces, then combining the small pieces into larger, more coherent structures. Fortunately, there are several object-oriented principles that assist us in this endeavor. As always, UML is used to visualize and communicate our decisions.

The following concepts are especially helpful.

- Packages
- Package dependency diagrams
- Subsystems
- Layers

The following sections examine each concept in detail, and provide the applicable UML notation.

Packages

In UML, a group of classes is known as a *package*. A package may also contain other packages, so that developers can construct arbitrarily complex groupings and sub-groupings.

Packages are valuable for several reasons. First, when classes are organized in logical groups, it is far easier to find classes and understand the system. Packages serve the same purpose as folders in an email system or directories in a file system; they help keep us sane.

There are two distinct approaches to grouping classes. Classes can be grouped according to similar responsibilities, even if they do not collaborate. Classes can be grouped because they collaborate to fulfill a larger responsibility, even if each of the classes has very different individual responsibilities.

Similar Responsibilities

It makes sense to group classes that have the same responsibility, but vary in their implementation. The classes form a group of alternatives, not a group of collaborators. For example, there are several implementations of the Border interface in Java's javax.swing.border package. Each implementation has a different way of drawing a border around a component. Figure 9.1 shows several of the alternative border classes and the interface that they all realize. Packaging the different borders together make sit easy for developers to find the right alternative for their needs.

In this case, all of the classes realize the same interface. While this is desirable in many cases, it is far from essential. A package may hold classes that have very similar responsibilities, but do not realize the same interface.

Collaborations

Another package may group more diverse classes because the classes collaborate to fulfill a significant responsibility. For example, all of the classes for compressing and

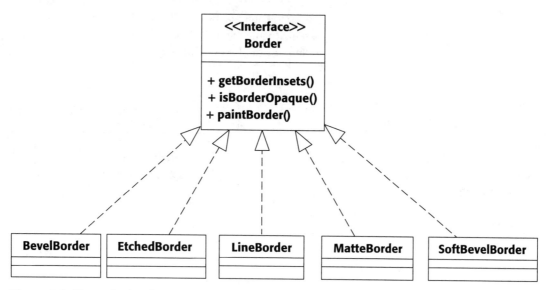

Figure 9.1 Alternative borders.

uncompressing data are held in the java.util.zip package. The classes have quite different responsibilities. The ZipOutputStream writes compressed data to an arbitrary output stream. It allows client objects to start a new entry, write data, and close the entry when they are done writing. This process may be repeated for any number of entries. A ZipInputStream object reads compressed data from an arbitrary input stream and uncompresses it, one entry at a time. A ZipFile uses a ZipInputStream to provide convenient functionality for reading compressed data from a file. Figure 9.2 shows the classes for compressing and uncompressing data using the Zip format. Each class has a separate responsibility, and collaborates with the others to meet a larger goal.

Notice that changes to the implementation of one class in this package may ripple to the other classes in the package. For example, any change to the compression logic in the ZipOutputStream causes a corresponding change in the uncompression logic in the ZipInputStream. However, no class outside of this package should need to depend on the implementation of any of these classes. Together, these classes fully encapsulate compression and uncompression within the package.

Packages are also a useful unit of work that can be designated to a small team. If a team takes responsibility for a package, that package must be sized appropriately, and all of the implementation technology must fall within the team's expertise. In order to divide up the effort in this way, each package must be fairly independent, so that it can be developed and tested separately.

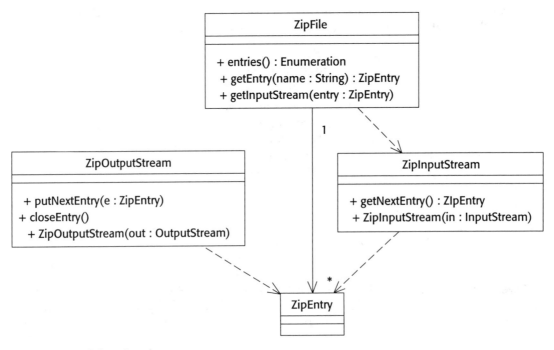

Figure 9.2 Collaborating classes.

Package Dependency

Package dependencies show how changes to classes can ripple throughout the system. A dashed dependency arrow from package A to package B indicates that there is at least one class in package A that uses at least one class in package B. This means that some changes to the classes in package B will ripple to affect the classes in package A. Other changes to package B may not affect package A at all. The absence of a dependency arrow from package B to package A would indicate that the classes in package A may change as much as you wish, with no effect on the classes in package B. Figure 9.3 shows package A depending on package B

Package dependencies may be direct, as in Figure 9.3, or indirect. If package A depends on package B, and package B depends on package C, then it is possible for a change to a class in package C to require a change to a class in package B, which requires a change to a class in package A. Package A indirectly depends on package C. This has tremendous implications when attempting to reuse a package in a new system. Trying to extract the desired package may require radical surgery, as each of its dependencies must be extracted, along with each of the dependency's dependencies. With this in mind, examining the package dependencies helps developers gauge the difficulty of reusing a package or a class from a package.

Package dependencies are often shown in high-level views, called *package dependency diagrams*, which ignore the individual classes and show all of the packages and their dependencies. These diagrams allow developers to measure the complexity of a system in a high-level view and help them evaluate the effects of a proposed change to the system.

TIP A package dependency diagram is like a road map. It only helps you if it is up to date.

Avoiding Mutual Dependency

We refer to packages that depend on one another, either directly or indirectly, as *mutually dependent*. Figure 9.4 shows the UserInterface package and the BusinessObjects packages depending directly on one another. Figure 9.5 shows the UserInterface package depending directly on the SessionManagement package, which depends on the BusinessObjects package, which completes the cycle by depending on the UserInterface package.

Figure 9.3 Package A depends on package B.

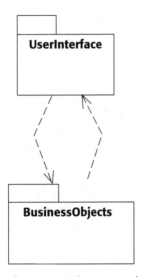

Figure 9.4 Direct mutual dependency.

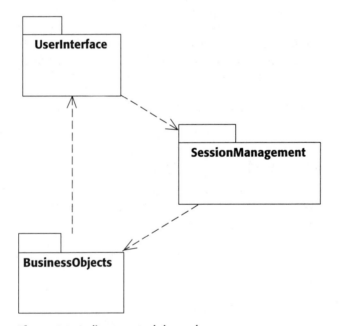

Figure 9.5 Indirect mutual dependency.

Mutual dependencies are definitely worth avoiding. Their presence dramatically decreases your ability to predict the effects of changes to the system, as a change in one package can ripple throughout the dependency cycle.

Mutual dependencies also reduce the architect's ability to limit and control the complexity of the system. Packages tend to intertwine over time, as the challenges and pressures of detailed design and code lead developers to discover ways in which the packages can cooperate to meet the needs of the system. A mutual dependency between packages gives free rein to this tendency. If the packages are already dependent on one another, it is difficult to fight the urge to add one more dependency. This process gradually increases complexity while decreasing extensibility and reusability.

TIP When creating package dependency diagrams, organize the packages so that the dependency arrows all point horizontally, down, or diagonally down. Following this convention makes it very easy to spot dependency cycles, as they will require an upward arrow.

Once you accept that mutual dependency is dangerous, you must break the cycle by reorganizing the classes within the packages or splitting some classes into new packages. The example in Figure 9.5 is a mutual dependency because the BusinessObjects package depends on the UserInterface package. This may seem necessary for some applications, as the user interface may demand notification whenever the business objects change. However, we can use the event model from JavaBeans to achieve this effect while removing the mutual dependency cycle. The user interface classes can implement the PropertyChangeListener interface as found in java.beans. The user interface objects can then be registered as listeners on the business objects. This allows business objects to notify registered listeners of changes without knowing their specific class. Figure 9.6 shows the new package dependency diagram without the mutual dependency cycle.

Subsystems

A *subsystem* is a package that completely encapsulates its implementation. Client objects access the subsystem's functionality through a narrowly defined interface. As long as the interface does not change, the dependent classes do not need to change.

For example, a project may need a logging subsystem. In UML, the subsystem is shown as a stereotyped package, and the subsystem directly realizes the interface. Of course, we know that there must be some implementation class hidden inside of the subsystem and that the running system needs an instance of the implementation class. We need to expose this instance to the objects that need it, without having them depend on its constructor or its specific type.

Fortunately, the Singleton design pattern [Gamma 1995] is a perfect match for this problem. We introduce a new class, LoggerSingleton, which has a public static method, called getLogger, that returns an ILogger reference. The LoggerSingleton instantiates the LoggerImplementation once, and passes that single instance to each caller.

Figure 9.7 shows the LoggingSubsystem and the ILogger interface in a class diagram. A more concise view of the same scenario is shown in 9.8.

To summarize, a subsystem hides functionality that can change—the implementation—behind something that will not change—the interface. Subsystems facilitate efficient development, support system configuration, and allow the system to evolve as requirements change.

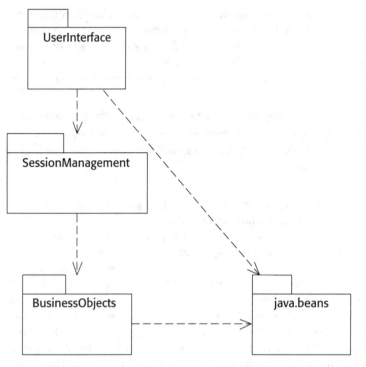

Figure 9.6 Breaking the dependency cycle.

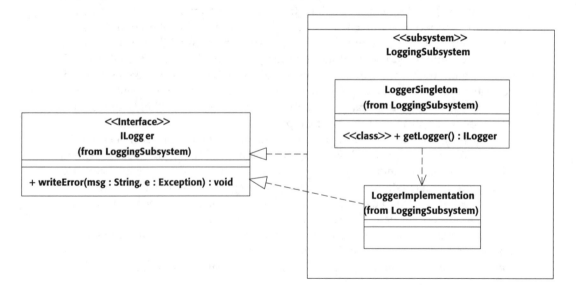

Figure 9.7 A logging subsystem.

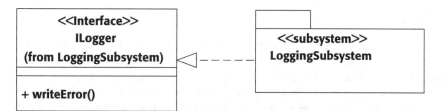

Figure 9.8 A logging subsystem with no details shown.

Efficient Development

Subsystems with well-established and consensual interfaces allow developers to work in parallel. The developers whose code depends on the subsystem do not actually need a fully functional version of the subsystem. All they need is a stub or trivial implementation of the subsystem and confidence that their code will integrate seamlessly with the real subsystem. This enables one set of developers to work on the subsystem without impeding the progress of the other developers.

To continue our logging subsystem example, the initial version of the subsystem simply writes the formatted messages to standard out. A subsequent version will write messages to a recycled error log file.

Variability and Configuration

Multiple subsystems may implement the same interface in very different ways. Once an implementation is selected, the rest of the system ignores the choice. This allows a development team to easily configure and deploy variations of a system.

For example, some clients for a system may want to log to an error file while others want to log to a database. One approach is to use a configuration file to tell the LoggerSingleton which implementation class to instantiate. This provides a lot of flexibility without breaking any existing code.

Extensibility

A subsystem's implementation is hidden. As long as the interface does not change, the implementation of the subsystem can freely evolve to meet new or expanding requirements.

For example, a requirement to add a timestamp to the formatted errors produced by our logging subsystem can be accommodated by changing the implementation class. There is no need to change the interface or alter the code that calls the logger's writeError method.

Guidelines for Software Architecture

As you develop a software architecture, you must keep some guiding principles in mind. The first, cohesion, helps you organize parts of the system into logical groups. The second, coupling, helps you keep groups independent and understandable.

Cohesion

Cohesion describes how members of the same group are related to one another. Strong cohesion indicates that the members of the group belong together. Weak cohesion indicates that the grouping is arbitrary or even illogical.

Cohesion can be applied to a group of methods inside of a class, a group of classes inside a package, and a group of packages. Given the members of the group, an outsider should be able to deduce the overall responsibility of a cohesive group. For instance, what is the responsibility of a class that has these methods: makeEggs, makeToast, makeHashBrowns, and makeJuice? The responsibility, make breakfast, is fairly clear, so these methods have strong cohesion within a class called Cook.

A similar level of cohesion should be demanded of classes within a package and packages in a layer. Groups with weak cohesion are hard to understand and to remember. They make a system more difficult to maintain and to extend.

Coupling

Coupling describes the level of dependence between different groups. Tight coupling indicates that the groups are very interdependent and that changes to one group may require a complex ripple of changes to the other groups. Loose coupling indicates that the groups are relatively independent. Loose coupling invariably makes the groups and their relationships easier to understand, maintain, and extend.

Coupling can be determined for a group of methods inside of a class, a group of classes inside a package, and a group of packages. However, the amount of permissible coupling varies greatly between the different types of groups. For instance, the methods in a class may be tightly coupled, as they interact with the same instance variables and frequently call one another. At the next level up, classes within a package should be less interdependent. They should not depend at all on one another's implementation, and they should depend on a fairly narrowly defined set of methods. The coupling between packages should be even looser. Whenever possible, they should depend on one another through interfaces rather than implementation.

Creating a Software Architecture

Creating a solid architecture requires a dedicated effort within the project. Choosing an architect and committing to a reasonably disciplined process for creating an architecture pays immense dividends throughout the life of the project.

The Architect

The software architect works with other senior developers to determine the architecture of the system, including technology selection and subsystem design. Architectural mechanisms, such as error-handling and caching strategies, must be defined before developers need them. Subsequent responsibilities include evaluating detailed designs for conformance with the architecture, revisiting the architecture, and encouraging developers to use good OO and software engineering practices. These practices include use of the UML, solid OO design principles, the educated use of design patterns, iterative development, and design and code reviews.

A software architect needs extensive experience developing object-oriented systems and mentoring technical people. Language and technology expertise are also required. It is impossible to select technology and decompose a solution into the right pieces without getting your hands dirtied in the details.

Strong communication and people skills are equally important. An architect must be able to hold and defend strong opinions, or the project will lack technical vision. On the other hand, architects must build consensus and mentor developers. They are obligated to push back against excessive and destructive schedule pressure, yet they must work closely with project mangers to manage risks and ensure the project's timely success.

Architecture also requires an odd mix of personality characteristics. To be successful in the short term, architects design a high-level solution with incomplete information while under schedule pressure. This requires them to be decisive, knowledgeable, and persuasive. To be successful over the life of the project, they must accept and improve their inevitably flawed ideas. They must be humble enough to admit their own failings in full view. They must also work with project management and highly technical people to resolve issues that range from risk mitigation and iteration planning to mechanisms and subsystem interfaces.

In my experience, this responsibility cannot be distributed among multiple architects for a system. Certainly, a good architect gathers input from many participants, and builds consensus among the senior technical people. However, the final responsibility cannot be shared. Cohesive and coherent solutions are not made by committee. Once the overall solution has been developed, individual parts can be delegated to designers, but there must be one coherent vision and one accountable person.

A Process

Creating a solid architecture involves several steps:

1. Set goals.
2. Group classes.
3. Show technologies.
4. Extract subsystems.
5. Evaluate against guidelines and goals.

The following sections discuss each step in detail.

Set Goals

Earlier in this chapter, we discussed goals for extensibility, maintainability, reliability, and scalability. Your system may have some of these, and perhaps other, goals. In any case, you must establish the goals and have some idea of their relative importance. Remember, architecture requires you to make a series of decisions based on incomplete information, and almost every decision has some unintended side effect.

Setting clear priorities is also a nice counterpoint to risk management. Risk management tracks all of the outcomes that you want to avoid. Goals are all of the outcomes that you want to foster. Either way, establishing priorities does not need to be an exhaustive process. Most projects need only a page or two of very informal text to get a huge benefit. Just discussing goals or risks on a regular basis is a healthy exercise, as it encourages people to think about the project as a whole.

Group Classes

Classes can be grouped into packages to keep collaborators together or to keep similar classes together. This choice is not easy. You must consider coupling and cohesion as well as the potential for variability and reuse. In general, classes that may be reused in different situations should be organized together by responsibility. Grouping them by responsibility rather than by collaboration helps to keep them independent of any one type of use. Classes that are dedicated to a single collaboration must be packaged with the other classes that they support.

I tend to group different types of analysis classes into layers by responsibility. For example, more than one control class can use each entity classes, so the entity classes belong in a layer. The same is true for the control classes, as each control class can interact with different versions of the same boundary class.

Within each layer, the classes often divide into packages. For example, the entity layer may contain several packages or even subsystems with clearly defined responsibilities. The control layer may be divided into groups of control classes that interact as part of a larger workflow for a particular type of user.

The layers and the packages within each layer must be shown in one or more package dependency diagrams.

Show Technologies

We selected technologies in Chapters 7 and 8, so this step is fairly mechanical. Each use of a technology must be added to the package dependency diagram(s) that shows the appropriate package.

Extract Subsystems

Remember that subsystems facilitate efficient development, support system configuration, and allow parts of the system to evolve independently as requirements change. Candidate subsystems can be found by looking for packages that have a clearly defined interface and loose coupling with the rest of the system. Within the candidates, look for packages that can be developed independently and/or that encapsulate volatile requirements.

Evaluate against Guidelines and Goals

You must periodically evaluate the architecture against the goals and against the guideline of high cohesion and loose coupling. UML and modeling tools allow you to review and revise a model with little waste. UML also allows you to efficiently communicate the structure of the system with other developers. Given these advantages, there is no reason not to review, collaborate, and revise the architecture.

> **TIP** You must accept the simple fact that, initially, all architectures are flawed. Software systems are horribly complex, and we have a finite capacity to manage complexity. You will not get it right the first time. You can fix it in a high-level tool or you can fix it in code.

Sample Architecture for the Timecard System

Now that we have discussed the theory and process for creating a software architecture, let's create the architecture for the example Timecard system. We'll walk through each of the steps:

1. Set goals.
2. Group classes.
3. Show technologies.
4. Extract subsystems.
5. Evaluate against guidelines and goals.

Set Goals

The first step is to set goals for the system. In some cases, a goal is given weight by an explicit requirement. For example, reliability and scalability requirements are often plainly stated in the supplementary requirements. Developers usually determine maintainability and extensibility goals. This makes sense, as the developers know how the system will be developed and can estimate the stability of the requirements.

Extensibility. While all systems change, the Timecard application seems fairly well focused. It gathers timecard data from the user. It does not analyze that data, bill clients, or calculate the pay for each employee. If I ever see such a well-defined system outside of a book, I may just dance a little jig. Caveats aside, we conclude that extensibility is not a huge priority.

Maintainability. The Timecard system must be easy to comprehend and to maintain. The company has separate teams for maintenance and for new projects, so the system will be transitioned to a new group.

Reliability. As part of the infrastructure of a company, the Timecard system must be reliable. However, it is not responsible for credit card processing or life support. Scheduled downtime is perfectly acceptable. Unanticipated downtime is not.

Scalability. The Timecard system must scale to accommodate more data and more users, as the company plans to grow rapidly.

Explicitly defining these goals and their relative importance helps shape subsequent architectural and design decisions. In this case, it is useful to know that we can sacrifice some extensibility to increase scalability, if the opportunity arises.

Group and Evaluate Classes

The next step is to group our classes into candidate packages and evaluate their cohesion. To do this, we'll identify some groups of classes from the analysis model and examine their responsibilities. We want each group of classes to be closely related, so that the resulting package has a clear and well-defined purpose.

Grouping Classes

In Chapter 5, "Analysis Model for the Timecard Application," we were able to identify five distinct groups of classes:

- Entity classes
- User interface classes
- Control classes
- System interface classes
- Locator classes

We will consider these groups as candidate packages and evaluate them for strong cohesion. If the packages exhibit strong cohesion, we will use the class diagrams created in analysis to evaluate them for loose coupling. In some cases, this simplistic layering approach will fail because the collaborations between classes of different types are stronger than the collaborations between classes of the same type. However, it is by far the easiest approach, and it is often sufficient.

Let's consider each candidate package separately.

Entity classes. This is our first group of classes, which were identified in Figure 5.2. Most of the classes describe a tightly related set of business concepts that are core to our understanding of a timecard. The only class that does not fit is ExportRequest, which has nothing to do with timecards in general. We decide to exclude ExportRequest from the package and look for a better fit.

We also need a name for this group of packages, as entity classes is simply too vague. Since all of the classes are part of our model of a timecard, the package name becomes TimecardDomain. Figure 9.9 shows the classes for the package.

User interface classes. This is our second set of classes, shown in Figure 5.3. These classes all encapsulate the logic needed to present data and interact with the user for time entry. In Chapter 7, we decided to use one user interface technology, servlets, for all user interface classes. Based on this decision, there is no reason to keep separate classes for the AdministrativeLoginUI and the RecordTimeAdministrativeUI.

The name for this package should reflect the application and the technology, so it becomes TimecardUI. Figure 9.10 shows the classes for the package.

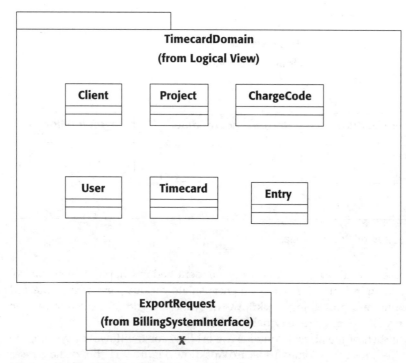

Figure 9.9 The TimecardDomain package.

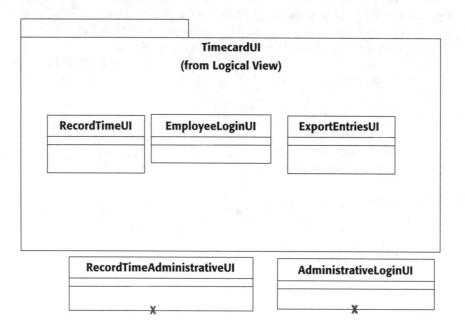

Figure 9.10 The TimecardUI package.

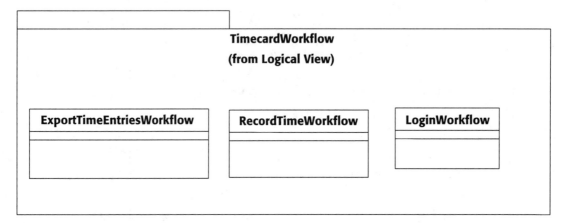

Figure 9.11 The TimecardWorkflow package.

Control classes. The third group of classes we identified in Chapter 5 were control classes, shown in Figure 5.4. These all encapsulate various parts of the timecard entry or timecard processing workflow. All of these workflows seem to use the same entity classes and are reasonably cohesive.

Since each of the classes contains a workflow for the timecard system, the name of the package becomes TimecardWorkflow. Figure 9.11 shows the classes for the package.

Billing system interface. The BillingSystemInterface class was the fourth group of classes, shown in Figure 5.3. This also seems like a good home for the Export-Request class, which was excluded from the TimecardDomain package. The package encapsulates the logic for generating the export data and also contains the export request. This seems to be reasonably strong cohesion.

Since the class is a system interface to the billing system, the package become the BillingSystemInterface. Figure 9.12 shows the classes for the package.

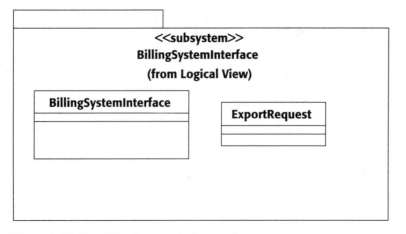

Figure 9.12 The BillingSystemInterface package.

Locator classes. Because we are using EJB to implement our entity classes, we will not need separate locator classes. The functionality is provided by the Home interface for each entity bean.

As described, each package has a clear purpose and strong cohesion between its classes. Next we need to see if the packages are tightly or loosely coupled.

Describe Coupling between Packages

In the next step, we use a package dependency diagram to evaluate the coupling between packages. Recall that package A depends on package B if there is a class in A that has a relationship with a class in B.

Fortunately, we collected a lot of information about the dependencies between classes during analysis. Figures 5.14 to 5.16 showed the dependencies between classes for each use case. We must merge these three diagrams into one class diagram, then summarize that diagram in a package dependency diagram.

Figures 9.13 to 9.15 show the diagrams exactly as they appeared in Chapter 5.

From these class diagrams, we can produce a single class diagram that shows all of the dependencies between all of the classes. This is a highly mechanical process, in

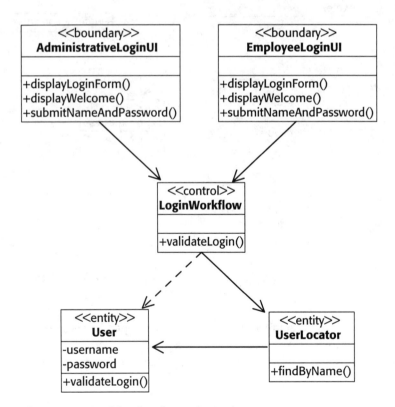

Figure 9.13 Participating classes for Login.

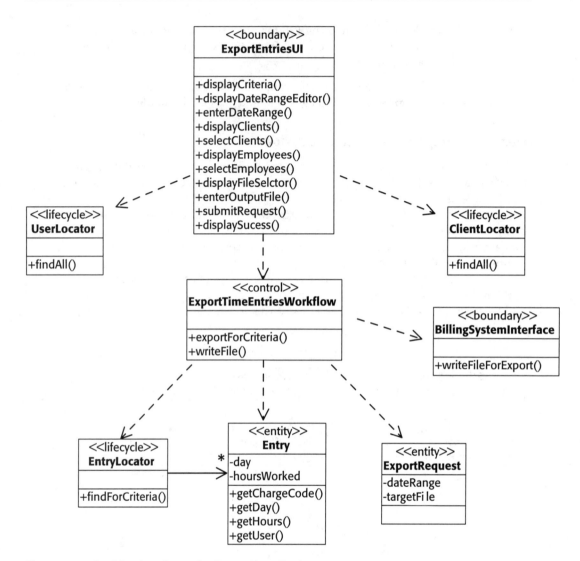

Figure 9.14 Participating classes for Export Time Entries.

which each relationship in each of the participating classes diagrams is added to a single diagram.

> **TIP** In real life, you need automated tool support to find dependencies. You just can't spend several days finding each relationship in a large model. Fortunately, this is exactly the sort of mindless drudgery that these tools were created to do.

Figure 9.16 shows the classes and their dependencies. Along the way, we notice that the ExportEntriesUI has direct dependencies on classes from the TimecardDomain

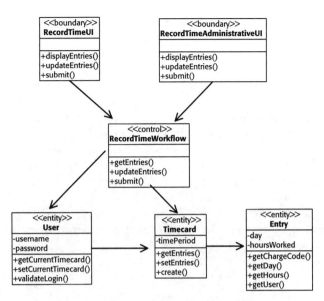

Figure 9.15 Participating classes for Record Time.

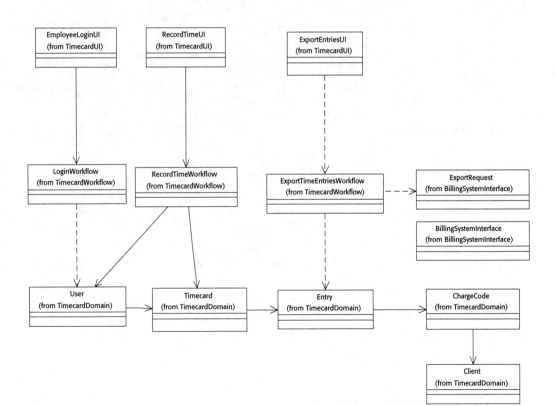

Figure 9.16 Classes and relationships.

package. This seems odd, as all of the other user interface classes depend on classes from the TimecardWorkflow package, which in turn depends on the TimecardDomain package. Our knowledge of EJB indicates that direct relationships from user interfaces to entity beans are not desirable, and we would like to keep the relationships consistent. This leads us to force the ExportEntriesUI to work through the classes in the TimecardWorkflow package.

The next step is to produce a package dependency diagram from the class relationships. Each relationship from a class to another class in a different package leads to a package dependency. For example, the relationship from RecordTimeUI (in the TimecardUI package) to the RecordTimeWorkflow (in the TimecardWorkflow package) leads to a dependency from the TimecardUI package to the TimecardWorkflow package. Again, this is a highly mechanical process, best left to a tool.

The package dependencies seem fairly reasonable. There are no circular dependencies. Also, the packages that we might expect to be reusable, such as TimecardDomain and BillingSystemInterface do not have any dependencies.

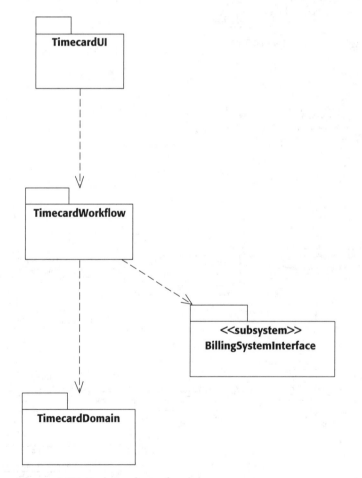

Figure 9.17 Package dependencies.

There is strong cohesion between the classes in each package, and loose coupling between the packages. We have a preliminary structure for our system.

Show Technologies

Fortunately, all of the technology selections for our Timecard system were made in Chapters 7 and 8. Recall that the entity and control classes will use Enterprise Java-Beans, while the user interface classes will become servlets. Also, the BillingSystem-Interface class will use XML. All we have to do is add a package for each technology to the package dependency diagram. Use of a technology is shown by drawing a dependency line from the original package to the technology package that it uses. For example, the TimecardUI package depends on the Servlets package. Figure 9.18 shows the updated diagram.

Extract Subsystems

The next step is to identify the candidate subsystems. These can be found by looking for packages that have a clearly defined interface and loose coupling with the rest of the system. Within the candidates, look for packages that can be developed independently and/or that encapsulate volatile requirements.

The most likely candidate subsystem is the BillingSystemInterface, which offers a very simple service to the rest of the system and is completely encapsulated. Also, since the billing system is an independent system, there is always a chance that the interface may change.

We decide to make the BillingSystemInterface into a Java interface, and make the ExportTimeEntriesWorkflow objects have a relationship through the interface. At this point in the process, this sort of decision is all but free. It takes longer to make the decision than to perform the changes in a UML modeling tool. How long would it take in code?

Figure 9.19 shows the BillingSystemInterface as a subsystem that realizes the IBillingSystemInterface interface. Notice that the TimecardWorkflow depends on the interface, not the subsystem directly.

Evaluate against Guidelines and Goals

Now that we have a reasonable draft architecture, we must evaluate it against our guidelines and our goals.

Recall that the goals for the Timecard system emphasized maintainability, reliability, and scalability. Extensibility was less significant, as the system has a very stable vision.

Maintainability and Extensibility

Each package has a very well-defined set of responsibilities, and the packages are well encapsulated. These factors are quite encouraging when planning for an easy-to-understand and easy-to-maintain system. Also, the system is based on reasonably

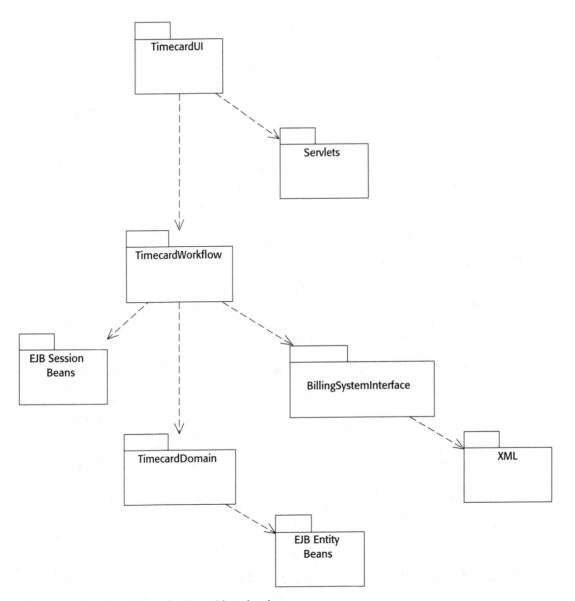

Figure 9.18 Package dependencies with technology.

standard technology, so the future developers will have a wealth of resources outside of the system documentation.

There is one concern. The user interface classes will be implemented as servlets, and the technology description for servlets warns us about producing HTML in a haphazard fashion (see Chapter 7). The following excerpt from the architect's role in servlet development summarizes the concern:

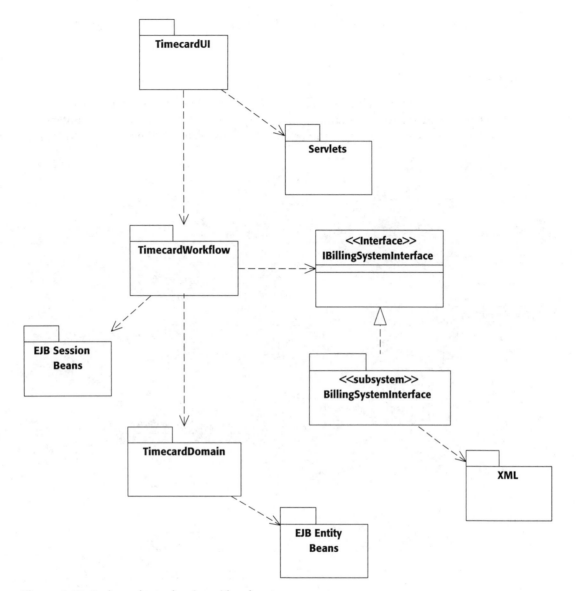

Figure 9.19 Package dependencies with subsystem.

Servlet-based user interfaces can degenerate into a series of unconnected works of art, with no two following the same format or producing HTML in the same way. An architect can reduce this effect by establishing reusable HTML production classes to produce everything from tables and trees to frames and the enclosing page. This allows developers to easily change the look of the entire application by altering the reusable HTML production classes. The alternative requires each servlet to be laboriously edited, perhaps for something as trivial as the background color or the space between buttons.

We decide to follow this advice, and add an HTMLProduction package to the architecture.

Reliability and Scalability

Most of the system's reliability and scalability concerns can be isolated to the TimecardDomain and TimecardWorkflow packages, which will be implemented as Enterprise JavaBeans. Picking the right server and allocating plenty of time for design and

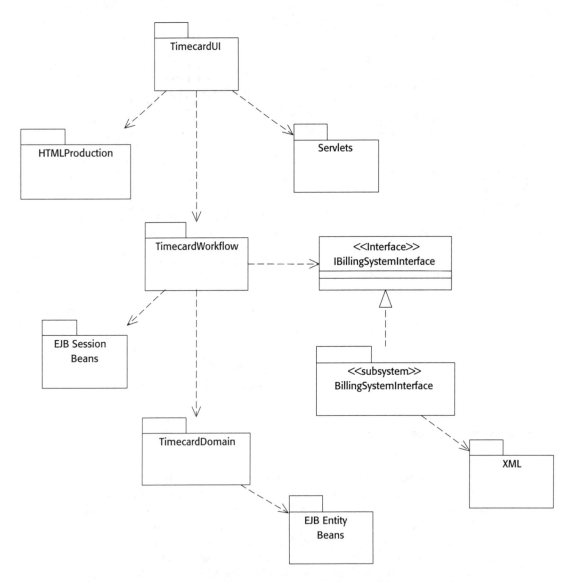

Figure 9.20 Package dependency diagram with HTMLProduction package.

prototyping with a real application server should address these concerns. These are tactical efforts within the design process; the architectural choice of EJB for these components is very sound.

The updated package dependency diagram in Figure 9.20 shows the TimecardUI package using the TimecardWorkflow package as well as the HTMLProduction package.

The Next Step

This chapter identified architectural goals, determined the structure of the system, and defined the relationships between the packages. These elements provide context and a solid foundation as we fill in the details of the solution during design. As we make decisions during design, we can evaluate them against the package dependency relationships that we have established.

Introduction to Design

Design builds on the understanding of the problem as developed during requirements gathering and analysis. It is an attempt to fully understand the solution as constrained by the structure developed during architecture. The goal of design is to make the next step, implementation, as simple and efficient as possible. It is your last chance to make changes quickly and efficiently in a tool and a notation, rather than in code and other deliverables.

What Is Design?

An object-oriented design is a detailed description of the objects that work together to fulfill the system's requirements. Design describes the solution, in great detail. It specifies instance variables, method parameters, return types, and technology details.

Design uses the same diagrams as analysis, and for the same purposes. Sequence diagrams show interactions between objects. Class diagrams show the structure, behavior, and relationships that objects of particular types have in common. With the added level of detail, the diagrams in design are much larger and more intricate.

Are You Ready?

Good designs are built on a solid foundation, including a clear system vision, a solid use case model, a fairly complete analysis model, careful and appropriate technology selection, and a resilient architecture.

Premature design risks project failure in several ways. If the system vision or use case model is incomplete or inaccurate, then even a brilliant design may solve the wrong problem. Omissions and inaccuracies in the analysis model lead to an incomplete architecture and poor technology selections, which in turn lead to a flawed design. If the analysis model is incomplete or inconsistent, the design model will probably perpetuate these omissions or errors.

Each step in the development process feeds the next, so that a good design is not possible unless the preceding steps are complete and of high quality.

The Need for Design

Omitting or neglecting design is prohibitively expensive and insanely risky. Without a good design, developer productivity and morale suffer. Inconsistent code and incompatible modules are a certainty. Discovery of deficiencies in the architecture is delayed because there is no way to see the larger picture. Accurate scheduling is impossible, since the problems are not well understood before coding begins. Flawed ideas and incompatible implementations that are not caught until integration or system test are incredibly expensive to fix.

My grandfather, who built residential and commercial buildings back in the days when they still laid bricks and cut lumber to fit, used to say, "Measure twice, cut once." This captures the essence of design for me. You are about to write code, which tends to resist change. A little extra effort in design often prevents painful rework later.

On the other hand, it is far cheaper and less time-consuming to make decisions in design than in code. Also, a clear design model enables more developers to understand and review more of the system, which makes it possible for them to understand their own responsibilities and contribute to the overall success of the project through design discussions and reviews. Moreover, project managers and senior developers can estimate effort more accurately if their estimates are based on a clear and concrete design.

Productivity and Morale

Implementing high-quality systems is a complicated process. New technology, complex requirements, and extreme schedule pressure create challenging and oftentimes frustrating puzzles for developers. Complex code must be developed, tested, and integrated with other developer's equally complex code. Anyone who has tried it knows that design and implementation are by turns daunting, exhilarating, frustrating, and at times addictive.

Momentum is an important key to thriving in this environment. Small successes lead to more successes and help the entire team build confidence and credibility. On the other hand, failure and wasted efforts destroy momentum. In order to gain and maintain momentum, developers must have a realistic and complete architecture and design for the system. This facilitates realistic expectations, partitions the project into reasonable and achievable parts, and avoids incompatibilities between different developers' modules.

Design helps developers succeed, and incremental success motivates developers more than any other stimulus. Okay, high salaries help, but a chance to produce high-quality work in a sane effort is a major motivator for most of us.

A Malleable Medium

UML in a modern tool can be shaped and reshaped very easily. It is a very malleable medium. Code is not so easy to work with. Code is dispersed over hundreds of files, with a very low level of detail obscuring the larger patterns. A UML model in a modern design tool is infinitely easier to assimilate, change, and extend.

Remember, the step after design is implementation. Mistakes that are not caught before implementation are often very expensive to fix. Fixing incompatible interfaces can take weeks, with developers alternating between coding, testing, and blaming. A poor architecture that survives into implementation often leads to months of rework or even to project failure.

Even radical surgery on a fairly large UML model can be completed in a hundred person-hours. Relationships between classes can be changed with a click of a mouse. Responsibilities easily migrate from class to class. A class becomes an interface with several concrete alternative implementations. Classes and packages split or merge with relative ease.

Moreover, a developer who knows UML can review the design for a large subsystem in a short day. Compare this to the weeks consumed developing a serious understanding of the code for a large subsystem. Consistent and thorough review of design artifacts is far more economically feasible than a similar review of code.

Scheduling and Delegation

A sound design makes estimation, scheduling, and delegation possible. Given a thorough design, a developer estimates the effort required for each class. The sum of these estimates is invariably more accurate than a rough guess based on the requirements. This gives the project manager something solid to work with. A solid design also allows developers to develop a few classes or a package and then integrate their code with the rest of the project. Delegation without a design is far less efficient, and generally requires a significant effort during integration.

Design Patterns

A *design pattern* is a well-defined, well-documented, and time-tested solution to a common problem in software design. Each pattern has a name, a problem description, a solution, a discussion of the consequences, a sample implementation, and a list of related patterns [Gamma 1995].

Problem description. Describes the specific problem that the pattern is intended to solve. This allows developers to quickly search through a catalog of patterns and extract the one or two that seem appropriate for more careful consideration.

Solution. Describes the objects and their interactions in a fairly abstract way, so that the pattern can be applied to a variety of designs. In most cases, a more concrete example is used to clarify and explain this generic solution.

Consequences. Discuss the positive and negative impact of using the pattern to achieve common design goals. This helps developers to determine which candidate pattern is best for their situation, and may lead them to modify the pattern when applying it to their own design.

Sample implementation. Shows how the solution can be implemented in at least one object-oriented language. This makes the solution more concrete for developers, and provides a solid proof of concept for cynical practitioners.

Related patterns section. Shows how other patterns can support or extend the pattern in question. In many cases, patterns can be combined to form very resilient and elegant designs.

Benefits

Without getting too mushy, I must say that learning and using design patterns radically changed the way I design software, and solidified my grasp of object-oriented theory more than any other experience.

Design patterns help developers design better software in two very significant ways:

- They provide a common language for collaboration and documentation.
- They reinforce object-oriented theory.

Common Language

Learning design patterns takes patience and effort. Each pattern takes time to assimilate, and there are a lot of patterns. However, the effort only adds to the incredible rush you get when you realize that the developer across the table shares a common language and that you just compressed three hours worth of design discussion into 15 incredibly productive minutes. A group of developers who all understand design patterns can communicate in a common language that is both expressive and compressed.

Design patterns help developers communicate their designs quickly and efficiently. Any uncertainty can be resolved by consulting a widely accepted source. This works in design meetings, design documents, and code comments.

WARNING In the same way a well-understood pattern enables you to communicate effectively, a misunderstood design pattern will confuse people just as effectively. You must know the patterns that you use.

Reinforces OO Theory

Object-oriented theory and practices are not intuitive for most people. They require us to think abstractly, analytically, and creatively—all at the same time. In my experience, exposure to good object-oriented design is the best way to refine your own understanding and to improve your own habits. Design patterns apply object-oriented practices to a clearly defined problem. This makes them excellent case studies for object-oriented design. It is interesting to see the consequences of different decisions and to see how the same techniques can be used in radically different ways.

Use

Fortunately for us, many design patterns have been captured in books, articles, and online repositories. An entire community of developers donates an enormous amount of time, effort, and expertise as they revise and extend a collective catalog of design patterns. The best single source for design patterns is the seminal book *Design Patterns: Elements of Reusable Object-Oriented Software*, by Erich Gamma, Richard Helm, Ralph Johnson, and John Vlissides (Addison-Wesley-Longman, 1995). These authors are often referred to as the Gang of Four; thus, their book is often referred to as the GoF book.

Design patterns are best applied to a well-defined problem. Fortunately, analysis and architecture identify lots of problems for us to solve. In many cases, you can apply a series of design patterns to a package or small group of packages. Each pattern helps provide some functionality or helps reach a design goal.

Planning for Design

To be successful, design must be a coherent and unified effort. Unfortunately, design is naturally a divisive process. Design breaks people into small teams or even isolates people by themselves. Each team or person is then immersed in the details of new technologies and the challenges of object-oriented design. Becoming absorbed in the design of his or her piece, to the exclusion of all other interests, is a natural part of the process, as the designer struggles to make sense out of complexity.

Once design begins, each design effort will go its own way for a while. Failure to accept this reality often leads to slow, painful progress, as developers are constantly expected to see the whole picture and ensure that their work fits with everyone else's work. In order to simulate a coherent and unified effort, we establish clear goals for the entire design before giving developers the freedom to work on their separate efforts. The following steps summarize this process:

1. Establish goals for the entire design.
2. Establish design guidelines.
3. Find independent design efforts.

Each of these steps is described in detail in the subsections that follow.

Establish Goals for the Entire Design

Every system contains a million decisions. Many of these decisions are more compromise than brilliant discovery of perfect truth. This is as true for design as it is for requirements and architecture. Establishing design goals before making decisions helps maintain the consistency of the system, and makes each decision easier.

One person's well-focused system is another person's overly restricted disappointment. An architecture or technology selection may trade performance for functionality and extensibility. Or it may partition subsystems to accommodate the development team's available skill set or to maximize the reuse potential of a subsystem. Design decisions often balance clarity, performance, reliability, extensibility, and reuse potential. We will refer back to these common goals as we discuss various techniques for creating a high-quality software design.

Clarity

Clarity and understandability is a key goal for every design. Developers cannot review or implement something that they cannot understand. Faced with an unclear design, most developers either attempt to follow the design and develop confusing code or simply ignore the design entirely. Clear and unambiguous designs often lead to code that is easy to maintain and to extend.

Clarity is increased by keeping strong cohesion for methods in classes and for classes in packages. Loose coupling makes the interfaces between packages tight and easy to understand. Encapsulation improves readability by limiting what you need to know to use a class.

Performance and Reliability

Many systems have demanding performance and reliability requirements. In most cases, performance and reliability goals can be reached by picking the right technology, then designing to the technology's strengths. Developers must understand how the technology exchanges data between different tiers and how the technology ensures data integrity. Establishing performance and reliability goals early in the design process encourages developers to consider these issues, rather than procrastinating and hoping for the best.

Extensibility

Extensibility is almost always a priority, even if the customer does not realize it. As the needs of the organization change, the system must be able to accommodate the new reality.

As a rule, loose coupling and strong cohesion make it more likely that the classes that need to change will reside in the same package and that the package will be loosely coupled with the rest of the system. This limits the ripple effect of each change.

If you can identify areas that are very likely to change, you may be able to design the variability into the system, by encapsulating the variability inside of a swappable subsystem or by designing the system to use configuration data. Of course, this requires a very clear vision of the future of the system; and if you are wrong, you have wasted time and increased the complexity of the system.

Reuse Potential

Reuse of classes, both within a project and between projects, is a tremendous selling point for object-oriented technology. Reusable classes must have a generically useful abstraction and well-encapsulated data. When aiming for reuse, keep classes small and well focused. Also, in order to reduce the burden on the person who wants to adopt or adapt your class or package, keep the dependencies to a minimum and make the abstraction easy to use and understand.

TIP Despite the hype, reuse never comes for free. You must design with reuse in mind, or be willing to clean up an existing design to gain reusability.

Establish Design Guidelines

It is important to have projectwide guidelines during design. This unifies the efforts of the different designers or teams of designers. Each design effort should use the same diagrams, describe the solution at the same level of detail, and follow the same naming conventions. The following guidelines form a reasonable starting point for most projects.

Diagrams for Each Use Case

Use several sequence diagrams to describe each use case, one for each significant flow of events. Also, a single class diagram should be used to capture the relationships between all of the classes that participate in the different sequence diagrams. In some cases, state diagrams can be used to show state-dependent behavior for a particular class.

Level of Detail

The level of detail for design is far lower than for analysis. Each method must be fully specified, complete with arguments and return types.

Also, any object that is used in a sequence diagram must be located or created, either in the same sequence diagram or in a supporting sequence. In analysis, sequences are often supported by a series of minor miracles, with objects simply appearing when needed. In design, objects are created, kept for future use, located, and finally destroyed.

Naming Conventions

Name each method with a well-selected verb or a combination of a verb and a noun; paint and open are good examples from the Java class libraries. The name of the method should match the return type, if any. For instance, a method that returns a reference to a Timecard object might be called getTimecard or getCurrentTimecard.

Each class should be named with a noun, a combination of nouns, or a combination of adjectives and nouns. String, MenuItem, and OutputStream are good examples from the Java class libraries.

The purpose of each class and each method must be clear and unambiguous to other developers. This usually precludes the use of filler class names, such as manager. Whenever possible, clearly defined terms from design patterns, such as Factory or Singleton, should be used as part of applicable class names.

Cohesion

Each set of methods within a class must form a cohesive whole. This requires them to have a common goal or responsibility. Similarly, the classes inside of each package must have a unifying purpose or nature. Classes and methods must not be grouped, arbitrarily or simply for convenience.

Find Independent Design Efforts

In order to divide up the design effort, you must identify packages or groups of packages that are loosely coupled with the rest of the system. This allows developers from different efforts to agree on the interfaces before starting independent design activities.

Packages that are tightly coupled must be designed together. Packages that are loosely coupled and well encapsulated are good candidates for independent development. Subsystems are perfect for independent development. By their very definition they are independent and well encapsulated.

Each independent design effort must fit the technical abilities of a single team. This may require an otherwise coherent design effort be divided into smaller efforts that more closely match the skill sets of existing teams. Otherwise, this may require reorganization and training of team members to improve skill sets.

Designing Packages or Subsystems

The design for a package or subsystem builds on the analysis model, including class diagrams and sequence diagrams. While each package is designed and implemented as a separate deliverable, all of the packages cooperate to realize the use cases. As part of the initial design of the package, developers must identify the use cases that include the package. This process highlights the interactions between the package and the other packages that are involved in the use case. At this point, the developers must cooperate with the developers of the other involved packages to finalize the interfaces between the packages.

A package or subsystem design is also constrained by the architecture and the overall goals for the system. Specifically, the architecture determines the permissible relationships between the system's packages. Each time a class in the package uses a class outside of the package, it establishes a dependency between these packages. These new relationships must be evaluated for compliance with the architecture.

Each package or subsystem may have its own goals. For instance, a package of user interface classes may need to be highly flexible and extensible, while a package of entity classes may need to be well encapsulated and meet demanding performance goals.

The following steps must be followed for each design effort:

1. **Identify goals and priorities.** While goals are established for the entire design, not every design effort can influence each goal. Each design effort must identify the goals and priorities that it can and cannot impact. This is usually clear from the technology involved and from the purpose of the package or subsystem. For instance, the design effort for the TimecardDomain and TimecardWorkflow packages will undoubtedly have a most noticeable effect on performance, as it controls persistence and the flow of data. On the other hand, the design efforts for the HtmlProduction framework and the TimecardUI package will have a greater effect on extensibility, since user interfaces are notoriously vulnerable to requirements changes.

2. **Review prior steps.** Previous steps created an analysis model, selected technologies, and established structural constraints for the design of the Timecard system. Each design effort must review, then follow these inputs and constraints. The analysis model describes the problem from the developer's perspective. As such, it is the best resource when designing packages and subsystems. In many cases, the responsibilities of a class or package can be directly extrapolated from the responsibilities of analysis classes.

3. **Design to goals.** In some cases, the high-level design is almost completely determined by the technology. For instance, Enterprise JavaBeans development completely determines much of your design. Decisions must be made for each use case to meet goals, but there are no sweeping design decisions left to the developer. In other cases, it is up to the developers to design the package or subsystem to meet the goals. Design patterns may serve as a valuable resource in this highly creative and iterative process.

4. **Apply design to use cases.** Applying the high-level design to the use cases validates and invariably improves the design. In this process, the high-level design developed in the previous step is applied to each use case in turn, until the design is fully fleshed out and all the applicable use cases are met or the design is proven intractable.

Design Efforts for the Timecard Application

The Timecard application seems to naturally break into four design efforts:

- TimecardDomain and TimecardWorkflow packages
- HtmlProduction framework
- TimecardUI package
- BillingSystemInterface subsystem

The TimecardDomain and TimecardWorkflow packages should be designed together, because they are so closely related. They depend on the same technologies, and are very tightly coupled.

The HtmlProduction framework should be designed as a separate package from the TimecardUI. It is the only package that produces the actual HTML for the system. The TimecardUI package clearly uses it and should drive its development, but the Html-Production framework should be able to evolve independently. One approach is to build a minimum set of functionality for the HtmlProduction framework before starting the design and implementation of the TimecardUI package. With this minimum functionality established, the HtmlProduction can grow in sophistication while the TimecardUI is designed and implemented.

The BillingSystemInterface subsystem is a natural independent design activity. Since the rest of the system does not depend on it, it can be developed concurrently or deferred until development resources are available.

The Next Step

We have spent the last 10 chapters building up to this point, improving our understanding of the problem, selecting technology, and structuring the solution. Now it is time to use UML to build a design model for the Timecard application.

Each of the following chapters shows how UML can be used to design a package or subsystem. The analysis model is used to determine each package's functionality and interfaces with other packages. Well-defined goals are met by applying object-oriented principles and design patterns. Finally, the design is evaluated for compliance with the architecture and the overall goals of the system.

In Chapters 11 through 14, the design is used as a basis for actual Java code. This is intended to reinforce the basic principles and to show how modeling in UML simplifies the coding process.

CHAPTER 11

Design for the TimecardDomain and TimecardWorkflow

The design for the TimecardDomain and TimecardWorkflow packages builds heavily on the analysis model, technology selection, and architecture we developed in Chapter 5, "Analysis Model for the Timecard Application," Chapter 8, "Evaluating Candidate Technologies for Control and Entity Classes," and Chapter 9, "Software Architecture." The analysis model in Chapter 5 showed how the boundary, control, and entity classes collaborate to fulfill the system's requirements. Chapter 8 described Enterprise Java-Beans and some of the decisions that must be made when developing with EJBs. Chapter 9 constrained the relationships between packages.

This chapter builds a sample design and implementation for the TimecardDomain and TimecardWorkflow packages. It follows the steps described in Chapter 10, "Introduction to Design":

1. Identify goals and priorities for the effort.
2. Review prior steps.
3. Design to goals.
4. Apply design to use cases.

The following sections apply each step to the TimecardDomain and TimecardWorkflow packages.

Establish Goals for the Effort

Establishing goals up front makes it easier to make consistent decisions during design. This is important, as design is all about making an endless series of decisions, generally under fairly strong schedule pressure.

The most important goals for the TimecardDomain and TimecardWorkflow packages are performance, reliability, and reuse potential. Extensibility is less of a priority, since the system is very well understood and has a narrow focus.

Performance and Reliability

Performance and reliability are important goals for the entire Timecard system. After all, a lot of people depend on a corporate Timecard system, and they do not have time to wait.

The classes in the TimecardDomain package contribute greatly to the performance and reliability of the entire system. The classes that reside in the TimecardDomain package are responsible for the availability and integrity of the timecard data itself. Design decisions for the TimecardDomain package dramatically impact the time required for data access and data updates. For instance, decisions on how the data is represented in the database and how the data maps to entity beans greatly impact the speed and efficiency of the EJB container as it services requests for data.

The classes of the TimecardWorkflow package have a different but equally significant impact on performance and reliability. The TimecardWorkflow classes contain the methods that client objects use to get access to the data and services provided by the TimecardDomain objects. The Workflow object may require the client object to make several requests, one large request, or some variation in between. Remember that the Client and TimecardWorkflow classes are invariably in separate virtual machines and are often on separate hosts. This makes the efficiency of the data flow very important, since even a fast network is far slower than the host's internal data bus, and the data must be serialized and deserialized at every turn.

Reuse

Reuse is another important goal for the TimecardDomain and TimecardWorkflow packages. To reach this goal, each entity bean in the TimecardDomain package should be useful in a wide variety of workflows within the Timecard application, and most of the session beans in the TimecardWorkflow package should be able to support new user interface classes as new views of the system evolve.

Extensibility

While extensibility is less of a priority, experience indicates that there are no static systems. Extensibility is improved by encapsulating potential variability and by keeping the classes small and narrowly focused.

Now that we have established some goals, we must review the prior decisions that affect the design effort.

Review Prior Steps

Several prior steps drive design. The analysis model describes exactly what the system will do, from a developer's perspective. The architecture describes the structural and technology decisions that constrain the design. In this section, we review the analysis model and the architectural decisions.

Review of the Analysis Model

Our first task requires us to work through each analysis diagram, first to refresh our understanding of the sequence of interactions between the objects and then to identify any important characteristics. We'll consider the Login, Record Time, and Export Time Entries use cases.

The Login Use Case

The Login use case contains several flows. First, there is the normal flow in which everything proceeds according to plan. Next there are alternate flows for invalid passwords and unknown users.

Normal Flow for Login (Analysis)

The actor asks the boundary EmployeeLoginUI object to display the login form, as shown in Figure 11.1. The actor then fills in username and password and submits them to the system. The EmployeeLoginUI object asks the control LoginWorkflow object to validate the login. In order to satisfy this request, the LoginWorkflow object asks the UserLocator object to find the User object that corresponds to the name. Once the LoginWorkflow object gets the correct User object, it asks it to validate the password. Once the LoginWorkflow object receives a response, it passes it back to the EmployeeLoginUI object. When the EmployeeLoginUI object receives the valid response, it displays a welcome message and the flow is complete.

The only object in this sequence that is outside of our current design effort is EmployeeLoginUI. There is only one request from the EmployeeLoginUI object to the LoginWorkflow object, validateLogin. This request includes very simple data and receives a simple yes/no response.

Alternate Flow for Invalid Password (Analysis)

The sequence for an invalid password proceeds exactly as in the normal flow, until the User object responds with INVALID to the validateLogin method. This response is propagated up to the EmployeeLoginUI, which must display an invalid password message to the actor. Figure 11.2 shows this sequence.

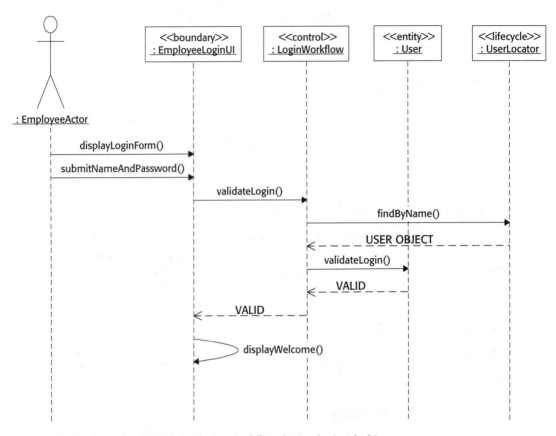

Figure 11.1 Sequence diagram for the normal flow for Login (analysis).

This sequence is incredibly similar to the normal flow. Within the TimecardDomain and TimecardWorkflow packages, there is no difference in what is done, only in the response values, so we will not need to develop a separate design sequence diagram for this flow of events.

Alternate Flow for Unknown User (Analysis)

The sequence for an unknown user proceeds exactly as in the normal flow, until the UserLocator responds with a NULL when asked to locate the User object by name. Obviously, the LoginWorkflow cannot ask an unknown User object to validate the password, so it returns INVALID to the EmployeeLoginUI object. As in the sequence for the invalid password, the EmployeeLoginUI calls its own displayErrorMessage method. Figure 11.3 shows this sequence.

Again, the sequence is incredibly similar to the normal flow. However, it does highlight the reaction of the LoginWorkflow object when the User object cannot be located. It is not an error or exception case, but rather a reasonable outcome.

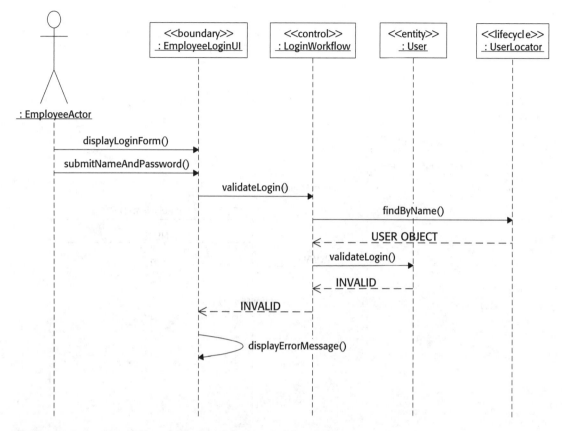

Figure 11.2 Sequence diagram for invalid password (analysis).

Participating Classes (Analysis)

The user interface objects use LoginWorkflow objects to validate the user's login data. The resulting relationship needs to be an association, so that the user interface objects can reuse the same LoginWorkflow object for login retries.

The LoginWorkflow object finds and uses a User object, but does not need to remember it for future use. So, the resulting relationship is a dependency. The Login-Workflow object uses a UserLocator object, and does keep it for future use, so the resulting relationship is an association. These relationships are shown in Figure 11.4.

The Record Time Use Case

The Record Time use case contains two flows of events. First, there is the normal flow in which everything proceeds according to plan. Next there is an alternate flow for Submit Timecard.

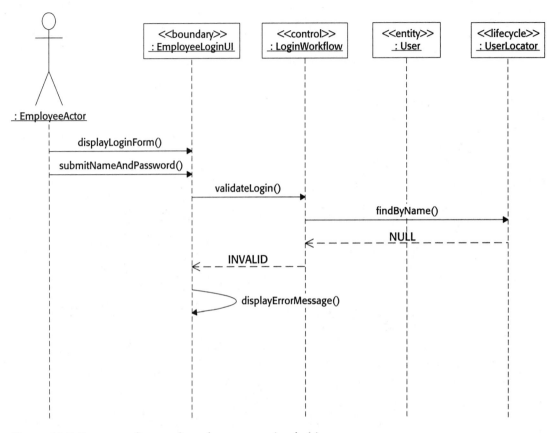

Figure 11.3 Sequence diagram for unknown user (analysis).

Normal Flow (Analysis)

The normal flow for the Record Time use case begins when the actor requests the current entries. The RecordTimeUI object calls the RecordTimeWorkflow object's getEntries method, which magically has a reference to the correct User object. Given the User object, the RecordTimeWorkflow object asks it for its current Timecard object. The RecordTimeWorkflow object can then ask the Timecard object for its entries and return them to the RecordTimeUI. After the Employee actor updates the time entries, the RecordTimeUI object uses the updateEntries method on the RecordTimeWorkflow to propagate the changes to the system. The RecordTimeWorkflow object calls the setEntries method on the previously stored reference to the Timecard object. These interactions are shown in Figure 11.5.

Submit Timecard (Analysis)

The Submit Timecard flow of events describes how the actor marks his or her current timecard as submitted and gets a new current timecard. Once the actor decides to sub-

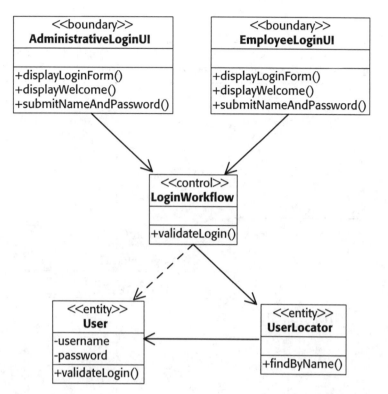

Figure 11.4 Participating classes for the Login use case (analysis).

mit his or her current timecard, the RecordTimeUI object calls the submit method on its RecordTimeWorkflow object, which knows the User and the Timecard objects. The RecordTimeWorkflow creates a new Timecard object and sets it as the current Timecard object for the user. The old Timecard object still exists, but it is not a current Timecard, so it cannot be edited by the user. These interactions are shown in Figure 11.6.

Participating Classes (Analysis)

Each method in the sequence diagrams requires some sort of relationship between the object calling the method and the object that contains the method. Each RecordTimeUI object is associated with an undetermined number of RecordTimeWorkflow objects. The undetermined multiplicity indicates that during analysis we did not know whether RecordTimeUI objects would have dedicated RecordTimeWorkflow objects or would share them. Each RecordTimeWorkflow object is associated with the User and Timecard objects. These relationships are shown in Figure 11.7.

The Export Time Entries Use Case

The Export Time Entries use case contains a single flow of events, the normal flow.

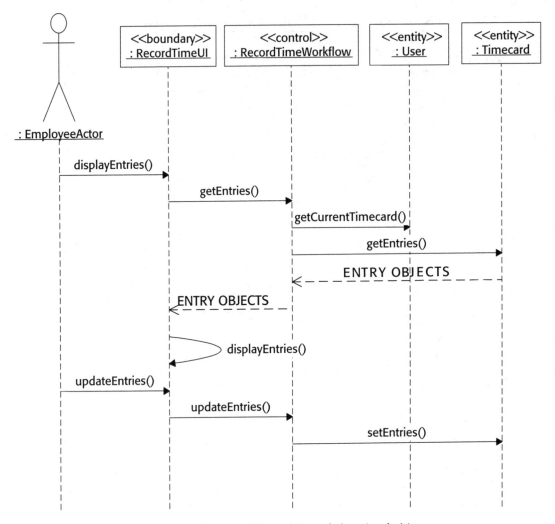

Figure 11.5 Sequence diagram for the normal flow of Record Time (analysis).

Normal Flow (Analysis)

The normal flow for the Export Time Entries use case begins when the ExportEntriesUI object builds the display by asking the ClientLocator for a list of clients and the User-Locator for a list of employees. The administrative user selects various criteria and submits the request. The ExportEntriesUI object calls the exportForCriteria method on the ExportTimeEntriesWorkflow object, which uses the EntryLocator's findForCriteria method to get a list of time entries that match the criteria. The details for each entry are extracted from each entry object and written to a file for export. This sequence is shown in Figure 11.8.

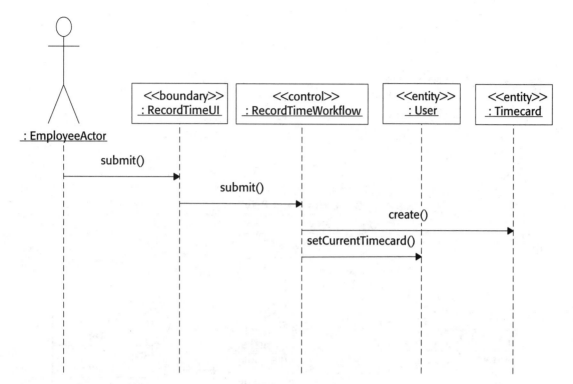

Figure 11.6 Sequence diagram for the submit Timecard flow of events (analysis).

Participating Classes (Analysis)

Each method call in the sequence diagram requires a dependency or association in the participating classes diagram. A fairly mechanical process yields the relationships, as shown in Figure 11.9.

The ExportEntriesUI does directly depend on the ClientLocator and the UserLocator; this dependency violates the structural constraints defined by the architecture. This must be remedied during design.

Review Architectural Constraints

For the Timecard application example, the server-side entity and control classes are implemented in Enterprise JavaBeans. The TimecardWorkflow package, which contains the control classes, depends on EJB session beans. The TimecardDomain package, which contains the entity classes, depends on EJB entity beans.

The architecture also precludes classes in the TimecardUI package from having direct relationships with classes in the TimecardDomain package. Instead, they must delegate any requests for information or services to a control class in the TimecardWorkflow. This is shown in the lack of a dependency from the TimecardUI directly to the TimecardDomain. Figure 11.10 shows these dependency relationships in a package diagram.

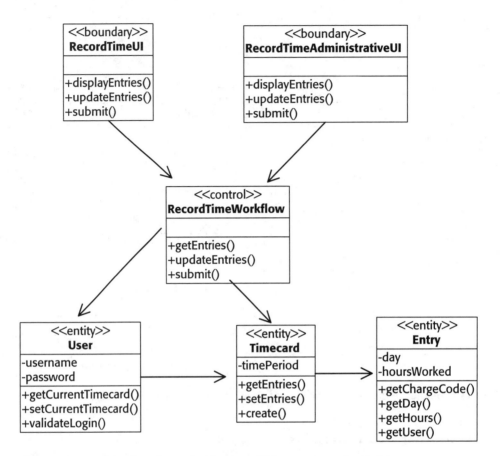

Figure 11.7 Participating classes for the Record Time use case (analysis).

WARNING If you are not familiar with Enterprise JavaBeans, review the technology description for EJB in Chapter 8.

Design for Goals

Enterprise JavaBeans constrains the developer to a fairly small number of decisions. In this section, we discuss some of the design decisions that are important in EJB development. In the next section, "Apply Design for Each Use Case," we will make these decisions for each bean involved in the use case.

Every technology forces the developer to make certain design decisions in order to meet his or her goals. EJB is no exception. It forces you to:

1. Choose between stateful or stateless for each session bean.
2. Choose between container-managed or bean-managed persistence for each entity bean.

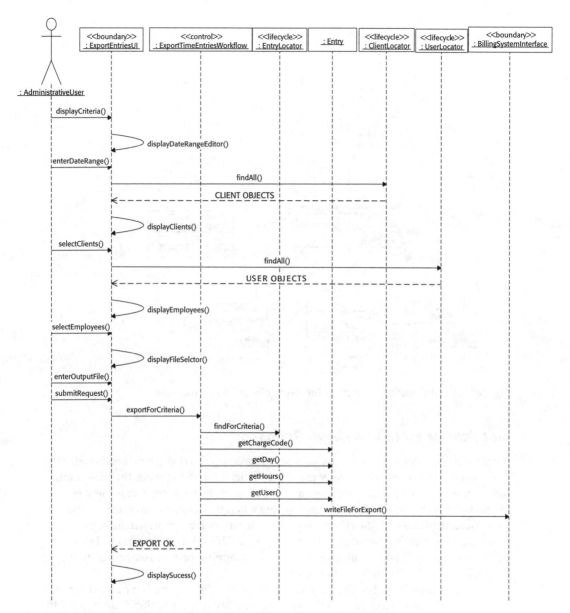

Figure 11.8 Sequence diagram for the normal flow of Export Time Entries use case.

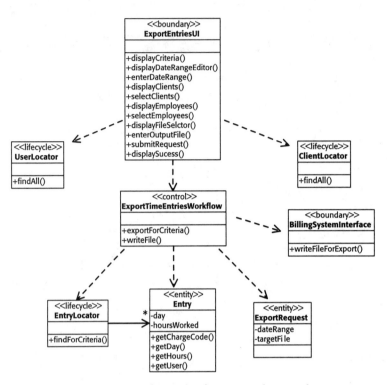

Figure 11.9 Participating classes for the Export Time Entries use case.

Stateless or Stateful Session Beans

Recall from Chapter 8 that stateless session beans do not hold any conversational state from request to request. This makes them very efficient, but decreases their usefulness for session beans that must moderate a series of requests from the same client object. Stateful session beans are far more appropriate when the session bean must maintain a conversational state with the client object, since it can remember information from previous requests that were made by the client object. This allows it to accumulate information for a consolidated transaction, such as a shopping cart, or remember previous results so it does not need to rebuild them.

For each session bean, the sequence diagrams reveal the pattern of requests from the client object to the session bean. If the session bean holds information from request to request, it is best modeled as a stateful session bean. Otherwise, the default choice should be stateless, since stateless session beans are much more efficient and place less of a burden on the bean container.

Container-Managed or Bean-Managed Persistence

Each entity bean has data that must be persisted to the database. Container-managed persistence allows the developer to isolate the persistence information in the deploy-

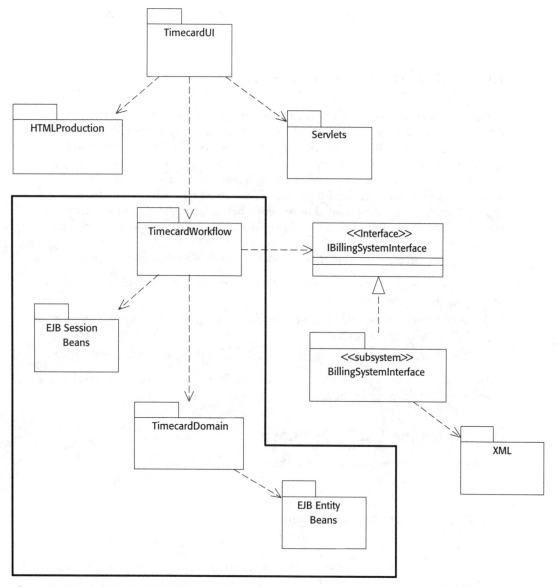

Figure 11.10 Architectural decisions and constraints.

ment descriptor. This allows the developer or deployer to specify the object-to-relational mapping and the transaction boundaries in a very concise form, without modifying any code. This is the default choice.

Bean-managed persistence forces you to write database access and transaction management code directly in the entity beans. However, it also provides unlimited flexibility. The most common reason to use bean-managed persistence is to achieve a tricky object-to-relational mapping that is not supported by the deployment tool. This is less preferable, but still fairly common.

Apply Design for Each Use Case

Remember, a design model is one step away from implementation. So, we need to carefully build a model that applies all of these decisions to all of the use cases in the requirements model. This model will provide a solid foundation for a clean and consistent implementation. As in analysis, the domain model includes sequence diagrams and a view of the participating classes for each use case. Unlike analysis, the design model is extremely detailed and thorough. Each return type and parameter must be shown. Each object must be created or retrieved before it is used. Significant mysteries and ambiguity in the design model lead to problems and poor solutions during implementation.

In designing an EJB-based solution for each use case, we follow these steps:

1. Consider each of the key design decisions for EJB development, as well as the goals for the package.

2. Build sequence diagrams for the normal and alternate flow of events as identified in the use case model.

3. Build a class diagram that shows all of the classes that participate in the use case.

We'll follow these steps for the Login, Record Time, and Export Time Entries use cases in the Timecard application.

Design for the Login Use Case

We are finally ready to start our design based on the first use case, Login. Let's walk through each of the steps.

Key Design Decisions for Login

We need to make two key design decisions for the Login use case.

- Is the LoginWorkflow object a stateless session bean or a stateful session bean?
- Is there any indication that bean-managed persistence is required for the User entity bean?

There is no indication in the sequence diagrams that the LoginWorkflow needs any data from or about previous attempts. A quick glance at the system's requirements reveals that there is no limit on the number of login attempts, so there is no need for a counter of login attempts. For performance reasons, we use stateless session beans by default. There is no reason not to follow that rule of thumb in this case.

The data for each User entity bean consists of a username and a password. Both fields are strings. There is no indication for bean-managed persistence, since the data is incredibly simple and the database schema is controlled by the development team.

Create Sequence Diagrams and Participating Classes for Login Use Case

Now that we have refreshed our memory of the analysis model and made some design decisions based on the architecture and on the analysis model, it is time to do the actual design for the Login use case. We will create sequence diagrams for the normal flow and for the alternate flow for an unknown user. Working from the analysis sequence diagram, we can simply apply the technology selections to each object. The messages are basically the same, just with more details.

Normal Flow

In the first part of the sequence diagram, shown in Figure 11.11, the login servlet asks the LoginWorkflow session bean to validate the user. The LoginWorkflow session bean calls the findByUsername method on the UserHome, which returns a remote reference to the appropriate User entity bean. The LoginWorkflow calls the isPasswordValid method on the User entity bean and returns the result.

Notice that this diagram does not attempt to show any behavior within the user interface object. For this design effort, we are mostly concerned with the interactions with the objects from the LoginWorkflow and LoginDomain packages.

Our earlier decision to make the LoginWorkflow a stateless session bean is validated by this sequence. There is no need for the LoginWorkflow to keep any information between method calls. It receives both the username and the password each time, and it uses the UserHome to find the right User entity bean each time.

> **NOTE** The Java Naming and Directory Interface (JNDI) lookups of the LoginWorkflow and the UserHome are not shown. This seems appropriate, as they are so incredibly repetitious and common.

Alternate Flow for Unknown User

Similar to the normal flow, the login servlet in the alternate flow asks the LoginWorkflow session bean to validate the user. The LoginWorkflow session bean calls the findByUsername method on the UserHome. Since the User object does not exist in the system, the UserHome returns a null reference. The LoginWorkflow session bean returns false, as the user's login information is clearly not valid. Figure 11.12 shows this sequence.

This sequence is very similar to the normal flow. Other than some internal logic within the LoginWorkflow session bean, there is no new information here.

Participating Classes

The validateLogin message from the LoginServlet to the LoginWorkflow requires a dependency relationship between the LoginServlet class and the LoginWorkflow class. The other messages in the sequence diagram lead to the dependency relationships shown in Figure 11.13. Notice that none of the objects retains any information between messages, so all of the relationships are dependencies.

It is always wise to verify that none of the relationships between the classes violates the structural decisions that were made during architecture. In this case, you can see

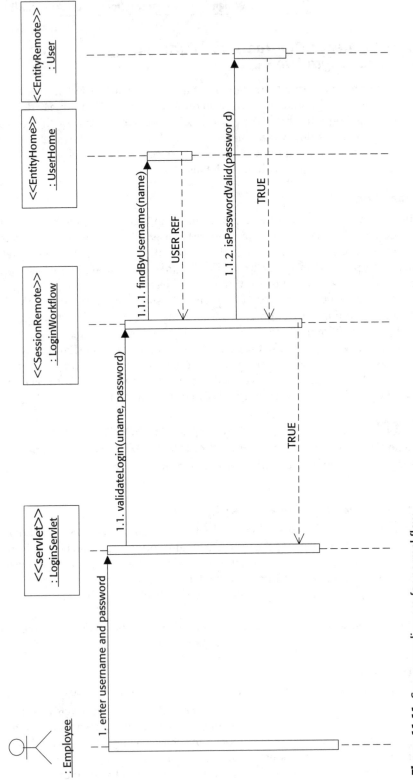

Figure 11.11 Sequence diagram for normal flow.

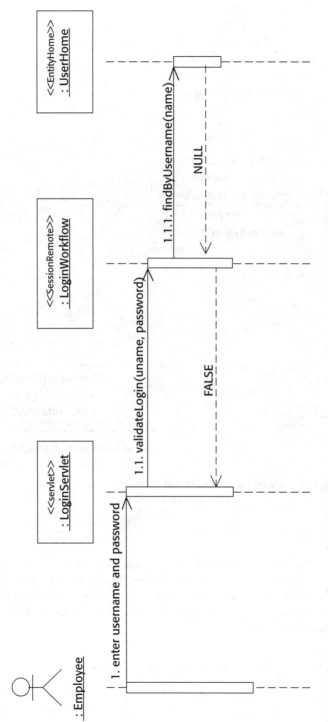

Figure 11.12 Sequence diagram for unknown user.

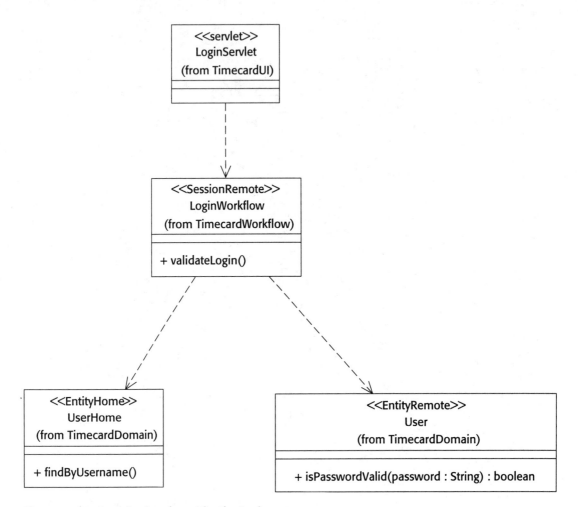

Figure 11.13 Participating classes for the Login use case.

that the dependencies exactly match the package dependencies specified in architecture. The user interface class depends on the Workflow class, which in turn depends on the user entity bean classes, which resides in the TimecardDomain package.

Now that we have a fairly complete design for the Login use case, the next step is to design the Record Time use case.

Design for the Record Time Use Case

To design the Record Time use case, we follow the same steps as those used for the Login use case design. First we consider the key design decisions, then create sequence diagrams and a class diagram.

Key Design Decisions for Record Time

We need to make three key design decisions for the Record Time use case:

- Is the RecordTimeWorkflow object a stateless session bean or a stateful session bean?
- How should data be returned from the session beans to the UI: as remote references or simple data?
- How should the persistent data be stored and mapped to entity beans?

Stateless or Stateful Session Bean?

In the analysis model, the RecordTimeWorkflow object appears to hold a reference to the Timecard object. If we carry this approach over to design, the RecordTimeWorkflow session bean must keep a reference to the Timecard entity bean, which means that it must be a stateful session bean.

Holding a reference to the Timecard entity bean would save the RecordTimeWorkflow from having to find the right User entity bean each time it needs to get the current Timecard bean. It almost certainly makes sense to avoid the extra database access and make RecordTimeWorkflow a stateful session bean.

Remote References or Simple Data?

RecordTimeWorkflow objects allow RecordTimeUI objects to obtain a lot of information about the current Timecard object. There are two fundamental ways that this goal can be accomplished. First, the RecordTimeWorkflow object can return remote references to any entity beans that the RecordTimeUI needs; alternatively, the RecordTimeWorkflow can return simple data.

Returning remote references allows the receiving object a lot of flexibility, because it can call any available method on the remote reference. For timecard data, this sort of flexibility seems excessive. The RecordTimeUI has very narrow needs. Also, allowing the RecordTimeUI object to have direct access to an entity bean violates the structural constraints established during architecture, as it introduces a direct dependency between the TimecardUI package and the TimecardDomain package.

> **TIP**   In EJB development, it is usually better to have the session beans return simple data or a collection of simple data. The client already has a remote reference to the session bean, and every remote reference introduces overhead on both the client and, more importantly, on the server.

Persistent Data and Design Implications

In the analysis model, each Timecard object contains many TimeEntry objects, one for each date/charge code combination. This is a reasonable way to express the relationship between hours, charge codes, and dates for an employee in the analysis model. However, it may not be a prudent design strategy.

A separate TimeEntry entity bean for each employee, charge code, and date combination can lead to an explosion of entity beans. Consider a typical employee, with four charge codes in each seven-day timecard. That employee's timecard is associated with 28 TimeEntry beans. As the system scales, to, say, 1,000 employees updating their timecards each hour on Friday morning, the application server must load 1,000 employee entity beans, 28,000 TimeEntry entity beans, and many charge code entity beans. Current experience with EJB systems indicates that creating tens of thousands of fine-grained entity beans has an adverse affect on performance and scalability. Each time an entity bean is loaded, a record must be read from the database, and a pooled object must be initialized with the data. This takes time, and forces the container to do more work tracking the objects and maintaining a pool of available entity objects.

What is the alternative? We need a way to hold charge codes, hours, and dates for each Timecard entity bean, without requiring a separate entity bean for each combination. Let's consider each type of data in turn.

Charge codes. We cannot store the timecard ID in each charge code, since each charge code is used by many timecards. Using a lookup table in the database is appealing but makes container-managed persistence (CMP) intractable. Since we really want CMP, we need to store all of the charge codes for a timecard in a single field. The solution is to serialize the charge code IDs into a string. Is this a kludge or is this an application of the classic maxim "keep it simple? "

On the one hand, the database no longer meets the criteria for first normal form; as a single row, column intersection is used to store multiple values. Database administrators throughout the organization may cringe, mock, then attack. They will rightly claim that we have ruined the reporting capabilities of the database, as the combined field is useless for queries. However, if the database is a subordinate tool for the application server, this may be irrelevant.

If breaking normalization is too high a price to pay, we can use bean-managed persistence (BMP) for the Timecard entity bean. This allows us to have a TimeEntry table with timecard ID, date index, charge code, and hours in the database. Each Timecard entity bean builds itself by reading entries from the table, and stores itself by writing entries to the table.

Hours. Each Timecard entity bean must also hold a list of hours, one for each combination of charge codes and day. Again, in order to use CMP, we need to store all of the hours in a single field. If we broke the database schema for charge codes, we can certainly store an ordered list of floats in a string field. Otherwise, the Timecard entity bean must use bean-managed persistence.

Again, the choice is the same: CMP provides convenience but reduces the flexibility of the database. BMP maintains the flexibility of the database, but requires the developers to write their own database access and transaction management code in the bean implementation.

Dates. Since we need only days, not hours or minutes, it is efficient to store the day of the year and the year for the start of the timecard. Also, we might want to store the length of the time period in days, in case the customer ever decides to move away from a standard seven-day time period.

There are three choices for persisting Timecard entity beans:

Use many fine-grained TimeEntry entity beans. This allows us to use CMP and keep the database in first normal form. However, it undoubtedly impacts the scalability of the system, since the system will require approximately 28 timecard entries per employee per week.

Normalize the database and use BMP to keep all of the data for a timecard within the Timecard entity bean. Keep the persistent data in well-normalized tables with a separate row for each time entry. BMP allows us to write the SQL to join the timecard and time entry data to build the consolidated Timecard entity bean. This is a bit harder to implement, but makes the database more useful for reporting and enables flexible queries against the time entry data.

Keep the data for a timecard within the Timecard entity bean. Keep the persistent data in one table that stores all of the hours in a single field and all of the charge codes in another field. This violation of first normal form allows us to use CMP, but it also reduces the database to a simple data store. Generating reports from the database becomes very painful. For example, if we want a list of all time entries for a particular client, we would have to extract the charge codes list out of every timecard and parse for the client.

Since we desire the convenience of CMP, and there is no requirement for extra reporting, there is no reason not to use the third option.

Create Sequence Diagrams and Participating Classes for Record Time Use Case

Now that we have refreshed our memory of the analysis model, and made some design decisions based on the architecture and on the analysis model, it is time to do the actual design for the Record Time use case. We will create sequence diagrams for the normal flow and the Submit Timecard alternate flow.

Normal Flow

The normal flow begins when the actor requests the current entries. The RecordTime-Servlet asks the RecordTimeWorkflow's home interface for a remote reference to a RecordTimeWorkflow session bean. The RecordTimeServlet can then ask the Record-TimeWorkflow session bean for the charge codes, dates, and hours that make up the current timecard. Notice that the first request for information requires the Record-TimeWorkflow to find the User object and ask for its current Timecard object. Subsequent requests use the references as held by RecordTimeWorkflow, which is a stateful session bean.

The interaction between the RecordTimeWorkflow session bean and the Timecard entity bean is quite straightforward. Each time the RecordTimeWorkflow receives a request for information, it passes the request on to the Timecard entity bean, and returns the result. Each time the RecordTimeWorkflow receives an update command, it passes it along to the Timecard entity bean. Figure 11.14 shows this sequence.

Submit Timecard

The Submit Timecard flow begins when the actor sends the submit command to the servlet. The RecordTimeServlet asks the RecordTimeWorkflow session bean to submit the timecard. No information is passed as part of this request. The RecordTimeWorkflow

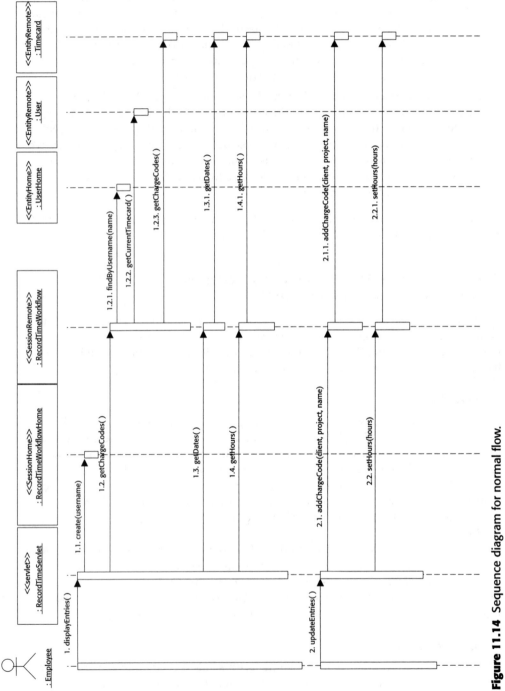

Figure 11.14 Sequence diagram for normal flow.

session bean uses a previously established reference to the User object to ask it to submit the current timecard. The User object uses the Timecard entity bean's home interface to create a new Timecard. It keeps this as the new current timecard. Figure 11.15 shows this sequence.

Participating Classes

As always, each message in the sequence diagram requires a relationship in the class diagram. Notice that the structural constraints established in architecture have been met, as the classes in the TimecardUI package depend on classes in the Timecard-Workflow package, which depend on classes in the TimecardDomain package. These exactly match the structural constraints that were introduced in architecture. Figure 11.16 shows the participating classes and their relationships.

Now that we have a fairly complete design for the Record Time use case, we turn our attention to the Export Time Entries use case.

Design for the Export Time Entries Use Case

To design the Record Time use case, we follow the same steps as used for the Login use case design. First we consider the key design decisions, then create sequence diagrams and a class diagram.

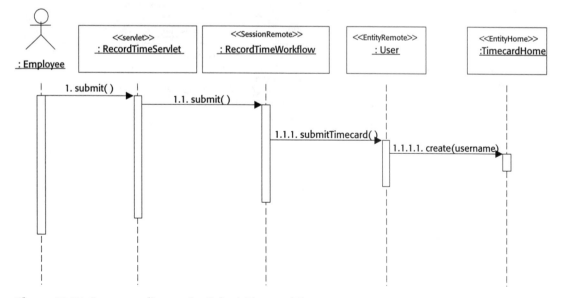

Figure 11.15 Sequence diagram for Submit Timecard flow.

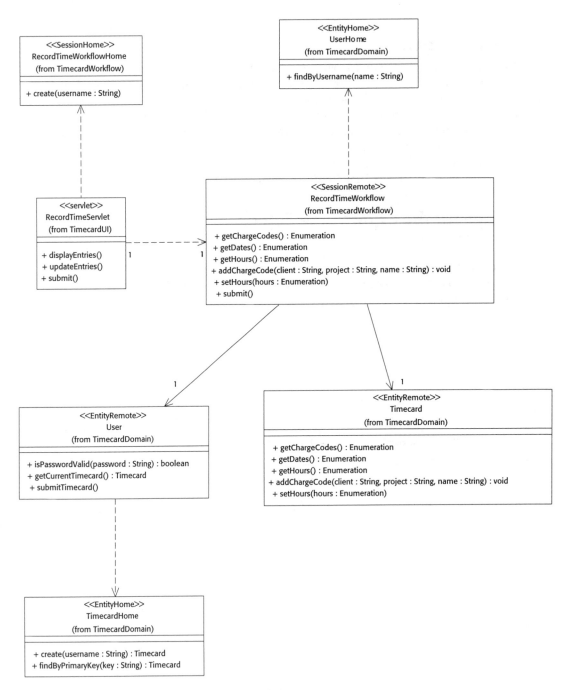

Figure 11.16 Participating classes for the Record Time use case.

Key Design Decisions for Export Time Entries

Only one key design decision remains: whether to use a stateless or a stateful session bean. The design for the other use cases has determined the design for all of the entity beans.

Stateless or Stateful Session Bean?

There is no indication in the sequence diagrams that the ExportTimeEntriesWorkflow needs any data from or about previous attempts. In fact, we expect export requests to be few and far between compared to other system functionality.

For performance reasons, we use stateless session beans by default. There is no reason not to follow that rule of thumb in this case.

Create Sequence Diagrams and Participating Classes for Export Time Entries Use Case

There is only one significant flow of events, the normal flow.

Normal Flow

In the normal flow, the ExportTimeEntriesServlet retrieves lists of users and clients from the ExportTimeEntriesWorkflow, which uses their respective home interfaces to actually find the relevant entity beans. The servlet uses the criteria entered by the user to build an ExportCriteria object, which it sends to the ExportTimeEntriesWorkflow as an argument to the exportForCriteria method.

The ExportTimeEntriesWorkflow is responsible for all interactions with the BillingSystemInterface. Each candidate time entry is sent to the BillingSystemInterface, which is responsible for using or rejecting the record. Figure 11.17 shows this sequence.

Participating Classes

Each ExportTimeEntriesServlet object depends on a ExportTimeEntriesWorkflow object and an ExportCriteria object, because it creates a ExportCriteria object and passes it along to the ExportTimeEntriesWorkflow object when it calls the exportForCriteria object.

Notice in the sequence diagram that the ExportTimeEntriesWorkflow depends on many entity beans, but does not keep any references to any of them. This indicates that the ExportTimeEntriesWorkflow is perfectly acceptable as a stateless session bean, as we planned. Figure 11.18 shows the participating classes and their relationships.

This concludes the design for the Login, Record Time, and Export Time Entries use cases. The next, and last step before implementation is to evaluate our design.

Evaluate the Design

Now that we have completed the exhausting and exhaustive design for each use case, we must evaluate the design against our goals and for compliance with the structural

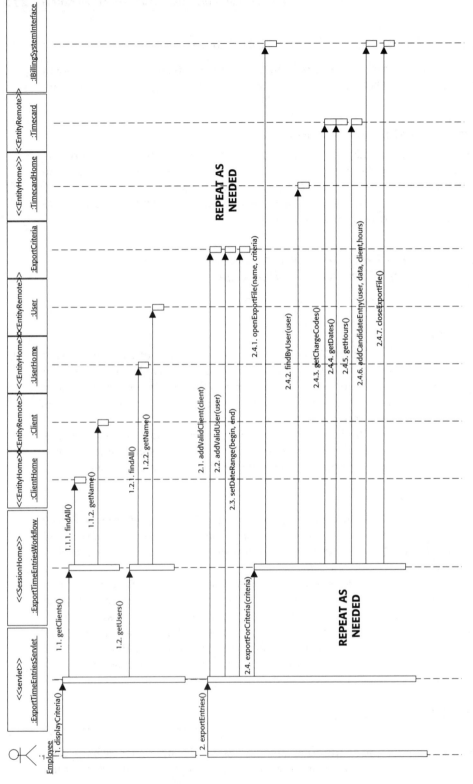

Figure 11.17 Sequence diagram for normal flow.

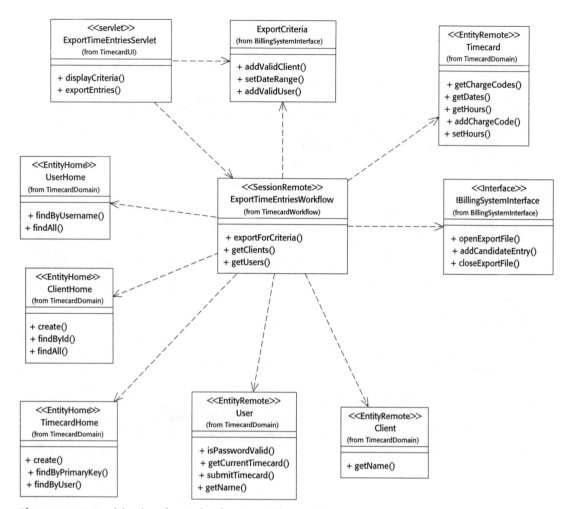

Figure 11.18 Participating classes for the Export Time Entries use case.

constraints from architecture. Recall that the primary goals for this design effort are reuse, performance, and reliability.

Performance and reliability. The design works toward our performance and reliability goals by leveraging EJB's strengths and by staying away from its weaknesses. Reviewing the sequence diagrams, we can see that remote connections are kept to a minimum and that the data access emphasizes speed for the Record Time use case, which is the most demanding of the common use cases.

Reuse. We have achieved a fairly high level of reuse within the system. The same entity beans, such as Timecard, are used by several session beans. Examining the methods for each bean, we can see that the methods are closely related and fulfill a clear responsibility. Based on these observations, we can use formal OO terminology and say that each bean is well encapsulated and has strong cohesion. Thus, there may be reuse opportunities with new systems within the organization.

The participating class diagrams show that the design fits the structural constraints in almost every case. The ExportTimeEntryServlet, from the TimecardUI package, depends on the ExportCriteria, which resides in the BillingSystemInterface package. This requires an updated package dependency diagram, as shown in Figure 11.19, but does not introduce any major issues, such as cyclical dependencies or tight coupling.

Finally, we are ready for implementation.

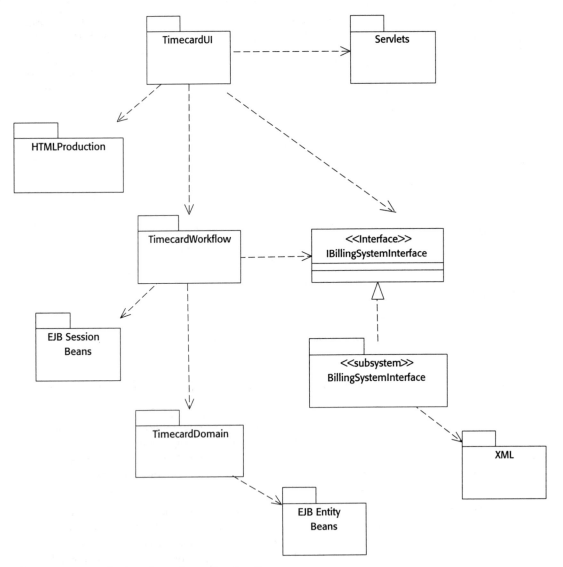

Figure 11.19 Revised package dependencies diagram.

Implementation

Now that the design is complete, and we have evaluated it, we have a solid foundation for implementation. We will make some important decisions during implementation, but we made most or all of the major structural decisions during analysis, architecture, and design. For example, we know each significant class, its responsibilities, and its relationships with other classes. We know how each entity bean holds data and how the session beans package that data for consumption by the user interface classes.

The implementation will be split into two parts. First, there are core classes, which are directly derived from the design model. Each section will show the derivation and code for the different parts of each bean. Second, described in the last section, are some helper classes. These classes are not in the design; they will be discovered as part of the implementation process.

> **NOTE** All of the code for this book is included on the CD-ROM. The package names in the book match the packages in the CD-ROM.

User Entity Bean

The User entity bean, like all entity beans, requires three files: a remote interface, a home interface, and an implementation class.

User.java

User.java is the remote interface for the User entity bean. It defines all of the remotely accessible business methods for the bean, as shown in Figure 11.20. This class consolidates behavior discovered in the Record Time and Login use cases.

All methods in User.java must throw RemoteException, since they are remotely accessible. Each method returns either void or a primitive. All of the data serialization rules we considered for RMI apply for EJB, so having primitive return values and parameters is desirable, to keep versioning simple.

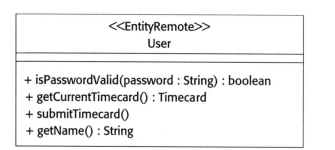

Figure 11.20 Remote interface for the User entity bean.

```
package com.wiley.compBooks.EJwithUML.TimeCardDomain;

import java.rmi.*;
import javax.ejb.*;

/**
 * The User bean holds descriptive information about
 * a user.
 *
 * User is the remote interface through which clients access
 * the underlying entity bean.
 *
 */
public interface User extends EJBObject
{

  /** Answers the name of this User bean. */
  public String getName() throws RemoteException;

  /** Answers true if the entered password matches this User's
      password. */
  public boolean isPasswordValid(String entered) throws
                                      RemoteException;

  /** Answers true if the password should be changed. */
  public boolean isPasswordChangeRequired() throws
                                      RemoteException;

  /** Sets the password of this User bean. */
  public void setPassword(String password) throws
                                      RemoteException;

  /** Answers the current timecard of this User bean. */
  public Timecard getCurrentTimecard() throws RemoteException;

  /** Sets the current timecard. */
  public void setCurrentTimecard(Timecard timecard) throws
                                      RemoteException;

}
```

UserHome.java

UserHome.java is the home interface for the User entity bean. It defines all of the methods needed to find, create, or destroy User entity beans, as shown in Figure 11.21.

Each of the methods in UserHome.java throws RemoteException and either CreateException or FinderException. RemoteExceptions are thrown for network, serialization, or class cast exceptions. CreateExceptions and FinderExceptions indicate logic errors or data errors in the implementation.

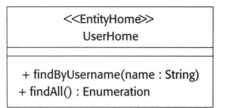

Figure 11.21 Home interface for the User entity bean.

Initially, it is quite surprising to see the findByUsername method returning an Enumeration. After all, logically, there should be only one User entity bean for each username. The Enterprise JavaBeans specification mandates that primary keys are unique. Any other criteria for a find method could yield more than one entity bean. So, the findByPrimaryKey method is the only find method that is permitted to return a single remote reference. It is up to the developers to verify that other criteria are unique when creating entity beans and to extract the entity bean's reference from the Enumeration returned by the find method.

```
package com.wiley.compBooks.EJwithUML.TimeCardDomain;

import java.util.*;
import java.rmi.*;
import javax.ejb.*;

/**
 * The User bean holds descriptive information about an
 * employee.
 *
 * UserHome is the remote interface through which clients find
 * and create the underlying entity beans.
 *
 */

public interface UserHome extends EJBHome
{

   /** Answers an Enumeration that contains references to
    * User beans that match the username. Should be unique. */
   public Enumeration findByUserName(String name) throws
                        FinderException,RemoteException;

   /** Answers an Enumeration that contains references to all
    *  User beans. */
   public Enumeration findAll() throws FinderException,
                                    RemoteException;

   /** Answers a reference to the User bean, if it exists.*/
```

```
        public User findByPrimaryKey(String userId) throws
                              FinderException, RemoteException;

        /** Answers a reference to the newly created User bean.*/
        public User create(String name, String password) throws
                              CreateException, RemoteException;

}
```

UserBean.java

UserBean.java is the implementation for the User entity bean. It provides implementations for the methods in the home and remote interfaces.

As a side effect of using container-managed persistence, all persistent data must be public. This is unnerving to developers who spend a fair amount of time convincing other developers that public data is vulnerable to corruption, due to concurrent access, and that making an instance variable public eliminates their ability to check values and propagate changes. With EJB, however, these very valid arguments are rendered irrelevant, as the container is the only object that deals directly with the bean implementation. If you want the benefits of CMP, you must follow the specification and trust your application server.

WARNING Enterprise JavaBeans should never be reused outside of an EJB context. Without the context, Enterprise JavaBeans are not even thread-safe, as the data is public, and use of the synchronized keyword is precluded by the specification.

The reference to the current Timecard entity bean is private. This is perfectly okay, since it is not persistent. Instead of keeping a persistent reference, the User bean holds the primary key of the current Timecard entity bean and uses it to obtain a reference on demand.

```
package com.wiley.compBooks.EJwithUML.TimeCardDomain;

import com.wiley.compBooks.EJwithUML.EjbUtil.*;
import java.util.*;
import java.rmi.*;
import javax.ejb.*;
import javax.naming.*;

/**
 * The User bean holds descriptive information about a user. *
 * UserBean is the actual entity bean implementation.
 *
 */
public class UserBean extends BasicEntityBean
{
  public String id;
  public String currentTimecardId;
```

```java
public String name;
public String password;
public boolean newUser;

private Timecard currentTimecard;

public UserBean ()
{
}

/** Creates a UserBean with the specified parameters. This is
 * never called directly. */
public String ejbCreate(String name, String password) throws
                                    RemoteException, CreateException
{
  this.id = "User" +IdGenerator.getId();
  this.name = name;
  this.password = password;
  this.newUser = true;

  checkForDuplicates();
  return null;
}

/** Actions performed after creation. This is never called
       directly. */
public void ejbPostCreate(String name, String password)
{
}

/** Answers the name of this User bean. */
public String getName()
{
  return this.name;
}

/** Answers true if the entered password matches this
User's password. */
public boolean is PasswordValid(String entered)
{
  return this.password.equals(entered);
}

/** Answers true if the password should be changed. */
public boolean isPasswordChangeRequired()
{
  return this.newUser;
}


/** Sets the password of this User bean. */
```

```java
public void setPassword(String password)
{
  this.password = password;
  this.newUser = false;
}


/** Answers the current timecard of this User bean. */
public Timecard getCurrentTimecard()
{
  try
  {
    if (this.currentTimecard == null)
    {
      Context initialContext = getInitialContext();
      TimecardHome thome =
          (TimecardHome)initialContext.lookup("TimecardBean");
      this.currentTimecard =
          thome.findByPrimaryKey(this.currentTimecardId);
    }
  }
  catch (NamingException e)
  {
    throw new EJBException(e.toString());
  }
  catch (FinderException e)
  {
    throw new EJBException(e.toString());
  }

  return this.currentTimecard;
}


/** Sets the current timecard. */public void
setCurrentTimecard(Timecard timecard)
{
  this.currentTimecard = timecard;
  this.currentTimecardId = (String) timecard.getPrimaryKey();
}



/** Checks for duplicates. Overrides method from
      BasicEntityBean.*/
public void doCheckForDuplicates() throws CreateException,
          FinderException,NamingException, RemoteException
{
  Context initialContext = getInitialContext();
  EmployeeHome ehome =
      (EmployeeHome)initialContext.lookup("EmployeeBean");

  Enumeration enum = ehome.findByUserName(this.name);
```

```
      if (enum.hasMoreElements())
      {
        throw new CreateException("Duplicate Employee: "
                +this.name);
      }

    }

    protected void doLoad() throws RemoteException,
                  NamingException, FinderException
    {
    }
  }
```

Timecard Entity Bean

The User entity bean, like all entity beans, requires three files: a remote interface, a home interface, and an implementation class.

Timecard.java

Timecard.java is the remote interface for the Timecard entity bean. It defines all of the remotely accessible business methods for the bean, as shown in Figure 11.22. This class consolidates behavior discovered in the Record Time, Export Time Entries, and Login use cases.

In the design, the methods to retrieve the current charge codes, dates, and hours each returned an Enumeration. This is an appealing design, but it does not always work well in practice. In many cases, the session bean passes the results of a request to an entity bean back to the client. This can lead to annoying versioning issues. The Enumeration for a Vector on an application server that is running within a VM from JDK 1.2 is *not* compatible with the Enumeration for a Vector in a servlet engine or Swing application that is running within a VM from JDK 1.1.

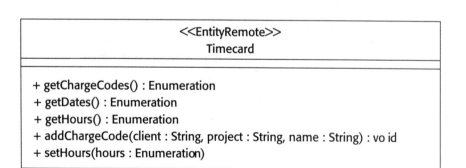

Figure 11.22 Remote interface for the Timecard entity bean.

TIP   It is prudent to have all remotely accessible methods return either primitives or a custom class that wraps a group of related primitives. The same is true for method parameters. This cannot be true for the find methods, as they automatically return a remote reference or a collection of remote references. However, in most cases, it is advisable to force clients to use session beans rather than accessing the entity beans through their find methods.

```java
package com.wiley.compBooks.EJwithUML.TimeCardDomain;

import java.util.*;
import java.rmi.*;
import javax.ejb.*;

/**
 * The Timecard bean holds time entries for a date range.
 *
 * Timecard is the remote interface through which clients
 * access the underlying entity bean.
 *
 * The order for hours is across the days for the first charge
 * code, then across for the next charge code, and so on.
 *
 */
public interface Timecard extends EJBObject
{
 /** Answers a list of ChargeCodes for this Timecard.*/
  public ChargeCode[] getChargeCodes() throws RemoteException;

   /** Answers a list of Dates for this Timecard. */
   public Date[] getDates() throws RemoteException;

   /** Answers a list of Floats of the hours of this Timecard.*/
   public float[] getHours() throws RemoteException;

   /** Adds a charge code to this Timecard*/
   public void addChargeCode(String clientName, String
                   projectName, String chargeCodeName) throws
                   RemoteException;

   /** Sets the hours for this Timecard. */
   public void setHours(float[] hours) throws RemoteException;
}
```

TimecardHome.java

TimecardHome.java is the home interface for the Timecard entity bean. It contains all of the methods for creating and finding Timecard entity beans, as shown in Figure 11.23.

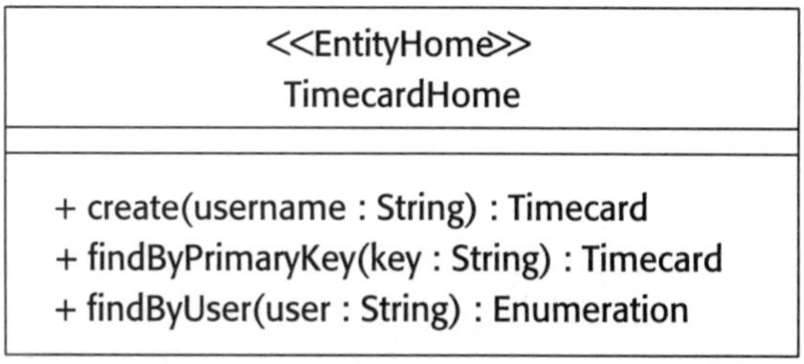

```
                    <<EntityHome>>
                    TimecardHome

    + create(username : String) : Timecard
    + findByPrimaryKey(key : String) : Timecard
    + findByUser(user : String) : Enumeration
```

Figure 11.23 Home interface for Timecard entity bean.

Note the variety of find methods that can be used for an entity bean. In more traditional Java development, each one-to-many relationship is kept in the containing
object. In EJB development, the containing object's primary key is often stored in each
object that it contains. At runtime, the containing object performs a reverse lookup on
the entity beans that it contains. For example, each Timecard entity bean contains the
primary key of the User entity bean to which it belongs. If the User entity bean needs
to find all of its Timecards, it uses a find method on Timecard's home interface.

This has a huge advantage, since relationships are kept in the data and are not realized unless they are needed. However, it also breaks the encapsulation of the containing entity bean. Any object can ask the Timecard's home interface for a list of all
Timecards for a given username. The User bean is not even involved.

```java
package com.wiley.compBooks.EJwithUML.TimeCardDomain;

import java.util.*;
import java.rmi.*;
import javax.ejb.*;

/**
 * The Timecard bean holds time entries for a date range.
 *
 * TimecardHome is the remote interface through which clients
 * find and create
 * the underlying entity beans.
 *
 * The order for hours is across the days for the first charge
 * code, then across
 * for the next charge code, and so on.
 *
 */
public interface TimecardHome extends EJBHome
{

    /** Answers a reference to the newly created Timecard bean.*/
    public Timecard create(String employeeId) throws
                            CreateException,RemoteException;

    /** Answers an Enumeration that contains references to all
```

```
 * Timecards for the specified Employee*/
public Enumeration findAllForEmployee(String employeeId)
                    throws FinderException, RemoteException;

/** Answers an Enumeration of references to Timecards that
 *  match the employee and start date. */
public Enumeration findTimecard(String employeeId, int
     startDayOfYear, int startYear) throws FinderException,
                                             RemoteException;

/** Answers a reference to the specified Timecard, if it
 * exists. */
public Timecard findByPrimaryKey(String timecardId) throws
                          FinderException, RemoteException;
}
```

TimecardBean.java

TimecardBean.java is the implementation class for the Timecard entity bean. As designed, it holds its charge codes as text in one string and its hours as text in another. To make matters even more complex, the charge codes are actually primary keys for actual ChargeCode entity beans. The rest of the data is fairly straightforward.

Again, all remotely accessible methods return a primitive or an array of primitives, to avoid versioning issues when the value is deserialized on the remote client.

```
package com.wiley.compBooks.EJwithUML.TimeCardDomain;

import com.wiley.compBooks.EJwithUML.EjbUtil.*;
import java.util.*;
import java.rmi.*;
import javax.ejb.*;
import javax.naming.*;

/**
 * The Timecard bean holds time entries for a date range.
 *
 * TimecardBean is the actual entity bean implementation.
 *
 * The order for hours is across the days for the first charge
 * code, then across for the next charge code, and so on.
 *
 */

public class TimecardBean extends BasicEntityBean
{
  public String employeeId;
  public String id;
  public String chargeCodeIds;
  public String hoursString;
  public int startDayOfYear;
```

```
  public int startYear;
  public int numberOfDays;

  private Vector chargeCodes = null;
  private Date[] dates = null;
  private float[] hours = null;

  public TimecardBean()
  {
  }


  /** Creates a TimecardBean with the specified parameters.
   *  This is never called directly. */
  public String ejbCreate(String employeeId) throws
                               RemoteException, CreateException
  {
    this.id = "Timecard" + IdGenerator.getId();
    this.employeeId = employeeId;
    this.chargeCodeIds = "";
    this.hoursString = "";
    initializeDates();

    checkForDuplicates();
    loadDates();
    loadHours();
    return null;
  }

  /** Actions performed after creation. This is never called
   *  directly. */
  public void ejbPostCreate(String employeeId) throws
                               RemoteException, CreateException
  {
  }

  public void ejbStore() throws RemoteException
  {
    storeHours();
    storeChargeCodes();
  }


public void doCheckForDuplicates() throws CreateException,
             FinderException, NamingException, RemoteException
  {
    Context initialContext = getInitialContext();
    TimecardHome thome =
          (TimecardHome)initialContext.lookup("TimecardBean");

    // Timecards must be unique for employee and start date
```

```
    Enumeration enum = thome.findTimecard(this.employeeId,
                          this.startDayOfYear, this.startYear);
    if (enum.hasMoreElements())
    {
      throw new CreateException("Duplicate Timecard: ");
    }
  }


protected void doLoad() throws RemoteException,
                        NamingException, FinderException
{
  loadChargeCodes();
  loadDates();
  loadHours();
}

/** Answers a list of ChargeCodes for this Timecard.*/
public ChargeCode[] getChargeCodes()
{
  ChargeCode[] codes=newChargeCode[this.chargeCodes.size()];
  for (int ctr=0; ctr < this.chargeCodes.size(); ctr++)
  {
    codes[ctr] = (ChargeCode)this.chargeCodes.elementAt(ctr);
  }
  return codes;
}

/** Answers an Enumeration of Dates for this Timecard. */
public Date[] getDates()
{
  return this.dates;
}

/** Answers a list of Floats for the hours of this Timecard.*/
public float[] getHours()
{
  return this.hours;
}

/** Adds a charge code to this Timecard*/
public void addChargeCode(String clientName, String
                          projectName, String chargeCodeName)
{
  try
  {


    if (this.chargeCodes == null)
    {
      this.chargeCodes = new Vector();
    }
```

```
Client client = null;
Project project = null;
ChargeCode chargeCode = null;

Context initialContext = getInitialContext();
ClientHome clientHome =
      (ClientHome)initialContext.lookup("ClientBean");
ProjectHome projectHome =
      (ProjectHome)initialContext.lookup("ProjectBean");
ChargeCodeHome chargeCodehome =
      (ChargeCodeHome)initialContext.lookup("ChargeCodeBean");

// Find the client
Enumeration clients = clientHome.findByName(clientName);
if (clients.hasMoreElements())
{
  client = (Client) clients.nextElement();
}
else
{
  throw new RemoteException("Client " +clientName+
                            " does not exist.");
}

// Find the project
Enumeration projects =
   projectHome.findProject((String)client.getPrimaryKey(),
   projectName);
if (projects.hasMoreElements())
{
  project = (Project) projects.nextElement();
}
else
{
  throw new RemoteException("Project " +projectName+
                            " does not exist.");

}

// Find the charge code
Enumeration chargeCodes =
      chargeCodehome.findChargeCode((String)
      project.getPrimaryKey(), chargeCodeName);

  if (chargeCodes.hasMoreElements())
{
  chargeCode = (ChargeCode) chargeCodes.nextElement();
}
else
{
```

```
        throw new RemoteException("ChargeCode "
          +chargeCodeName+ " does not exist.");
      }

      this.chargeCodes.addElement(chargeCode);
    }
    catch (NamingException e)
    {
      throw new EJBException(e.toString());
    }
    catch (FinderException e)
    {
      throw new EJBException(e.toString());
    }

  }


  /** Sets the hours for this Timecard. */
  public void setHours(float[] newHours)
  {
    this.hours = new float[newHours.length];
    for (int ctr=0; ctr < newHours.length; ctr++)
    {
      this.hours[ctr] = newHours[ctr];
    }
  }

  private void loadChargeCodes() throws NamingException,
                          FinderException, RemoteException
  {
    this.chargeCodes = new Vector();
    Context initialContext = getInitialContext();
    ChargeCodeHome chargeCodehome =
(ChargeCodeHome)initialContext.lookup("ChargeCodeBean");

    StringTokenizer tokenizer = new
        StringTokenizer(this.chargeCodeIds, "|");
    while (tokenizer.hasMoreTokens())
    {
      String id = tokenizer.nextToken();
      ChargeCode code = chargeCodehome.findByPrimaryKey(id);
      this.chargeCodes.addElement(code);
    }
  }

  private void storeChargeCodes()
  {
    try
    {
      StringBuffer buffer = new StringBuffer();
```

```java
    Enumeration codes = this.chargeCodes.elements();
    while (codes.hasMoreElements())
    {
      ChargeCode nextCode = (ChargeCode) codes.nextElement();
      buffer.append((String)nextCode.getPrimaryKey());
      buffer.append("|");
    }

    this.chargeCodeIds = buffer.toString();
  }
  catch (RemoteException e)
  {
    System.out.println("e: " +e);
  }
}

private void loadDates()
{
  this.dates = new Date[this.numberOfDays];

  Calendar calendar = Calendar.getInstance();
  calendar.setLenient(true);
  calendar.set(Calendar.YEAR, this.startYear);

  for (int delta = 0; delta < this.numberOfDays; delta++)
  {
    calendar.set(Calendar.DAY_OF_YEAR,
            this.startDayOfYear+delta);
    this.dates[delta] = calendar.getTime();
  }
}

private void storeHours()
{
  StringBuffer buffer = new StringBuffer();
  for (int ctr=0;this.hours != null && ctr <
                  this.hours.length; ctr++)
  {
    buffer.append(""+this.hours[ctr]+"|");
  }
  this.hoursString = buffer.toString();

}

private void loadHours()
{
  if (this.hoursString == null ||this.hoursString.equals(""))
  {
    float[] hours = {0f,0f};
  }
  else
```

```
    {
      StringTokenizer tokenizer = new
         StringTokenizer(this.hoursString, "|");

      int numTokens = tokenizer.countTokens();
      this.hours = new float[numTokens];

      for (int ctr=0; ctr < numTokens; ctr++)
      {
        String hourString = tokenizer.nextToken();
        this.hours[ctr] = Float.parseFloat(hourString);
      }
    }
  }
}

private void initializeDates()
{
  Calendar calendar = Calendar.getInstance();
  this.startDayOfYear = calendar.get(Calendar.DAY_OF_YEAR);
  this.startYear = calendar.get(Calendar.DAY_OF_YEAR);
  this.numberOfDays = 7;
}


}
```

LoginWorkflow Stateless Session Bean

The LoginWorkflow stateless session bean consists of three files: a remote interface, a home interface, and an implementation class.

LoginWorkflow.java

LoginWorkflow.java contains the one remotely accessible method for the LoginWorkflow session bean, as shown in Figure 11.24.

Since LoginWorkflow is a stateless session bean, each method includes all of the information needed to perform the request. For example, setPassword must specify the user, since the LoginWorkflow session bean does not remember who is logged in. In fact, consecutive calls to a stateless session bean are frequently received by different bean implementations. The container pools implementations, and can do as it pleases with stateless session beans between method invocations.

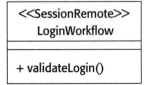

Figure 11.24 Remote interface for the LoginWorkflow stateless session bean.

```
package com.wiley.compBooks.EJwithUML.TimeCardWorkflow;

import java.rmi.*;
import javax.ejb.*;


/**
 * The LoginWorkflow allows client objects to validate users
 * and update their paswords.
 *
 * LoginWorkflow is the remote interface through which clients
 * access the underlying
 * session bean.
 *
 */
public interface LoginWorkflow extends EJBObject
{
  /** Answers true if the password is correct for the specified
   *  user. */
  public boolean isUserValid(String username, String password)
                                        throws RemoteException;

  /** Answers true if the password is due to be changed. */
  public boolean isPasswordChangeRequired(String username)
                                        throws RemoteException;

  /** Sets the password, if the old password is valid. */
  public void setPassword(String username, String oldPassword,
      String newPassword) throws RemoteException;
}
```

LoginWorkflowHome.java

LoginWorkflowHome.java is the home interface for the LoginWorkflow session bean.
It contains the method by which LoginWorkflow session beans are created.

Since LoginWorkflow is a stateless session bean, there would not be much point to
including parameters in the create method. Nevertheless, we must specify the method.

```
package com.wiley.compBooks.EJwithUML.TimeCardWorkflow;

import java.util.*;
import java.rmi.*;
import javax.ejb.*;


/**
 * The LoginWorkflow allows client objects to validate users
 * and update their paswords.
 *
 * LoginWorkflowHome is the remote interface through which
 * clients find and create the underlying session beans.
 *
```

```
    */
public interface LoginWorkflowHome extends EJBHome
{
    /** Answers a reference to the newly created Activity bean.*/
    public LoginWorkflow create() throws CreateException,
                                                RemoteException;

}
```

LoginWorkflowBean.java

LoginWorkflowBean.java is the implementation class for the LoginWorkflow session bean.

As you can see in the code here for the isPasswordValid method, LoginWorkflow-Bean obtains and uses remote references to entity beans as it needs them. There is no way for one entity or session bean to directly get at an implementation bean. Instead, the entity or session bean must obtain a remote reference. Performance between two local beans is dramatically better than the performance between a client object in a different VM and a bean in an application server, even if both VMs are on the same host. Otherwise, local access and remote access of a bean use the same remote and home interfaces and very similar name resolution code.

```
package com.wiley.compBooks.EJwithUML.TimeCardWorkflow;

import com.wiley.compBooks.EJwithUML.EjbUtil.*;
import com.wiley.compBooks.EJwithUML.TimeCardDomain.*;
import java.util.*;
import java.rmi.*;
import javax.ejb.*;
import javax.naming.*;


/**
 * The LoginWorkflow allows client objects to validate users
 * and update their paswords.
 *
 * LoginWorkflowBean is the actual session bean implementation.
 *
 */
public class LoginWorkflowBean extends BasicSessionBean
{
    public void ejbCreate() throws CreateException
    {
    }

    public void ejbPostCreate()
    {
    }

    /** Answers true if the password is correct for the specified
```

```
 * user. */
public boolean isUserValid(String username, String password)
{
  try
  {
    Context initialContext = getInitialContext();
    UserHome ehome =
        (UserHome)initialContext.lookup("EmployeeBean");

    Enumeration employees = ehome.findByUserName(username);
    if (!employees.hasMoreElements())
    {
      return false;
    }

    Employee employee = (User) employees.nextElement();
    return employee.isPasswordValid(password);
  }
  catch (NamingException e)
  {
    throw new EJBException("" +e);
  }
  catch (FinderException e)
  {
    throw new EJBException("" +e);
  }
}

/** Answers true if the password is due to be changed. */
public boolean isPasswordChangeRequired(String username)
{
  try
  {
    Context initialContext = getInitialContext();
    UserHome ehome =
        (UserHome)initialContext.lookup("EmployeeBean");

    Enumeration employees = ehome.findByUserName(username);
    if (!employees.hasMoreElements())
    {
      throw new EJBException("User does not exist.");
    }

    User employee = (User) employees.nextElement();
    return employee.isPasswordChangeRequired();
  }
  catch (NamingException e)
  {
    throw new EJBException("" +e);
  }
  catch (FinderException e)
```

```
   {
     throw new EJBException("" +e);
   }

  }

  /** Sets the password, if the old password is valid. */
  public void setPassword(String username, String oldPassword,
                          String newPassword)
  {
    try
    {
      Context initialContext = getInitialContext();
      UserHome ehome =
          (UserHome)initialContext.lookup("UserBean");

      Enumeration employees = ehome.findByUserName(username);
      if (!employees.hasMoreElements())
      {
        throw new EJBException("User does not exist.");
      }

      User employee = (Employee) employees.nextElement();

      if (!employee.isPasswordValid(oldPassword))
      {
        throw new EJBException("Old password is invalid.");
      }

      employee.setPassword(newPassword);
    }
    catch (NamingException e)
    {
      throw new EJBException("" +e);
    }
    catch (FinderException e)
    {
      throw new EJBException("" +e);
    }
  }

}
```

RecordTimeWorkflow Stateful Session Bean

The RecordTimeWorkflow stateless session bean consists of three files: a remote interface, a home interface, and an implementation class.

RecordTimeWorkflow.java

RecordTimeWorkflow.java contains all of the remotely accessible methods for the RecordTimeWorkflow session bean, as shown in Figure 11.25.

Since RecordTimeWorkflow is a stateful session bean, each method assumes a particular session, which involves a single user and a single current timecard. This allows the getChargeCodes to have an empty parameter list.

Again, notice that each return type is an array of primitives or an array of custom wrapper objects that wrap primitives. This eliminates versioning issues when the remote client object deserializes the object.

```java
package com.wiley.compBooks.EJwithUML.TimeCardWorkflow;

import java.rmi.*;
import javax.ejb.*;
import java.util.*;

/**
 * The RecordTimeWorkflow allows client objects to record their
 * time.
 *
 * RecordTimeWorkflow is the remote interface through which
 * clients access the underlying session bean.
 *
 */
public interface RecordTimeWorkflow extends EJBObject
{
  /** Answers an array of charge code wrappers. */
  public ChargeCodeWrapper[] getChargeCodes() throws
                                        RemoteException;

  /** Answers an array of the dates for the current timecard.*/
  public Date[] getDates() throws RemoteException;

  /** Answers an array of the hours for the current timecard.*/
  public float[] getHours() throws RemoteException;
```

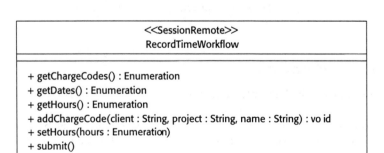

Figure 11.25 Remote interface for RecordTimeWorkflow session bean.

```
    /** Adds the specified charge code to the current timecard. */
    public void addChargeCode(String client, String project,
                             String name) throws RemoteException;

    /** Sets the hours for the current timecard. */
    public void setHours(float[] hours) throws RemoteException;

    /** Submits the current timecard. */
    public void submitTimecard() throws RemoteException;

}
```

RecordTimeWorkflowHome.java

RecordTimeWorkflowHome.java contains the methods for creating RecordTimeWorkflowHome session beans.

The create method requires a username. This associates the RecordTimeWorkflow session bean with a single user for the life of the session.

```
package com.wiley.compBooks.EJwithUML.TimeCardWorkflow;

import java.util.*;
import java.rmi.*;
import javax.ejb.*;

/**
 * The RecordTimeWorkflow allows client objects to record their
 * time.
 *
 * RecordTimeWorkflowHome is the remote interface through which
 * clients find and create the underlying session beans.
 *
 */
public interface RecordTimeWorkflowHome extends EJBHome
{
    /** Answers a reference to the newly created Activity bean.*/
    public RecordTimeWorkflow create(String username) throws
                             CreateException,RemoteException;
}
```

RecordTimeWorkflowBean.java

RecordTimeWorkflowBean.java is the implementation class for the RecordTimeWorkflow session bean.

Most of this code should be somewhere between familiar, and monotonous, by this point. However, there is one new wrinkle, as the ejbCreate method finds a User entity bean based on the username parameter. This bean reference is kept for the duration of the stateful session.

The RecordTimeWorkflow session bean wraps the data for a charge code into a custom ChargeCodeWrapper object. This avoids the versioning issues, while providing a convenient interface for the client object.

```java
package com.wiley.compBooks.EJwithUML.TimeCardWorkflow;

import com.wiley.compBooks.EJwithUML.TimeCardDomain.*;
import com.wiley.compBooks.EJwithUML.EjbUtil.*;
import java.util.*;
import java.rmi.*;
import javax.ejb.*;
import javax.naming.*;


/**
 * The RecordTimeWorkflow allows client objects to record their
 * time.
 *
 * RecordTimeWorkflowBean is the actual session bean
 * implementation.
 *
 */
public class RecordTimeWorkflowBean extends BasicSessionBean
{
  private Timecard timecard;
  private Employee employee;


  public void ejbCreate(String username) throws
                          RemoteException, CreateException
  {
    try
    {
      Context initialContext = getInitialContext();
      UserHome ehome =
          (UserHome)initialContext.lookup("UserBean");
      Enumeration employees = ehome.findByUserName(username);
      if (employees.hasMoreElements())
      {
        this.employee = (Employee) employees.nextElement();
        this.timecard = employee.getCurrentTimecard();
      }
    }
    catch (NamingException e)
    {
      throw new RemoteException("" +e);
    }
    catch (FinderException e)
    {
      throw new RemoteException("" +e);
```

```
        }
    }

    public void ejbPostCreate(String username)
    {
    }

    /** Answers an array of charge code wrappers. */
    public ChargeCodeWrapper[] getChargeCodes()
    {
      ChargeCode[] codes = this.timecard.getChargeCodes();
      ChargeCodeWrapper[] wrappers = new
          ChargeCodeWrapper[codes.length];

      for (int ctr=0; ctr < codes.length; ctr++)
      {
        String codeName = codes[ctr].getName();
        Project project = codes[ctr].getProject();
        String projectName = project.getName();
        String clientName = project.getClient().getName();

        wrappers[ctr] = new ChargeCodeWrapper(clientName,
            projectName, codeName);
      }

      return wrappers;
    }

    /** Answers an array of the dates for the current timecard.*/
    public Date[] getDates()
    {
      return this.timecard.getDates();
    }

    /** Answers an array of the hours for the current timecard.*/
    public float[] getHours()
    {
      return this.timecard.getHours();
    }

    /** Adds the specified charge code to the current timecard. */
    public void addChargeCode(String clientName, String
                              projectName, String name)
    {
      this.timecard.addChargeCode(clientName, projectName, name);
    }

    /** Sets the hours for the current timecard. */
    public void setHours(float[] hours)
    {
      this.timecard.setHours(hours);
```

```
  }

  /** Submits the current timecard. */
  public void submitTimecard()
  {
    try
    {
      Context initialContext = getInitialContext();
      TimecardHome thome =
          (TimecardHome)initialContext.lookup("TimecardBean");
      Timecard timecard = thome.create((String)
          this.employee.getPrimaryKey());
      this.employee.setCurrentTimecard(timecard);
    }
    catch (NamingException e)
    {
      throw new EJBException("" +e);
    }
    catch (CreateException e)
    {
      throw new EJBException("" +e);
    }
  }
}
```

Supporting Classes

The rest of the classes for this chapter support the classes that were found in the design. While implementing a design, developers often discover classes that capture common functionality or provide significant functionality. As long as these new classes do not significantly impact the architecture by introducing new dependencies between packages, this discovery process is a healthy refinement of the design.

BasicSessionBean.java

The BasicSessionBean class removes some of the drudgery from creating implementation classes for session beans. It provides default implementations for all of the required EJB methods. Except for the initial context, all of the methods are empty.

```
package com.wiley.compBooks.EJwithUML.EjbUtil;

import java.rmi.*;
import javax.ejb.*;
import javax.naming.*;


public abstract class BasicSessionBean implements SessionBean
{
  protected SessionContext context;
```

```java
    public void ejbRemove() throws RemoteException
    {
    }

    public void ejbPassivate() throws RemoteException
    {
    }

    public void ejbActivate() throws RemoteException
    {
    }

    public void setSessionContext(SessionContext context)
    {
      this.context = context;
    }

    protected Context getInitialContext() throws NamingException
    {
      return new InitialContext();
    }
}
```

BasicEntityBean.java

The BasicEntityBean.java class removes some of the drudgery from creating implementation classes for entity beans. It provides default implementations for all of the required methods. Except for the initial context, all of the required methods are empty.

BasicEntityBean also provides a checkForDuplicates method that can be called from the create method in each bean implementation. The checkForDuplicates calls doCheckForDuplicates, which must be implemented in the subclass. This allows BasicEntityBean to do the boring exception handling, while each subclass fills in the interesting duplicate checking logic.

```java
    package com.wiley.compBooks.EJwithUML.EjbUtil;

    import java.rmi.*;
    import javax.ejb.*;
    import javax.naming.*;

    public abstract class BasicEntityBean implements EntityBean
    {
      protected EntityContext context;

      public BasicEntityBean()
      {
      }

      public void setEntityContext(EntityContext context) throws
```

```
                                          RemoteException
{
  this.context = context;
}

public void unsetEntityContext() throws RemoteException
{
  this.context = null;
}

public void ejbPassivate() throws RemoteException
{
}

public void ejbRemove() throws RemoteException
{
}

public void ejbLoad() throws RemoteException
{
  try
  {
    doLoad();
  }
  catch (NamingException e)
  {
    throw new RemoteException(e.toString());
  }
  catch (FinderException e)
  {
    throw new RemoteException(e.toString());
  }
}

public void ejbStore() throws RemoteException
{
}

public void ejbActivate() throws RemoteException
{
}

public void checkForDuplicates() throws CreateException
{
  try
  {
    doCheckForDuplicates();
  }
  catch (FinderException e)
  {
    throw new CreateException("BasicEntityBean: Unable to
```

```
              check for duplicates. " +e);
      }
      catch (NamingException e)
      {
        throw new CreateException("BasicEntityBean: Unable to
            check for duplicates. " +e);
      }
      catch (RemoteException e)
      {
        throw new CreateException("BasicEntityBean: Unable to
            check for duplicates. " +e);
      }
    }

    protected Context getInitialContext() throws NamingException
    {
      return new InitialContext();
    }

    protected abstract void doCheckForDuplicates() throws
        CreateException, FinderException, NamingException,
        RemoteException;

    protected abstract void doLoad() throws NamingException,
        FinderException, RemoteException;
}
```

Activity Entity Bean

The Activity entity bean is a simple data repository with no behavior beyond a simple check for uniqueness. An activity is a unit of work that can be used for a charge code.

Activity.java

Activity.java is the remote interface for the Activity entity bean. It defines all of the remotely accessible methods for the Activity entity bean.

```
package com.wiley.compBooks.EJwithUML.TimeCardDomain;

import java.rmi.*;
import javax.ejb.*;

/**
 * The Activity bean holds simple descriptive information on a
 * common activity that is performed by development teams. This
 * activity may be used to create a ChargeCode.
 *
 * Activity is the remote interface through which clients
 * access the underlying entity bean.
 *
```

```
 */
public interface Activity extends EJBObject
{

  /** Answers the name of this Activity. */
  public String getName() throws RemoteException;

  /** Answers the description of this Activity. */
  public String getDescription() throws RemoteException;

  /** Answers the state data for this Activity. */
  public String getStateData() throws RemoteException;


}
```

ActivityHome.java

ActivityHome.java is the home interface for the Activity entity bean. It defines the
methods for finding and creating Activity entity beans.

```
package com.wiley.compBooks.EJwithUML.TimeCardDomain;

import java.util.*;
import java.rmi.*;
import javax.ejb.*;

/**
 * The Activity bean holds simple descriptive information on a
 * common activity that is performed by development teams. This
 * activity may be used to create a ChargeCode.
 *
 * ActivityHome is the remote interface through which clients
 * find and create the underlying entity beans.
 *
 */
public interface ActivityHome extends EJBHome
{
  /** Answers an Enumeration containing references to each
    * Activity bean.*/
  public Enumeration findAll() throws FinderException,
                                      RemoteException;

  /** Answers an Enumeration containing references to all
    * Activity beans that match the name. Should only return
    * one. */
  public Enumeration findByName(String name) throws
                            FinderException, RemoteException;

  /** Answers a reference to the Activity bean, if it exists.*/
  public Activity findByPrimaryKey(String activityId) throws
```

```
                              FinderException, RemoteException;

  /** Answers a reference to the newly created Activity bean.*/
  public Activity create(String name, String description)
                         throws CreateException,RemoteException;

}
```

ActivityBean.java

ActivityBean.java is the implementation class for the Activity entity bean. It contains the actual data and logic for the bean. There is not much to it, just an ID, a name, and a description.

```
package com.wiley.compBooks.EJwithUML.TimeCardDomain;

import com.wiley.compBooks.EJwithUML.EjbUtil.*;
import java.util.*;
import java.rmi.*;
import javax.ejb.*;
import javax.naming.*;


/**
 * The Activity bean holds simple descriptive information on a
 * common activity
 * that is performed by development teams. This activity may be
 * used to create a ChargeCode.
 *
 * ActivityBean is the actual entity bean implementation.
 *
 */
public class ActivityBean extends BasicEntityBean
{
  public String id;
  public String name;
  public String description;

  public ActivityBean()
  {
  }

  /** Creates an ActivityBean with the specified parameters.
   *  This is never called directly. */
  public String ejbCreate(String name, String description)
                    throws RemoteException, CreateException
  {
    this.id = "Activity" + IdGenerator.getId();
    this.name = name;
    this.description = description;
```

```java
    checkForDuplicates();

  return null;
}

/** Actions performed after creation. This is never called
 *   directly. */
public void ejbPostCreate(String name, String description)
{
}

/** Answers the name of this ActivityBean. */
public String getName()
{
  return this.name;
}

/** Answers the description of this ActivityBean. */
public String getDescription()
{
  return this.description;
}

/** Answers the state data for this Activity. */
public String getStateData()
{
  String data = "\nId = "+this.id+ "\nName = " +this.name+
                "\nDescription = " +this.description;
  return data;
}


/** Checks for duplicates. Overrides method from.
 *   BasicEntityBean. */
protected void doCheckForDuplicates() throws CreateException,
                FinderException, NamingException, RemoteException
{
  Context initialContext = getInitialContext();
  ActivityHome home =
      (ActivityHome)initialContext.lookup("ActivityBean");

  Enumeration enum = home.findByName(name);
  if (enum.hasMoreElements())
  {
    throw new CreateException("Duplicate Activity: " +name);
  }
}

/** Overrides method from BasicEntityBean. */
protected void doLoad() throws RemoteException,
                               NamingException, FinderException
```

```
      {
      }
   }
```

ChargeCode Entity Bean

The ChargeCode entity bean is a simple data repository with no behavior beyond a simple check for uniqueness. A charge code is a billable unit of work.

ChargeCode.java

ChargeCode.java is the remote interface for the ChargeCode entity bean. It defines all of the remotely accessible methods for the ChargeCode entity bean.

```
package com.wiley.compBooks.EJwithUML.TimeCardDomain;

import java.rmi.*;
import javax.ejb.*;

/**
 * The ChargeCode bean holds descriptive information about a
 * billable charge code.
 * Since each ChargeCode is part of a larger project, the parent
 * project can be accessed from the charge code.
 *
 * ChargeCode is the remote interface through which clients
 * access the underlying entity bean.
 */
public interface ChargeCode extends EJBObject
{

  /** Answers the name of this ChargeCode. */
  public String getName() throws RemoteException;

  /** Answers the description of this ChargeCode. */
  public String getDescription() throws RemoteException;

  /** Answers the parent Project of this ChargeCode. */
  public Project getProject() throws RemoteException;
}
```

ChargeCodeHome

ChargeCodeHome.java is the Home interface for the ChargeCode entity bean. It defines the methods for finding and creating ChargeCode entity beans.

```
package com.wiley.compBooks.EJwithUML.TimeCardDomain;

import java.util.*;
```

```java
import java.rmi.*;
import javax.ejb.*;

/**
 * The ChargeCode bean holds simple descriptive information on
 * a common Activity that is performed for a client.
 *
 * ChargeCodeHome is the remote interface through which clients
 * find and create the underlying entity beans.
 *
 */
public interface ChargeCodeHome extends EJBHome
{

  /** Answers an Enumeration containing references to each
   *  ChargeCode bean that has the specified project as its
   *  parent.*/
  public Enumeration findByProject(String projectId) throws
                              FinderException, RemoteException;

  /** Answers an Enumeration containing references to each
   *  ChargeCode bean. Should be unique. */
  public Enumeration findChargeCode(String projectId,
                              String name)
                  throws FinderException,RemoteException;

  /** Answers reference to the ChargeCode bean,if it exists.*/
  public ChargeCode findByPrimaryKey(String chargeCodeId)
                      throws FinderException,RemoteException;

  /** Answers reference to the newly created ChargeCode bean.*/
  public ChargeCode create(String projectId, String name,
       String description) throws RemoteException,
                              CreateException;

}
```

ChargeCodeBean.java

ChargeCodeBean.java is the implementation class for the ChargeCode entity bean. It provides the data and logic for the bean. Again, there is not much to it. Each ChargeCode entity bean holds an ID, a name, a description, and the ID of the project entity bean to which it belongs.

```java
package com.wiley.compBooks.EJwithUML.TimeCardDomain;

import com.wiley.compBooks.EJwithUML.EjbUtil.*;
import java.util.*;
import java.rmi.*;
import javax.ejb.*;
import javax.naming.*;
```

```java
/**
 * The ChargeCode bean holds descriptive information about a
 * billable charge code.
 * Since each ChargeCode is part of a larger Project, the
 * parent Project can be accessed from the charge code.
 *
 * ChargeCodeBean is the actual entity bean implementation.
 */
public class ChargeCodeBean extends BasicEntityBean
{
  public String id;
  public String name;
  public String description;
  public String projectId;

  private Project project;

  public ChargeCodeBean()
  {
  }

  /** Creates an ChargeCodeBean with the specified parameters.
   *  This is never called directly. */
  public String ejbCreate(String projectId, String name, String
                          description) throws RemoteException,
                                                  CreateException
  {
    this.id = "ChargeCode" + IdGenerator.getId();
    this.projectId = projectId;
    this.name = name;
    this.description = description;

    this.checkForDuplicates();
    return null;
  }

  /** Actions performed after creation. This is never called
   *  directly. */
  public void ejbPostCreate(String projectId, String name,
                      String description) throws RemoteException
  {
  }

  /** Answers the name of this ChargeCode. */
  public String getName()
  {
    return this.name;
  }
```

```
/** Answers the description of this ChargeCode. */
public String getDescription()
{
  return this.description;
}

/** Answers the parent Project of this ChargeCode. */
public Project getProject()
{
  try
  {
    if (this.project == null)
    {
      Context initialContext = getInitialContext();
      ProjectHome phome =
          (ProjectHome)initialContext.lookup("ProjectBean");
      this.project = phome.findByPrimaryKey(this.projectId);
    }
  }
  catch (NamingException e)
  {
    throw new EJBException(e.toString());
  }
  catch (FinderException e)
  {
    throw new EJBException(e.toString());
  }

  return this.project;
}

/** Checks for duplicates. Overrides method from
  * BasicEntityBean.*/
public void doCheckForDuplicates() throws CreateException,
                  FinderException, NamingException, RemoteException
{
  Context initialContext = getInitialContext();
  ChargeCodeHome home =
      (ChargeCodeHome)initialContext.lookup("ChargeCodeBean");

  Enumeration enum = home.findChargeCode(this.projectId,
                                         this.name);
  if (enum.hasMoreElements())
  {
    throw new CreateException("Duplicate ChargeCode: ");
  }
}

protected void doLoad() throws RemoteException,
                               NamingException, FinderException
```

```
        {
        }
    }
```

Client Entity Bean

The Client entity bean is a simple data repository with no behavior beyond a simple check for uniqueness. A client represents an organization that hires the company to perform some task or tasks.

Client.java

Client.java is the remote interface for the Client entity bean. It defines all of the remotely accessible methods for the Client entity bean.

```
package com.wiley.compBooks.EJwithUML.TimeCardDomain;

import java.util.*;
import java.rmi.*;
import javax.ejb.*;

/**
 * The Client bean holds descriptive information about a
 * client.
 *
 * Client is the remote interface through which clients access
 * the underlying entity bean.
 *
 */
public interface Client extends EJBObject
{

  /** Answers the name of this Client. */
  public String getName() throws RemoteException;

  /** Answers the description of this Client. */
  public String getDescription() throws RemoteException;

}
```

ClientHome.java

ClientHome.java is the home interface for the Client entity bean. It defines the methods for finding and creating Client entity beans.

```
package com.wiley.compBooks.EJwithUML.TimeCardDomain;

import java.util.*;
import java.rmi.*;
```

```
import javax.ejb.*;

/**
 * The Client bean holds descriptive information about a
 * client.
 *
 * ClientHome is the remote interface through which clients
 * find and create the underlying entity beans.
 *
 */
public interface ClientHome extends EJBHome
{

  /** Answers an Enumeration that holds references to all of
   *  the Client beans. */
  public Enumeration findAll() throws FinderException,
                                      RemoteException;

  /** Answers an Enumeration that holds references to all of
   *  the Client beans that match the name parameter. */
  public Enumeration findByName(String name) throws
                          FinderException, RemoteException;

  /** Answers a reference to the Client bean, if it exists. */
  public Client findByPrimaryKey(String clientId) throws
                          FinderException, RemoteException;

  /** Answers a reference to the newly created Client bean. */
  public Client create(String name, String description) throws
                          CreateException, RemoteException;

}
```

ClientBean.java

ClientBean.java is the implementation class for the Client entity bean. It contains the data and logic for the bean.

```
package com.wiley.compBooks.EJwithUML.TimeCardDomain;

import com.wiley.compBooks.EJwithUML.EjbUtil.*;
import java.util.*;
import java.rmi.*;
import javax.ejb.*;
import javax.naming.*;

/**
 * The Client bean holds descriptive information about a
 * client.
 *
 * ClientBean is the actual entity bean implementation.
```

```
 *
 */
public class ClientBean extends BasicEntityBean
{
  public String id;
  public String name;
  public String description;

  public ClientBean()
  {
  }

  /** Creates an ClientBean with the specified parameters. This
   *  is never called directly. */
  public String ejbCreate(String name, String description)
                          throws RemoteException, CreateException
  {
    this.id = "Client" +IdGenerator.getId();
    this.name = name;
    this.description = description;

    checkForDuplicates();

    return null;
  }

  /** Actions performed after creation. This is never called
   *  directly. */
  public void ejbPostCreate(String name, String description)
                                            throws RemoteException
  {
  }

  /** Answers the name of this Client. */
  public String getName()
  {
    return this.name;
  }

  /** Answers the description of this Client. */
  public String getDescription()
  {
    return this.description;
  }

  /** Checks for duplicates. Overrides method from
   *  BasicEntityBean.*/
  public void doCheckForDuplicates() throws CreateException,
                FinderException, NamingException, RemoteException
  {
```

```
        Context initialContext = getInitialContext();
        ClientHome home =
            (ClientHome)initialContext.lookup("ClientBean");

        Enumeration enum = home.findByName(name);
        if (enum.hasMoreElements())
        {
          throw new CreateException("Duplicate Client: ");
        }
    }

    protected void doLoad() throws RemoteException,
                                    NamingException, FinderException
    {
    }
}
```

Project Entity Bean

The Project entity bean is a simple data repository with no behavior beyond a simple check for uniqueness. A project represents a large-scale task or deliverable that may contain many charge codes for a client.

Project.java

Project.java is the remote interface for the Project entity bean. It defines the remotely accessible methods for the Project entity bean.

```
package com.wiley.compBooks.EJwithUML.TimeCardDomain;

import java.util.*;
import java.rmi.*;
import javax.ejb.*;

/**
 * The Project bean holds descriptive information about a
 * project.
 *
 * Project is the remote interface through which clients access
 * the underlying entity bean.
 *
 */
public interface Project extends EJBObject
{
  /** Answers the name of this Project. */
  public String getName() throws RemoteException;

  /** Answers the description of this Project. */
  public String getDescription() throws RemoteException;
```

```
  /** Answers the parent Client of this Project. */
  public Client getClient() throws RemoteException;
}
```

ProjectHome.java

ProjectHome.java is the home interface for the Project entity bean. It defines the methods for finding and creating Project entity beans.

```
package com.wiley.compBooks.EJwithUML.TimeCardDomain;

import java.util.*;
import java.rmi.*;
import javax.ejb.*;

/**
 * The Project bean holds descriptive information about a
 * project.
 *
 * ProjectHome is the remote interface through which clients
 * find and create the underlying entity beans.
 *
 */

public interface ProjectHome extends EJBHome
{

  /** Answers an Enumeration that contains references to all
   *  Project beans that have the specified client id. */
  public Enumeration findByClientId(String clientId) throws
                            FinderException,RemoteException;

  /** Answers an Enumeration that contains references to
   * Project beans that have the specified name. Should be
   * unique. */
  public Enumeration findProject(String clientId, String name)
                        throws FinderException,RemoteException;

  /** Answers a reference to the Project if it exists. */
  public Project findByPrimaryKey(String projectId) throws
                            FinderException,RemoteException;

  /** Answers a reference to the newly created Project. */
  public Project create(String clientId, String name, String
              description) throws CreateException,RemoteException;
}
```

ProjectBean.java

ProjectBean.java is the implementation class for the Project entity bean. It holds the
data and logic for the bean.

```java
package com.wiley.compBooks.EJwithUML.TimeCardDomain;

import com.wiley.compBooks.EJwithUML.EjbUtil.*;
import java.util.*;
import java.rmi.*;
import javax.ejb.*;
import javax.naming.*;

/**
 * The Project bean holds descriptive information about a
 * Project.
 *
 * ProjectBean is the actual entity bean implementation.
 *
 */

public class ProjectBean extends BasicEntityBean
{
  public String id;
  public String clientId;
  public String name;
  public String description;

  private Client client;

  public ProjectBean()
  {
  }

  /** Creates an ProjectBean with the specified parameters. This
   * is never called directly. */
  public String ejbCreate(String clientId, String name, String
               description) throws RemoteException, CreateException
  {
    this.id = "Project" +IdGenerator.getId();
    this.name = name;
    this.description = description;
    this.clientId = clientId;

    return null;
  }

  /** Actions performed after creation. This is never called
   * directly. */
  public void ejbPostCreate(String clientId, String name,
```

```
                 String description) throws RemoteException,CreateException
{
}

/** Answers the name of this Project. */
public String getName()
{
  return this.name;
}

/** Answers the description of this Project. */
public String getDescription()
{
  return this.description;
}


/** Answers the parent Client of this Project. */
public Client getClient()
{
  try
  {
    if (this.client == null)
    {
      Context initialContext = getInitialContext();
      ClientHome chome =
          (ClientHome)initialContext.lookup("ClientBean");
      this.client = chome.findByPrimaryKey(this.clientId);
    }
  }
  catch (NamingException e)
  {
    throw new EJBException(e.toString());
  }
  catch (FinderException e)
  {
    throw new EJBException(e.toString());
  }

  return this.client;
}

public void ejbStore() throws RemoteException
{
}

/** Checks for duplicates. Overrides method from
 *  BasicEntityBean.*/
public void doCheckForDuplicates() throws CreateException,
          FinderException, NamingException, RemoteException
```

```
  {
    Context initialContext = getInitialContext();
    ProjectHome phome =
         (ProjectHome)initialContext.lookup("ProjectBean");

    // projects must be unique for all clients
    Enumeration enum = phome.findProject(this.clientId,
this.name);
    if (enum.hasMoreElements())
    {
      throw new CreateException("Duplicate Project: ");
    }
  }

  protected void doLoad() throws RemoteException,
      NamingException, FinderException
  {
  }
}
```

ChargeCodeWrapper.java

ChargeCodeWrapper.java encapsulates the details of a specific charge code inside a simple data container. This allows methods of Enterprise JavaBeans to return a small serializable chunk of data, rather than a less efficient remote reference. Of course, the wrapper is less flexible than the remote reference.

```
package com.wiley.compBooks.EJwithUML.TimeCardWorkflow;

import java.io.*;

public class ChargeCodeWrapper implements Serializable
{
  private String clientName;
  private String projectName;
  private String chargeCodeName;

  public ChargeCodeWrapper(String clientName, String
                           projectName, String chargeCodeName)
  {
    this.clientName = clientName;
    this.projectName = projectName;
    this.chargeCodeName = chargeCodeName;
  }

  public String getClientName()
  {
    return this.clientName;
  }
```

```
public String getProjectName()
{
  return this.projectName;
}

public String getChargeCodeName()
{
  return this.chargeCodeName;
}
}
```

Node.java

A Node holds child nodes and may be a child of another Node object. It allows the composition of arbitrary tree structures.

```
package com.wiley.compBooks.EJwithUML.TimeCardWorkflow;

import java.util.*;
import java.io.*;

public class Node implements Serializable
{
  private String name;
  private String description;
  private Vector children = new Vector();

  public Node(String name, String description)
  {
    this.name = name;
    this.description = description;
  }

  public void addChild(Node child)
  {
    this.children.addElement(child);
  }

  public Node[] getChildren()
  {
    int size = this.children.size();
    Node[] nodes = new Node[size];
    for (int ctr=0; ctr < size; ctr++)
    {
      nodes[ctr] = (Node) this.children.elementAt(ctr);
    }
    return nodes;
  }
```

```
    public String getName()
    {
      return this.name;
    }

    public String getDescription()
    {
      return this.description;
    }

}
```

The Next Step

The design and implementation for the TimecardDomain and TimecardWorkflow packages are now complete. Now we move on to the next design effort: the HTML Production class library.

Design for HTML Production

Much of our system's functionality will be obtained via Web browsers, so we will be producing a huge volume of moderately complex HTML. This can be a daunting task, as HTML and its surrounding technologies are often a capricious and unforgiving lot. There are details to learn for each browser, and a frighteningly large number of potential solutions for any problem. HTML documents can be both disturbingly large and incomprehensibly dense. Many large-scale Web-based systems are composed of hundreds of different screens, each sharing some common elements, and many with unique aspects.

One effective approach to these issues is to develop a class library that is dedicated to the production of HTML. Servlet developers will use this framework as they build the user interface classes. Ideally, the servlet developers should not even need to directly produce any HTML. Instead, they will depend on HTML production classes to handle this tedious task.

Designing a class library is quite different from designing a package based on use cases; therefore, we will deviate a bit from the normal design steps. First, we will establish goals for the design. Next, we will attempt to design to one or more goals. It may help to consider existing design patterns or existing products as guides in this effort. Then we will measure the resulting design against the goals. Finally, we will flesh out our design to support our particular user interface needs.

NOTE Remember, design is an iterative process; doing refactoring or even completely changing your mind is a natural part of the process.

Design Goals

Before we can design a clever solution to our problem, it is essential to formally determine the design goals for the HTML production framework. After all, how can we hit an undefined target? Think of the goals for a subsystem or framework as a technically oriented internal requirements document. The goals detail how other parts of the system will interact with the framework, and what these parts can expect from it.

You must establish concrete examples and very specific criteria for your goals before you begin to design. Clear and quantifiable goals can drive a design and provide a valuable measure of success. Vaguely defined goals do not provide direction for the design, and tend to frustrate developers more than they help. For example, it is far more useful to require the framework to support new versions of Internet Explorer than to require the framework to be extensible in some generic sense.

Let's take a look at the design goals for the HTML production class library.

Goal 1: Support Modular Construction of Views

It can be useful to nest one HTML component inside another HTML component to form a more complex page. A page might contain a table, an input form, and some text. One cell in the table might contain an image while another cell contains another complete table. Component nesting allows a patient developer to assemble arbitrarily complex pages from a small number of relatively simple building blocks. We want our underlying HTML production classes to allow a presentation developer to easily nest and combine structures.

Consider a page that contains a table, which in turn contains an image and some text. This moderately complex view is built by combining these three simple elements. The pseudocode for this table might look like the following:

1. Get a new table from the framework.
2. Get a new image from the framework, and set its source.
3. Add the image to the table.
4. Add text to the table.
5. Get a new page from the framework.
6. Add the table to the page.

Graphical interface programmers use this sort of bottom-up composition to stay sane while they create elaborate screens. Even the most complex screen is composed from a relatively small number of components, which are creatively combined. Our framework must provide the same capability.

Goal 2: Keep HTML Production Simple

We want the majority of our developers to remain focused on the intricacies of the business and to ignore the painful details that can be involved in generating the actual

HTML. Presentation developers must be able to add data to views without knowing about differences between browsers or which arcane option on a particular HTML tag does what.

In short, we want to keep HTML production simple. To do this, there are three specific criteria:

Hide the actual tags and options. Outside of the framework team, developers should not need more than a casual familiarity with HTML syntax.

Hide all browser-specific behavior. Application and presentation logic that uses the HTML production framework must be able to completely ignore browser-specific behavior. Developers trust the underlying framework to tailor the generated HTML for the user's browser.

Enable natural development of user interface. Adding content or data should be natural from the perspective of the view developer. It should not necessarily be dictated by the structure of the resulting HTML.

An example of how a view might use the class library might be helpful. Let's consider a view that extracts some data from the domain and displays it in a table. The pseudocode might look like the following:

1. Retrieve raw data from the domain.

2. Format the data into a two-dimensional array of strings.

3. Retrieve the user's context, including browser type, from the request.

4. Get a new page from the framework.

5. Set the title of the page.

6. Add some instructional text to the page.

7. Get a new table from the framework.

8. Set the column headings for the table.

9. Set the formatted data from step 2 as the table's data.

10. Add the table to the page.

11. Ask the page for its HTML.

Notice that the view does not know how the HTML is produced. It just wires the data into the elements that are provided by the framework.

By encapsulating the dirty details of HTML production, we allow staff specialization. Presentation developers can keep their data manipulation logic separate from the complexities of the actual HTML. This helps keep the code base smaller and easier to understand.

This is a very valuable form of reuse. It may not be as stunning or politically impressive as a cross-corporate domain infrastructure, but it is really nice when everyone can add data to a table and have it produce the same HTML. Without such a framework, developers must create their own unique and often incompatible solutions. When allowed to compound over time, this trend leads to chaos and terminal code bloat.

Goal 3: Support Preferences

Preferences allow the look and feel of a system to be modified to meet the user's wants or needs. For example, the user might want to change the color scheme, or draw solid lines around each cell of a table. This can involve changing a configuration file and restarting the system, but it should never require a change to the source code. Many users expect to change preferences while the system is running.

Since there are many types of screen elements, we must allow for many preference options. A page might allow customization of the background color and text color, while a table might allow customization of its colors, as well as the width of the border and various alignments. A system could use preferences to allow customization of tens or even hundreds of screen characteristics.

Preferences have one more interesting wrinkle. Different systems offer customization at different levels. A system with many anonymous customers would probably have a single look and feel that could be customized by the Web master. A complicated corporate intranet might allow each user to override these default choices with his or her own preferences. Some systems have a complicated preference scheme in which user choices override department choices that override the system defaults.

For simplicity and to enable reuse, our underlying HTML production framework must be oblivious to how the preferences are created, edited, and selected for a user. The framework will allow view objects to set the preferences for an element. It is up to the view to build the right preferences for a given circumstance. If no preference is set for an element, the preference for the enclosing element will be used. The framework will:

- Only apply preferences; it will not determine the correct preference for a situation.
- Allow preferences to be set at any level.
- Make it easy to extend preferences and to support entirely new types of preferences.

The framework will support preferences without losing its independence and reuse potential.

Goal 4: Extensibility and Encapsulation

Class library developers must be able to extend the framework easily and without impacting existing views. The presentation logic will not change to accommodate each new version of Internet Explorer or Netscape Navigator. These changes must be isolated to the framework.

Framework developers must be free to change the framework to take advantage of new browser features, to fix rendering anomalies, and to make changes to the look and feel of the system. These changes must not break the interface on which the presentation developers depend. The framework must accommodate the following changes without impacting existing client code or existing framework code:

- New browsers
- Changes to the HTML specification for an element
- Changes to the preferred look of an HTML element

The presentation layer is protected from changes in the HTML production classes, so the HTML production classes must be protected from changes in the application or presentation layers. To ensure this, the HTML production classes should depend only on primitives and standard Java classes. For instance, the framework must not know anything about timecards or employees. The user interface developer would need to extract data from any domain-specific classes before using it to configure any HTML production classes.

Meeting these specific design goals will allow the framework developers to keep the presentation developers happy over time. The encapsulation also will make it easier for other projects to reuse the entire framework.

Design to Goals

Once we have developed specific goals, the next step is to develop high-level designs that meet them. It is difficult to design for all of the goals simultaneously. Instead, we will design for one goal at a time and periodically check for contradictions.

Design for Goal 1: Support Modular Construction of Views

Supporting modular construction of views captures the flavor of the HTML production classes. The class library exists because it lets developers build elaborate structures from simple primitives.

The Composite Design Pattern

Goal 1 is also especially meaningful because it is a perfect fit for an existing design pattern. Gamma and his co-authors describe the Composite pattern's intent as follows: "Compose objects into tree structures to represent part-whole hierarchies. Composite lets clients treat individual objects and compositions of objects uniformly" [Gamma, et al.1995].

A tree structure that represents a part-whole hierarchy sounds applicable. We can represent our page as the following tree:

- Page
  - Table
    - Image
    - Text

The next part of the intent, "Composite lets clients treat individual objects and compositions of objects uniformly," is a bit more interesting. It implies that Composite objects implement the same interface as their children. So, the client does not care if it holds a reference to a Composite or an individual object. Similarly, a Composite does not care if a child is a Composite or an individual object.

Gamma and his colleagues demonstrate the pattern with graphical primitives, such as lines, rectangles, text, and pictures. These primitives can be combined to form elaborate pictures. As the intent states, the payoff comes when we draw the picture by asking the topmost container to draw itself. It in turn asks each of its children to draw itself. If it is a leaf, the child draws itself and is done. If it is a container, it draws itself then asks each of its children to draw itself. What a nice generic and recursive solution to a very common problem.

Applying Composite

Consider the potential for using the Composite pattern for the HTML production class library. The Composite pattern can be used to construct very complex HTML pages by combining relatively simple HTML producers.

For example, a table contains text, images, forms, and other tables. A page might contain a table, a form, images, and some miscellaneous text. A form might contain input fields, descriptive text, and one or more Submit buttons. Notice that some elements, such as forms and tables, can contain other elements. Other elements, such as text, cannot contain any other elements.

To access the elements, we need a common interface that the Composites and individual objects can implement. Since this is an HTML production framework, let's call the interface IHtmlProducer. Each Composite will have methods that add any IHtml-Producer. To keep names consistent, we'll name each class that implements IHtml-Producer with its type and the suffix Producer. For the example, we invent PageProducer, TextProducer, ImageProducer, and TableProducer. Each class formats its own HTML; and except for TextProducer, all can contain any other IHtmlProducer. So, we create the HTML page by creating a PageProducer object then adding a TableProducer to it. Next, we'll add an ImageProducer and a TextProducer to the TableProducer. Figure 12.1 shows how a composite page can be built from simple pieces. Note that each Composite can accept any IHtmlProducer.

Each type of producer has a different way to add a producer. The PageProducer adds one producer after another. The TableProducer allows control over the relative positioning of producers, by allowing us to add each producer to a separate cell in the table.

While each type of element needs different methods for adding data, all of them should support a simple way to retrieve the formatted HTML. Once the page has been constructed, getting the HTML is simple: The page asks each child for its HTML; then each child asks its children for their HTML. Notice in Figure 12.2 that each parent does not need to know much about its children. It just expects nicely formatted HTML when it asks for it. Figure 12.3 shows the producer classes and the common IHtmlProducer interface. Notice that the TableProducer and PageProducer may have many IHtmlProducers, but are completely unconcerned as to the type of any particular producer.

Design Evaluation

Let's express our design in terms of the Composite design pattern and evaluate our effectiveness. PageProducer and TableProducer are Composites since they implement the IHtmlProducer interface and contain objects that implement IHtmlProducer. This allows us to easily build complex HTML pages by combining IHtmlProducers. Also,

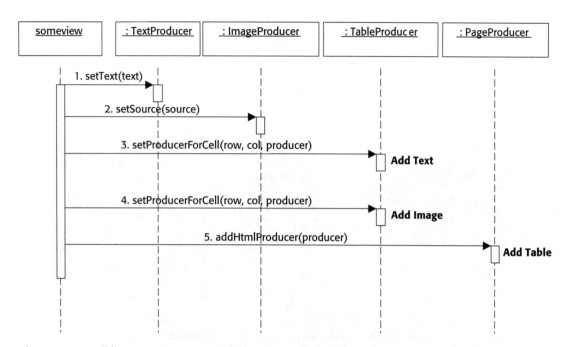

Figure 12.1 Building an IHTML page with the Composite pattern.

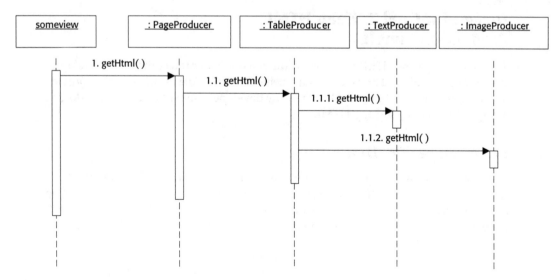

Figure 12.2 Retrieving HTML from a Composite.

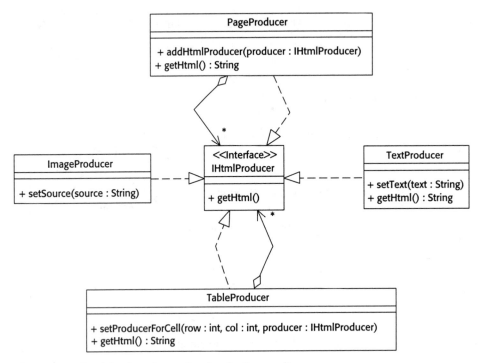

Figure 12.3 Participating classes for simple Composite.

when we add a new HTML producer, existing HTML producers are not affected. We used the Composite pattern to build a very modular class library.

Design for Goal 2: Keep HTML Production Simple

The first goal for the HTML production framework is to protect the view developers from HTML details and browser-specific behavior. So far, the design seems to provide a level of abstraction above HTML. The view developer can build a table and add it to a page without knowing any HTML.

Browser-Specific HTML

Although the design supports modular composition, it does not make any provision for browser-specific HTML production. It would be fairly simple, if tedious, to develop a separate class for each browser-specific version of each element. This might be worth the effort, since you can inherit common behavior and thus reuse it and still encapsulate any pesky and subtle differences.

Creating a separate class for each browser for HTML tables we end up with a hierarchy similar to that shown in Figure 12.4. Since HTML tables are fairly standardized in recent browsers, the generic TableProducer might do most of the work. Any browser-specific behavior can be overridden in the subclasses. This may seem like overkill for a TableProducer, but consider the differences between an Internet Explorer and a Netscape implementation of a TabbedPaneProducer. Notice that a view can populate and configure any TableProducer by using the public methods in the base class. Browser-specific implementations have different behavior behind the scenes, but never change the public interface.

The browser-specific behavior is encapsulated within the implementation classes. Once a view has the correct implementation, it can interact with it through the generic base class. We are making progress. Unfortunately, each view still needs to know which implementations are available and which is best for a particular situation. This means that to add support for a new browser requires changes in each view. This is clearly not acceptable.

The Abstract Factory Design Pattern

The Abstract Factory design pattern lets us hide the varying implementations behind a common interface. Its intent: "Provide an interface for creating families of related or

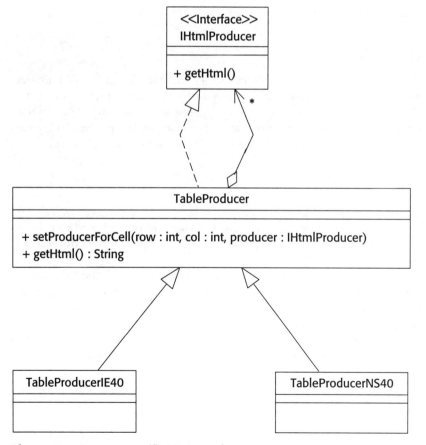

Figure 12.4 Browser-specific HTML producers.

dependent objects without specifying their concrete classes" is perfect [Gamma, et al. 1995]. Let's examine some participants as defined in the pattern and see how they apply to the example.

First, an AbstractProduct is an interface that is common to all implementations of a particular type of product. In this example, TableProducer is an AbstractProduct. A ConcreteFactory creates actual implementations of AbstractProducts for a particular family of products. For example, there might be separate ConcreteFactory classes for Netscape 4.0 and Internet Explorer 4.0. Each actual implementation, such as TableProducerIE40, is known as a ConcreteProduct.

Figure 12.5 shows the Abstract Factory pattern applied to some of the products in our application. The Netscape40Factory overrides AbstractFactory's interface by creating Netscape-specific objects that extend either TableProducer or PageProducer. When a client requests a product, the AbstractFactory identifies the right ConcreteFactory and asks it to create a ConcreteProduct. It is important to remember that the client never sees the ConcreteFactory or the ConcreteProduct. The presentation code has a reference to some arbitrary implementation of AbstractFactory. When the presentation code asks for a particular type of producer, the ConcreteFactory builds a very specific producer, but returns a reference to the producer's abstract base class, such as PageProducer or TableProducer.

Design Evaluation

There is one drawback to using the Abstract Factory pattern. We must have a different ConcreteProduct for each combination of family and product. In our example, where some HTML constructs are quite standard across browsers and completely standard within one company's offerings, this is excessive. For instance, it is possible to produce a generic PageProducer since the HTML for the page header is pretty standard.

Producer Factory

Let's revise the design so that there is a single ProducerFactory that is responsible for finding the best-fit implementation for a given browser and type of producer. This is more efficient, since many of the combinations of vendor, version, and producer would have been redundant.

Now for the tricky part: How will the ProducerFactory determine the best concrete producer for a combination? Figure 12.6 shows that the ProducerFactory has a list of concrete producers. It would need to ask each concrete producer a series of questions: "Are you of type X?" Then, "Do you support browser vendor Y?" If so, "How close are you to version Z?" Based on the answers, it could ask the best one to copy itself. This practice of creating new objects by copying an existing one is documented as the Prototype pattern.

Notice that the ProducerFactory does not depend on the concrete implementations. Instead, it has a list of objects whose classes implement the IConcreteHtmlProducer interface.

Let's reconsider the earlier example in which we added a table to a page. This time, let's assume that the HTML is intended for an Internet Explorer 4.0 browser. The view

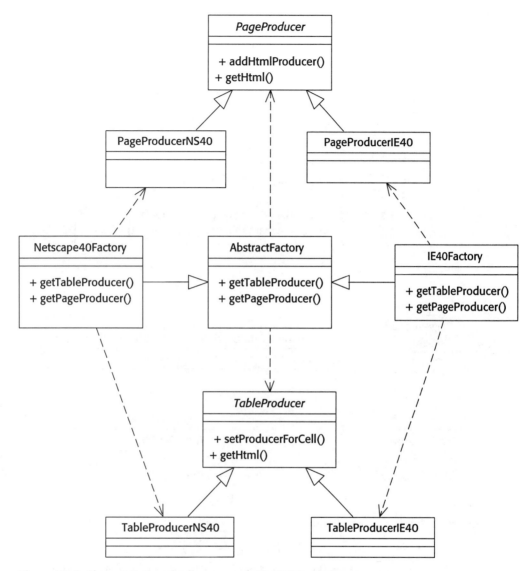

Figure 12.5 Abstract Factory for browser-specific HTML producers.

object uses the ProducerFactory to obtain a TextProducer, an ImageProducer, a TableProducer, and a PageProducer. The text and image producers are added to the table, and the table to the page, as before. The view object does not need to construct the producers directly. Instead, it delegates this chore to the ProducerFactory. The sequence diagram in Figure 12.7 shows this scenario.

All of the logic for determining the correct concrete producer and returning a new instance of that concrete producer is left to the ProducerFactory. When the view asks the factory for a TextProducer, the ProducerFactory uses the browser information to find a match. Since there is only one TextProducer, this decision is simple. Notice that,

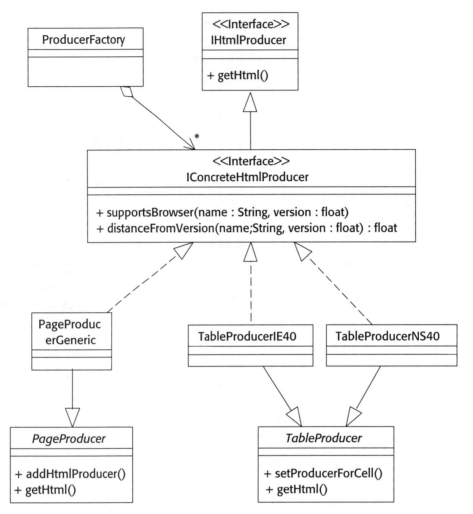

Figure 12.6 Criteria-based Factory.

from the view's perspective, the returned object is a TextProducer, not a TextProducer-Generic. Views do not need to know the specific implementation. Next, the view asks for a TableProducer. The ProducerFactory knows it has two candidates, so it asks them if they support the browser name, which in this case would be "IE" for Internet Explorer. Since only one candidate answers appropriately, it creates a copy and returns it. The view uses the PageProducer and TableProducer interfaces to populate the view. Figure 12.8 shows this sequence.

Reevaluation

Have we met the first design goal? View developers can create HTML pages without knowing HTML; and the logic for finding the most suitable concrete producer is well

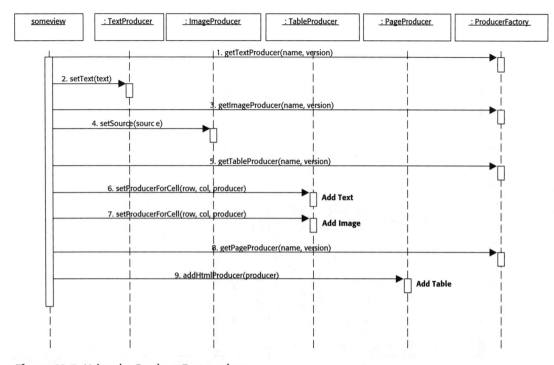

Figure 12.7 Using the ProducerFactory class.

hidden in the ProducerFactory. The current design achieves the first goal of keeping HTML production simple.

Before we forge ahead, we need to make sure that our design changes have not compromised our previously realized goals. It seems that, from the view developer's perspective, we have simply replaced the direct instantiation of producers with requests to the ProducerFactory. The flow for retrieving HTML is unchanged. Goal 2 was met without losing any ground.

Design for Goal 3: Support Preferences

To meet the third goal, support user preferences, we need to look at how preferences are captured and how they are applied to different elements.

Preferences Alternatives

There are two major alternatives for capturing preferences. First, we could design a separate class for each type of preference. Table preferences would be encapsulated in a TablePreference class, with specific methods for setting colors, cell borders, and spacing. Every element would have a corresponding preference class, and every preference would have a corresponding access method. For example, the framework might determine the background color of the page with the following code:

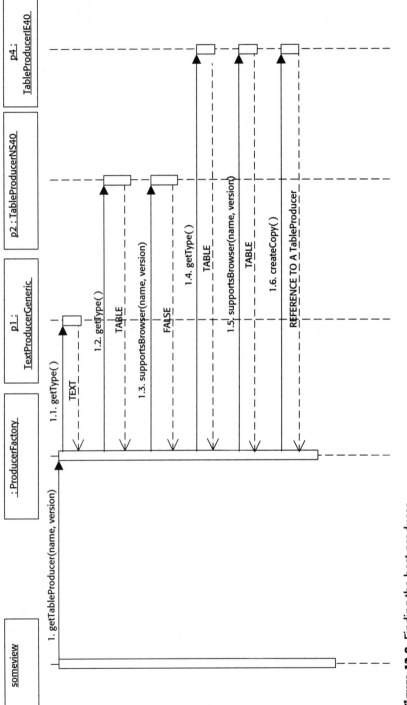

Figure 12.8 Finding the best producer.

```
String colorName = pageProperties.getBackgroundColor();
```

The other design alternative is to include a simple list of name and value pairs in a java.util.Properties object. For example, page.backgroundColor = LightGray sets the background color to gray. In order to retrieve the preference, the framework code would access the properties object with this code:

```
String colorName = theProperties.getProperty("page.backgroundColor");
```

Trade-offs

The first approach uses the compiler to protect against typing errors. For instance, the compiler will catch an error such as pageProperties.getBsckgroundColor. In the second design, the equivalent error of:

```
String colorName = theProperties.getProperty("page.bsckgroundColor");
```

compiles and runs fine. Unfortunately, it returns a null String instead of "LightGray."

On the other hand, the first design is rather cumbersome, with potentially hundreds of incredibly simple preference access methods. Loading or editing the preference objects will be complicated since each preference has its own method. Using the standard Properties class allows us to easily load preferences from files.

Also, in order to add a new preference type or even a new preference to an existing type in the first design requires changes to the preference class, the code that loads the preference class, and the framework code that reads the preference. A similar change in the second design will require only a change in the preference data and in the framework code that uses the preference.

After considering both possibilities, I prefer the second method. Though it does introduce some potential for errors, I like the simplicity and its use of a standard Java idiom. We can add a method in the IHtmlProducer, as shown in Figure 12.9, that uses a Properties object to hold preferences. It is up to each concrete implementation of the interface to use the preferences appropriately. Composite objects must propagate the Properties object to their child IHtmlProducer objects.

NOTE Keeping the preferences in a properties file works well for simple or moderately complex preferences. However, if you have very complex preferences, with different values for the same preference for different types of

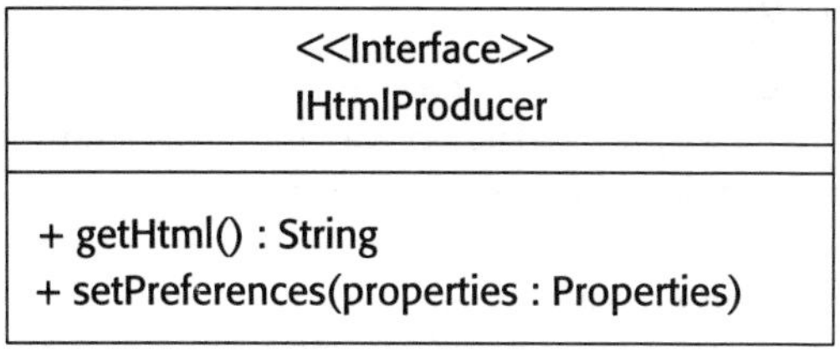

<<Interface>>
IHtmlProducer
+ getHtml() : String + setPreferences(properties : Properties)

Figure 12.9 HtmlProducer interface

producers, the properties become very difficult to read. One solution is to use an XML file to hold the preferences. This lets you edit the preferences in your favorite XML editor, which is a major advantage.

Design for Goal 4: Extensibility and Encapsulation

In addition to the first three goals, we must ensure that the design can survive the tests of time. Requirements inevitably evolve over time, and a resilient system must accommodate them.

Encapsulation

Changes within the framework, excluding the public interfaces, must not be allowed to propagate to the presentation layer that depends on it. The view package depends on the generic HtmlProduction package with its generic HTML producers, but not on any actual implementations.

To be really encapsulated, the generic HTML producers also should not depend on their concrete implementations. This allows us to add new concrete implementations or change existing concrete implementations without fear of cascading changes. Remember, the ProducerFactory in the HtmlProduction package must pick the correct concrete implementation for a given user and element. Does this mean that the Html-Production package depends on the concrete implementations? Not necessarily, since each concrete implementation implements the IConcreteProducer interface and the ProducerFactory can use those methods to determine the best fit. All we need is a way to register concrete producers with the factory. To do so, we add a method to the ProducerFactory, as shown in Figure 12.10. Notice that the addConcreteProducer method does not introduce any dependency on the concrete implementations. The only dependency is on the IConcreteProducer interface.

Let's use table production to look at the dependencies between classes. Notice that the SomeServlet class depends only on the ProducerFactory and the abstract producer classes in the HtmlProduction package. Neither of these classes has any dependencies on the concrete producer classes. Notice that each concrete producer implements the IConcreteProducer interface and recall from Figure 12.6 that each concrete producer extends an abstract producer class. Figure 12.11 shows these relationships.

Evaluation of Package Dependencies

The class dependencies can be consolidated into package dependencies. The concrete implementation packages for Internet Explorer and Netscape Navigator depend on the HtmlProduction package, since they implement interfaces from that package. The HtmlProduction package does not depend on the concrete implementations, since they register using the IConcreteProducer interface; and each extends one of the generic producers. This demonstrates how changes can ripple from one package to another. Notice that changes to the generic classes and interfaces will require

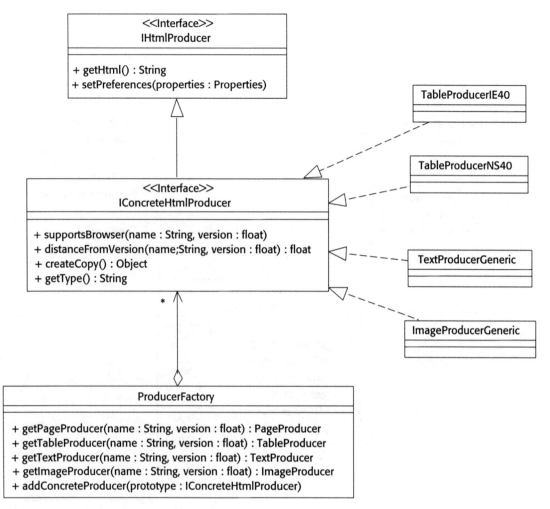

Figure 12.10 ProducerFactory with producer registration.

the concrete implementations to evolve to meet the changes. The converse is not true! Concrete implementations may be created, destroyed, and modified without impacting the HtmlProduction classes and interfaces. The last goal, extensibility and encapsulation, has been met. Figure 12.12 shows the package dependencies for HTML production.

Filling in the Details

Now that we have a high-level design that meets our high-level goals, we need to flesh out the details. Our goal for this section is to develop detailed sequence diagrams and class diagrams for several screens in the user interface prototype.

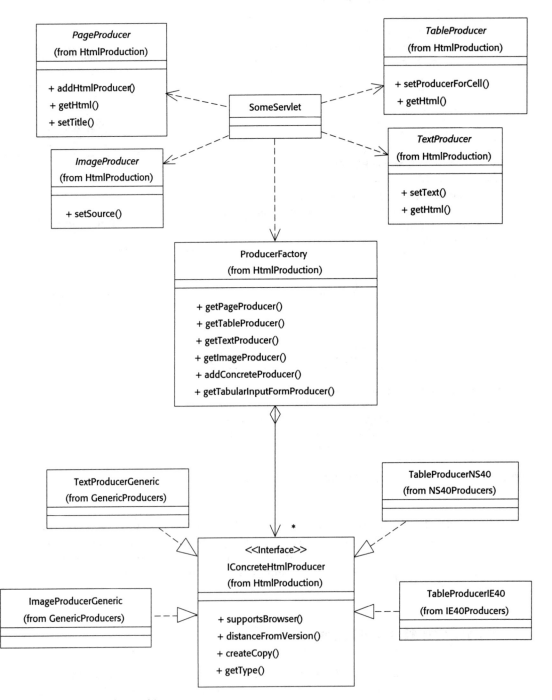

Figure 12.11 Class relationships.

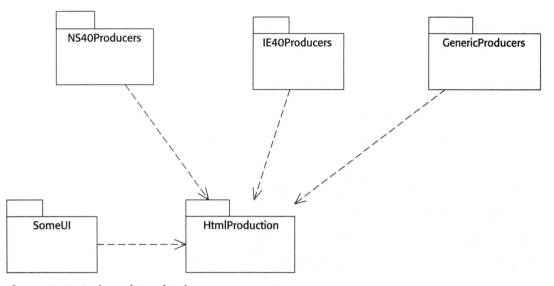

Figure 12.12 Package dependencies

NOTE Perfect initial designs are as common as perfect people. It is important to remember that you will always discover some flaws in your design, and identify some areas that you simply had not considered. Additional classes will be discovered. Interfaces will be modified. It is far more efficient to discover the inevitable issues in a modeling tool. Code has inertia, too; once code is written, it tends to stay written.

Login Screen

From the login screen, it is clear that we will need a quick way to produce very simple text input forms. The form consists of input boxes and a Submit button. Each input box needs a label, a name, and an initial default value. The Submit button requires a label. Figure 12.13 shows an input form and a new generic producer class.

The sequence diagram in Figure 12.14 shows how a LoginServlet object builds this HTML. The LoginServlet object obtains a TabularInputFormProducer object from the ProducerFactory. It then configures it with the correct submission target and the correct submission label. Next, it adds fields for the username and the password. A similar process is used to build and configure a page. The TabularInputFormProducer is added to the PageProducer, and the preferences are set on the PageProducer.

It is important to note how little the view needs to know. There is no knowledge of HTML or browser versions or any nasty details in the servlet. All in all, it looks like a nice payoff for our hard work in high-level design.

Nevertheless, there are still questions to answer: How does an actual concrete TabularInputFormProducer do its job? Should it independently produce the HTML, or should it use internal FormProducer and TableProducer objects? Figure 12.15 shows

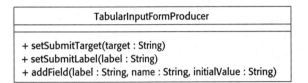

TabularInputFormProducer
+ setSubmitTarget(target : String) + setSubmitLabel(label : String) + addField(label : String, name : String, initialValue : String)

Figure 12.13 Login form and TabularInputFormProducer.

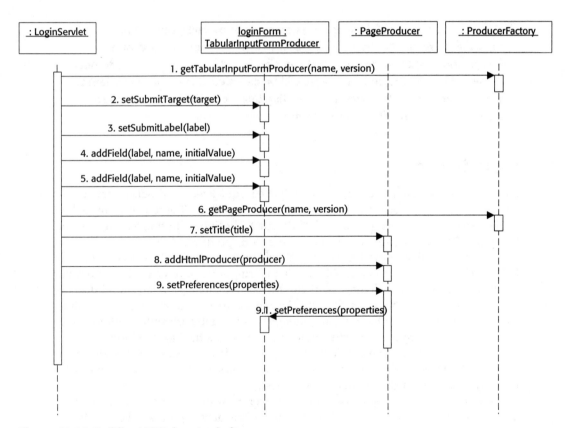

Figure 12.14 Building HTML for a Login form.

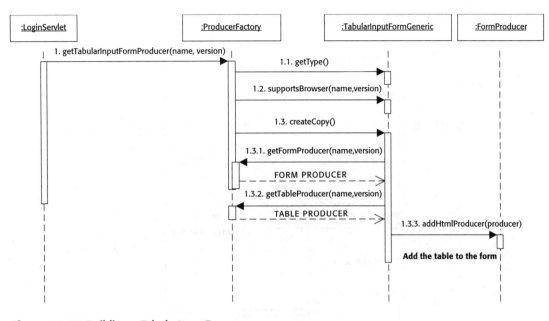

Figure 12.15 Building a TabularInputForm.

how the TabularInputFormProducer is constructed. For this example, assume that the concrete producer is a TabularInputFormProducerGeneric. The factory creates a copy of a Prototype object. (See Prototype pattern in [Gamma, et al. 1995].) In the construction of the copy, a table producer is added to a form producer. The TabularInputFormProducerGeneric contains a FormProducer and adds a TableProducer to the FormProducer. Notice that the TabularInputFormProducerGeneric gets concrete producers the same way everything else does, through the ProducerFactory.

Many messages from the view to the TabularInputFormProducer are passed along to other objects. When the view adds a field, the TabularInputFormProducer adds a corresponding text label and a text field to the TableProducer. Also, notice in Figure 12.16 how the setPreferences and getHtml messages cascade down from the Tabular-InputFormProducer to the FormProducer and on to the TableProducer, because TableProducer is a child of the FormProducer. Then, the messages cascade from the TableProducer to the TextProducer and TextFieldProducer since they are children of the TableProducer. This cascading effect is typical of the Composite pattern.

As sequence diagrams become complex, we use notes to annotate them. For example, one method may be called for two very different reasons. Notes allow us to tie the low-level method calls together. In many cases, the notes may resemble pseudocode that describes the intent behind a series of methods calls.

Figure 12.17 shows how each TabularInputFormProducer object is associated with a single FormProducer object and a single TableProducer object. It also highlights the way the TabularInputFormProducer depends on the other producers, while not bothering to keep track of them. It is clear that many objects, including the views and any TabularInputFormProducer objects, will need a reference to a ProducerFactory object. It is also clear that a single factory will be sufficient. We can implement this by

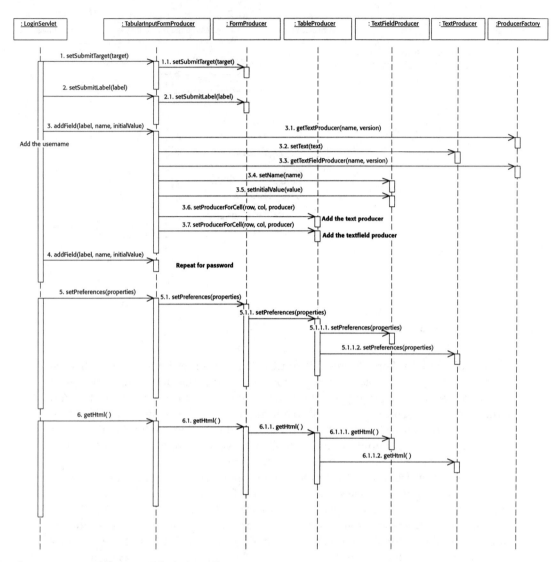

Figure 12.16 Adding to a TabularInputForm.

using the Singleton pattern. Specifically, we add a static getFactorySingleton method to the ProducerFactory class.

Evaluation

It seems logical to have the TabularInputFormProducer use the TableProducer. However, there is one drawback: Normal tables may look very different from the simple input forms. For instance, a simple input form blends in with the screen. We would not want borders or a different background color to draw attention to the table. Data tables, on the other hand, need

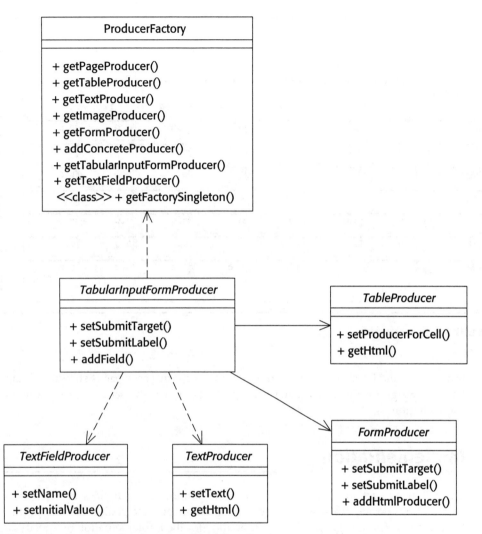

Figure 12.17 Classes for the TabularInputFormProducer

to clearly distinguish rows and columns. Since we are merely using the table to get the layout right, we may need different preferences for the internal TableProducer. So, the preferences must be altered by the TabularInputFormProducer before they are passed down to the TableProducer.

Time Entry

Our next challenge is the Timecard form itself. As you can see in Figure 12.18, this form consists of text and text entry fields in a table. We already have producers for the enclosing table and the text. It is a fairly simple exercise to add TextProducers and TextFieldProducers to a TableProducer. Because there is no new behavior within the

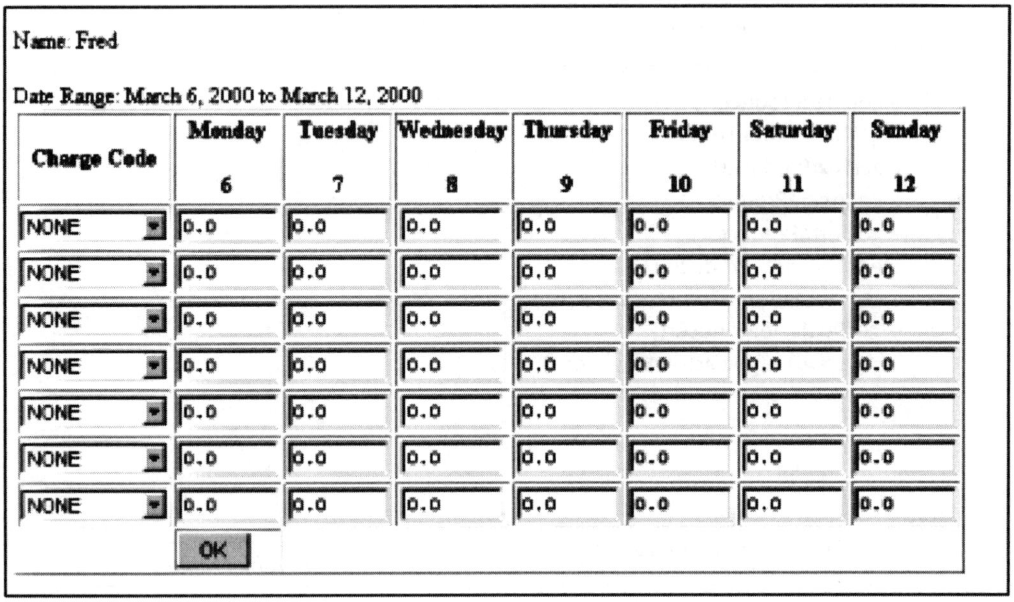

Name: Fred

Date Range: March 6, 2000 to March 12, 2000

Charge Code	Monday 6	Tuesday 7	Wednesday 8	Thursday 9	Friday 10	Saturday 11	Sunday 12
NONE ▾	0.0	0.0	0.0	0.0	0.0	0.0	0.0
NONE ▾	0.0	0.0	0.0	0.0	0.0	0.0	0.0
NONE ▾	0.0	0.0	0.0	0.0	0.0	0.0	0.0
NONE ▾	0.0	0.0	0.0	0.0	0.0	0.0	0.0
NONE ▾	0.0	0.0	0.0	0.0	0.0	0.0	0.0
NONE ▾	0.0	0.0	0.0	0.0	0.0	0.0	0.0
NONE ▾	0.0	0.0	0.0	0.0	0.0	0.0	0.0

OK

Figure 12.18 Timecard form.

framework, and because the use of the framework for this scenario is shown in Chapter 13, "Design for the TimecardUI Package," I omit here the sequence diagram and class diagram.

Implementation

The following section shows sample implementations for each class in the design. Based on our design goals, we created a design to meet these goals while supporting the use cases. This design provides a foundation for the implementation by specifying the responsibilities for each class and the relationships between classes. While there are still many decisions left for implementation, the design provides a coherent structure during implementation.

IHtmlProducer.java

There is no difference between the design interface and its implementation, as you can see from the following code. If only all implementations were this straightforward.

```
package com.wiley.compBooks.EJwithUML.HtmlProduction;

import java.util.*;

/**
```

```
 *
 * The IHtmlProducer interface defines the methods provided by
 * all classes that produce HTML in the framework. This framework
 * uses the Composite pattern, and
 * IHtmlProducer is the common interface that allows you to treat
 * Composite and
 * leaf objects the same.
 */
public interface IHtmlProducer
{
    /** Answers the formatted HTML for this producer. */
    public String getHtml();

    /** Sets the preferences for this producer. */
    public void setPreferences(Properties preferences);
}
```

ComboBoxProducer.java

The ComboBoxProducer is an abstract class that provides some concrete and final behavior. It has public final methods that allow a client to set the producer's preferences, set the name of the combo box, and add values for the combo box. The access methods for this data are all protected and final. This means that any client can use the set and add methods to configure the producer. Since the methods are final and the underlying instance variables are private, subclasses of ComboBoxProducer cannot change the underlying data or the way it is held. Subclasses only override the getHtml method. Any other changes, such as adding a new method, will not be visible through the base ComboBoxProducer class, and therefore would be useless within the framework.

It is considered good practice to narrowly define the responsibilities of the subclasses and enforce these decisions through the use of final methods and private data.

```
package com.wiley.compBooks.EJwithUML.HtmlProduction;

import java.util.*;

/**
 *
 * The ComboBoxProducer abstract class is a configurable HTML
 * producer
 * for HTML combo boxes. It captures the data that is needed for
 * combo boxes in general, but does not build them. This is left
 * to the concrete implementations.
 */
public abstract class ComboBoxProducer implements IHtmlProducer
{
  private Properties preferences;
  private Collection values = new ArrayList();
  private String name;
```

```java
/** Answers the HTML for this producer. */
public abstract String getHtml();

/** Sets the preferences of this producer. */
public final void setPreferences(Properties preferences)
{
  this.preferences = preferences;
}

/** Answers the preferences of this producer..*/
protected final Properties getPreferences()
{
  return this.preferences;
}

/** Sets the name of the combo box. */
public final void setName(String name)
{
  this.name = name;
}

/** Answers the name of the combo box. */
protected final String getName()
{
  return this.name;
}

/** Adds a value to the combo box. */
public final void addValue(String value)
{
  this.values.add(value);
}

/** Answers the values for the combo box. */
protected final Iterator getvalues()
{
  return this.values.iterator();
}

}
```

FormProducer.java

Like ComboBoxProducer, FormProducer is an abstract class that provides some concrete and final behavior. Its final methods and private data encapsulate the configuration of a combo box. Subclasses must override getHtml to provide browser-specific behavior.

Client objects can add any object that implements IHtmlProducer to the FormProducer's running list of producers through the addHtmlProducer method. This is what makes the FormProducer a Composite.

Notice that a private ArrayList is used to keep the HTML producers in order.

```
package com.wiley.compBooks.EJwithUML.HtmlProduction;

import java.util.*;

/**
 *
 * The FormProducer abstract class is a configurable Composite
 * HTML producer for HTML forms. It captures the data that is
 * needed for forms in general, but does not build them. This is
 * left to the concrete implementations.
 */
public abstract class FormProducer implements IHtmlProducer
{
  private String submitTarget;
  private Collection producers = new ArrayList();
  private Properties preferences;
  private String method = "POST";

  /** Answers the HTML for this producer. */
  public abstract String getHtml();

  /** Sets the submit target for the form. Must be a valid url.*/
  public final void setSubmitTarget(String target)
  {
    this.submitTarget = submitTarget;
  }

  /** Sets submission method to GET or POST. A value of true
    * indicates POST.*/
  public final void setPostMethod(boolean post)
  {
    this.method = (post) ? "POST":"GET";
  }

  /** Adds a HTML producer to this Composite. */
  public final void addHtmlProducer(IHtmlProducer producer)
  {
    producers.add(producer);
  }

  /** Sets the preferences. */
  public final void setPreferences(Properties preferences)
  {
    this.preferences = preferences;
  }

  /** Answers the submission target. */
  protected final String getSubmitTarget()
  {
```

```
      return this.submitTarget;
    }

    /** Answers the IHtmlProducers that have been added to this
     *  Composite.*/
    protected final Iterator getProducers()
    {
      return this.producers.iterator();
    }

    /** Answers the preferences.*/
    protected final Properties getPreferences()
    {
      return this.preferences;
    }

    /** Answers the submission method. */
    protected final String getMethod()
    {
      return this.method;
    }
}
```

PageProducer.java

Subclasses are limited to overriding getHtml. Like FormProducer, PageProducer is a Composite with producers added through the addHtmlProducer method.

There is no limit to the number of producers, and they are kept in the order in which they are added.

```
package com.wiley.compBooks.EJwithUML.HtmlProduction;

import java.util.*;

/**
 *
 * The PageProducer class is a Composite HTML producer for pages.
 */
public abstract class PageProducer implements IHtmlProducer
{
  private Collection producers = new ArrayList();
  private String title;
  private Properties preferences = new Properties();

  /** Answers the HTML for this producer. */
  public abstract String getHtml();

  /** Sets the title of this page. */
  public final void setTitle(String title)
  {
```

```
    this.title = title;
  }

  /** Adds an IHtmlProducer to this Composite producer. */
  public final void addHtmlProducer(IHtmlProducer producer)
  {
    producers.add(producer);
  }

  /** Sets the preferences for this page and its children. */
  public final void setPreferences(Properties preferences)
  {
    this.preferences = preferences;
  }

  /** Answers the HTML producers for this page. */
  protected final Iterator getProducers()
  {
    return this.producers.iterator();
  }

  /** Answers the title for the page. */
  protected final String getTitle()
  {
    return this.title;
  }

  /** Answers the preferences for this page. */
  protected final Properties getPreferences()
  {
    return this.preferences;
  }
}
```

SubmitButtonProducer

As always, subclasses are limited to overriding the getHtml method. SubmitButton-Producer provides the methods and attributes for storing the label and preferences for the actual concrete producer. Notice that the attributes are private, so the subclasses must access them through the public methods.

SubmitButtonProducer is not a Composite.

```
package com.wiley.compBooks.EJwithUML.HtmlProduction;

import java.util.*;

/**
 *
 * The SubmitButtonProducer class is a configurable HTML producer
 * that produces a form submission button.
```

```
    */
  public abstract class SubmitButtonProducer implements IHtmlProducer
  {
    private String label;
    private Properties preferences;

    /** Answers the HTML for this producer. */
    public abstract String getHtml();

    /** Sets the label for the submit button. */
    public final void setSubmittLabel(String label)
    {
      this.label = label;
    }

    /** Sets the preferences for this producer.*/
    public final void setPreferences(Properties preferences)
    {
      this.preferences = preferences;
    }

    /** Answers the label of the submit button. */
    protected final String getLabel()
    {
      return this.label;
    }

    /** Answers the preferences of this producer. */
    protected final Properties getPreferences()
    {
      return this.preferences;
    }
  }
```

TableProducer.java

TableProducer restricts subclasses to overriding the getHtml method. TableProducer is a Composite HTML producer. HTML producers are added to the TableProducer through the setHtmlProducerForCell method, which specifies a position and an IHtml-Producer. Producers are kept in SortedMaps, with one SortedMap per row. This keeps the producers in order by column index. Each SortedMap for a row is kept in another SortedMap, so that the rows stay in order by row index.

Subclasses retrieve producers by row and column index. This simple interface has one shortcoming. Notice that the subclass is free to request a producer for a cell that does not exist. Therefore, it must be prepared to receive null as a response.

It is important that this fairly complex logic be kept in the base class. This encapsulates complexity and ensures that all subclasses behave in the same way.

```
package com.wiley.compBooks.EJwithUML.HtmlProduction;
```

```java
import java.util.*;

/**
 *
 * The TableProducer abstract class is a configurable Composite
 * HTML producer for HTML tables. It captures the data that is
 * needed for tables in general, but does not build them. This is
 * left to the concrete implementations.
 */
public abstract class TableProducer implements IHtmlProducer
{
  private SortedMap rows = new TreeMap();
  private Properties preferences;
  private int maxRow = 0;
  private int maxColumn = 0;


  /** Answers the HTML for this producer. */
  public abstract String getHtml();

  /** Sets the producer for the specified cell. */
  public final void setHtmlProducerForCell(int row, int column,
          IHtmlProducer producer)
  {
    Integer rowKey = new Integer(row);
    Integer columnKey = new Integer(column);

    this.maxRow = Math.max(row, this.maxRow);
    this.maxColumn = Math.max(column, this.maxColumn);

    if (!rows.containsKey(rowKey))
    {
      rows.put(rowKey, new TreeMap());
    }

    SortedMap currentRow = (SortedMap) rows.get(rowKey);
    currentRow.put(columnKey, producer);
  }

  /** Sets the preferences for this producer. */
  public final void setPreferences(Properties preferences)
  {
    this.preferences = preferences;
  }

  /** Answers the producer for the specified cell. */
  protected final IHtmlProducer getHtmlProducer(int row,
          int column)
  {
    IHtmlProducer producer = null;
```

```
        Integer rowKey = new Integer(row);
        Integer columnKey = new Integer(column);

        if (rows.containsKey(rowKey))
        {
          SortedMap currentRow = (SortedMap) rows.get(rowKey);
          if (currentRow.containsKey(columnKey))
          {
            producer = (IHtmlProducer) currentRow.get(columnKey);
          }
        }

        return producer;
      }

      /** Answers the greatest row index. */
      protected final int getMaxRowIndex()
      {
        return this.maxRow;
      }

      /** Answers the greatest column index. */
      protected final int getMaxColumnIndex()
      {
        return this.maxColumn;
      }
    }
```

TabularInputFormProducer.java

TabularInputFormProducer is quite different from the other producers. It is a Composite, but it mostly constructs itself. Its constructor obtains a FormProducer, a TableProducer, and SubmitButtonProducer from the ProducerFactory. These are wired together to form the TabularInputFormProducer. Unlike the other producer classes, its getHtml method is not abstract. Subclasses do not override the getHtml method. Instead, the getHtml method in TabularInputFormProducer produces formatted HTML, in part by calling the getHtml method on its FormProducer.

```
package com.wiley.compBooks.EJwithUML.HtmlProduction;

import java.util.*;

/**
 *
 * TabularInputFormProducer is a self-constructing Composite. It
 * obtains producers from the ProducerFactory, just like any
 * other object.
 *
```

```
 */
public abstract class TabularInputFormProducer implements IHtmlProducer
{
  private ProducerFactory factory =
ProducerFactory.getFactorySingleton();
  private FormProducer formProducer;
  private TableProducer tableProducer;
  private SubmitButtonProducer submitButtonProducer;

  private Properties preferences;
  private int rowIndex = 0;

  public TabularInputFormProducer()
  {
    String browserName = this.getBrowserName();
    float browserVersion = this.getBrowserVersion();

    this.formProducer =           factory.getFormProducer(browserName,
                                  browserVersion);
    this.tableProducer =
        factory.getTableProducer(browserName, browserVersion);
    this.submitButtonProducer =
        factory.getSubmitButtonProducer(browserName,browserVersion;

    this.formProducer.addHtmlProducer(this.tableProducer);
    this.formProducer.addHtmlProducer(this.submitButtonProducer);
  }

  /** Answers the HTML for this producer. */
  public final String getHtml()
  {
    StringBuffer buffer = new StringBuffer();
    buffer.append("\n<!--" +this+ "-->\n");
    buffer.append(this.formProducer.getHtml());

    return buffer.toString();
  }

  /** Adds a labeled input field.*/
  public final void addField(String label, String name,
                             String initialValue)
  {
    String browserName = this.getBrowserName();
    float browserVersion = this.getBrowserVersion();

    TextProducer textProducer =
        factory.getTextProducer(browserName, browserVersion);
    textProducer.setText(label);

    TextFieldProducer fieldProducer =
        factory.getTextFieldProducer(browserName,browserVersion);
```

```
      fieldProducer.setName(name);
      fieldProducer.setInitialValue(initialValue);

      this.tableProducer.setHtmlProducerForCell(this.rowIndex, 0,
                                                  textProducer);
      this.tableProducer.setHtmlProducerForCell(this.rowIndex, 1,
                                                  fieldProducer);
      this.rowIndex++;
  }

  /** Sets the submit label for this TabularInputFormProducer. */
  public final void setSubmitLabel(String label)
  {
      this.submitButtonProducer.setSubmittLabel(label);
  }

  /** Sets the submit target for this TabularInputFormProducer. */
  public final void setSubmitTarget(String target)
  {
      this.formProducer.setSubmitTarget(target);
  }

  /** Sets the preferences for this producer. */
  public final void setPreferences(Properties preferences)
  {
      this.preferences = (Properties) preferences.clone();
      this.customizePreferences(preferences);

      this.formProducer.setPreferences(preferences);
  }

  /** Answers the name of the browser for which the producer is
        tailored. */
  protected abstract String getBrowserName();

  /** Answers the version of the browser for which the producer
        is tailored. */
  protected abstract float getBrowserVersion();

  /** Customizes the properties so that the Composite producers
        look right. */
  protected abstract void customizePreferences(Properties
      properties);
}
```

TextFieldProducer.java

As always, subclasses are limited to overriding the getHtml method. TextFieldProducer contains the attributes and methods needed to set the name and initial value of the text field, as well as the preferences. Since these attributes are private, the subclasses must access the attributes through the public methods.

TextFieldProducer is not a Composite.

```
package com.wiley.compBooks.EJwithUML.HtmlProduction;

import java.util.*;
/**
 *
 * The TextFieldProducer class is a configurable HTML producer
 * that produces a text field.
 */
public abstract class TextFieldProducer implements IHtmlProducer
{
  private Properties preferences;
  private String name;
  private String initialValue;

  /** Answers the HTML for this producer. */
  public abstract String getHtml();

  /** Sets the preferences for this producer. */
  public final void setPreferences(Properties preferences)
  {
    this.preferences = preferences;
  }

  /** Sets the name of the TextField*/
  public final void setName(String name)
  {
    this.name = name;
  }

  /** Sets the initial value of the text field*/
  public final void setInitialValue(String initialValue)
  {
    this.initialValue = initialValue;
  }


  /** Answers the properties of this producer. */
  protected final Properties getPreferences()
  {
    return this.preferences;
  }

  /** Answers the name of the text field. */
  protected final String getName()
  {
    return this.name;
  }

  /** Answers the initial value for the text field.*/
  protected final String getInitialValue()
```

```
    {
      return this.initialValue;
    }
}
```

TextProducer.java

As always, subclasses are limited to overriding the getHtml method. TextProducer contains the attributes and methods needed to set the text of the text, as well as the preferences. Since these attributes are private, the subclasses must access the attributes through the public methods.

TextProducer is not a Composite.

```
package com.wiley.compBooks.EJwithUML.HtmlProduction;

import java.util.*;

/**
 *
 * The TextProducer class is a configurable HTML producer that
 * produces arbitrary HTML.
 */

public abstract class TextProducer implements IHtmlProducer
{
  private String text;
  private Properties preferences;

  /** Answers the HTML for this producer. */
  public abstract String getHtml();


  /** Sets the text for this TextProducer. */
  public final void setText(String text)
  {
    this.text = text;
  }

  /** Sets the properties for this producer. */
  public final void setPreferences(Properties preferences)
  {
    this.preferences = preferences;
  }

  /** Answers the properties for this producer*/
  protected final Properties getPreferences()
  {
    return this.preferences;
  }
```

```
  /** Answers the text for this producer. */
  protected final String getText()
  {
    return this.text;
  }
}
```

IConcreteProducer.java

IConcreteProducer is a simple interface that allows the ProducerFactory to treat all registered concrete producers the same. It allows a concrete producer to reveal how suitable it is for a certain browser. It also contains constants that identify different types of producers.

```
package com.wiley.compBooks.EJwithUML.HtmlProduction;

/**
 *
 * The IConcreteProducer interface defines the methods needed to
 * determine if a concrete producer is appropriate to produce
 * HTML for a particular browser.
 */
public interface IConcreteProducer
{
  /** Answers true if this concrete supports the browser.*/
  public boolean supportsBrowser(String browserName,
       float version);

 /** Answers how much older the input browser is compared to
  * the producer.
  * The formula is: (producer's version - input version). *
    * So, newer input browsers may yield negative numbers. */
  public float distanceFromVersion(String browserName,
       float version);

  /** Answers the type of the producer, for example
    * PAGE_PRODUCER. */
  public String getProducerType();

  /** Answers a copy of this producer. */
  public Object createCopy();

  // Constants for producer types
  public final static String PAGE_PRODUCER = "PAGE_PRODUCER";
  public final static String TABLE_PRODUCER = "TABLE_PRODUCER";
  public final static String TEXT_PRODUCER = "TEXT_PRODUCER";
  public final static String FORM_PRODUCER = "FORM_PRODUCER";
  public final static String SUBMIT_BUTTON_PRODUCER =
       "SUBMIT_BUTTON_PRODUCER";
  public final static String TEXTFIELD_PRODUCER =
```

```
        "TEXTFIELD_PRODUCER";
    public final static String TABULAR_INPUT_FORM_PRODUCER =
        "TABULAR_INPUT_FORM_PRODUCER";
    public final static String SELECTABLE_TABLE_DATA_PRODUCER =
        "SELECTABLE_TABLE_DATA_PRODUCER";
    public final static String RADIO_BUTTON_PRODUCER =
        "RADIO_BUTTON_PRODUCER";
    public final static String MENU_BUTTON_PRODUCER =
        "MENU_BUTTON_PRODUCER";
    public final static String COMBO_BOX_PRODUCER =
        "COMBO_BOX_PRODUCER";
}
```

ProducerFactory.java

ProducerFactory allows client objects to obtain the best concrete producer for a given browser. For efficiency and convenience, it is a Singleton that is exposed through a static retrieval method. The static getFactorySingleton method makes sure that an instance of ProducerFactory exists and returns a reference to the caller. Notice that the constructor is private, so the Singleton pattern cannot be subverted.

Concrete producers are registered with the factory through the addConcrete-Producer method. Any object that implements the IConcreteProducer interface may be registered. Since concrete producers are frequently configured, they cannot be shared by different clients. When a client requests a particular kind of producer, the Producer-Factory determines the best match, then asks it to copy itself. The copy is then returned to the client.

The best match for a particular browser is determined by asking each registered concrete producer a series of questions. First, the concrete producer must be of the same type, and support the browser. So, the ProducerFactory asks the concrete producer if it supports the browser. Once the list is narrowed down to compatible producers, the ProducerFactory determines which concrete producer is the best fit by asking each producer how far it is from the specified version.

The same matching logic is used for all types of producers. The specific get method simply casts the resulting producer to the specified type, and returns it.

```
package com.wiley.compBooks.EJwithUML.HtmlProduction;

import java.util.*;

/**
 *
 * The ProducerFactory finds the best HTML producer for a given
 * browser.
 *
 * ProducerFactory is a Singleton.
 * Producers are registered with the factory.
 */
public final class ProducerFactory
{
```

```
private Vector concreteProducers = new Vector();
private static ProducerFactory factory;

/** Answers a reference to a unique ProducerFactory object. See
 *  Gamma, et al. for Singleton pattern. */
public static ProducerFactory getFactorySingleton()
{
  if (ProducerFactory.factory == null)
  {
    ProducerFactory.factory = new ProducerFactory();
  }
  return ProducerFactory.factory;
}


/** Private constructor to protect singleton status. */
private ProducerFactory()
{

}


/** Registers a concrete producer with this factory. */
public void addConcreteProducer(IConcreteProducer producer)
{
  this.concreteProducers.addElement(producer);
}


/** Answers the best TableProducer for the browser, version.*/
public TableProducer getTableProducer(String browser,
     float version)
{
  IConcreteProducer match =
      findBestProducer(IConcreteProducer.TABLE_PRODUCER, browser,
                       version);
  return (TableProducer) match;
}

/** Answers the best TabularInputFormProducer for the browser,
                       version.*/
public TabularInputFormProducer
     getTabularInputFormProducer(String browser, float version)
{
  IConcreteProducer match =
    findBestProducer(IConcreteProducer.TABULAR_INPUT_FORM_PRODUCER,
                    browser, version);
  return (TabularInputFormProducer) match;
}


/** Answers the best TextProducer for the browser, version.*/
public TextProducer getTextProducer(String browser,
```

```
                              float version)
{
  IConcreteProducer match =
      findBestProducer(IConcreteProducer.TEXT_PRODUCER, browser,
                            version);
  return (TextProducer) match;
}


/** Answers the best TextFieldProducer for the browser, version. */
public TextFieldProducer getTextFieldProducer(String browser,
                                                  float version)
{
  IConcreteProducer match =
     findBestProducer(IConcreteProducer.TEXTFIELD_PRODUCER,
                         browser, version);
  return (TextFieldProducer) match;
}


/** Answers the best SubmitButtonProducer for the browser, version. */
public SubmitButtonProducer getSubmitButtonProducer(
                                      String browser, float version)
{
  IConcreteProducer match =
      findBestProducer(IConcreteProducer.SUBMIT_BUTTON_PRODUCER,
                         browser, version);
  return (SubmitButtonProducer) match;
}


/** Answers the best SelectableTableDataProducer for the browser,
 * version. */
public SelectableTableDataProducer
     getSelectableTableDataProducer(String browser,
                                    float version)
{
  IConcreteProducer match =
   findBestProducer(IConcreteProducer.SELECTABLE_TABLE_DATA_PRODUCE,
                      browser, version);
  return (SelectableTableDataProducer) match;
}


/** Answers the best RadioButtonProducer for browser, version.*/
public RadioButtonProducer getRadioButtonProducer(String browser,
                                                  float version)
{
  IConcreteProducer match =
      findBestProducer(IConcreteProducer.RADIO_BUTTON_PRODUCER,
                         browser, version);
  return (RadioButtonProducer) match;
}


/** Answers the best MenuButtonProducer for browser, version.*/
```

```
public MenuButtonProducer getMenuButtonProducer(String browser,
                                         float version)
{
  IConcreteProducer match =
      findBestProducer(IConcreteProducer.MENU_BUTTON_PRODUCER,
                    browser, version);
  return (MenuButtonProducer) match;
}


/** Answers the best ComboBoxProducer for browser, version. */
public ComboBoxProducer getComboBoxProducer(String browser,
                                         float version)
{
  IConcreteProducer match =
      findBestProducer(IConcreteProducer.COMBO_BOX_PRODUCER,
                    browser, version);
  return (ComboBoxProducer) match;
}


/** Answers the best PageProducer for the browser, version. */
public PageProducer getPageProducer(String browser, float version)
{
  IConcreteProducer match =
      findBestProducer(IConcreteProducer.PAGE_PRODUCER, browser,
                    version);
  return (PageProducer) match;
}


/** Answers the best FormProducer for the browser, version. */
public FormProducer getFormProducer(String browser, float version)   {
  IConcreteProducer match =
      findBestProducer(IConcreteProducer.FORM_PRODUCER, browser,
                    version);
  return (FormProducer) match;
}


private IConcreteProducer findBestProducer(String type,
                          String browser, float version)
{
  IConcreteProducer match = null;

  Enumeration producers = this.concreteProducers.elements();
  while (producers.hasMoreElements())
  {
    IConcreteProducer concreteProducer = (IConcreteProducer)
        producers.nextElement();
    if (concreteProducer.getProducerType().equals(type))
    {
      if (concreteProducer.supportsBrowser(browser, version))
      {
        if (match == null)
```

```
                    {
                      match = concreteProducer;
                    }
                    else
                    {
                      float newDistance =
                          concreteProducer.distanceFromVersion(browser,version);
                      float oldDistance =
                          match.distanceFromVersion(browser, version);

                      if (newDistance == 0.0)
                      {
                        match = concreteProducer;
                      }
                      else if ( newDistance < 0.0 && oldDistance < 0.0 &&
                                  newDistance > oldDistance)
                      {
                        match = concreteProducer;
                      }
                      else if ( newDistance > 0.0 && oldDistance < 0.0 &&
                                  newDistance < oldDistance)
                      {
                        match = concreteProducer;
                      }
                      else if (newDistance < 0.0 && oldDistance > 0.0)
                      {
                        match = concreteProducer;
                      }
                    }
                  }
                }
              }

          if (match != null)
          {
            return (IConcreteProducer) match.createCopy();
          }
          else
          {
            return null;
          }
        }
      }
```

FormProducerGeneric.java

FormProducerGeneric produces HTML forms that are not tuned to any particular browser. It produces a lowest common denominator that works in any modern browser.

As expected, FormProducerGeneric overrides getHtml and all of the methods from
IConcreteProducer. In getHtml, FormProducerGeneric uses protected methods to
access the configurable properties that are common to all FormProducers. These properties are used to build the actual HTML.

```java
package com.wiley.compBooks.EJwithUML.HtmlProduction.GenericProducers;

import com.wiley.compBooks.EJwithUML.HtmlProduction.*;
import java.util.*;

/**
 *
 * The FormProducerGeneric is a concrete implementation of
 * FormProducer that produces HTML for all modern browsers.
 *
 * It implements IConcreteProducer so that it can be registered
 * with the ProducerFactory.
 *
 */
public class FormProducerGeneric extends FormProducer implements
IConcreteProducer
{
  public String getHtml()
  {
    StringBuffer buffer = new StringBuffer();

    buffer.append("\n<!--" +this+ "-->\n");
    buffer.append("<form method=" +this.getMethod()+
                " action=\""+ this.getSubmitTarget()+ "\" >\n");

    Iterator producerIterator = this.getProducers();
    while (producerIterator.hasNext())
    {
      IHtmlProducer producer =
          (IHtmlProducer) producerIterator.next();
      buffer.append("" +producer.getHtml()+ "\n\n");
    }

    buffer.append("</form>");
    return buffer.toString();
  }

  public String getProducerType()
  {
    return IConcreteProducer.FORM_PRODUCER;
  }

  public Object createCopy()
  {
    FormProducerGeneric copy = new FormProducerGeneric();
```

```
      return copy;
    }

    public float distanceFromVersion(String browserName,
       float version)
    {
      return Float.MIN_VALUE;
    }

    public boolean supportsBrowser(String browserName,
       float version)
    {
      return true;
    }
  }
```

PageProducerGeneric.java

PageProducerGeneric is very similar to FormProducerGeneric. It too overrides
getHtml to produce lowest-common-denominator HTML. In addition to the configurable properties that are held in the superclass, PageProducer, PageProducerGeneric
also uses the preference data.

Looking at the short, but rather gross, code required to build HTML highlights the
wisdom in our decision to encapsulate HTML production to a few dedicated classes.
Picture a system with customized HTML production code and domain access for each
view. Now consider the differences between each developer's code and the effects of
time and changing requirements. Now aren't you glad we took some time for design?

```java
package com.wiley.compBooks.EJwithUML.HtmlProduction.GenericProducers;

import java.util.*;
import com.wiley.compBooks.EJwithUML.HtmlProduction.*;

/**
 *
 * The PageProducerGeneric is a concrete implementation of
 * PageProducer that produces HTML for all modern browsers.
 *
 * It implements IConcreteProducer so that it can be registered
 * with the ProducerFactory.
 *
 */
public class PageProducerGeneric extends PageProducer implements
IConcreteProducer
{
  public String getHtml()
  {
    StringBuffer buffer = new StringBuffer();
```

```
      buffer.append("\n<!--" +this+ "-->\n");

buffer.append("<html><head><title>"+this.getTitle()+"</title></head>\n")
;

      String backgroundColor = "";
      if(this.getPreferences().containsKey("page.backgroundColor"))
      {
        backgroundColor = " bgcolor=" +
            this.getPreferences().get("page.backgroundColor");
      }
      buffer.append("<body" +backgroundColor+ ">");

      Iterator producerIterator = this.getProducers();
      while (producerIterator.hasNext())
      {
        IHtmlProducer producer = (IHtmlProducer)
            producerIterator.next();
        buffer.append("\n<!-- Producers: -->\n");
        buffer.append("" +producer.getHtml()+ "\n\n");
      }

      buffer.append("</body></html>");
      return buffer.toString();
    }

    public boolean supportsBrowser(String browserName,
                                   float version)
    {
      return true;
    }

    public float distanceFromVersion(String browserName,
                                     float version)
    {
      return Float.MIN_VALUE;
    }

    public String getProducerType()
    {
      return IConcreteProducer.PAGE_PRODUCER;
    }

    public Object createCopy()
    {
      PageProducerGeneric copy = new PageProducerGeneric();
      return copy;
    }
}
```

TableProducerGeneric.java

As with the PageProducer, getHtml contains the interesting code. It traverses each row of the table, by calling the getHtmlProducer method defined in the superclass TableProducer. Each producer is retrieved for a particular row index and column index. As before, the TableProducer encapsulates a narrowly defined piece of fairly complex logic.

```java
package com.wiley.compBooks.EJwithUML.HtmlProduction.GenericProducers;

import java.util.*;
import com.wiley.compBooks.EJwithUML.HtmlProduction.*;

/**
 *
 * The TableProducerGeneric is a concrete implementation of
 * TableProducer that produces HTML for all modern browsers.
 *
 * It implements IConcreteProducer so that it can be registered
 * with the ProducerFactory.
 *
 */
public class TableProducerGeneric extends TableProducer implements
IConcreteProducer
{
  public String getHtml()
  {
    StringBuffer buffer = new StringBuffer();
    buffer.append("\n<!--" +this+ "-->\n");
    buffer.append("<table>\n");

    for (int rowCtr=0; rowCtr <= this.getMaxRowIndex(); rowCtr++)
    {
      buffer.append(" <tr>\n");
      for (int columnCtr=0; columnCtr <=this.getMaxColumnIndex();
          columnCtr++)
      {
        buffer.append("   <td>");
        IHtmlProducer cellProducer = this.getHtmlProducer(rowCtr,
                                                 columnCtr);
        if (cellProducer != null)
        {
          buffer.append(cellProducer.getHtml());
        }
        buffer.append("   </td>\n");
      }
      buffer.append(" </tr>\n");
    }

    buffer.append("</table>");
```

```
      return buffer.toString();
  }

  public boolean supportsBrowser(String browserName,
                                      float version)
  {
    return true;
  }

  public float distanceFromVersion(String browserName,
                                        float version)
  {
    return Float.MIN_VALUE;
  }

  public String getProducerType()
  {
    return IConcreteProducer.TABLE_PRODUCER;
  }

  public Object createCopy()
  {
    TableProducerGeneric copy = new TableProducerGeneric();
    return copy;
  }
}
```

TabularInputFormProducerGeneric.java

TabularInputFormProducerGeneric is interesting because it does not override getHtml. Remember, TabularInputFormProducer is a self-constructing Composite. It builds itself from other producers, each of which has a concrete implementation of getHtml. TabularInputFormProducer's getHtml simply retrieves the HTML from its internal FormProducer. There is nothing to override.

Notice that it does override the getBrowserName and getBrowserVersion methods that were defined as abstract in the superclass.

```
package com.wiley.compBooks.EJwithUML.HtmlProduction.GenericProducers;

import com.wiley.compBooks.EJwithUML.HtmlProduction.*;
import java.util.*;

/**
 *
 * The TabularInputFormProducerGeneric is a concrete
 * implementation of TabularInputFormProducer that produces HTML
 * for all modern browsers.
 *
 * TabularInputFormProducerGeneric is a self-constructing
```

```
 * Composite. It obtains producers from the ProducerFactory, just
 * like any other object.
 *
 *
 * It implements IConcreteProducer so that it can be registered
 * with the ProducerFactory.
 *
 */
public class TabularInputFormProducerGeneric extends
TabularInputFormProducer implements IConcreteProducer
{

  public boolean supportsBrowser(String browserName,
                                 float version)
  {
    return true;
  }

  public float distanceFromVersion(String browserName,
                                   float version)
  {
    return Float.MIN_VALUE;
  }

  public String getProducerType()
  {
    return IConcreteProducer.TABULAR_INPUT_FORM_PRODUCER;
  }

  public Object createCopy()
  {
    TabularInputFormProducerGeneric copy = new
        TabularInputFormProducerGeneric();
    return copy;
  }

  /** Answers the name of the browser for which the producer is
   *  tailored. */
  protected final String getBrowserName()
  {
    return "GENERIC";
  }

  /** Answers the version of the browser for which the producer
   *  is tailored. */
  protected final float getBrowserVersion()
  {
    return 1.0f;
  }

  /** Customizes the properties so that the Composite producers
```

```
  *   look right. */
  protected void customizePreferences(Properties properties)
  {

  }
}
```

The Next Step

In this chapter we defined goals for the design of our HTML production class library, designed to those goals, and finally implemented our design in Java. This design and implementation is used as a foundation for Chapter 13, "Design for the TimecardUI Package," which follows the same design and implementation process for the Time-card system's servlet-based user interface.

Design for the TimecardUI Package

The TimecardUI package contains the servlets that provide a Web front end to the Login and Record Time use cases of the Timecard application. These servlets obtain and update system data by using the session beans in the TimecardWorkflow package, and use the HTML production framework from the HtmlProduction package to format the results into HTML. The Sun Microsystems servlet class library is used to interpret the HTTP request and to build the HTTP response.

As in earlier design efforts, we must identify goals and priorities, review prior steps, design to goals, and apply design to use cases.

Establish Design Goals

To develop a solid design, we need clear goals. Establishing clear goals before you begin to design helps designers avoid hasty decisions. After all, design forces a developer to compromise or pick between competing goals. Establishing clear goals up front makes this easier and less arbitrary.

Extensibility

User interfaces always evolve over time, as the users' needs mature. To keep the code base small, each new feature should reuse existing components or introduce new modular components that can be used on other features. At times, users also may desire different appearances for particular screens or for the system as a whole. In some cases, the customer might want to update the look of the entire site to emphasize a brand or to produce a fresh look.

Because of these two factors, the servlets in our system should never produce their own HTML. Instead, this tedious activity is always delegated to the classes of the HtmlProduction framework. If a new feature cannot be created by combining existing HTML producers, then a new HTML producer must be added to the framework. Once in the framework, the new producer becomes available for use in other servlets. A new look for the entire site should be accomplished by changing the preferences and a few key producers, without altering the servlets themselves. Preventing the servlets from producing their own HTML, and forcing them to depend on the HTML production framework, keeps the system smaller and easier to understand and to extend.

Testability

The servlets tie together much of the system to provide direct benefit to the customer, so they are a logical place to start for system and integration testing. While final testing involves Web browsers going against the Web server and the application server, it is useful to test the servlets inside an integrated development environment. This allows quick edit and rebuild cycles, and the use of a debugger. The alternative, whereby developers recompile classes and restart or notify the servlet engine after each change, is demoralizing and time-consuming. If the servlets are testable outside of the servlet engine, developers can perform independent and isolated load testing, which is useful to determine scalability and to locate performance bottlenecks.

Review Prior Steps

Before proceeding, we must review the architectural constraints as well as the analysis model.

Review Architectural Constraints

At the end of Chapter 9, "Software Architecture," we determined that the TimecardUI depends directly on the HtmlProduction package and on the TimecardWorkflow package. It must not directly depend on any other package in the system. Rather than depend on the specifics of the HtmlProducers, it should depend upon the Producer-Factory and the abstract producer classes. Also, TimecardUI must never directly access any entity beans. In addition, no other package depends on the TimecardUI package. Together, these restrictions help make the system more extensible and easier to understand and to maintain. For example, even radical changes in the way data is stored or in the business logic for validating timecards will not affect the servlets, as long as they

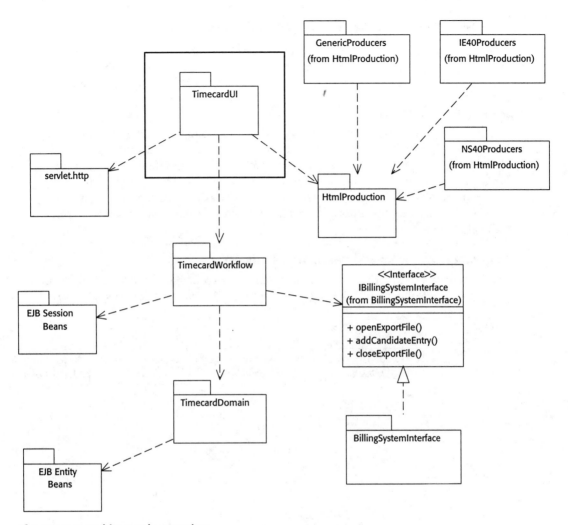

Figure 13.1 Architectural constraints.

do not affect the public interface of the TimecardWorkflow session beans. Figure 13.1 shows the architecture as it affects the TimecardUI package.

Each use case dynamically builds several HTML pages and processes that are input from one or more HTML forms. Since page production and form processing are tightly intertwined, it seems logical to encapsulate those tasks for each use case in a single servlet. This results in two servlets: LoginServlet and RecordTimeServlet.

Review Analysis Model

In this step, we review the analysis model for the Login and Record Time use cases.

Review Analysis Model for Login Use Case

The Login use case allows users to validate themselves to the system as a precursor to any use of the system. The login use case has one normal flow and two alternate flows. The alternate flows show different ways that the user's information can be invalid.

Normal Flow (Analysis)

The sequence begins when the employee asks the EmployeeLoginUI to display the login form. The employee then uses the form to submit his or her username and password. The EmployeeLoginUI asks the LoginWorkflow to validate the login information. Since the LoginWorkflow does not have the information needed to perform the validation, it uses the UserLocator to find the User object, and the resulting User object to finally validate the login information. Figure 13.2 shows the sequence diagram from the analysis model.

Alternate Flow for Invalid Password (Analysis)

The sequence for the alternate flow for an invalid password begins when the employee asks the EmployeeLoginUI to display the login form. The employee then uses the form

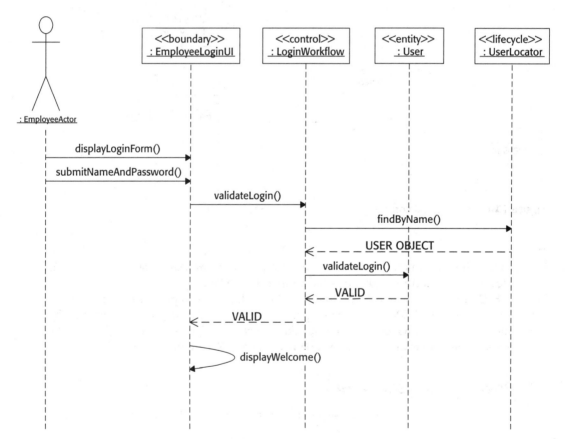

Figure 13.2 Sequence diagram for normal flow of Login (analysis).

to submit his or her username and password. The EmployeeLoginUI asks the Login-Workflow to validate the login information. Since the LoginWorkflow does not have the information needed to perform the validation, it uses the UserLocator to find the User object, and the resulting User object to finally validate the login information. In this case, the User object responds that the user's information is invalid; the Employ-eeLoginUI displays an error message, and the sequence is complete. Figure 13.3 shows the sequence diagram from the analysis model.

Alternate Flow for Unknown User (Analysis)

When the user is unknown, the sequence for the alternate flow begins when the employee asks the EmployeeLoginUI to display the login form. The employee then uses the form to submit his or her username and password. The EmployeeLoginUI asks the LoginWorkflow to validate the login information. Since the LoginWorkflow does not have the information needed to perform the validation, it uses the User-Locator to find the User object. In this flow of events, no matching User object can be found, so the LoginWorkflow responds that the user's information is invalid. The EmployeeLoginUI displays an error message, and the sequence is complete. The return value of invalid does not seem to convey the reason why the login information is

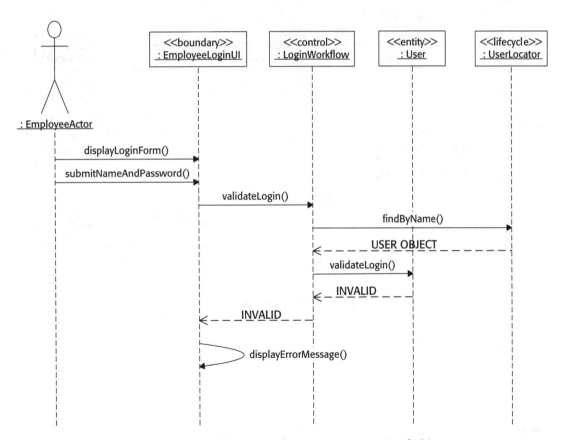

Figure 13.3 Sequence diagram for invalid password for Login use case (analysis).

invalid to the EmployeeLoginUI. Figure 13.4 shows the sequence diagram from the analysis model.

Participating Classes for the Login Use Case (Analysis)

The user interface objects use LoginWorkflow objects. The resulting relationship needs to be an association, so that the user interface objects can reuse the same LoginWorkflow object for login retries. The LoginWorkflow object uses a User object, but does not need to remember it for future use; therefore, the resulting relationship is a dependency. The LoginWorkflow object uses a UserLocator object and keeps it for future use, so the resulting relationship is an association. These relationships are shown in Figure 13.5.

Review Analysis Model for Record Time Use Case

In the Record Time use case, an employee views his or her current hours, edits existing hours, adds new hours, and optionally submits the timecard. The normal flow is the only significant flow of events from a user interface based on user interface complexity and processing.

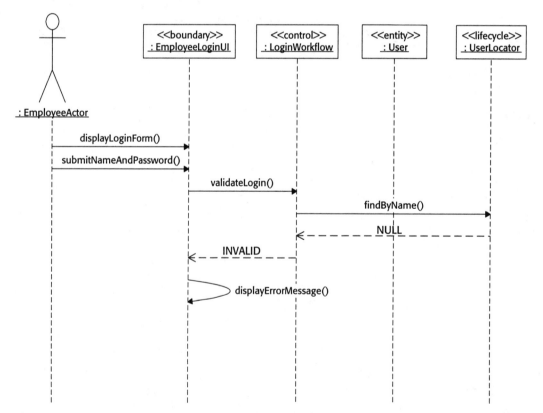

Figure 13.4 Sequence diagram for unknown user for Login use case (analysis).

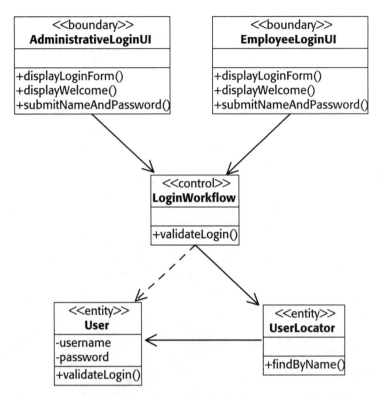

Figure 13.5 Participating classes for the Login use case (analysis).

Normal Flow for Record Time Use Case (Analysis)

The sequence for the normal flow of events begins when the employee actor asks the RecordTimeUI object to display his or her current timecard. The RecordTimeUI object passes the request along to the RecordTimeWorkflow object, which finds the user's current timecard and extracts the current timecard data. The RecordTimeUI uses this raw data to build a display. The employee actor uses the display to update the entries. The RecordTimeUI sends the updated entries back to the RecordTimeWorkflow, which applies them to the current timecard. Figure 13.6 shows this sequence.

Design to Goals

Our design is fairly constrained, since we know that we will use servlets and the HTML production classes. However, we must still consider our two goals: extensibility and testability.

Extensibility can be achieved by keeping each servlet well focused and by always depending on the HTML production classes. If the desired functionality does not exist within the HTML production class library, we must either create a new HTML producer that can live within the library or wait for a HTML production developer to do

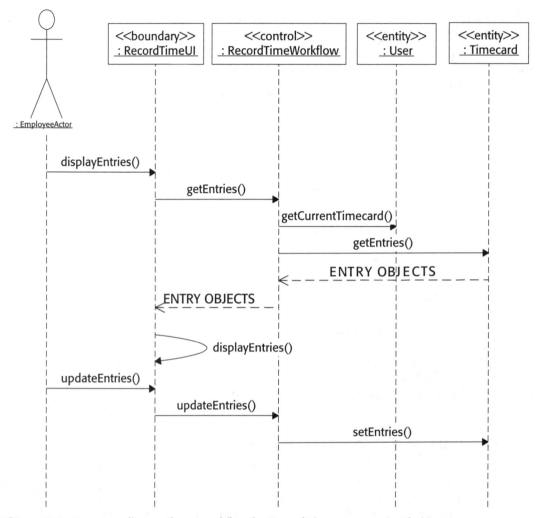

Figure 13.6 Sequence diagram for normal flow for Record Time use case (analysis).

so. Creating our own custom HTML production code that lives within a servlet is not acceptable, as it gradually leads away from standardization and reusable HTML production code.

Stressing testability determines how we write each servlet. First of all, we want the doGet method to be as small as possible. It should simply retrieve any parameters and session data before calling private methods to perform any interesting logic. This allows us to test the bulk of the servlet's functionality from a static main entry point, perhaps even from the debugger of our choice. The code, compile, deploy, and test cycle is significantly more difficult for most servlet engines than for an application in an integrated development environment (IDE). It pays to minimize the amount of time spent testing deployed servlet code.

Design for Each Use Case

We need to create a design for both the Login and the Record Time use cases.

Create Design for the Login Use Case

Our design for the Login use case considers three major flows: building the empty form, processing valid login data, and processing invalid login data.

Build the Login Form

The first step is to build an empty login form in HTML. While it is certainly possible to use a static HTML page for this purpose, producing dynamic HTML for static pages helps ensure the same look for all of the pages.

The LoginServlet knows to produce the empty form because the username parameter is not set in the HttpRequest object. Note that the servlet calls an internal method, buildForm, to produce the form. Separating the actual form production logic makes it easier to test the use case inside of a debugger or within a performance test harness.

Next, a TabularInputFormProducer is obtained from the ProducerFactory. Note from the earlier HTML production design that TabularInputFormProducer is an abstract class. The actual object reference is an instantiation of a class that extends TabularInputFormProducer. Only the ProducerFactory knows which concrete implementation of TabularInputFormProducer is used. We are protected from such details.

The submit target is set to the URL for the LoginServlet. Fields for the name and password are added to the TabularInputFormProducer before the TabularInputFormProducer is added to the PageProducer. Next, the preferences Properties object is retrieved from the PreferenceManager and set in the PageProducer. Finally, formatted HTML is extracted from the PageProducer and written to the HttpResponse's output stream. Figure 13.7 shows the sequence of messages that produces an empty login form.

Process Valid Login Data

In the sequence for processing valid login data, the username and password parameters exist in the HttpRequest. The LoginServlet asks the LoginWorkflow to validate the username and password combination. When the true response is received, the LoginServlet stores the username in the HttpSession.

Next, the LoginServlet builds a page with links to the user's options. For now, there is only one option, record time. In any case, the link is built by obtaining a LinkProducer from the ProducerFactory. Since there is no existing LinkProducer in the HTML production framework, we must design one. As we might expect, the target for the LinkProducer is set to the URL of the RecordTimeServlet. Notice that the contents of the link are encapsulated inside of a TextProducer. Allowing client code to add any sort of IHtmlProducer provides limitless flexibility. For instance, adding an Image-

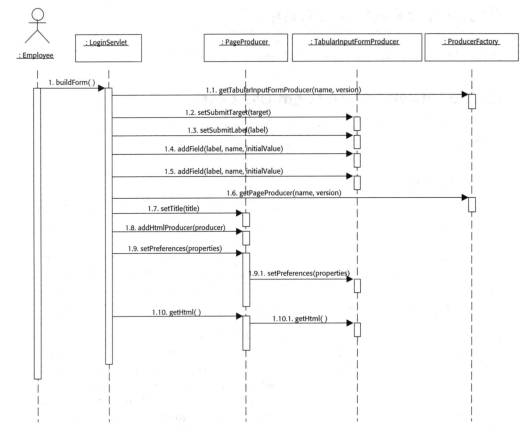

Figure 13.7 Sequence to build Login form.

Producer would produce a clickable image. While this requires us to wrap the text for the link inside of a TextProducer, the extra flexibility is well worth the inconvenience.

The LoginServlet adds the LinkProducer to the PageProducer, sets the preferences in the PageProducer, and extracts the formatted HTML from the PageProducer. This sequence is shown in Figure 13.8.

Process Invalid Login Data

As in the sequence for valid data, the username and password parameters exist in the HttpRequest. However, in this scenario, the validateUser method in the Login-Workflow returns false, so the LoginServlet builds a page with a TabularInputForm-Producer, as in the build empty form, and adds a TextProducer with some explanatory error text. Figure 13.9 shows this sequence.

Participating Classes for the Login Use Case

LoginServlet sits in the middle of the action, like a frantic Hollywood agent, knowing all of the players but unable to accomplish anything on its own. This is a very common

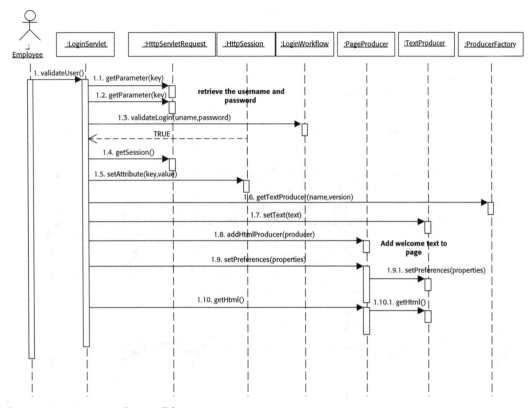

Figure 13.8 Sequence for a valid user.

and powerful concept: One thin class combines the talents of many other classes to form a new and interesting whole. Luckily, classes and objects are truly egoless, so the HtmlProducers do not mind the servlets' time in the limelight while they perform the tedious HTML formatting.

Notice the complete lack of association relationships in the class diagram. Remember, each sequence begins when the servlet engine calls the doPost method of the LoginServlet and the same LoginServlet object is used to validate any number of users. Everything that the LoginServlet needs to produce the HTML is passed into the doPost method inside of the HttpRequest object. Figure 13.10 shows the classes for the Login use case.

Create Design for the Record Time Use Case

Based on our recently refreshed memory of the analysis model for the Record Time use case and our knowledge of the Servlet class library and the HTML production classes, we can develop a design for the Record Time user interface. There are two main sequences: building the Record Time form and updating the timecard based on a submitted form.

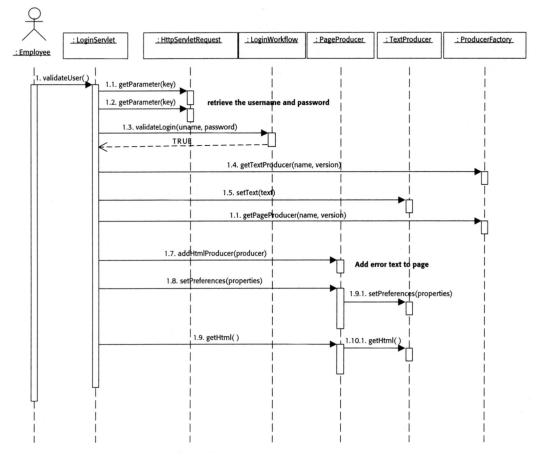

Figure 13.9 Sequence for Invalid login data.

Build the Record Time Form

The sequence begins when the employee actor asks the RecordTimeServlet to build the time entry form. The RecordTimeServlet extracts the username from the HttpSession, and uses it to create a RecordTimeWorkflow object. The RecordTimeServlet asks the RecordTimeWorkflow for the charge codes, dates, and hours for the current timecard. With the raw data in hand, the RecordTimeServlet obtains a FormProducer and a TableProducer from the ProducerFactory. The TableProducer will hold the data and the input text fields, so it must be added to the FormProducer. Each TextProducer to hold the charge codes and the dates must be obtained from the ProducerFactory, configured with correct text, and added to the correct cell in the TableProducer. A similar process populates the table with TextfieldProducers for the hours. Finally, the Form-Producer is configured with the appropriate submit target and is added to the Page-Producer. Figure 13.11 shows this sequence.

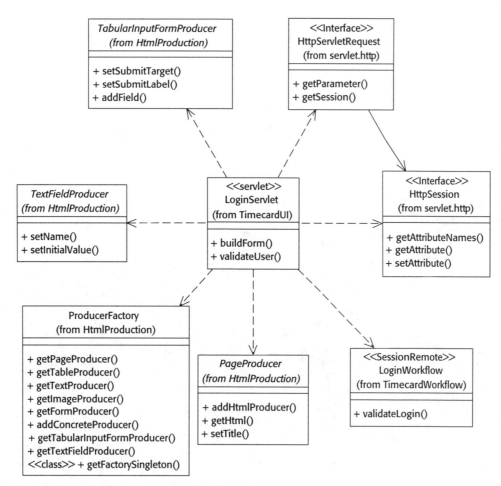

Figure 13.10 Participating classes for the Login use case.

Update the Timecard

The sequence for updating the timecard begins when the employee updates his or her time entries and submits the form to the servlet. The RecordTimeServlet extracts the HttpSession from the HttpServletRequest. The RecordTimeServlet pulls the username out of the session and uses it to get a remote reference to the appropriate RecordTime-Workflow. Next, the RecordTimeServlet pulls parameters out of the request for the hours, charge codes, and dates. The hours are then used to update the RecordTime-Workflow. Figure 13.12 shows this sequence.

Participating Classes for the Record Time Use Case

Many classes help realize the Record Time use case, but most are independent of the others. As in the Login use case, the servlet ties the disparate objects together. Again, it

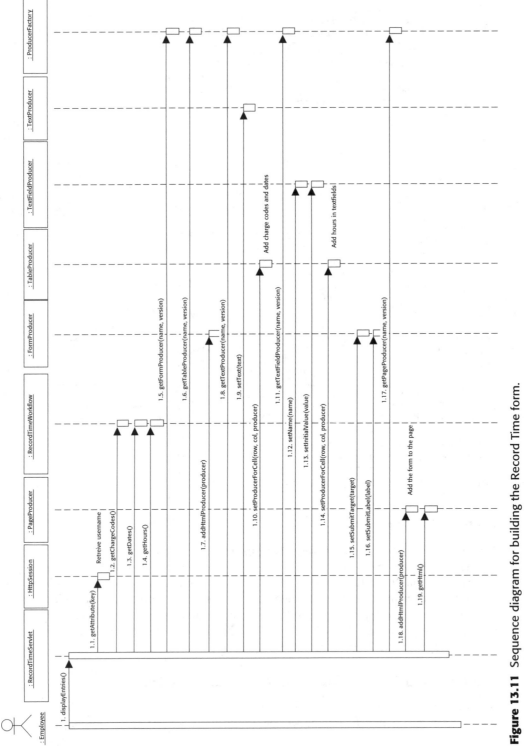

Figure 13.11 Sequence diagram for building the Record Time form.

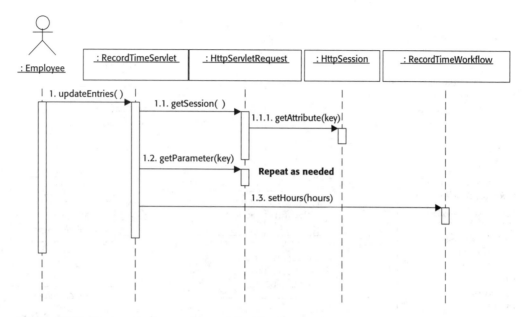

Figure 13.12 Sequence diagram for updating the timecard.

is worth noting that the RecordTimeServlet does not do any real work: It does not retrieve any data from the database, it does not format any HTML, and it certainly does not hold any business logic. It just knows where to go to ask.

At first glance, it seems odd that the RecordTimeServlet class depends on many classes, yet does not have any lasting relationship with any classes. For instance, where is the one-to-one or one-to-many association between the RecordTimeServlet class and the RecordTimeWorkflow class? Remember that all of the work done by a servlet is initiated when the servlet engine calls either the servlet's doPost or doGet method. Also recall that many users may share a servlet. So, the HttpRequest contains all of the information that the RecordTimeServlet needs, including form data and the RecordTimeWorkflow that is embedded within the HttpSession. Figure 13.13 shows this sequence.

Now that we have a solid design for the servlets for the Login and Record Time use cases, we can implement them in Java.

Implementation

The following sections show the implementation for the LoginServlet, the Record-TimeServlet, and a BasicServlet class that serves as a useful base class for both.

LoginServlet.java

The LoginServlet does not directly format any HTML. Instead, it extracts information from the LoginWorkflow class and uses the HtmlPoduction package to format all of the HTML.

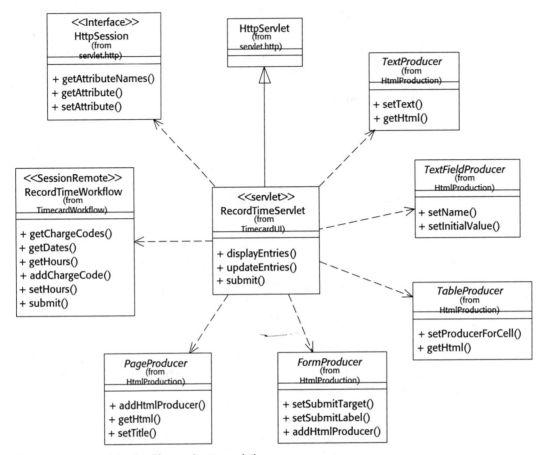

Figure 13.13 Participating classes for Record Time use case.

If the username parameter is not set, then the LoginServlet knows that the user needs to enter his or her information in an HTML form. The static main entry point is used to test the servlet's functionality.

```
package com.wiley.compBooks.EJwithUML.TimeCardServlets;

import javax.servlet.http.*;
import javax.servlet.*;

import javax.naming.*;
import javax.ejb.*;
import java.rmi.*;
import javax.rmi.PortableRemoteObject;

import java.io.*;

import com.wiley.compBooks.EJwithUML.HtmlProduction.*;
```

```java
import com.wiley.compBooks.EJwithUML.TimeCardWorkflow.*;

/**
 *
 * The LoginServlet class uses the TimecardWorkflow and
 * HtmlProduction packages to create the formatted HTML
 * for the Login form, and to validate the user.
 *
 */
public class LoginServlet extends BasicServlet
{
  /** Overrides method from HttpServlet - doPost allows the
   * code to interact with the system. */
  public void doPost(HttpServletRequest request,
                     HttpServletResponse response)
                     throws ServletException, IOException
  {
    PageProducer pageProducer = null;
    String browser = this.getBrowserName(request);
    float version = this.getBrowserVersion(request);

    try
    {
      // extract user name and password
      String username = request.getParameter("username");
      String password = request.getParameter("password");

      if (username == null)
      {

        pageProducer = buildLoginPage(browser,version);
      }
      else
      {
        if (this.isLoginValid(username, password))
        {
          HttpSession session = request.getSession(true);
          session.putValue("username", username);
          pageProducer=buildWelcomePage(browser,
                                    version,username);
        }
        else
        {
          pageProducer =
              buildLoginInvalidPage(browser,version);
        }
      }

    }
    catch (NamingException e)
    {
```

```
          pageProducer =
              this.getRemoteErrorPage("Error During Login\n", e);
      }
      catch (CreateException e)
      {
          pageProducer =
              this.getRemoteErrorPage("Error During Login\n", e);
      }

      pageProducer.setPreferences(this.getPreferences());
      response.getWriter().println(pageProducer.getHtml());
      response.getWriter().flush();
      response.getWriter().close();
  }

  /** Builds page for display on succesful login.*/
  PageProducer buildWelcomePage(String browserName,
                    float browserVersion, String username)
  {
      PageProducer pageProducer =
      this.producerFactory.getPageProducer(browserName,
                                                  browserVersion);

      pageProducer.setTitle("Welcome "+ username);

      LinkProducer linkProducer =
          this.producerFactory.getLinkProducer(browserName,
                                              browserVersion);

                  TextProducer linkText =
          this.producerFactory.getTextProducer(browserName,
                                              browserVersion);

                  linkText.setText("Enter Hours");
      linkProducer.setTarget("./RecordTimeServlet");
      linkProducer.addHtmlProducer(linkText);
      pageProducer.addHtmlProducer(linkProducer);

      return pageProducer;
  }

  /** Builds page for user input */
  PageProducer buildLoginPage(String browserName,
                              float browserVersion)
  {
      String host = this.getHost();

      TabularInputFormProducer formProducer =
        this.producerFactory.getTabularInputFormProducer(browserName,
                                                  browserVersion);
      formProducer.setSubmitTarget("./servlets/login");
```

```
        formProducer.setSubmitLabel("Login");
        formProducer.addField("User Name", "username", "");
        formProducer.addField("Password", "password", "");

        PageProducer pageProducer =
            this.producerFactory.getPageProducer(browserName,
                                                 browserVersion);
        pageProducer.setTitle("Login");
        pageProducer.addHtmlProducer(formProducer);

        return pageProducer;
    }

    /** Builds page with error message when login trades. */
    PageProducer buildLoginInvalidPage(String browserName,
                                       float browserVersion)
    {
        PageProducer pageProducer =
            buildLoginPage(browserName, browserVersion);
        pageProducer.setTitle("Login Failed. Try Again.");

        TextProducer textProducer =
            this.producerFactory.getTextProducer(browserName,
                                                 browserVersion);
        textProducer.setText("<p>Invalid username or
                        password.<p>Remember, case matters.");
        pageProducer.addHtmlProducer(textProducer);

        return pageProducer;
    }

    /** Answers true if the login data matches the database.*/
    boolean isLoginValid(String username, String password) throws
NamingException, RemoteException, CreateException
    {
        Context initial = new InitialContext();
        Object lwobjref = initial.lookup("LoginWorkflow");
        LoginWorkflowHome loginWorkflowHome =
            (LoginWorkflowHome)PortableRemoteObject.narrow(lwobjref,
                                       LoginWorkflowHome.class);
        LoginWorkflow loginWorkflow = loginWorkflowHome.create();

        return loginWorkflow.isUserValid(username, password);
    }

    public static void main(String[] args)
    {
      try
      {
        LoginServlet ls = new LoginServlet();
```

```
      PageProducer pageProducer = ls.buildLoginPage("Netscape",
                                                     4.0f);
      FileOutputStream fos = new FileOutputStream("LoginForm.html");
      BufferedOutputStream bos = new BufferedOutputStream(fos);
      PrintStream ps = new PrintStream(bos);
      ps.println(pageProducer.getHtml());
      ps.flush();
      ps.close();


      pageProducer = ls.buildWelcomePage("Netscape", 4.0f,"Joe");
      fos = new FileOutputStream("Welcome.html");
      bos = new BufferedOutputStream(fos);
      ps = new PrintStream(bos);
      ps.println(pageProducer.getHtml());
      ps.flush();
      ps.close();

      pageProducer = ls.buildLoginInvalidPage("Netscape", 4.0f);
      fos = new FileOutputStream("Invalid.html");
      bos = new BufferedOutputStream(fos);
      ps = new PrintStream(bos);
      ps.println(pageProducer.getHtml());
      ps.flush();
      ps.close();
    }
    catch (IOException e)
    {
      System.out.println("e: " +e);
    }
  }

}
```

RecordTimeServlet.java

RecordTimeServlet.java does not directly format any HTML. Instead, it extracts information from the RecordTimeWorkflow class and uses the HtmlPoduction package to format all of the HTML. If the hours are not set, it knows that it needs to build a form for display. The form shows the current data and allows the user to update it. If the hours are present in the request data, then the RecordTimeServlet extracts the data from the form and passes it to the RecordTimeWorkflow for processing. Then it builds the Time Entry form so the users can see their changes and make further updates.

```
package com.wiley.compBooks.EJwithUML.TimeCardServlets;

import javax.servlet.http.*;
import javax.servlet.*;
```

```java
import javax.naming.*;
import javax.ejb.*;
import java.rmi.*;
import javax.rmi.PortableRemoteObject;

import java.io.*;
import java.util.*;

import com.wiley.compBooks.EJwithUML.HtmlProduction.*;
import com.wiley.compBooks.EJwithUML.TimeCardWorkflow.*;

/**
 * The RecordTimeServlet uses the TimecardWorkflow and
 * HtmlProduction packages to create the formatted HTML
 * for the time entry form and to capture the entered hours.
 */
public class RecordTimeServlet extends BasicServlet
{
  /** Overrides method from HttpServlet.
      doPost is called by the servlet engine. */
  public void doPost(HttpServletRequest request,
                     HttpServletResponse response)
                     throws ServletException, IOException
  {
    PageProducer pageProducer = null;

    try
    {
      // extract username from session
      HttpSession session = request.getSession(false);
      String username = (String) session.getValue("username");

      // obtain remote reference to RecordTimeWorkflow session
      // bean
      Context initial = new InitialContext();
      Object rtwobjref = initial.lookup("RecordTimeWorkflow");
      RecordTimeWorkflowHome home =
          (RecordTimeWorkflowHome)PortableRemoteObject.narrow(
          rtwobjref,RecordTimeWorkflowHome.class);
      RecordTimeWorkflow rtw = home.create(username);

      // if hours are set in request, extract and set in
      // workflow
      String hour = request.getParameter("hours1");
      if (hour != null)
      {
        float hours[] = extractHours(request);
        rtw.setHours(hours);
      }

      // retrieve values from workflow
```

```java
        ChargeCodeWrapper[] codes = rtw.getChargeCodes();
        Date[] dates = rtw.getDates();
        float[] hours = rtw.getHours();

        // build the time entry page producer
        pageProducer =
            this.buildRecordTimeForm("",4.0f, codes,dates, hours);
    }
    catch (NamingException e)
    {
      pageProducer =
          this.getRemoteErrorPage("Error During Login\n", e);
    }
    catch (CreateException e)
    {
      pageProducer =
          this.getRemoteErrorPage("Error During Login\n", e);
    }

    pageProducer.setPreferences(this.getPreferences());
    response.getWriter().println(pageProducer.getHtml());
    response.getWriter().flush();
    response.getWriter().close();
  }


  /** Builds the time entry page producer*/
  PageProducer buildRecordTimeForm(String browserName, float
browserVersion, ChargeCodeWrapper[] codes, Date[] dates, float[] hours)
throws RemoteException, CreateException, NamingException
  {
    ProducerFactory factory =
        ProducerFactory.getFactorySingleton();

   PageProducer pageProducer =
        factory.getPageProducer(browserName, browserVersion);
    FormProducer formProducer =
        factory.getFormProducer(browserName, browserVersion);
    TableProducer tableProducer =
        factory.getTableProducer(browserName, browserVersion);

    // populate table producer with charge codes down side
    TextProducer text =
        factory.getTextProducer(browserName, browserVersion);
    text.setText("Charge Codes");
    tableProducer.setHtmlProducerForCell(0, 0, text);
    for (int ctr = 0; ctr < codes.length; ctr++)
    {
      ChargeCodeWrapper ccw = codes[ctr];
      String name = ccw.getChargeCodeName();
      text =
```

```
        factory.getTextProducer(browserName, browserVersion);
    text.setText(name);
    tableProducer.setHtmlProducerForCell(ctr+1, 0, text);
  }

  // populate table producer with dates across top
  for (int ctr = 0; ctr < dates.length; ctr++)
  {
    Date d = dates[ctr];
    String dateString = d.toString();
    text =
          factory.getTextProducer(browserName, browserVersion);
    text.setText(dateString);
    tableProducer.setHtmlProducerForCell(0, 1+ctr, text);
  }

  // populate table producer with hours in middle
  for (int cc_ctr = 0; cc_ctr < codes.length; cc_ctr++)
  {
    for (int date_ctr=0; date_ctr < dates.length; date_ctr++)
    {
      int index = cc_ctr*dates.length +date_ctr;
      String initValue = "" + hours[index];

      TextFieldProducer tfp =
        factory.getTextFieldProducer(browserName, browserVersion);
      tfp.setInitialValue(initValue);
      tfp.setMaxLength(5);
      tfp.setSize(5);
      tfp.setName("hours"+index);

      tableProducer.setHtmlProducerForCell(cc_ctr+1,
                                           date_ctr+1, tfp);
    }
  }

  formProducer.addHtmlProducer(tableProducer);
  formProducer.setSubmitTarget("./RecordTimeServlet");

  SubmitButtonProducer submitButtonProducer =
    factory.getSubmitButtonProducer(browserName, browserVersion);
  submitButtonProducer.setSubmittLabel("OK");
  formProducer.addHtmlProducer(submitButtonProducer);

  pageProducer.addHtmlProducer(formProducer);

  return pageProducer;
}

/** Extracts hours from the request. */
float[] extractHours(HttpServletRequest request)
```

```
{
  Vector v = new Vector();

  int ctr=0;
  String hour = request.getParameter("hours" +ctr);
  while (hour != null)
  {
    v.addElement(new Float(hour));

    ctr++;
    hour = request.getParameter("hours" +ctr);
  }

  float hours[] = new float[v.size()];
  Enumeration enum = v.elements();
  int index = 0;
  while (enum.hasMoreElements())
  {
    Float f = (Float) enum.nextElement();
    hours[index] = f.floatValue();
  }

  return hours;
}

public static void main(String[] args)
{
  try
  {
    RecordTimeServlet rts = new RecordTimeServlet();

    ChargeCodeWrapper[] codes = new ChargeCodeWrapper[4];
    for (int ctr = 0; ctr < 4; ctr++)
    {
      codes[ctr] =
      new ChargeCodeWrapper("ford", "mustang", "code" +ctr);
    }

    Date[] dates = new Date[7];

    Calendar calendar = Calendar.getInstance();
    calendar.setLenient(true);
    calendar.set(Calendar.YEAR, 2000);
    int startDayOfYear = calendar.get(Calendar.DAY_OF_YEAR);

    for (int delta = 0; delta < 7; delta++)
    {
      calendar.set(Calendar.DAY_OF_YEAR,
                  startDayOfYear+delta);
      dates[delta] = calendar.getTime();
    }
```

```
        float[] hours = new float[28];
        for (int ctr=0; ctr< 28; ctr++)
        {
          hours[ctr] = (float) (ctr % 10);
        }

        PageProducer pageProducer =
            rts.buildRecordTimeForm("Netscape", 4.0f, codes, dates,
                                    hours);
        FileOutputStream fos =
            new FileOutputStream("RecordTimeForm.html");
        BufferedOutputStream bos = new BufferedOutputStream(fos);
        PrintStream ps = new PrintStream(bos);
        ps.println(pageProducer.getHtml());
        ps.flush();
        ps.close();
      }
    catch (Exception e)
    {
      System.out.println("e: " +e);
    }
  }
}
```

BasicServlet.java

The BasicServlet.java holds functionality that can be used by every servlet in the system. The functionality includes populating the ProducerFactory, initializing preferences, and formatting errors.

```
package com.wiley.compBooks.EJwithUML.TimeCardServlets;

import javax.servlet.http.*;
import java.util.*;
import java.io.*;

import com.wiley.compBooks.EJwithUML.HtmlProduction.*;
import com.wiley.compBooks.EJwithUML.HtmlProduction.GenericProducers.*;

/**
 * The BasicServlet provides a consistent mechanism for
 * handling preferences, populating producers, and producing
 * error messages.
 */
class BasicServlet extends HttpServlet
{
  private static Properties preferences = null;
  private static boolean populatedProducers = false;
```

```java
protected ProducerFactory producerFactory;

BasicServlet()
{
  if (!BasicServlet.populatedProducers)
  {
    BasicServlet.populatedProducers = true;
    producerFactory = ProducerFactory.getFactorySingleton();

    IConcreteProducer cp = new FormProducerGeneric();
    producerFactory.addConcreteProducer(cp);

    cp = new PageProducerGeneric();
    producerFactory.addConcreteProducer(cp);

    cp = new SubmitButtonProducerGeneric();
    producerFactory.addConcreteProducer(cp);

    cp = new TableProducerGeneric();
    producerFactory.addConcreteProducer(cp);

    cp = new TabularInputFormProducerGeneric();
    producerFactory.addConcreteProducer(cp);

    cp = new TextFieldProducerGeneric();
    producerFactory.addConcreteProducer(cp);

    cp = new TextProducerGeneric();
    producerFactory.addConcreteProducer(cp);

    cp = new LinkProducerGeneric();
    producerFactory.addConcreteProducer(cp);
  }
}

protected String getHost()
{
  return "localhost";
}

protected Properties getPreferences()
{
  // in an actual impementation, this should be a resource bundle.
  this.preferences = new Properties();
  this.preferences.setProperty("page.backgroundColor",
                               "lightGrey");

  return preferences;
}
```

```
protected String getBrowserName(HttpServletRequest request)
{
  // Just a test stub. This should parse the browser out
  // of the request
  return "Netscape";
}

protected float getBrowserVersion(HttpServletRequest request)
{
  // Just a test stub. This should parse the browser version
  // out of the request
  return 4.0f;
}

protected PageProducer getRemoteErrorPage(String message,
                                          Exception e)
{
  TextProducer textProducer =
      this.producerFactory.getTextProducer("GENERIC", 1f);
  textProducer.setText("Request failed due to failure of
                       remote service.\n" +message+ "\n"+e);

  PageProducer pageProducer =
      this.producerFactory.getPageProducer("GENERIC", 1f);
  pageProducer.setTitle("ERROR");
  pageProducer.addHtmlProducer(textProducer);
  pageProducer.setPreferences(this.getPreferences());

  return pageProducer;

}

}
```

The Next Step

In this chapter, we used session beans, as designed in Chapter 11, and the HTML production classes, as designed in Chapter 12, to produce the dynamically generated HTML for the Timecard system. At this point, we have completed the core functionality for the Timecard system. The last step is the interface with the BillingSystem, which we cover in Chapter 14.

Design for BillingSystemInterface

The design for the BillingSystemInterface subsystem builds heavily on the analysis model, architecture, and technology selection, and the design for the TimecardWorkflow packages, as developed in Chapter 5, "Analysis Model for the Timecard Application," Chapter 8, "Evaluating Candidate Technologies for Control and Entity Classes," Chapter 9, "Software Architecture," and Chapter 11, "Design for the TimecardDomain and TimecardWorkflow." The analysis model developed in Chapter 5 will help to determine the behavior of the BillingSystemInterface subsystem, while the content in Chapters 8, 9, and 11 will help to determine the technologies and existing packages that it will use.

As in the preceding design chapters, the goal here is to develop a design that is quite close to code and that is also constrained by the functional, architectural, and technological decisions made in those chapters. In this chapter, we will establish design goals, review the analysis model to recall the required functionality, then review the architecture to remind us of the architectural constraints. Based on this foundation, we will build a design that fits the use case.

Identify Goals

The design for the BillingSystemInterface should support the goals established for the entire system in Chapter 10, "Introduction to Design." Clarity, performance and reliability, extensibility, and reuse potential are all considered goals for the BillingSystem-Interface.

Clarity

Clarity is always an important goal, and the BillingSystemInterface is no exception. Both the design and the code must be understood by a wide variety of developers, from reviewers to maintenance developers. Adherence to design guidelines and code standards is very important.

Performance and Reliability

Performance and reliability are less important for the BillingSystemInterface than for the system in general. The BillingSystemInterface is intended for occasional use, and can be limited to off-peak hours if necessary.

Extensibility

Extensibility is fairly important for the BillingSystemInterface, since the Billing System itself is outside of our control and subject to change. The BillingSystemInterface must be able to evolve to meet different requirements for the format or content of the interchange data. Also, the BillingSystemInterface must be flexible in the criteria used to include or exclude time entries.

At the very least, these two areas must be kept well encapsulated, so that any changes are confined to a few closely related classes.

Reuse Potential

Reuse potential is relatively unimportant. No other part of the Timecard system needs any of this logic, and the BillingSystemInterface is not solving a generally applicable problem that might be shared by other systems.

Review of Analysis Model

There is only one use case that uses the BillingSystemInterface subsystem, Export Time Entries. The sequence begins when the administrative user asks the ExportEntriesUI to display the criteria that can be used to filter time entries. Once the administrative user selects the criteria, the control object, ExportTimeEntriesWorkflow, delegates the actual work to the locator objects and the entity objects. Figure 14.1 shows this sequence.

Review of Architecture

In the architecture developed in Chapters 8 and 9, the BillingSystemInterface uses XML to package the data for transfer to the actual billing system. The BillingSystem-

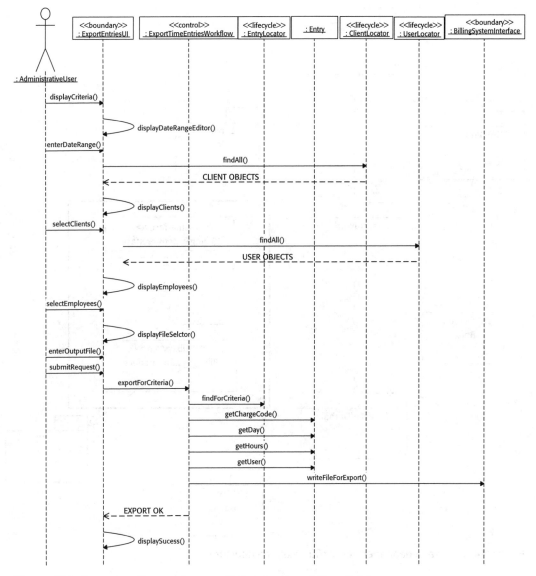

Figure 14.1 Sequence diagram for normal flow for Export Time Entries.

Interface is used by a class or classes in the TimecardWorkflow package, shown in Figure 14.2.

Design

The architecture and analysis diagrams indicate that the BillingSystemInterface subsystem is accessed from a GUI and uses XML. In designing the subsystem, we

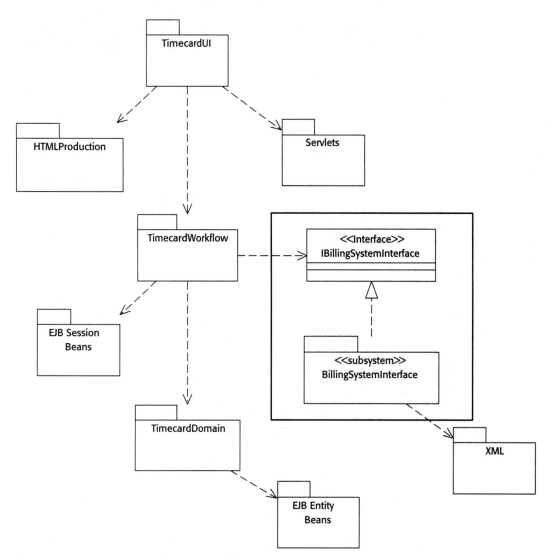

Figure 14.2 Package dependencies for Timecard architecture.

reconsider the first assumption. There is no need for a fancy user interface for a data export utility. Also, it may be useful to run the export as a scheduled task, so it can run at off peak hours without inconveniencing anyone. This approach suggests a command-line application that extracts all of the information that it needs from a configuration file. A fancy graphical user interface would be unnecessary and perhaps an obstacle.

The BillingSystemInterface could easily use the existing beans from the Timecard-Workflow and TimecardDomain packages to gather the raw data that it needs. This change, as shown in Figure 14.3, keeps the rest of the system independent of the

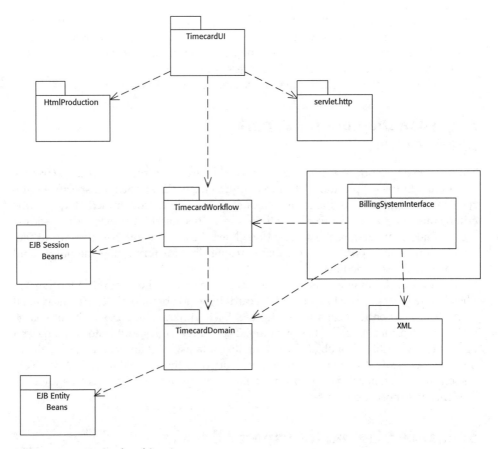

Figure 14.3 Revised architecture.

BillingSystemInterface package. Classes in the BillingSystemInterface depend on classes in the TimecardWorkflow and TimecardDomain packages, but nothing depends on the BillingSystemInterface package.

> **NOTE** Changes of this magnitude cannot be made lightly, and must be reviewed by the developers who are responsible for the architecture. However, in many cases, the developers who create the detailed design for a package or subsystem gain a more thorough understanding of the problem and of the solution. They must be allowed to apply this deeper understanding as they create the solution. Judicious changes to the architecture are an inevitable and healthy part of the design process.

Recall from Chapter 11 that individual time entries are not stored separately. Instead, each Timecard entity bean encapsulates all of the hours for an employee during a particular pay period. The TimecardHome interface lets a client object find all timecards for a given user. So, if the users are specified in the criteria, the timecards for those users can be retrieved and the data extracted for comparison with the other criteria. If the criteria include all users, then the UserHome interface can be used to obtain a list of all users. The rest of the process is the same.

We will develop two sequence diagrams, one for each variation.

Sequence Diagram for Export Specific Users

The sequence to export specific users begins when the AdministrativeActor starts the ExportTimeEntriesApplication. The input arguments to the application specify a criteria file and a results file for the formatted output. The application immediately uses the criteria filename to build an ExportCriteria object. This object is responsible for reading the file and encapsulating the criteria data. Next the application uses the output filename to build an ExportFile object that is responsible for formatting the output and writing it to the specified file.

A list of users is obtained from the ExportCriteria object. The ExportTimeEntriesApplication then uses an existing class, TimecardHome, to obtain remote references to all of the Timecard entity beans for each user. Each Timecard exposes a list of charge codes, a list of dates, and a list of hours. The charge codes and dates are checked against the ExportCriteria object by calling its containsClient and containsDate methods. The entries that match the criteria are added to the ExportFile, which is solely responsible for formatting and writing them to the output file. Figure 14.4 shows the sequence to export specific users.

Sequence Diagram for Export All Users

As in the sequence for Export Specific Users, the sequence to export all users begins when the AdministrativeUser starts the ExportTimeEntriesApplication. The ExportTimeEntriesApplication object creates the ExportCriteria and ExportFile objects. However, in this sequence, ExportCriteria answers the getUsers method with all users. This leads the ExportTimeEntriesApplication to ask the UserHome for a list of all users. The remainder of the sequence is the same as before, with the ExportTimeEntriesApplication object using the ExportCriteria object to determine if each entry meets the criteria, and adding the matching entries to the ExportFile object. Figure 14.5 shows the sequence diagram for Find All Export Time Entries.

Participating Classes

Each ExportTimeEntriesApplication object keeps exactly one ExportFile object and exactly one ExportCriteria object. No other objects use these two objects. Each ExportTimeEntriesApplication object uses many remote references to User and Timecard entity beans. Figure 14.6 shows the participating classes for Export Time Entries.

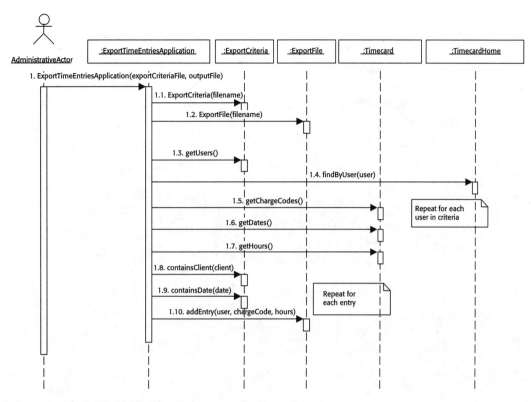

Figure 14.4 Sequence diagram for Export Specific Users.

Implementation

The implementation of these classes is fairly straightforward. We begin with the ExportCriteria and ExportFile, then proceed to the ExportTimeEntriesApplication class that uses them.

ExportCriteria.java

ExportCriteria's entire purpose is to completely encapsulate the criteria file. The private method loadCriteria loads the criteria from the file. It loads the included users and clients into separate hashtables for fast and convenient lookup. It also loads begin and end dates for the included date range.

The loadCriteria method is called from each criteria-checking method, although it only does the actual load on the first occurrence. Since loadCriteria can throw exceptions, it is better to accept this slightly clumsy approach than to call it once from the constructor.

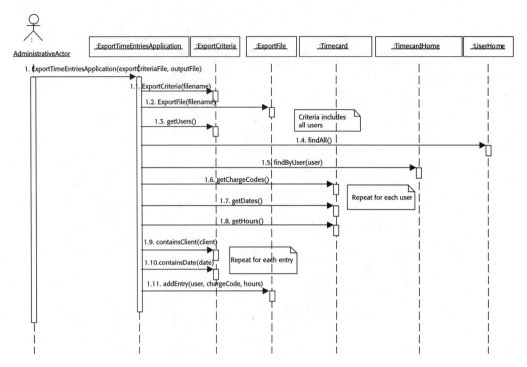

Figure 14.5 Sequence diagram for Find All Export Time Entries.

There are several methods for checking criteria. None of them allows the calling code to change the criteria or to discover how criteria are determined. Our goal of encapsulation is well served by this discipline.

The class itself has default visibility, which is visibility to the other classes in the package and no other classes. This reflects the architectural decision that no other classes in the system use any classes in the BillingSystemInterface package.

```java
package com.wiley.compBooks.EJwithUML.ExportEntries;

import java.util.*;
import java.io.*;
import java.text.*;


/**
 * The ExportCriteria class loads criteria from a file and
 * determines if they are met.
 *
 */
class ExportCriteria
{
  private Hashtable clients = new Hashtable();
```

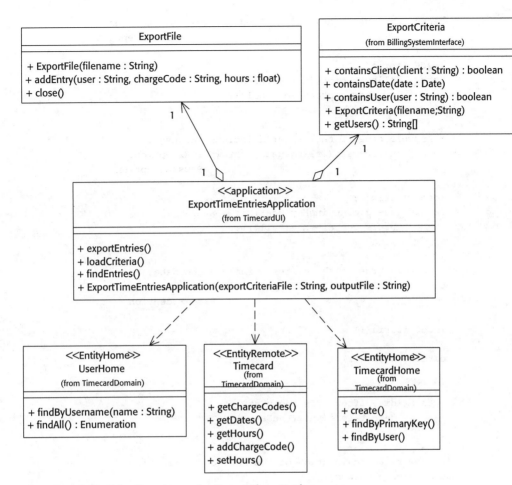

Figure 14.6 Participating classes for Export Time Entries.

```
private Hashtable users = new Hashtable();
private Date beginDate;
private Date endDate;

private String filename;
private boolean loaded = false;

/** Creates a ExportCriteria using the raw criteria found
    in the file */
ExportCriteria(String filename)
{
  this.filename = filename;
}

/** Answers true if the criteria include the client. */
```

```java
boolean containsClient(String client) throws IOException,
                                             ParseException
{
  loadCriteria();
  return (clients.containsKey(client) ||
          clients.containsKey("all"));
}

/** Answers true if the criteria include the user. */
boolean containsUser(String user) throws IOException,
                                          ParseException
{
  loadCriteria();
  return (users.containsKey(user) ||
          users.containsKey("all"));
}

/** Answers true if the criteria include the date. */
boolean containsDate(Date date) throws IOException,
                                       ParseException
{
  loadCriteria();

  date.setHours(12);


  return (date.after(this.beginDate) &&
          date.before(this.endDate));
}

/** Answers an Enumeration of the included users. */
Enumeration getUsers()
{
  return this.users.keys();
}

/** Loads the criteria, if needed. */
private void loadCriteria() throws IOException,
                                   ParseException
{
  if (loaded)
  {
    return;
  }

  FileInputStream fis = new FileInputStream(this.filename);
  BufferedInputStream bis = new BufferedInputStream(fis);


  Properties rawProperties = new Properties();
  rawProperties.load(bis);
```

```java
    String rawUsers = rawProperties.getProperty("users","");
    String rawClients= rawProperties.getProperty("clients","");
    String rawBegin = rawProperties.getProperty("beginDate");
    String rawEnd = rawProperties.getProperty("endDate");

    Calendar calendar = Calendar.getInstance();
    calendar.setLenient(true);
    SimpleDateFormat sdf = new SimpleDateFormat("dd MMM yyyy");
    this.beginDate = sdf.parse(rawBegin);
    this.endDate = sdf.parse(rawEnd);

    this.beginDate.setHours(1);
    this.endDate.setHours(20);

    this.users = buildHash(rawUsers);
    this.clients = buildHash(rawClients);
    bis.close();

    this.loaded = true;
}

private Hashtable buildHash(String raw)
{
  Hashtable hash = new Hashtable();
  StringTokenizer st = new StringTokenizer(raw, "|");

  while (st.hasMoreTokens())
  {
    String token = st.nextToken();
    hash.put(token,token);
  }

  return hash;
}

/** Test harness. */
public static void main(String[] args)
{
  try
  {
    ExportCriteria ec =
        new ExportCriteria("./criteria.properties");
    boolean b = ec.containsUser("fred");
    b = ec.containsClient("IBM");
    Date d = Calendar.getInstance().getTime();
    b = ec.containsDate(d);
    int a =1;
  }
  catch (IOException e)
  {
    e.printStackTrace();
```

```
      }
      catch (ParseException e)
      {
        e.printStackTrace();
      }

   }
}
```

ExportFile.java

The ExportFile class holds all logic for formatting time entries into XML. As with ExportCriteria, ExportFile's constructor just captures the filename. The more complex code that may lead to an exception is not called until someone calls addEntry. In addEntry, open is called if it has not been called before, then the new time entry is formatted and added to the file.

```java
package com.wiley.compBooks.EJwithUML.ExportEntries;

import java.io.*;
import java.util.*;
import com.wiley.compBooks.EJwithUML.TimeCardWorkflow.*;

/**
 * The ExportFile class encapsulates the formatting logic
 * for producing XML for time entries.
 *
 */
class ExportFile
{
  private PrintWriter writer;
  private String filename;
  private boolean open = false;

  /** Creates a new ExportFile that writes to the specified
      filename.*/
  ExportFile(String filename)
  {
    this.filename = filename;
  }

  /** Closes this ExportFile. */
  void close() throws IOException
  {
    if (writer != null && this.open)
    {
      writer.flush();
      writer.close();
      this.open = false;
    }
```

```
  }

/** Adds an entry to the output file. */
void addEntry(String user, ChargeCodeWrapper chargeCode,
              float hours, Date date) throws IOException
{
  if (!this.open)
  {
    open();
  }

  this.writer.println("<TimeEntry>");

  this.writer.println("  <User>");
  this.writer.println("    " +buildNode("Name", user));
  this.writer.println("  </User>");

  this.writer.println("  <ChargeCode>");
  this.writer.println("    "+buildNode("Client",
      chargeCode.getClientName()));
  this.writer.println("    "+buildNode("Project",
      chargeCode.getProjectName()));
  this.writer.println("    "+buildNode("Name",
      chargeCode.getChargeCodeName()));
  this.writer.println("  </ChargeCode>");

  this.writer.println("  " +buildNode("Hours", ""+hours));
  this.writer.println("  " +buildNode("Date", ""+date));

  this.writer.println("</TimeEntry>");

}

private void open() throws IOException
{
  FileWriter fw = new FileWriter(this.filename);
  this.writer = new PrintWriter(fw);

  this.open = true;
}

private String buildNode(String eName, String contents)
{
  return "<" +eName+ ">" +contents+ "</" +eName+ ">";
}

/** Tests harness*/
public static void main(String[] args)
{
  try
  {
```

```
      ExportFile ef = new ExportFile("./export.xml");

      ChargeCodeWrapper cc =
          new ChargeCodeWrapper("IBM", "AS400", "Assembly");
      ef.addEntry("fred", cc, 9.5f, new Date());
      ef.close();
    }
    catch (IOException e)
    {
      e.printStackTrace();
    }
  }
}
```

ExportTimeEntriesApplication.java

ExportTimeEntriesApplication retrieves the User and Timecard entity beans. Included users are determined by retrieving the included users from the ExportCriteria object. Each included user is used to get potential Timecards. Each entry within each Timecard is compared to the included clients and included date range. Entries that match are sent to the ExportFile for formatting.

Again, the constructor does not have to do much. All of the interesting processing, which can throw exceptions, is left to the exportEntries method.

```
package com.wiley.compBooks.EJwithUML.ExportEntries;

import javax.naming.*;
import javax.ejb.*;
import java.rmi.*;
import javax.rmi.PortableRemoteObject;

import java.io.*;
import java.text.*;
import java.util.*;

import com.wiley.compBooks.EJwithUML.TimeCardWorkflow.*;
import com.wiley.compBooks.EJwithUML.TimeCardDomain.*;

/**
 * The ExportTimeEntriesApplication class allows time entry
 * exports to be run from the command line. The criteria for
 * the export are read from a properties file, and the
 * formatted XML is written to a flat file.
 * This combination lets us run the exports as batch jobs.
 *
 * @see ExportCriteria
 * @see ExportFile
 */
class ExportTimeEntriesApplication
{
```

```
private String criteriaFile;
private String exportFile;
private ExportCriteria criteria;
private ExportFile file;

/** Creates a ExportTimeEntriesApplication object with the
    specified files. */
ExportTimeEntriesApplication(String criteriaFile,
  String exportFile)
{
  this.criteriaFile = criteriaFile;
  this.exportFile = exportFile;
}

/** Initiates the export. */
void exportEntries() throws IOException, NamingException,
        RemoteException, FinderException, ParseException
{
  // load the export criteria and prepare the output file
  this.criteria = new ExportCriteria(this.criteriaFile);
  this.file = new ExportFile(this.exportFile);

  // get references to the Home interfaces
  Context initial = new InitialContext();
  Object objref = initial.lookup("EmployeeHome");
  EmployeeHome ehome =
    (EmployeeHome)PortableRemoteObject.narrow(objref,
    EmployeeHome.class);

  objref = initial.lookup("TimecardHome");
  TimecardHome thome =
    (TimecardHome)PortableRemoteObject.narrow(objref,
    TimecardHome.class);

  // retreive a list of included users
  Enumeration users = this.criteria.getUsers();
  while (users.hasMoreElements())
  {
    String username = (String) users.nextElement();

    // find the Employee beans that match the current name
    Enumeration employees = null;
    if (username.equalsIgnoreCase("ALL_USERS"))
    {
      employees = ehome.findAll();
    }
    else
    {
      employees = ehome.findByUserName(username);
    }
```

```
      // extract the Timecard beans for each Employee bean
      while (employees.hasMoreElements())
      {
        Employee employee = (Employee) employees.nextElement();
        String employeeId = (String) employee.getPrimaryKey();

        Enumeration timecards =
            thome.findAllForEmployee(employeeId);
        while (timecards.hasMoreElements())
        {
          Timecard timecard =
                (Timecard) timecards.nextElement();
          addTimecard(timecard, username);
        }
      }
    }

}


/* Adds the matching entries from the timecard. */
private void addTimecard(Timecard timecard, String username)
                  throws RemoteException, IOException,
                          ParseException
{
  float[] hours = timecard.getHours();
  Date[] dates = timecard.getDates();
  ChargeCode[] codes = timecard.getChargeCodes();

  // loop through the dates
  for (int date_ctr = 0; date_ctr < dates.length; date_ctr++)
  {
    Date currentDate = dates[date_ctr];

    // if the current date is not included, continue loop
    if (!this.criteria.containsDate(currentDate))
    {
      continue;
    }

    // loop through charge codes
    for (int cc_ctr=0; cc_ctr < codes.length; cc_ctr++)
    {
      // find project and client for code
      ChargeCode code = codes[cc_ctr];
      Project project = code.getProject();
      Client client = project.getClient();

      // retrieve names and build wrapper
      String codeName = code.getName();
      String projectName = project.getName();
      String clientName = client.getName();
```

```
            ChargeCodeWrapper wrapper =
              new ChargeCodeWrapper(clientName, projectName,
              codeName);

            // if final criteria met, add entry
            if (this.criteria.containsClient(clientName))
            {
              int index = cc_ctr * dates.length + date_ctr;
              float currentHour = hours[index];
              this.file.addEntry(username, wrapper, currentHour,
              currentDate);
            }
          }
        }
      }
    }

    public static void main(String[] args)
    {
      try
      {
        if (args.length < 2)
        {
          System.out.println("Usage:java
            ExportTimeEntriesApplication criteriafile
            outputfile");
          System.exit(-1);
        }

        ExportTimeEntriesApplication application =
          new ExportTimeEntriesApplication(args[0], args[1]);
        application.exportEntries();
      }
      catch (Exception e)
      {
        e.printStackTrace();
      }
    }
}
```

Conclusion

This chapter completed the implementation of the Timecard application. Throughout
the development process, UML helped us describe the problem and the solution in a
clear and comprehensible form. In a real project, this allows a community of developers and stakeholders to evolve a consensus on what the system should do and how it
should do it. Less time is lost in communicating ideas. This time is more profitably
spent debating the merits of the ideas.

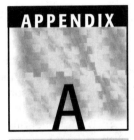

APPENDIX

A

Visual Glossary

The following glossary shows how several important object-oriented concepts are shown in the UML and how they can be implemented in Java. Each section describes a concept, provides a sample UML diagram that uses the concept, implements the UML in Java, and offers some guidance on the proper use of the concept.

Generalization

One or more subclasses may share the attributes and behavior that are defined for the base class. There are two ways to describe this relationship in proper object-oriented terminology. First, a class inherits all of the attributes and behaviors from a superclass or base. From the opposite perspective, the superclass is a generalization of the attributes and behaviors that are common to all of its subclasses. In UML, the relationship is described as a generalization and is denoted by a solid line with a hollow arrow pointing to the base class.

UML Example

Consider a brief example of generalization. Vehicle is a generalization of both Car and Truck. The two subclasses, Truck and Car, inherit all of the attributes and behavior from the base class. Figure A.1 shows the two subclasses, with generalization arrows pointing to the base class. In this case, there is no default go behavior for vehicles, so the base class must be abstract. Each concrete subclass of Vehicle must provide an implementation of the go method. Each concrete subclass may accept the default behavior for startEngine, stopEngine, and isEngineOn. If the default implementation is inappropriate, the subclass may override the default implementation by providing its own implementation.

In UML, rendering the abstract class name in italics indicates that the class is abstract. Showing a method in both the base class and in the subclass indicates that the subclass overrides that method.

Java Example

The following Java files show how the UML model in Figure A.1 can be implemented in Java.

Vehicle.java

Vehicle.java is the abstract base class in Figure A.1. This is reflected in the source code, as the class and the go method are both abstract. The other methods have implementations, but are not final, so they may be overridden by subclasses.

```
/**
 * The Vehicle class contains the data and behavior that
 * is common to all Vehicles.
 */
```

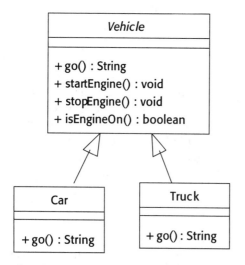

Figure A.1 Generalization example.

```
public abstract class Vehicle
{
  private boolean engineStarted;

  /** Answers the noise made when the Vehicle goes.
      Must be overridden by all concrete implementations
      of Vehicle. */
  public abstract String go();

  /** Starts engine. */
  public void startEngine()
  {
    this.engineStarted = true;
  }

  /** Stops engine. */
  public void stopEngine()
  {
    this.engineStarted = false;
  }

  /** Answers true if engine is started. */
  public boolean isEngineOn()
  {
    return this.engineStarted;
  }
}
```

Car.java

Car.java is a subclass of Vehicle, which in Java is indicated by the reserved word "extends." Car overrides the go method and uses the base class implementation of the isEngineOn method.

```
/**
 * The Car class inherits from Vehicle and overrides the go method.
 * It encapsulates all data and behavior that is specific to Cars.
 */
public class Car extends Vehicle
{
  /** Answers the noise made by the Car when it goes. */
  public String go()
  {
    if (this.isEngineOn())
    {
      return "Vroom";
    }
    else
    {
```

```
        return "...";
      }
    }
  }
```

Truck.java

Truck.java is a subclass of Vehicle, which in Java is indicated by the reserved word "extends." Truck overrides the go method and uses the base class implementation of the isEngineOn method. Truck is almost identical to Car, with a different implementation of the go method.

```
/**
 * The Truck class inherits from Vehicle and overrides the go method.
 * It encapsulates all data and behavior that is specific to Trucks.
 */
public class Truck extends Vehicle
{
  /** Answers the noise made by the Truck when it goes. */
  public String go()
  {
    if (this.isEngineOn())
    {
      return "Rumble";
    }
    else
    {
      return "...";
    }
  }
}
```

Guidelines

It is extremely important for the generalization relationship to be an accurate description of the underlying reality that you are modeling. Each subclass must really be a refinement of the superclass. Do not subclass a class just to get useful behavior or attributes. Doing so makes the system significantly more difficult to understand, and may result in strange errors as the system evolves.

Realization

A class realizes an interface by implementing each method that is defined in the interface. By realizing the interface, the class is promising to make the interface real. In UML, the realization relationship is denoted by a dashed line, with a hollow arrow pointing to the interface.

UML Example

Continuing the earlier example, some Vehicles can carry cargo, some cannot. Also, some classes that are not "normal" vehicles may also carry cargo. So, rather than introducing a separate subclass for all cargo-carrying vehicles, we introduce an interface, ICargoTransport. Our design allows any class to realize the ICargoTransport by providing an implementation for the loadCargo method. Figure A.2 shows Truck realizing the ICargoTransport interface, while Car does not.

Java Example

The following Java files show how the UML model in Figure A.2 can be implemented in Java. Only the files that have changed from the generalization example are shown.

Truck.java

Truck.java is a subclass of Vehicle, which in Java is indicated by the reserved word "extends." Truck overrides the go method and uses the base class implementation of the isEngineOn method. Truck also realizes the ICargoTransport interface, as indicated by the "implements" reserved word in the class definition.

```
/**
 * The Truck class inherits from Vehicle, and overrides the go method.
 * It encapsulates all data and behavior that is specific to Trucks.
 */
```

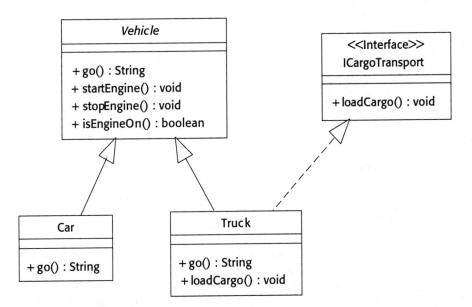

Figure A.2 Realization example.

```
public class Truck extends Vehicle implements ICargoTransport
{
  /** Answers the noise made by the Truck when it goes. */
  public String go()
  {
    if (this.isEngineOn())
    {
      return "Rumble";
    }
    else
    {
      return "...";
    }
  }

  /** Adds cargo to this Truck.*/
  public void loadCargo()
  {
  }
}
```

ICargoTransport.java

ICargoTransport.java simply defines the name and signature for the loadCargo method. As an interface, it is precluded from providing an implementation.

```
/**
 * The ICargoTransport interface defines the methods
 * that must be implemented by all classes that
 * transport cargo.
 */
public interface ICargoTransport
{
  /** Loads cargo for transport. */
  public void loadCargo();
}
```

Guidelines

All of the methods in an interface must combine to describe a coherent responsibility.

Association

An association is a long-term relationship between objects. In an association, an object keeps a reference to another object, and can call the object's methods as it needs them. Real life is replete with association relationships. Consider a person with his or her own automobile. As long as he or she remembers where it is parked, the car will let the person in to drive to his or her destination. In the UML, a solid line between the two classes represents an association.

In some cases, an object may instantiate another object and keep a reference to it for future use. An object may also receive an object as a parameter to a configuration method and keep a reference to the object.

UML Example

Consider an association relationship in which each Person object knows about zero or more Vehicle objects. Figure A.3 shows this relationship in a class diagram. The relationship is read as "every Person object is associated with zero or more Vehicle objects," and "every Vehicle object is associated with one or more Person objects." It may help to think of this as a "knows-about-a" relationship, as in "each Person object knows about some Vehicle objects."

Java Example

Person.java shows how the association relationship shown in Figure A.3 between Person and Vehicle can be implemented in Java. Each reference to a Vehicle object is kept in a Vector.

Person.java

The Person class simply holds the vehicles for a person.

```
import java.util.*;

/**
 * The Person class contains all data and logic for a person
 * in the system.
 */
public class Person
{
  public Vector vehicles = new Vector();

  /** Adds a vehicle to this person. */
  public void addVehicle(Vehicle v)
  {
     this.vehicles.addElement(v);
  }
}
```

Guidelines

Association is the default long-term relationship between objects. If you are in doubt as to which long-term relationship to use, use association.

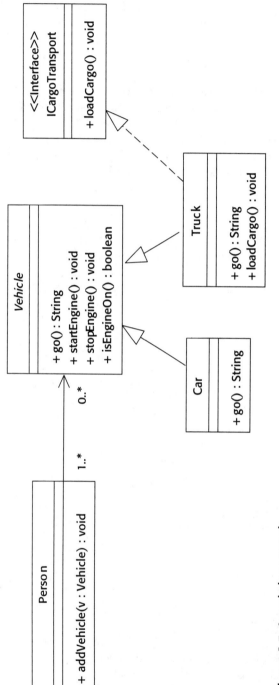

Figure A.3 Association example.

Aggregation

Aggregation indicates a long-term relationship, with the additional restriction that some of the objects are part of another object. It is this whole-part nature of the relationship that distinguishes aggregation from association.

UML Example

To continue the example, each Vehicle object may contain zero or one Engine objects. There is a clear whole-part relationship, as the engine is part of the car or truck. Figure A.4 shows a modified association from Vehicle to Engine, with the hollow diamond at the Vehicle indicating aggregation. The hollow diamond is always drawn next to the enclosing whole.

Java Example

The following Java files show how the UML model in Figure A.4 can be implemented in Java. Only the files that have changed from the previous running example are shown.

Vehicle.java

Vehicle no longer determines whether it is running or not. Instead, this behavior is delegated to an Engine object.

```
/**
 * The Vehicle class contains the data and behavior that
 * is common to all Vehicles.
 */
public abstract class Vehicle
{
  private Engine engine;

  /** Sets the engine */
  public void setEngine(Engine e)
  {
    this.engine = e;
  }

  /** Answers the noise made when the Vehicle goes.
      Must be overridden by all concrete implementations
      of Vehicle. */
  public abstract String go();

  /** Starts engine. */
  public void startEngine()
  {
```

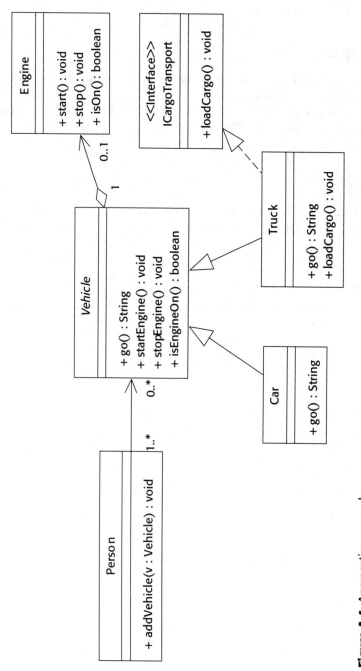

Figure A.4 Aggregation example.

```
   if (this.engine != null)
   {
     this.engine.start();
   }
 }

 /** Stops engine. */
 public void stopEngine()
 {
   if (this.engine != null)
   {
     this.engine.stop();
   }


 }

 /** Answers true if engine is started. */
 public boolean isEngineOn()
 {
   if (this.engine != null)
   {
     return this.engine.isOn();
   }

   return false;
 }
}
```

Engine.java

Engine.java provides very simple behavior for starting, stopping, and checking the current value.

```
/**
 * The Engine class contains the data and behavior for all engines
 * for use with Vehicles.
 */
public class Engine
{
  private boolean on;

  /** Starts this engine. */
  public void start()
  {
    this.on = true;
  }

  /** Stops this engine. */
  public void stop()
  {
```

```
      this.on = false;
  }

  /** Answers true if the engine is running. */
  public boolean isOn()
  {
    return this.on;
  }
}
```

Guidelines

Aggregation requires a clear whole-part relationship. Any uncertainty about the need for aggregation or ambiguity over which object is the whole and which is the part should lead you to use association instead.

Composition

Composition is an even stronger relationship, with one object essentially owning the other object or objects. The subordinate objects are created when the whole is created, and are destroyed when the whole is destroyed. Also, an object cannot play the role of a subordinate part in two composition relationships.

UML Example

Every engine contains many wheels, cogs, and gears that are integral and indivisible parts of the greater whole. Figure A.5 shows that each Engine object contains zero or many Cog objects. The filled-in diamond next to the enclosing class indicates the composition relationship.

Java Example

The following Java files show how the UML model in Figure A.5 can be implemented in Java. Only the files that have changed from the previous running example are shown.

Engine.java

The Cog objects are created when the Engine is created, and become eligible for garbage collection along with their enclosing Engine.

```
import java.util.*;

/**
 * The Engine class contains the data and behavior for all engines
 * for use with Vehicles.
 */
```

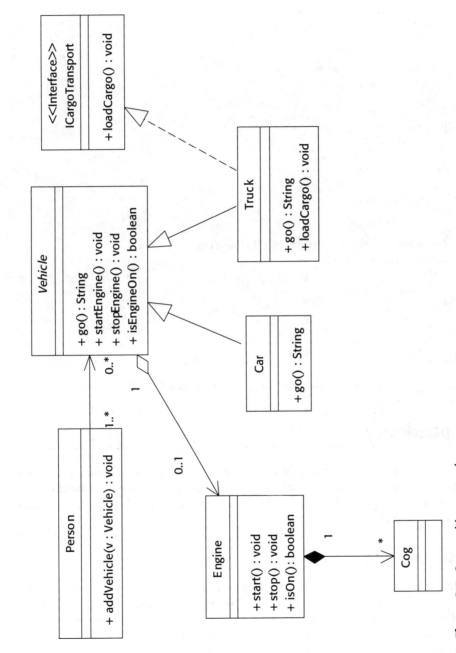

Figure A.5 Composition example.

```
public class Engine
{
  private boolean on;
  private Vector cogs = new Vector();

  public Engine()
  {
    this.cogs.addElement(new Cog());
    this.cogs.addElement(new Cog());
  }

  /** Starts this engine. */
  public void start()
  {
    this.on = true;
  }

  /** Stops this engine. */
  public void stop()
  {
    this.on = false;
  }

  /** Answers true if the engine is running. */
  public boolean isOn()
  {
    return this.on;
  }
}
```

Guidelines

As with aggregation, when in doubt, do not use composition.

Dependency

Objects often need to use another object. An object may receive a reference as a parameter to a method, or it may create the object, use it, and lose it before the end of the current method. The key idea is that the dependent object acquires, uses, and forgets the object within a single method.

UML Example

Continuing the example, people use gas pumps to get gas, but most people do not keep track of every pump that they have used. The Person object receives a reference to a GasPump object as a parameter to the purchaseGas method. The reference is used within the method; it is not kept. The resulting dependency relationship can be seen as the dashed line from Person to GasPump in Figure A.6.

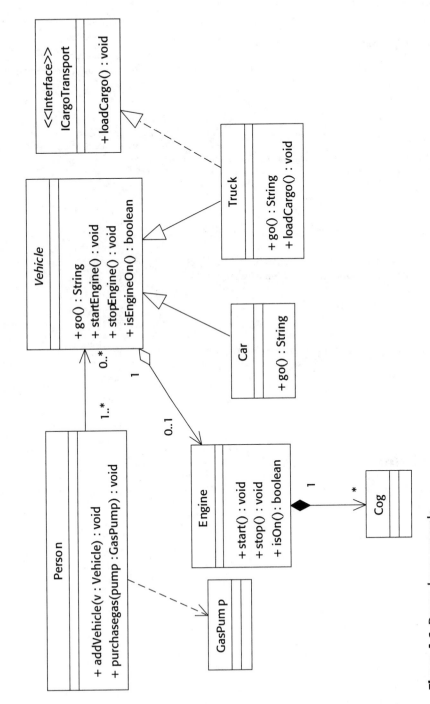

Figure A.6 Dependency example.

Java Example

Person.java shows how the dependency relationship between Person and GasPump can be implemented in Java.

Person.java

Now, the Person class has a purchaseGas method that accepts a reference to a GasPump object as a parameter.

```java
import java.util.*;

/**
 * The Person class contains all data and logic for a person
 * in the system.
 */
public class Person
{
  public Vector vehicles = new Vector();

  /** Adds a vehicle to this person. */
  public void addVehicle(Vehicle v)
  {
     this.vehicles.addElement(v);
  }

  public void purchaseGas(GasPump pump)
  {
    // use pump
    // forget about pump
  }
}
```

Guidelines

Dependency should be used whenever an object is used and forgotten within a single method.

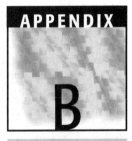

Additional Resources

This appendix describes additional resources for several categories.

Object-Oriented Analysis and Design

Booch, Grady. *Object-Oriented Analysis and Design with Applications.* Reading, MA: Addison-Wesley-Longman, Inc., 1994.
This is still the classic text for OO analysis and design. It has a unique combination of academic precision and clear explanations.

Booch, Grady, James Rumbaugh, and Ivar Jacobson. *The Unified Modeling Language User Guide.* Reading, MA: Addison-Wesley-Longman, Inc., 1999.
Excellent reference for the UML and its application.

Coad, Peter, and Mark Mayfield. *Java Design.* Upper Saddle River, NJ: Prentice-Hall PTR, 1997.
A very concise and readable book that stresses design by composition.

Fowler, Martin, with Kendall Scott. *UML Distilled: Applying the Standard Object Modeling Language.* Reading, MA: Addison-Wesley-Longman, Inc., 1997.
A very concise guide to the UML.

Patterns

Buschmann, Frank, Regine Meunier, Hans Rohnert, Peter Sommerlad, and Michael Stal. *Pattern-Oriented Software Architecture: A System of Patterns.* West Sussex, England: John Wiley & Sons, Ltd., 1996.

Introduces several important architectural patterns, including MVC and layers.

Fowler, Martin. *Analysis Patterns: Reusable Object Models.* Reading, MA: Addison-Wesley-Longman, Inc., 1997.

Very interesting book on analysis and domain modeling. Contains a lot of examples and clear explanations of the author's thought process as he creates his designs.

Gamma, Erich, Richard Helm, Ralph Johnson, and John Vlissides. *Design Patterns Elements of Reusable Object-Oriented Software.* Reading, MA: Addison-Wesley-Longman, Inc., 1995.

The book for design patterns. Invaluable resource.

Software Development Process

Jacobson, Ivar, Grady Booch, and James Rumbaugh. *The Unified Software Development Process.* Reading, MA: Addison-Wesley-Longman, Inc., 1999.
Excellent reference for the proprietary process and for OO software engineering in general.

Kruchten, Philippe. *The Rational Unified Process: An Introduction.* Reading, MA: Addison-Wesley-Longman, Inc., 1999.
Concise guide to the RUP.

McConnell, Steve. *Rapid Development.* Redmond, WA: Microsoft Press, 1996.
Incredibly easy-to-read coverage of some difficult and important topics. This is not an OO book, rather the definitive software engineering book for the practitioner.

McConnell, Steve. *Software Project Survival Guide.* Redmond, WA: Microsoft Press, 1998.
Contains a lot of the same material as *Rapid Development*, above, but in a convenient easy-to-gift-wrap size. Makes a great gift for your favorite unenlightened manager or customer.

Webster, Bruce F. *Pitfalls of Object-Oriented Development.* New York: M&T Books, 1995.
A clearly organized and easy-to-read guide to the dangers inherent in OO software development. It contains excellent advice for both managers and developers as they adopt OO technology.

XML

Megginson, David. *Structuring XML Documents.* Upper Saddle River, NJ: Prentice-Hall, Inc., 1998.
    Goes way beyond the basics for a complete discussion of XML DTDs and how to construct them.

St. Laurent, Simon. *XML: A Primer.* Foster City, CA: MIS Press, 1998.
    Concise guide to creating XML DTDs and documents.

Java

Asbury, Stephen, and Scott R. Weiner. *Developing Java Enterprise Applications.* New York: John Wiley & Sons, Inc., 1999.
    An excellent introduction to Sun's Enterprise Java class libraries.

Chan, Patrick, Rosanna Lee, and Douglas Kramer. *The Java Class Libraries Second Edition, Volumes 1, 2, and Supplemental edition for the Java 2 Platform.* Reading, MA: Addison-Wesley-Longman, Inc., 1998.
    An amazing series of books, with the best low-level explanations of the packages and classes that make up the core class libraries for Java.

Eckstein, Robert, Marc Loy, and Dave Wood. *Java Swing.* Sebastopol, CA: O'Reilly & Associates, Inc., 1998.
    Very readable explanations of a complex topic. Exhaustive and evenly written coverage of a huge amount of material.

Flanagan, David. *Java in a Nutshell.* Sebastopol, CA: O'Reilly & Associates, Inc., 1996.
    Excellent guide and reference for the language, tools, and basic classes.

Hamilton, Graham, Rick Cattell, and Maydene Fisher. *JDBC Database Access with Java: A Tutorial and Annotated Reference.* Reading, MA: Addison-Wesley-Longman, Inc., 1997.
    Thorough coverage of JDBC, but a little heavy on the reprinted JavaDocs for my taste.

Hunter, Jason, with William Crawford. *Java Servlet Programming.* Sebastopol, CA: O'Reilly & Associates, Inc., 1998.
    Solid coverage of servlets, from fundamentals to advanced topics.

Oaks, Scott, and Henry Wong. *Java Threads.* Sebastopol, CA: O'Reilly & Associates, Inc., 1997.
    Excellent coverage of multi-threaded programming in Java, with a good balance of theory and details.

Reese, George. *Database Programming with JDBC and JAVA.* Sebastopol, CA: O'Reilly & Associates, Inc., 1997.

Excellent coverage of JDBC, and a thought-provoking introduction to the design of object-to-relational frameworks.

Roman, Ed. *Mastering Enterprise JavaBeans and the Java 2 Platform, Enterprise Edition.* New York: John Wiley & Sons, Inc., 1999.

Excellent coverage of a wide range of enterprise technologies.

The CD-ROM

The CD-ROM contains a read-only HTML version of the UML design model for the Timecard application, as well as the Java source code and deployment instructions that can be used to deploy the application. If the model fails to load in your browser, please try the Netscape version. Also, your browser must be configured to support Java applets in order to view the model. The model file was created by using Rational Rose "Web Publisher" feature to produce a read-only HTML version of the model. This is a great way to distribute your designs to a larger audience, such as customers who do not have a copy of Rose.

The model is intended to provide a coherent picture of the design that was developed over many chapters in the book. Some figures that are in the book are not in the model, and vice versa.

In order to view the contents of the model, simply use the tree control on the left. If you are in the frames version, the main view frame on the right will display the selected diagram. Otherwise, the selected diagram will appear in a second browser window. For example, click on the plus sign to the left of the Logical view folder. Double-click on the "main" diagram symbol.

The Java source code and deployment instructions allow the reader to see one possible implementation of the design and to experiment with various alternatives. These instructions guide you as you install the required software and deploy the Timecard application. The instructions are broken into several sections, with each section shown in its own table. The leftmost column of the table shows the major steps required for the section. The middle column describes the details for each step. Finally, the right-most column describes any expected results.

If your interest and patience are high, you may wish to deploy the Enterprise Jav-aBeans from scratch. An additional page of custom installation instructions guides you through this tedious process. You can also view the deployment instructions or the custom installation instructions as Word documents.

Hardware Requirements

To use this CD-ROM, your system must meet the following requirements:

Platform/processor/operating system: Windows NT or 2000

RAM: 128 MB

Hard drive space: 120 MB

Processor: 300 Mhz Pentium or equivalent

Installing the Software

To install the software, follow these steps:

1. Start Windows on your computer.
2. Place the CD-ROM in your CD-ROM drive.
3. You can browse the model from the CD-ROM by opening X:\Models\Design\index.htm in Internet Explorer or X:\Models\Design\contents.html in Netscape Navigator.
4. If you want to deploy the application, open **X:\INDEX.HTM** file on the CD-ROM for detailed instructions (where **X** is the correct letter of your CD-ROM drive).

User Assistance and Information

The software accompanying this book is being provided as is without warranty or support of any kind. Should you require basic installation assistance, or if your media is defective, please call our product support number at (212) 850-6194 weekdays between 9AM and 4PM Eastern Standard Time. Or, we can be reached via e-mail at: **techhelp@wiley.com**.

To place additional orders or to request information about other Wiley products, please call (800) 879-4539.

Index

To use this CD-ROM, your system must meet the following requirements:

Platform/Processor/Operating System: Windows NT or 2000 on atleast a 300 Mhz Pentium
RAM: 128 MB
Hard Drive Space: 120 MB

Developing
User Interfaces